LAUGHING FIT
TO KILL

LAUGHING FIT TO KILL

Black Humor in the Fictions

of Slavery

GLENDA R. CARPIO

OXFORD
UNIVERSITY PRESS

2008

OXFORD
UNIVERSITY PRESS

Oxford University Press, Inc., publishes works that further
Oxford University's objective of excellence
in research, scholarship, and education.

Oxford New York
Auckland   Cape Town   Dar es Salaam   Hong Kong   Karachi
Kuala Lumpur   Madrid   Melbourne   Mexico City   Nairobi
New Delhi   Shanghai   Taipei   Toronto

With offices in
Argentina   Austria   Brazil   Chile   Czech Republic   France   Greece
Guatemala   Hungary   Italy   Japan   Poland   Portugal   Singapore
South Korea   Switzerland   Thailand   Turkey   Ukraine   Vietnam

Published by Oxford University Press, Inc.
198 Madison Avenue, New York, New York, 10016

www.oup.com

Oxford is a registered trademark of Oxford University Press

A version of chapter 3 was previously published as "Conjuring the Mysteries of Slavery:
Voodoo, Fetishism, and Stereotype in Ishmael Reed's *Flight to Canada*," *American
Literature* 77, no. 3 (2005): 563–89. Reproduced courtesy of *American Literature*.

Library of Congress Cataloging-in-Publication Data
Carpio, Glenda.
Laughing fit to kill : black humor in the fictions
of slavery / by Glenda R. Carpio.
p.   cm.
Includes bibliographical references and index.
ISBN 978-0-19-530470-1; 978-0-19-530469-5 (pbk.)
1. American literature—African American authors—History
and criticism. 2. African American wit and humor—History and
criticism. 3. Black humor. 4. Slavery in literature. 5. Comic, The, in literature.
6. African Americans in literature. I. Title.
PS153.N5C373 2008
817.009'352996073—dc22   2007041364

1 3 5 7 9 8 6 4 2

Printed in the United States of America
on acid-free paper

for Samuel Otter

Procurad también que, leyendo vuestra historia, el melancólico se mueva a risa, el risueño la acreciente, el simple no se enfade, el discreto se admire de la invención, el grave no la desprecie, ni el prudente deje de alabarala.

Another thing to strive for: reading your history should move the melancholy to laughter, increase the joy of the cheerful, not irritate the simple, fill the clever with admiration for its invention, not give the serious reason to scorn it, and allow the prudent to praise it.

—Miguel de Cervantes, *Don Quixote*

ACKNOWLEDGMENTS

I am not the first to call Werner Sollors a great scholar and a gentleman, nor am I the first to thank him for setting a stellar example and for providing his sustaining and inspiring guidance. But it well merits stating it all again and I do it with much warmth and gratitude. This book would not have been possible without his sharp, witty insights and wise encouragement. Indeed, many of my esteemed colleagues at Harvard and beyond have been instrumental in the completion of this project. Aside from embodying much of the essence of African American humor, Henry Louis Gates Jr. has been both fuel and fire, always expecting the best of me. Marcyliena Morgan and Lawrence Bobo have been not only incredibly generous hosts and incisive critics, but also friends with whom I have shared much laughter fit to kill.

Several people have given me their support in small ways (a passing but insightful conversation in the hall) and big ways (revelatory references, generous readings). Vincent Brown has been a brother in the struggle, he generously read much of this manuscript and offered extremely helpful criticism, advice, and laughter. Colleagues in the English Department, especially Larry Buell, Daniel Albright, John Stauffer, and Gordon Teskey, have all been encouraging. Thank you, Daniel, for reminding me of Beckett's "risus purus"! Others have clarified my thinking and given me encouragement in moments of doubt. Barbara Rodriguez has been a supremely generous and supportive friend. Cheryl Finley and Robin Bernstein who, along with Vincent and Barbara, constituted the Mourning Group, provided incisive commentary on drafts of chapters. Conversations with Adam Bradley about African American popular culture (and Ellison) proved illuminating, as did talks about comedy with Pierre Marks. Toward the end, Jeffrey Ferguson's intellectual integrity and wry sense of humor were both enlightening and absolutely necessary. At Oxford University Press, I thank Niko Pfund for believing in this project. My editor, Shannon McLachlan, has provided great enthusiasm and support, and I thank her for it. Other staff members at the press, especially Christina Gibson, have been wonderful. I also wish to extend my deep thanks to the anonymous readers of the manuscript for their insightful comments.

The Center for Comparative Studies in Race and Ethnicity at Stanford University generously provided indispensable funds to write a large portion of this manuscript and to test much of its contents; many thanks to its executive director, Dorothy M. Steele, to her staff, and other members of the Center, especially Hazel Markus. While at Stanford, I also had the pleasure of meeting Harry J. Elam Jr. and Michele Elam, who kindly read, heard, and critiqued portions of this book. The New York Public Library has been a haven for me since the days of my dissertation, and I thank everyone who works there for their daily support. I also wish to thank the W. E. B. Du Bois Institute for African and African American Research at Harvard, where I read an early version of "The Tragicomedy of Slavery in Suzan-Lori Parks's Early Plays" and where I am now starting a new project. Many thanks to the staff at the Institute for its help with research and to its directors for generously providing the means to use the image of Richard Pryor that graces this book's cover. Thank you, Jennifer Lee Pryor, for granting permission and to Trudy Claiborne for making all else possible. My gratitude also goes to Susan Lively and Rebecca Wassarman at Harvard for facilitating the fine printing of the images in "'A Comedy of the Grotesque': Robert Colescott, Kara Walker and the Iconography of Slavery" through the Faculty of Arts and Science Tenure-Track Publication Fund.

My students have been an unending source of inspiration. Special thanks go to C. Namwali Serpell and Cameron Leader-Picone, two of the brightest stars that I have had the pleasure to know and guide, for reading drafts of this book with their characteristic astuteness and brilliance. I look forward to seeing their books in print. My other students, especially those in African American Literature to the 1920s, Black Humor, Contemporary African American Literature, and Black Women Writers, provided me with fresh, unadulterated perspectives on much of the context for this book. I could not have wished for a brighter set of students with which to share literature and culture. I also wish to thank my students at Davis Middle School and Rosecrans Elementary in Compton, California, for teaching me how to teach and for opening my eyes to the true state of America.

I am happy to finally have the opportunity to thank my teachers. At Vassar College, Peter Antelyes introduced me to the power of incorporating literary criticism and research in popular culture, and Susan Brisman first showed me the pleasures of close reading. At the University of California at Berkeley, Saidiya Hartman worked with me on the initial stages of the dissertation from which this book has grown and provided a model of scholarship early on. Similarly,

Stephen Best raised the bar high and therefore transformed much of what is now "'A Comedy of the Grotesque': Robert Colescott, Kara Walker, and the Iconography of Slavery" in this book. The late Barbara Christian shared much time in her office and thus allowed me to explore the roots of this project in her wise company. Waldo Martin kindly stepped in when Barbara could no longer be there. When she was at Berkeley, Katherine C. Bassard taught me early African American literature in ways that revolutionized how I think about American culture. Other professors in the English Department at Berkeley provided inspiration and support. I wish to thank Stephen Greenblatt, with whom I now have the pleasure to be at Harvard, Genaro Padilla, Jennifer Miller, Catherine Gallagher, Katherine Snyder, Hertha D. Sweet Wong, and Sue Schweik.

Without the wise counsel and spiritual guidance of teachers of a different kind, this book would not have been possible. I thank Lynn Tracy, Ralph Klein, and Larry Schultz for helping me see when I could not. My thanks go also to my family and friends *who are* family. Eva Lydia Carpio made tremendous sacrifices for me, and for this I will always be thankful. Arnaldo, Franca, Andrea, and Matteo Bardi replenished my faith in family with love. My debt to them is tremendous. I also thank Linda and Bill Berliner for being guardian angels. I am fortunate, too, to have friends who are not only generous and supportive but also some of the funniest people I know. I have shared many a deep belly laugh with Marissa Sanchez, mi comadre for life, Michele Asselin, Kevin Greer, Robyn Coval, May Woo, Deborah "Ashaka" Wefer, Mechel Thompson, Dennis Teston, Joseph Meltzer, and Miguel Ortiz. I wish also to thank the staff at Paladar restaurant for having dined and wined a tired scholar on many a night.

For his faith in me, for his deep, sustaining love and his great sense of humor, I thank Aarón Sanchez. Our dog Bhakti has sat at my feet first through a dissertation and then through a book, while our other dog, Placido, has forced me to take long walks during which I often gained much needed clarity. My love goes to all three—of course, not equally!

The dedication does not begin to acknowledge my debt to Samuel Otter, who has long been advisor, exemplar, and rich source of knowledge and faith. If anyone has taught me the importance of being able to laugh at oneself, especially when the going gets tough, it has been he. And what an amazing lesson, indeed!

CONTENTS

LAUGHING FIT
TO KILL

INTRODUCTION

Race is not only real, but also illusory. Not only is it common sense; it is also common nonsense. Not only does it establish our identity; it also denies us our identity.—HOWARD WINANT, "Racial Dualism at Century's End," in Lubiano, *The House That Race Built,* 90

How does anyone navigate the contradictions of race, so succinctly described by Winant? Without a sense of humor, they might just drive one crazy. Race, of course, has not always been deemed illusory or common nonsense. Far from it. The belief in biologically determined differences in race has generated atrocities such as genocide, enslavement, and colonization. While today we live in the more "enlightened" state in which race is understood for the construction that it is, old-fashioned racism not only persists but also creates new, strange fictions around its concept. In the United States, the last decades of the twentieth century witnessed a pendulum swing in which, after playing a crucial role in the making of the American nation and throughout the nation's history, race became so purportedly insignificant that broad sectors of the country could claim the end of institutional racism and the achievement of a color-blind society.[1] In many ways this swing constituted a backlash against the gains made by the civil rights movement of the 1960s. A great reversal occurred almost as soon as the major civil rights acts passed: the focus was no longer on white racism—because segregation in public accommodations and proscribed discrimination in employment and disenfranchisement had been outlawed—but on the moral deficiencies of minorities.[2]

For African Americans, such backlash included the reemergence of long-standing stereotypes regarding their character. Stereotypes of blacks as lazy, irresponsible, and "in violation of core American values"[3] have been used to explain the undeniable inequalities that persist in this brave new world in which racial discrimination apparently no longer exists. Differences in wages, access to health care, housing, family income, and more have been constantly attributed to the cultural and individual failures of African Americans. The "welfare queen," the "career criminal," and the "deadbeat dad" became, especially during the intense poverty besieging American inner cities during the 1970s and 1980s, synonymous with black femininity and masculinity. These developments happened against the background of a staggering widening in income between blacks and whites. By 1978, "30.6 percent of black families earned income below the official poverty line, compared with 8.7 percent of white families." Matters grew worse during Ronald Reagan's administration. By Reagan's second term, "about one out of every three African Americans, most of whom were women and children, lived below the poverty line."[4] And, while affirmative action made equal opportunity possible for some African Americans, it also came to be considered by many to be a form of reversed discrimination. Reflecting on the "ideology of victimization" that has come to characterize white anti–affirmative action, Winant writes, the "situation would be farcical if it were not so dangerous."[5]

What if we were to focus precisely on the farcical nature of race in America? Certainly none of the facts that I have just listed are humorous in and of themselves. Yet to confront the maddening illusions of race and the insidiousness of racism we may just need to laugh long and hard, perhaps in the tragicomic notes of the blues or in the life-affirming spirit of righteous insurgency. For centuries, in fact, African Americans have faced racism, in its various manifestations and guises, with a rich tradition of humor that, instead of diminishing the dangers and perniciousness of racism, highlights them. Consider a well-known folk story in which a slave is caught eating one of his master's pigs. The slave admits his guilt, saying, "Yes, suh, Master, you got less pig now but you sho' got more nigger."[6] The tale effectively burlesques "the entire notion of ownership in human beings," as the slave carries the master's objectification of his body to its outmost absurdity.[7] No doubt the tale takes a risky gambit. As Mel Watkins notes, the tale could also be interpreted as "an example of self-effacement, a groveling attempt to amuse in order to stave off punishment as well as an affirmation of black masochism and self-emasculation." At the same time, it could be seen "as an example of a calculated ploy to acquire a prized treat" with impunity.[8] The difference in interpretation is a matter of how much one knows about the nature of African American humor in the context of slavery and segregation.

Black American humor began as a wrested freedom, the freedom to laugh at that which was unjust and cruel in order to create distance from what would otherwise obliterate a sense of self and community. Until well into the twentieth century, it had to be cloaked in secrecy lest it be read as transgressive and punished by violence. Hence the popular slave aphorism "Got one mind for white folk to see / 'Nother for what I know is me."[9] In the tale just cited, the slave was likely "puttin' on Massa," catering to whites' beliefs in the inferiority of blacks in order to mask the aggressive message of his retort. Despite the life-threatening injunctions against black laughter, African American humor flourished, at first under the mask of allegory and increasingly in more direct forms. It developed a Janus-face identity: on the one hand, it was a fairly nonthreatening form that catered to whites' belief in the inferiority of blacks but that usually masked aggression; on the other, it was a more assertive and acerbic humor that often targeted racial injustice but that was generally reserved for in-group interactions. For black Americans, humor has often functioned as a way of affirming their humanity in the face of its violent denial.

By most accounts, African American humor, like other humor that arises from oppression, has provided a balm, a release of anger and aggression, a way of coping with the painful consequences of racism. In this way, it has been linked to one of the three major theories on humor: the relief theory made popular by Freud, which posits that we laugh as a way to release pent-up aggression. Freud claimed that "tendentious jokes," of which he identified two main kinds, the obscene and the hostile, allow the joker and his or her audience to release energy used for the purposes of inhibition. Much, but certainly not all, African American humor can be understood as a kind of relief-inducing humor. Indeed, under the violent restrictions of slavery and segregation, African Americans developed the art of tendentious jokes so well, in particular those that mask aggression, that often they left whites "with the baffled general feeling that [they had] been lampooned [before their very eyes] without quite knowing how."[10] Among themselves, however, African Americans have expressed aggression against their oppressors much more openly. For instance, in a tale that became popular during the postbellum period, when slavery was often portrayed in the public sphere in mythic and picturesque modes (full of paternalistic masters, benevolent mistresses, and happy, loyal "darkies"), a slave owner bids a sentimental farewell to his slave, Uncle Tom, soon after emancipation. "Ah, dear, faithful, loyal Uncle Tom!" the master says. "Lincoln has forced you to accept freedom—against my wishes, and, I am sure against yours. Dear old friend and servant, you need not leave this plantation. Stay here with us." To which Uncle Tom replies, "Thank you, deah, kine, lovin', gen'rous Massa. I reckon I'll leave. But befo' I go I wants you ter know I will allus 'membuh you ez de son uv a bitch you is an' allus wuz!"[11]

While African American humor addresses many topics other than black and white relations, it frequently marks the multifaceted nature of those relations, both how much they have changed and how much they have stayed the same over time. Thus, in another well-known tale, a black man gets off in a strange town in Mississippi sometime in the early twentieth century. Seeing no members of his race, he asks a white man, "Where do the colored folks hang out here?" Pointing to a large tree in the public square, the white man replies, "Do you see that limb?"[12] Jokes about lynching and other forms of racial violence *in the aftermath* of slavery attest to the perversion of freedom. At the same time, they express the quintessential quality of gallows humor, which Freud called the "triumph of narcissism" because it asserts the ego's invulnerability in the face of death.[13]

African American humor is also, although less commonly, linked to a second major theory on humor, the superiority theory, which posits that we laugh at other people's misfortunes. In some ways, the tradition of signifyin', including the play of the dozens, of boasting and toasting, belongs to this kind of humor, although the verbal battle of capping and "yo mamma" jokes savor verbal wit over any mean-spirited competition or put-down. The signifying tradition is generally known as mother wit and departs significantly from the Freudian model of humor, which stresses sublimation, in that it relishes exposure and does not depend on the joke form. Instead, it is mainly visual and depends on the verbal dexterity of the dozens, the toasts (long, metrically and rhythmically complex compositions), and the telling of "lies," or stories. Signifying remained largely segregated until Richard Pryor broke out of his original image as a slim, mild-mannered comedian who, believe it or not, never cursed and usually told charming jokes patterned after Bill Cosby's material. But Pryor began performing revolutionary acts for mixed audiences in the late 1960s and thus was largely responsible for desegregating African American humor. Black comedians before Pryor, most notably Moms Mabley, Dick Gregory, Godfrey Cambridge, Flip Wilson, Redd Foxx, and Bill Cosby, had introduced aspects of black humor to mixed audiences, but it was Pryor, after a remarkable self-transformation, who brought all aspects of black humor to the stage. In a sense, he "outed" black humor from the closely guarded circles within which black folk had kept it since slavery.

Rarely is black humor connected to a third and, for me, the most interesting theory on humor: the incongruity theory. Simply put, this theory suggests that we laugh when our expectations are somehow disturbed. Such a simple definition hardly argues for why I am interested in this theory, so allow me to explain. The humor of incongruity generally entails the playing of "what if" games that suspend normativity. They are games that momentarily reconfigure habits of mind and language and that can lead to what Ralph Ellison called "perspective by incongruity" (after Kenneth Burke).[14] At its best, the humor of incongruity allows us to see the world inverted, to consider transpositions of time and place and to get us, especially when the humor is hot enough to push our buttons, to question the habits of mind that we may fall into as we critique race. The kind of humor that I am invoking is not the kind that has been romanticized and thus normalized, as in some interpretations of Mikhail Bakhtin and his theories of carnival. In the context of African American expressive culture, and particularly in the hands of the writers and artists that I have selected, the humor of incongruity allows us to appreciate the fact that, far from being *only* a coping mechanism, or a means of "redress," African American humor has been and continues to be both a bountiful source of creativity and pleasure and an energetic mode of social and political critique.

Laughing Fit to Kill explores how a set of late twentieth- and early twenty-first-century writers and artists mine the rich tradition of African American humor—from the trickster tales of Brer Rabbit and Brer Fox to the John and Master slave stories and the tradition of signifying, of toasting, of playing the dozens—to represent both the distance that separates us from American slavery and the often imperceptible ways slavery has mutated. How do the ideologies that supported slavery continue to shape our national modes of belief and behavior? This question is not, of course, meant to ignore the obvious fact that African Americans have made considerable political and economic gains over time, especially since the civil rights movement.[15] But it is meant to suggest that the legacy of slavery underwrites the post–civil rights backlash against African Americans and the new forms of segregation and institutionalized poverty to which they have been subjected.[16] It is meant to suggest, too, that a spectacle such as the Bush administration's lack of response to the disaster of Hurricane Katrina in New Orleans and the thinly veiled poverty that the hurricane made obvious are but two examples of how the racism of antebellum and Jim Crow America persists, albeit in different forms. The writers and artists of this book do not so much protest against the sociological manifestations of this racism as probe into the subtle and sometimes difficult-to-define ways that the concept of chattel slavery, especially the stereotypical imagery that it produced, influences the individual identities, social relations, and artistic production of African Americans.

How can slavery, the sorrow and anger that it has signified for African Americans and the devastation that it caused Africa, serve as the subject of humor? It becomes such a subject only in the most piercing tragicomedy, one in which laughter is disassociated from gaiety and is, instead, a form of mourning. The short fiction of Charles W. Chesnutt, especially his tales in *The Conjure Woman* (1899), particular performances in Richard Pryor's stand-up, and the early plays of Suzan-Lori Parks are all uniquely eloquent instances of such tragicomedy. However, throughout this book, I also explore an eviscerating humor, one that is bawdy, brutal, horrific, and insurgent and that does not take as its subject the tragedy of slavery per se. Rather, it pillories the ideologies and practices that supported slavery and that, in different incarnations, continue to support racist practices. Yet, a moralizing discourse it is not. Debunking the all too familiar dichotomies of slavery—master and slave, oppressor and oppressed, enslavement and freedom—the humor that I here examine exposes how racial conflict, and the obsessive ways that it colonizes American minds, can divest *everyone*, albeit at different registers, of a sense of reality.

Laughing Fit to Kill argues that black writers and artists have utilized hetero-geneous forms of humor across two centuries as a uniquely invigorating kind of epistemological response to the situation of forced migration and transatlantic alienation. The book takes its main title from a phrase commonly repeated in Chesnutt's short fiction, where it appears in the vernacular, "laffin' fit ter kill." The phrase succinctly expresses the extremes of humor and violence that I ex-plore throughout the book since it marks a particular kind of tragicomedy, one that creates tension between the comedy produced at the expense of African Americans, primarily through minstrelsy, and its present-day manifestations, and the humor that African Americans have created with respect to slavery and its legacy. It becomes the unifying concept of the first chapter, in which I provide a historical context for the twentieth-century textual, visual, and dramatic repre-sentations of slavery and its legacy on which the rest of the book focuses.

In the subtitle and throughout I employ the term "black" rather than African American humor, intending to draw attention to the overlap between two types of humor. Normally understood as a species of gallows humor or a kind of dark satire, black humor, as William Solomon notes, was first coined "at the end of the 1930s by André Breton in the course of putting together an anthology of writings designed to exemplify the surrealist idea of humor" and became, in the 1960s, a term used to describe the work of a number of American authors, largely white, who wanted to explore "the vicissitudes of whiteness . . . the extent to which this social construct takes shape, by and large, in relation to hallucinatory impressions of blackness."[17] Whereas Solomon investigates how "black humor" was used to describe the work of writers now more commonly known as postmodernists, I use the term to invoke both the long tradition in African American culture of critiquing "the vicissitudes of whiteness" and its "relation to hallucinatory im-pressions of blackness" and to explore how different generations of writers and artists improvise on that tradition as they symbolically create redress for slavery.

For all its concreteness as a "historical sequence" and "scene of pulverization and murder," slavery is also an experience for which historical evidence is both abundant and problematic (for instance, in the great imbalance in accounts by captors and captives), an experience that many have vigorously wished to deny, forget, or distort but that, ironically, constitutes a foundational feature of the "New World."[18] How and why slavery comes to be symbolically redressed through black humor, specifically during the late twentieth and early twenty-first century, depends in part on the nature and politics of redress as it pertains to slavery in the United States. Taking a cue from Victor Turner's work on social dramas, American slavery may be seen as a breach in relationship to which the Civil War and emancipation and Reconstruction become, respectively, crisis and redressive action without resolution—as evidenced by the legalized extension of slavery during the long career of Jim Crow segregation. In *Dramas, Fields, and*

Metaphors (1974), Turner defines social dramas as entailing four main phases: (1) breach, an event that creates a schism in a community; (2) crisis, which brings the breach into a climax; (3) redressive action, conceived as retribution, correction, and reparations; and (4) "reintegration of the disturbed social group or the social recognition and legitimation of irreparable schism between contesting parties."[19] Turner argues that sometimes "a phase of a social drama may seethe for years and years with nothing much happening on the surface," and sometimes, too, "there is no resolution even after a climactic series of events."[20] "When redress fails," writes Turner, "there is usually regression to crisis. At this point direct force may be used, in the varied forms of war, revolution, intermittent acts of violence, repression, or rebellion. Where the disturbed community is small and relatively weak vis-à-vis the central authority, however, regression to crisis tends to become a matter of endemic, pervasive, smoldering factionalism, without sharp, overt confrontations."[21] The civil rights and Black Power movements are two instances of regression to crisis that did not lead to a resolution of the originating breach, indeed because such a resolution is impossible given the magnitude of the breach: the genocide and dehumanization of people of African descent. Americans will continually return to the breach of slavery without resolving it. This is not a cynical declaration that the nation is forever doomed to rehearse its painful past. As I have already stressed, both the civil rights and Black Power movements did achieve certain measures of redress. Yet, given both the impossibility of full redress and the lasting impact of slavery, each generation of Americans needs to map its own relationship to a breach that has fundamentally shaped the nation. Thus, while the return to crisis that the civil rights and Black Power movements propelled has now arguably "become a matter of endemic, pervasive, smoldering factionalism, without sharp, overt confrontations," the returns to crisis that generations in the past few decades and in the future have enacted and will enact may have different, hopefully more positive outcomes. The original breach, however, can never be completely resolved and forgotten.[22]

New World slavery constituted such a tremendous crime against humanity that, from its inception, it could not be properly redressed. What has remained in the aftermath of this crime is what Stephen Best and Saidiya Hartman call the "limited scope of the possible in the face of the irreparable."[23] The impetus for redress has shuttled between grievance, the seeking of legal remedies for the crimes of slavery and the injustices perpetuated by Jim Crow segregation and other racist practices, and grief, the expression of the deep sorrow occasioned by the suffering, loss, and death that has constituted slavery and its legacy. Pointing to recent cases in the debate over legal reparations for the crimes of slavery, Best and Hartman argue that this kind of shuttling "has been lost in pursuit of what is possible within a liberal conception of law and property," and further, that what is "sacrificed in this approach" is the expression of "black noise." "Black noise," Best and Hartman write, "represents the kinds of political aspirations that are inaudible and illegible within the prevailing formulas of political rationality; these yearnings are illegible because they are so wildly utopian and derelict to capitalism (for example, 'forty acres and a mule,' the end of commodity production and restoration of the commons, the realization of 'the sublime ideal of freedom,' the resuscitation of the socially dead). Black noise is always already barred from the court."[24] Black noise is barred from court because it urges a radical transformation of society in which the court itself would have to undergo an overhaul, as would the liberal conceptions of law and property that guide the current reparations debates. Reflecting on the struggle for equality that the civil rights movement represented, Howard Winant notes, "'Equality' has had many meanings since the nation was founded; it was hardly unprecedented to redefine it in terms of formal and legal standing rather than in terms of redistribution of resources, compensation for past wrongs, or forceful efforts to reshape the material conditions of minorities." He adds, "In retrospect, we can see that to have undertaken these measures . . . would have required not only the dismantling of segregated neighborhoods, workplaces, and schools, but the transformation of the status of white workers as well. Substantive equality would have meant massive redistribution of resources; it would have clashed with fundamental capitalist class interests; such dramatic social change was never even on the table."[25] Such dramatic social change may not have been on the table for everyone, especially for those in power, but it *was* the major goal fueling sectors of the liberation movement. As Robin D. G. Kelley observes, black revolutionaries in groups such as the Black Panther Party and the Revolutionary Action Movement (and in earlier groups such as the Congress of Racial Equality, founded in 1942) not only sought a radical transformation of their country but also "viewed the emerging freedom movement in the United States as part of a global assault on empire" and looked to the Third World (especially Africa, Asia, and Latin America) for models of black liberation in America.[26] And precisely because their goals "clashed with fundamental capitalist class interests," their revolutionary impulse had to be destroyed or driven underground.[27]

In the decades after the civil rights and Black Power movements, maintaining the dream of a radical social transformation has been difficult, to say the least. The backlash against civil rights policies arrived in concert with a liberal retreat from racial politics and the development of new forms of racisms that, because of their subtlety compared with the outright bigotry of the past, have been more difficult to battle. Instead of returning to overtly exclusionary practices, "the forces of 'racial reaction' . . . sought to reinterpret the [civil rights] movement's victories, to strip it of its more radical implications, to rearticulate its vision of a substantively egalitarian society in conservative and individualistic terms."[28] As I have noted, racism began to be coded in the language of color-blind policies and antiwelfare, anti–affirmative action arguments. This is not to say that old-fashioned racism became a thing of the past. If, as Orlando Patterson observes, estimates suggest that in the post–civil rights era only one in four whites is a bigot, this still means that there are two bigots for every black person in the United States.[29] Aside from suffering the worst effects of economic recessions, black Americans in the post–civil rights era also saw a rise in police brutality. In 1975 they "constituted forty-six percent of people killed by police."[30]

Today, the expression of both grievance and grief is crucial in working toward and keeping alive the dream of a radical social transformation. To mute grief or otherwise ignore it is to implicitly deny the monumental impact of an irreparable crime against humanity. As I show throughout this book, however, grief need not always be expressed in traditional forms of lament. In African American expressive culture, grief often assumes a tragicomic mode, best known through the blues. But this tragicomic mode also finds stunning expression in black humor. Thus, for instance, Richard Pryor's performance as the Wino and Junkie in *Live and Smokin'* (1971) combines the power of humor as cathartic release and politically incisive mode of critique with deep pathos. In this performance, as throughout his career, Pryor exposes the legacy of slavery in the police brutality, lack of employment, drug addiction, and poverty that assailed African American communities in the late twentieth century, transforming tropes of black humor to express both grievance and grief. Like the other black humorists in this book, Pryor makes clear that grief over the immense tragedy of slavery is necessary, not out of melancholic attachment to a traumatic past, but because slavery remains ingrained in the sociopolitical and economic fabric of America. Saidiya Hartman has eloquently given voice to this insight in *Lose Your Mother* (2007), and Robin D. G. Kelley has explored the "freedom dreams" toward which the dual acts of grievance and grief have been and continue to be enacted. If to effect grievance is to work within what is possible in the world as it is, grief can keep us focused *not* on ameliorating its corrupt systems (based on slavery, other forms of labor exploitation, and racism) but on dreams of a better world altogether.[31]

By enacting symbolic rituals of redress with respect to the breach of slavery, the black humorists in this book keep such "freedom dreams" alive. In the chapters that follow, I explore how different generations of black humorists enact symbolic rituals of redress with respect to the breach of slavery. I pair one artist or writer from the civil rights and Black Power generation with another from the post–civil rights decades (Pryor with Dave Chappelle, Robert Colescott with Kara Walker) or examine them on their own (Ishmael Reed, Suzan-Lori Parks). I start, however, with the ways in which William Wells Brown, an ex-slave, and Charles W. Chesnutt, born free in 1858, set templates for the use of black humor to represent the violence of slavery. Through various modes of "conjuring," through gothic, grotesque, and absurdist comedies of the body, through stinging satirical narrative defamiliarization, through hyperbole, burlesque, and, perhaps most important, through what Hortense Spillers might call the "cultural vestibularity" of the racial stereotype itself, these black humorists have enacted oral, discursive, and corporeal rituals of redress with respect to the breach of slavery.[32]

Writers and artists from the civil rights and Black Power generation began to enact such rituals in the context of highly publicized racial struggles and bicentennial celebrations, both of which provoked a great deal of reflection regarding the nation's history and highlighted the contradiction between the country's profession of democracy and its history of racial oppression. During this time, slavery assumed a central role in public discourses in America. As Ashraf H. A. Rushdy notes, social activists, artists, writers, and scholars began to explore the connections between acts of black empowerment in 1965 and those before the end of the Civil War in 1865. The popular television miniseries *Roots* (1977), based on Alex Haley's book of the same name (1976), made widely available a history of the Middle Passage and plantation slavery. Meanwhile scholars dramatically changed the historiography of slavery. They vindicated the slave narrative from its earlier status as an unreliable historical and weak literary source and generally called for a rewriting of history in which the testimony and perspective of the enslaved would figure prominently.[33] Rushdy argues, in fact, that the social climate of the United States during and directly after the 1960s, in particular arguments about slavery and history, gave rise to a new kind of fiction, "neo-slave narratives" or "contemporary novels that assume the form, adopt the conventions, and take on the first-person voice of the antebellum slave narrative."[34]

Preferring not to constrain my focus to the genre of the novel, or the generic categorization implied by the term "neo-slave narrative," I examine how, from the late 1960s to the present, slavery has continued to be a major focus of artistic production for African Americans in a variety of forms, including not only novels and short stories but also plays, visual art, and comic performances. Contemporary fiction and art on slavery is characterized by formally innovative ways of connecting America's slave past with the concerns of the late twentieth and early twenty-first century. Hence, in Richard Pryor's performances, the art of signifying becomes a way of oscillating between the past and the present, linking, for instance, police brutality or the taboo against miscegenation to analogous practices during slavery. Similarly, Ishmael Reed's *Flight to Canada* (1976) operates by anachronism, mapping the flight of three fugitive slaves within a fictional space that merges the past (antebellum and Civil War America) and the novel's present (the years after the civil rights movement). In the early plays of Suzan-Lori Parks, experiments with language and dramatic structure become a way of emphasizing the lack of structural change between the slave past and present racial conditions. The transpositions of time in Pryor, Reed, Parks, and the other black humorists here included not only corrupt putative temporal boundaries, thus exposing the impact of slavery on contemporary culture, but also challenge conventional and ossified interpretations of slavery so that we gain fresh perspectives from which to assess the past.

In challenging historical positivism and the linear notions of time that support it, the subjects of my study are certainly not alone. In much contemporary African American literature, "non-linear time is juxtaposed with linear processes, to the effect that they intersect with and perspectivize each other." In particular, fictional revisions of the history of slavery, as in, for instance, Gayl Jones's novel *Corregidora* (1975) and Toni Morrison's *Beloved* (1987), intertwine the traumatic repetition of the past "with a tentative progressive movement: by repeating the past, by revisiting it imaginatively and dialogically, they sketch a possible future that might help their characters to break out of . . . the after-effects of the past of slavery."[35] Rather than adopt the language of trauma, as much contemporary fiction on slavery does, the black humorists I have chosen expose the murderous *and* ridiculous effects of slavery in the present. They focus in particular on how the stereotypes produced by slavery—the evil master, the submissive or rebellious slave, the perfect abolitionist, the overbearing mammy, the lascivious Jezebel—have attained new, sometimes not easily discernible reincarnations that need to be exposed and criticized. They underscore how the "presence of a *system* of . . . stereotypes," is not only a "permanent feature of U.S. culture," but one that is "essential" and "integral" to its social order.[36] Thus, while they conjure the stereotypes produced by slavery and suggest how they have changed over time and attained new meanings for new purposes, they ultimately underscore their persistence as a system. Their work highlights, for instance, how pernicious stereotypes regarding black people's innate ability and intelligence may no longer be particularly relevant for the current political climate, yet they can resurface suddenly: thus stereotypes regarding the purported unwillingness of blacks to work have come to the forefront of the debate on welfare and the persistence of black poverty.[37] Particular stereotypes are resuscitated and adjusted depending on the kind of politics they are made to serve, but the system of stereotypes remains.

In drawing our attention to the tenacity of the stereotypes produced by slavery, the black humorists in this study urge us to confront, rather than avoid, their legacy by exploring their theatricality and their appeal across differences of race, class, and gender. Through parody and caricature, and invoking the practices of conjure, these artists set stereotypes in disturbing motion. They inhabit the images, exaggerate them, and dislocate them from their habitual contexts. Certainly the act of "appropriating a language of stereotypes in order to undermine the dominant order is an age old device employed by persecuted groups to subvert the status quo."[38] But it is also true that such appropriations are not always performed with the same kind of artistry, nor are their effects examined with sophistication, mainly because stereotypes tend to elicit knee-jerk reactions. Like curse words, stereotypes are not owned by anyone and invoke the past history of their use each time they are reiterated. They are often vulgar, especially when they are stereotypes of race and sexuality, and as such bring up powerful feelings, feelings not only of embarrassment, anger, and shame, but also of desire, affiliation, and recognition. Quite often, stereotypes can evoke a host of contradictory feelings all at once. Through confrontation, and complex forms of laughter, the black humorists in this book channel and "defang" the potency of stereotypes, always risking the possibility that the conjured stereotypes may take lives of their own and exceed their efforts to control them. This is no doubt a volatile artistic gambit. The appropriation of stereotypes carries the possibility of confirming popular, if tacitly held, racist beliefs. But the risk can be mitigated through the kind of formal experimentation that these humorists so expertly perform. The risk also opens up the possibility of investigating the fetishistic force of stereotypes in American culture and, ultimately, of exploring the impact of slavery through a new lexicon for historical reconstruction.

When used as the source or object of humor, stereotypes can provide the kind of catharsis of emotion that Freud examined in his *Jokes and Their Relation to the Unconscious* (1905/1960). They can give voice to that which is taboo and allow the energy involved in keeping it in place to be released through laughter. But they also bring up thorny questions: Who is allowed to laugh? Who is allowed to tell the joke? Take the following exchange from the extensive cycle of John and Master slave stories, which depicts a clever slave, John—sometimes also called Nehemiah, Pompey, Jack, or Golias—who generally bests the Master in word and deed:

> Master got his slave with the longest dick and said, "I don't want no black screwing my daughter, but she wants sixteen inches."
>
> John said, "Nah, suh, boss. Not even for a white woman. I wouldn't cut two inches off my dick for nobody."[39]

The tale begins by exaggerating the stereotype of black male genital superiority and, rather than deny it, quite literally exaggerates it even more. It also insinuates the "wrong" kind of desire ("she wants," "not even for a white woman") in one of the most potent of American taboos, interracial sex ("I don't want no black").[40] While this tale may, in certain environments, provide cathartic release through laughter, it remains relatively safe because its racial and sexual stereotypes are only invoked. The story provokes many questions: In what company can this tale be retold? What kind of laughter would it create in a community such as the white, affluent, suburban one where I happened to attend high school in the late 1980s (my mother worked as a servant for a wealthy family with whom we both lived) and where at least one teen, a generally well-regarded young man, had what he called a "nigger-be-good" bat in his car (he kept it as "protection" for his excursions to New York City, where he went to score drugs)? What kind of laughter would it produce in a racially mixed crowd? The use of stereotypes in jokes, as this example suggests, produces interesting questions about the joke act but not necessarily about stereotypes, mainly because these remain at the level of description.

In this book, by contrast, stereotypes are not merely described or joked about. Rather, they are conjured, brought to life, made bigger than life, through words, images, and performances. Brown and Chesnutt, Pryor and Chappelle, Colescott and Walker, Reed and Parks all signify on the vulgarity of racism by amplifying the distortions that crystallize in stereotypes. They are conjurers who use the complicated dynamics of race and humor to set the denigrating history of antebellum stereotypes against their own humorous appropriation of those images. Improvising on the verbal, visual, and performative aspects of African American humor, they give life, through characters, images, scenarios, and even their own bodies, to the most taboo aspects of race and sexuality in America, ultimately seeking to effect a liberating sabotage of the past's hold on the present. Directly or indirectly, they all employ the aesthetics and principles of voodoo and conjure, but not in any nostalgic or essentializing manner. Rather, they do so through formally innovating means that incorporate aspects of popular culture (images produced by television or by advertisement, for example), of other art forms (modern art, film and comic strips, for instance), and postmodern techniques. In the process, they raise a central question of this book: can stereotypes be used to critique racism without solely fueling the racist imagination?

In embracing conjure, the black humorists in this study give their work a diasporic sensibility. African American conjure derives from voodoo, a practice that was transported by enslaved Africans across the Middle Passage, which is a form of ancestor worship in which the souls of the dead—known as *loa* or *mysteries*—are evoked and made manifest through ritual. The loa are said to re-enter the world by "taking possession" of practitioners in what is called a *crise de loa*, the moment in which the soul of an ancestor "mounts" the body of the devotee and through which he or she attains a physical presence.[41] In the New World, especially in Haiti, voodoo's rituals recall and restage the brutality of cultural rupture and enslavement. In the American South, voodoo became known as conjure, as well as hoodoo, and has been associated less with "possession" and more with the ability to transform people into things or objects, as in magic. In this and other ways, voodoo and conjure are different; one is more rooted in African and Haitian practices, the other is more informed by the cultural mixtures specific to the United States. Yet they are similar in that both practices emphasize the use of a person's body: possession in voodoo and metamorphosis in conjure.[42]

As I demonstrate throughout this book, for centuries black humorists have used these aspects of voodoo and conjure to signify on chattel slavery's transformation of people into objects. In Charles W. Chesnutt's short fiction, for instance, conjure is not only a mode of narration in which to tell a story is to cast a spell, but also a way of creating a comedy of the body that highlights the lack of control that the enslaved had over their own bodies. His stories often feature a conjurer who turns people into objects, animals, or spirits in attempts at counteracting the dispossession of the body that chattel slavery constituted. Chesnutt draws a dark comedy out of these transformations and puts it in the service of tragedy, showing how attempts to repossess the dispossessed body are almost always defeated by the institutionalized violence of slavery. Thus laughter in his tales is often the sound of the tragic recognition of dispossession. At another level, conjure in Chesnutt also entails the appropriation and transformation of racial stereotypes as a way of thwarting and rearranging his readers' racial assumptions and expectations. The result is an entropic form of humor that constantly puts in tension the experience and interpretation of slavery.

This tension is also key in the work of William Wells Brown, in particular the dramatic plays he performed on the abolitionist circuit. An expert mimic, Brown used only his body and voice to conjure the racial stereotypes and distorted depictions of slavery that the minstrel stage produced. For instance, in his performances of his play *The Escape; or, A Leap for Freedom* (1858/2001), Brown, playing every role in the play, parodied the stereotypes of race and gender produced by slavery—the wicked overseer, the tragic mulatta, the lascivious slave master, the heroic slave, the buffoonish "coon"—in a hyperbolic mode that sabotaged their power. During his performances, Brown transformed into stereotypes across differences of race, gender, and class lines not only to lampoon racist ideologies but also to show the nonsensical nature of race and its identities.

Neither Brown nor Chesnutt ever seriously acknowledged conjure as part of their own belief or as an influence on their work—an unsurprising move since both needed to fashion a "civilized" self against the stereotypes of heathenism that defined blackness in nineteenth- and early twentieth-century America. And yet they were conjurers of the first order. Brown's strategy of caricaturing the caricatures that minstrelsy produced, of animating them in a hyperbolic mode, and Chesnutt's use of black vernacular forms, especially his transliteration of conjure, serve as model strategies for the writers and artists whose works I analyze in the rest of the book. Certainly, other African American writers have used different forms of humor to address slavery and racism in America—from the burlesques that Frederick Douglass performed on the abolitionist stage during the early years of his career, to the sharp satire of David Walker, Harriet Jacobs, and Harriet Wilson and the expert mimicry of Bert Williams, the burlesque acts of Josephine Baker, the hearty comedy of Langston Hughes and Zora Neale

Hurston, the wicked parodies and satire of George Schuyler, to the biting sarcasm of Chester Himes, the mix of warmth and righteousness in Toni Cade Bambara, and, more recently, the intricate layering of humor and postmodern techniques in the work of Charles Johnson, Paul Beatty, and Colson Whitehead. The list, no doubt, could be expanded. The black humorists I have gathered here, however, focus on the theatricality and tenacity of stereotypes and use aesthetic practices derived from conjure in ways that produce a particular kind of humor: a humor that outrageously brings to life America's most cherished racial obsessions; a humor that, paradoxically, arises in a reactionary climate comparable to that of the Reconstruction decades and extends through what Nelson George and others have called the "post-soul" era.[43]

In many respects, the generations belonging to this era, those born roughly between the March on Washington in 1963 and the landmark case *The Regents of the University of California v. Bakke* (1978), have experienced a deepening sense of cynicism, even nihilism.[44] Reflecting on the climate of the post–civil rights decades, Saidiya Hartman writes that the "narrative of liberation had ceased to be a blueprint for the future, the decisive break the revolutionaries had hoped to institute between the past and the present failed. The old forms of tyranny, which they had endeavored to defeat, were resuscitated and the despots live long and vigorous lives."[45] There was nothing particularly new in the backlash and retreat of liberal support that occurred in the immediate post–civil rights years. As Stephen Steinberg notes, "Essentially the same thing had happened during Reconstruction. In both cases advancements made by blacks were followed by periods of racism and reaction."[46] Yet, because many African Americans had believed with fervor that the civil rights movement and later the Black Power movement were redirecting the history of their country and the world, because many hoped that the movement would put an end to the endless process of advancement and reaction, the disappointment of the post–civil rights decades had particular force. Other momentous events had given black Americans reason to hope for change. The Second World War, for instance, highlighted the contradiction between America's fight against the racism of fascism abroad and its own racist practices at home. "The democratic ideology and rhetoric with which the war was fought stimulated a sense of hope and certainty in black Americans that the old race structure was destroyed forever."[47] Yet that hope never came to fruition. The war did effect some change in racist attitudes toward black Americans; it did lessen the production of racist images and some of the more overt racist practices, such as lynching. But these changes were brought about due to concerns about America's image abroad. The real hope for change was driven underground and flourished in the civil rights movement.[48]

When the movement itself also became a source of disillusion, the country erupted in violent rioting during the mid-1960s, not only as a response to the assassination of Malcolm X in 1965 and of Martin Luther King in 1968, but also in protest against numerous acts of violence perpetrated against African Americans. Court-sanctioned police brutality—expressed both in the context of the riots and in random acts of murder—gave clear evidence that the U.S. government would not only fail to protect black Americans against violent injustice but that it would, in fact, promote and condone it. The rioting of the mid-1960s was also fueled by black anger at the poverty and inequality left untouched by civil rights legislation. As has been well documented, the Black Power movement drew its force precisely from this anger. But that force would be vigilantly restrained. Between 1956 and 1971 the FBI conducted a massive counterintelligence program known as COIN-TELPRO that took 295 actions, often brutal and sometimes lethal, against black militant groups. Coupled with problems within such groups and government-sanctioned suppression, revolutionary groups dissolved.

This brief recap of backlash against the achievements of black activists and radicals only begins to hint at the reasons for the cynicism and political apathy that besieged black communities in the last decades of the twentieth and the beginning of the twenty-first century. In *Race Matters* (1993), a book written in the aftermath of the Rodney King riots, Cornel West focuses on "the profound sense of psychological depression, personal worthlessness, and social despair widespread in Black America."[49] For him, the psychology of despair, so rooted in the consistency of racial oppression even after centuries of struggle, is a better way of explaining the state of affairs in black communities; it is better than either liberal structuralism, which places blame on socioeconomic conditions, or conservative behaviorism, which blames lapses in morals. Others have focused on the cultural escapism and instant gratification that perpetual consumerism has provided the postsoul generations to explain the political apathy of young people. "In a world where so many youth believe that 'getting paid' and living ostentatiously was the goal of the black freedom movement," writes Robin D. G. Kelley, "there is little space to even *discuss* building a radical democratic public culture."[50]

How, then, is it possible for humor to flourish in this post–civil rights context? Arguably, the picture I have been sketching is imbalanced for, although the post-soul generations have experienced great challenges, not all of them have had negative outcomes. Mark Anthony Neal, whose work focuses on the "post-soul aesthetic" in contemporary black popular culture, notes that, while the "children of soul" have experienced "the change from urban industrialism to deindustrialism, from segregation to desegregation, from essential notions of blackness to metanarratives on blackness," they have done so "without any nostalgic allegiance to the past . . . but firmly in grasp of the existential concerns of this brave new world," one that demands a "radical reimagining of the contemporary African-American experience."[51] Mounting a critique of essential notions of black identity, once so useful to radical black groups in closing ranks against racist practices, has made it more difficult to discern how black people can act collectively toward sociopolitical and economic advancement, given differences in class, gender, geography, and sexual orientation; yet it has also allowed for greater freedom of expression. Thus challenges against essential notions of black identity have gone hand in hand with critiques of reified concepts of black art, as defined, for instance, by writers such as Addison Gayle, Amiri Baraka, and Larry Neal in the anthology *The Black Aesthetic* (1971), one of many manifestos for the black arts movement, the artistic sister to the Black Power movement.

Gayle, Baraka, Neal, and others insisted, as had W. E. B. Du Bois earlier in the century, that black art must have a utilitarian function, one of celebrating the African roots of African American identity and culture and, more generally, of distinguishing these from Euro-American concepts of self and art. For them, black artists had the responsibility of "isolating and evaluating the artistic works of black people which reflect the special character and imperatives of black experience," to quote Hoyt Fuller in his essay "Towards a Black Aesthetic."[52] The black arts movement inspired the development of art driven by identity politics and the multicultural trends of the 1980s, but its tenets have proven too constricting for younger generations of artists and writers, who see themselves as "cultural mulattos" (Trey Ellis's term) and who, while steeped in black culture, are also willing and able to draw from and reassemble a wide array of cultural knowledge across racial and class divides.[53] Nelson George's *Buppies, B Boys, Baps and BoHos: Notes on Post-Soul Black Culture* (1992) and *Post-Soul Nation* (2004), Mark Anthony Neal's *Soul Babies*, Trey Ellis's seminal essay "The New Black Aesthetic" (1989), various essays by Greg Tate, Thelma Golden's use of the term "Post-Black" to define new trends in black visual practices, and Madhu Dubey's meditation on black postmodernism in *Signs and Cities* (2003) are but a few prominent instances of an increasingly growing body of work examining the ways in which artists and writers aesthetically represent the variety of perspectives and experiences of black life in America in the late twentieth and early twenty-first centuries.

Not that there weren't artists and writers working along this vein during the black arts movement. Indeed, Trey Ellis identifies a minority within the black arts community who, rather than espouse propaganda, "produced supersophisticated black art that either expanded or exploded the old definitions of blackness, showing us as the intricate, uncategorizeable folks we have always known ourselves to be."[54] His list includes Ishmael Reed and Richard Pryor, Clarence Major, John Edgar Wideman, George Clinton, Toni Morrison, and David Hammons. Unlike these pioneers (and Ellis's list no doubt could be expanded to include Robert Colescott and others), artists emerging in the postsoul decades must contend with the marketing and commodifying of black culture. While Ellis, writing in 1989, was enthusiastic about the fact that black culture was increasingly becoming synonymous with popular culture, seeing it as an advantage that new generations of artists had over the pioneers of the mid-1970s, today we have many reasons to be more than leery of the consumerist impulse that affects the production and reception of black art.

Still, Ellis identified a major shift in tone and attitude in the art of postsoul generations, one that is central to the work of the black humorists I examine. The new artists, Ellis observes, are "not shocked by the persistence of racism as were those of the Harlem Renaissance," nor are they "preoccupied with it as were those of the Black Arts Movement." A novelist in his own right, Ellis speaks as one of these artists, stating, for "us, racism is a hard and little-changing constant that neither surprises nor enrages."[55] Some might call this position cynical, yet implicit in it is a view of racial struggle that is not dependent on illusions of revolution but that nonetheless is deeply invested in fighting for freedom, both politically and artistically.

In their recognition that racial struggle is "little-changing," the postsoul generations have reclaimed the central role that humor has played in African American culture for centuries but that was largely underplayed within the moral and militant culture of the civil rights and Black Power movements and the climate of political correctness that followed. Certainly, it is due to the fact that earlier generations fought tooth and nail for basic civil rights that the postsoul generations can afford to reclaim African American humor in its full variety. But this reclaiming is also in tragicomic recognition of the apparent endlessness of the struggle and the dire need, therefore, to keep the tradition of African American humor alive, given the central role it has played as a form of release, a medium of protest, and a source of artistic freedom.

The civil rights and Black Power movements were, of course, not *devoid* of humor. In fact, Joseph Boskin discusses the role of gallows humor in the marches of the civil rights movement and the often caustic humor with which black folk responded to white violence.[56] Indeed, as Boskin also notes, some of the first studies on black humor appeared during the mid-1960s: Langston Hughes and Arna Bontemps's *The Book of Negro Folklore* (1965), Philip Sterling's *Laughing on the Outside* (1965), Langston Hughes's *The Book of Negro Humor* (1966), and Richard Dorson's *American Negro Folktales* (1967). In 1964 Roger D. Abrahams published *Deep Down in the Jungle*, a seminal study of African American folklore in the streets of Philadelphia, and in the 1970s there were two other important texts, Alan Dundes's *Mother Wit from the Laughing Barrel* (1973/1990) and Lawrence Levine's *Black Culture and Black Consciousness* (1977), which includes the excellent chapter, "Black Laughter." This was also the time in which many older black comedians became nationally known (artists such as Redd Foxx, Moms Mabley, and Pigmeat Markham) and younger ones flourished (Dick Gregory, Godfrey Cambridge, Flip Wilson, Bill Cosby, Garrett Morris, and, of course, Richard Pryor). But this is a moment in which mainstream American culture is only beginning to discover African American humor and struggling to accept some of its edgier political, more risqué, and culturally specific aspects.

In addition, the civil rights and Black Power eras produced tacit forms of censorship that resulted in the suppression of stereotype-based humor. Protest against the proliferation of stereotypical imagery has been a constant throughout African American history, but it took particular force in the 1960s and 1970s. Through adamant remonstration, through acts of exorcism and reappropriation of figures such as Uncle Tom, Sambo, and Mammy, artists and activists in the 1960s and 1970s declared the death of stereotypes of submission, complicity, and clownish behavior. Artist Betye Saar's mixed-media collage *The Liberation of Aunt Jemima* (1972) is emblematic, featuring Mammy in her typical roles as nurse and house servant yet she is reconceived as a revolutionary. Other artists, among them Jeff Donaldson, Murry DePillars, and Jon Lockard, transformed the Mammy figure by questioning her popularity as a visual icon and, like Saar, using her to represent black rage against the racial oppression embodied by her.[57] In *Sambo: The Rise & Demise of an American Jester* (1986), Joseph Boskin locates the death of Sambo, in his various incarnations (the plantation "darky," the minstrel man, the postcard buffoon, the movie chauffeur), in the mid-1960s, when African Americans increasingly gained more access to mass-media forms such as television.

In this context, many preferred the "clean" Richard Pryor of the early 1960s to the "crazy nigger" of the 1970s, who refused to sanitize black culture in the name of integration; others welcomed the "essentially colorless" comedy of Bill Cosby and Godfrey Cambridge.[58] If by the end of the 1970s mainstream culture had incorporated the less risqué aspects of African American humor, the climate of censorship that developed during the black arts movement would impact the production and reception of African American culture for decades. For instance, in a 1991 introduction to a new edition of Langston Hughes and Zora Neale Hurston's play *Mule Bone: A Comedy of Negro Life* (1931), George Houston Bass notes the difficulties of producing the play in the late twentieth century, given its embrace of "politically incorrect" characters and tropes. "The expansion of moral and aesthetic consciousness that has occurred in American society since 1960," he writes, "has produced a social climate that does not allow one to laugh easily at broad comic interpretations of black people." He adds, "Many of the comic characters, comic devices, and forms of laughter that were sources of renewal and release within the black community before 1960 are now inhibited by the politics of race and gender. Forms of parody and self-parody which were once a way of dealing with the stress and pain of a bad situation and finding a way to change it are now quite often viewed as assaults and insults."[59] Although stereotype-derived humor was a staple of in-group interactions in many African American communities, after segregation African Americans became, and arguably remain, leery of sharing this aspect

of black humor with mixed audiences. Some have turned to policing the use of stereotypes by other African Americans in literature, the visual arts, and popular culture. Acts of protest against the ubiquity of stereotypical imagery in the American public sphere were much needed, of course, but as Bass's comments suggest, the political correctness underwriting some of that protest ultimately proved too restrictive.

The death of Sambo constituted the waning of minstrel performances, which emerged in the early 1830s and were popular in America until the early twentieth century, surviving through the 1950s not only in theaters, but also on radio in fraternities and high school and civic auditoriums. Sambo-like images were ultimately removed and banned from public spaces, claims Boskin, because, after centuries of struggle, "blacks had finally shoved and laughed [them] off the stages, the screens, the comic strips, the cartoons, the front lawns, the children's stories, the knickknacks, the advertisements, the radio and televisions programs."[60] And good riddance. Except, of course, that Sambo and Mammy and all of the racial stereotypes produced by slavery and perpetuated by Jim Crow segregation were only banned from the public sphere and not destroyed in the American psyche. Also, racial stereotypes were not entirely driven from the public sphere, as evident in the many hypersexualized and violent pimps and light-skinned Jezebels of blaxploitation films and the more buffoonish stereotypes that the television sitcoms of the late twentieth century promoted.[61] It took a lot more than laughter to shove Sambo and Mammy out of the public arena—indeed, the NAACP had a lot of legislating to do toward the cause—and it would take more than acts of protest and exorcism to cleanse the American id of their power. In fact, as the prominence of stereotype-derived art in the late twentieth and early twenty-first centuries attests, the idea of forever cleansing the American psyche of its racial fetishes may be not only a futile project but one that might fuel the power of the fetish all the more by making it taboo and therefore seductive.

While political correctness suppressed the use of stereotypical imagery in mainstream culture, in alternative settings such as experimental theaters and avant-garde art galleries, artists, both white and black, featured stereotypical imagery in what Shawn-Marie Garrett has called the Freudian "return of the repressed."[62] Garrett cites a few prominent instances: in 1981 the Wooster Group, a widely respected and influential theater group staged *Route 1&9*, a startlingly controversial juxtaposition of *Our Town* and a Pigmeat Markham blackface routine; other alternative theater groups, such as the Drama Dept., have given plays such as *Uncle Tom's Cabin* "new life in politically conscious productions with multicultural casts"; starting in the 1990s, the painter Michael Ray Charles has reassembled racial stereotypes drawn from a history of American advertising, product packaging, billboards, radio jingles, and television commercials to comment on contemporary racial attitudes; artist Fred Wilson designed installations that explored the whole range of racial stereotypes; the white photographer David Leventhal has created Polaroid portraits of racist memorabilia (salt and pepper shakers, cookie jars) and, along with other artists, opened up a dialogue about the value that some see in such memorabilia; in 2000, Spike Lee produced *Bamboozled*, a film that, while clearly highlighting the disturbing and violent aspects of minstrelsy, also underscores its artistry and attraction.[63] Trey Ellis's novel *Platitudes* (1988), Darius James's *Negrophobia* (1992), and Paul Beatty's *The White Boy Shuffle* (1996) in different ways investigate the power of stereotypes. Without fail, discussions of contemporary stereotype-centered art includes the work of two black humorists that I examine: Kara Walker's silhouettes, which conjure the whole array of racial and gender stereotypes from plantation slavery against bizarre but often puzzlingly beautiful contexts, and Suzan-Lori Parks's plays, in particular *The Death of the Last Black Man in the Whole Entire World* (1990), in which the leading figures are Black Man with Watermelon and Black Woman with Fried Drumstick, and *Venus*, first performed in 1996, in which Parks imaginatively renders the painful history of the Venus Hottentot.

As Garrett notes, many professional critics and scholars have condemned the new art of stereotype for "not establishing distance between themselves and their material, for underestimating the destructive power of these images, for failing to put them in context or view them critically or unambiguously."[64] In the chapters that follow, I do not argue *for* this new stereotype-centered art, nor do I provide a detailed overview of the work of its practitioners. Rather, having selected some of the most powerful conjurers in African American culture, I explore how they transform stereotypes into vehicles for black humor and use them to illuminate the reach of slavery's long arm into our contemporary culture. Their effort to transform, subvert, and transfigure racial stereotypes evolves directly out of the culture of slavery, in particular through African Americans' response to and appropriation of the imagery of the minstrel stage.

As one of the first mass-media forums to claim to represent African Americans for the nation as a whole, the minstrel stage had a tremendous impact on racial discourse since its emergence in the 1830s and its full-fledged development in the 1840s. Originally performed by white men in blackface, minstrel shows lampooned African Americans through grossly drawn out stereotypes of laziness, superstition, lasciviousness, and buffoonish behavior. They consisted of a three-part structure: an opening section featuring a semicircle of performers who combined songs and dances with broad jokes and riddles, a middle or "olio" section offering comic or novelty set-speeches such as burlesque sermons or pun-filled "stump speeches," and a final section usually consisting of an extended skit set in the South. White women and African Americans adopted and altered the form, the latter as early as the 1850s and especially after the Civil War, the former in the early 1870s.

The origins, nature, and impact of the minstrel show have been the subject of critical debate especially during the 1990s, when several prominent studies of the form were published. Earlier studies of minstrelsy, such as Nathan Huggins's powerful chapter on the subject in *Harlem Renaissance* (1971) and Robert Toll's *Blacking Up: The Minstrel Show in Nineteenth-Century America* (1974), explore how the humor of minstrelsy viciously distorted the black body and black vernacular forms. Yet several critics, including Eric Lott, Michael Rogin, and W. T. Lhamon Jr., have made the case that, before the mid-1840s, white blackface minstrelsy contained the possibility of creating cross-racial alliances along class lines. But with increasing racial tensions that culminated in the Civil War and white working-class unrest, minstrel shows became violent expressions of white racism. Garrett succinctly summarizes the questions guiding this scholarship: "To what extent did minstrel shows imitate extant black folk traditions? Was minstrelsy a white invention created out of hatred and fear, or out of admiration and cross-cultural desire, or some combination? Or a black invention stolen and then distorted by whites for the purpose of perpetuating the ideologies of slavery and race? Or a black invention stolen and then distorted by whites for the purposes of invoking carnivalesque license toward the creation of the first subversive, even bohemian, alternative American multiculture?"[65] The extent to which minstrelsy continues to shape American popular culture is also a prominent element in recent scholarship. Lhamon, for instance, examines what he calls the "lore cycle" of minstrelsy from its marketplace origins to present-day music videos, concentrating on the form's development in the 1830s through its impact on contemporary popular music forms such as hip-hop.[66] And Lott provocatively explores the pleasure involved in the production and consumption of minstrel shows, noting the "giddy pleasure that actors and audiences of all types experience in the performance of stereotypes."[67] Similarly, in *Racechanges: White Skin, Black Face in American Culture* (1997), Susan Gubar examines the complicated dynamics of cross-racial impersonations in contemporary culture in a variety of cultural forms (film, photography, literature, painting) through which she traces the legacy of minstrelsy.

Minstrelsy certainly produced an abiding source of racist iconography and vulgar forms of humor, but it has also proven to be an enduring American cultural form because, as I have already suggested, it afforded a variety of strange or taboo pleasures. The characters that formed its core—the dimwitted slave and his dandy counterpart, Zip Coon, the mammy, the octoroon—were outlandish buffoons, or, as in the case of the mammy, overtly sentimental types in costumes that emphasized huge lips and eyeballs, overly wide noses, and, in the case of the "wench" characters, huge behinds. As Lott argues, audiences were able to sublimate "repressed pleasures in the body" such as those experienced during infancy (the "gorging and mucus-mongering of early life"), as well as cross-racial homosexual desire. They could also play out murderous misogynist fantasies (female roles were almost always played by men in drag, even though women were active in other theater forms) and explicit reassertions of racial violence. Lott notes in particular "the relentless transformation of black people into things" in, for instance, the minstrel stage's "sheer overkill of songs in which black men are roasted, fished for, smoked like tobacco, peeled like potatoes, planted in the soil or dried and hung up as advertisements."[68] Disgust and desire coalesced in "lubricious dances, jokes [and] lyrics" that at times barely disguised "culturally prohibited forms of pleasure."[69]

In its early years minstrelsy portrayed slavery in inconsistent ways; during the 1850s, when William Wells Brown began performing his dramatic readings of *The Escape*, the minstrel stage turned decidedly proslavery, often presenting grossly exaggerated images of black life with happy-go-lucky slaves who always yearned to please their master. Concentrating on Brown's novel *Clotel*, Paul Gilmore has shown how Brown highlighted the antislavery possibilities of minstrelsy. For Brown, Gilmore writes, "the minstrel show offered expansive representational possibilities because its commercialized images foregrounded the slippage between performative and essential notions of blackness and manliness."[70] In chapter 1, I examine how, in *The Escape*, Brown, rather than argue against the minstrel show's distorted depictions of slavery, appropriated and lampooned minstrel images in order to sabotage the denigrating comedy of minstrelsy. Similarly, Chesnutt exploited stereotypes about African Americans common on the minstrel stage, including the figure of the loyal retainer embodied in Joel Chandler Harris's Uncle Remus, to highlight its violence, particularly its obsession with transforming people into things. In later chapters, I examine how Richard Pryor and Suzan-Lori Parks, unlike many other contemporary artists who resurrect minstrel tropes, experiment with form to highlight the libidinal subtext of minstrelsy without replicating the bodily contortions and verbal nonsense through which it represented blackness.

For a time, however, Pryor was willing to embrace one of the most commonly spoken words of the minstrel stage, "nigger." In chapter 2, I examine how Pryor attempted to purge the word of its toxicity while conjuring and manipulating the racial and sexual stereotypes that flourished under slavery. A brilliant, gifted performer and mimic, Pryor, like Brown, used only his body and voice to give life to racial stereotypes across differences of gender and class. He culled his style and humor from the streets of black communities and was able to speak about the mutations that slavery has undergone in the language of the pool hall (his grandfather and uncle each owned one), the whorehouse (which he knew well, having grown up in his grandmother's brothel), the stoop, the barbershop, the jive of juke joints and Black Panther meetings—in short, in the verbal flourish that characterizes African American folklore. His stand-up performances, anecdotal and often autobiographical, give a sense of time, place, and people: Peoria, Illinois (where he grew up), his family members (especially his father and grandmother), characters of his youth, and the many different people that he met through show business (especially black athletes and actors), his many marriages, his addictions (to cocaine, to alcohol), and the comedian's travels (especially in Africa). At the height of his career, however, Pryor became concerned that he was reaffirming rather than sabotaging the stereotypes he was so adept at conjuring. Dave Chappelle now finds himself in a similar situation. Unlike Pryor, he largely relies on sets and costumes to conjure stereotypes, yet he too is a powerful performer whose show became phenomenally successful in the market. First produced by the cable channel Comedy Central in 2003, *Chappelle's Show* has also been released in DVD form. The first season of the show sold 1.7 million copies, making it the best-selling DVD of all time and a record for any television show.[71] What kind of success is this for stereotype-derived humor? Surely the success depends on Chappelle's numerous gifts as a performer. But, as Chappelle himself suspects, it could signal the co-optation of his power to conjure stereotypes.

In chapter 3, I explore how Ishmael Reed conjures stereotypes through a comic book–like graphicness that exaggerates the caricature to the point of the grotesque. Like Robert Colescott and Kara Walker, whose works I examine in chapter 4, Reed makes vivid the infinitely complex layers of associations embedded in stereotypes and gives access to the emotions, often conflicting and violent, that they provoke. Colescott's trademark is to transpose easily recognizable stereotypes, usually from the mythology of slavery, onto images that he appropriates from the work of master European painters such as Manet and Picasso. Through this conceit he creates a comedy of the grotesque that resembles Reed's. Walker also works through a process of appropriation. Transforming the nineteenth-century polite form of silhouette portraiture, she makes explicit the murderous, sexual, and even scatological subtexts of stereotypes. Cut from black cardboard, mounted on white walls, and displayed in installations that take over entire rooms, or even the space of huge opera curtains (in Vienna), Walker's images have both the zany energy of cartoons—their busy, speedy action—and the alluring beauty of finely crafted art. Making use of insights gathered from the work of Bakhtin and Baudelaire on the comic grotesque, I examine how Colescott and Walker give life to the whole storehouse of fantasies produced in the hothouse of a racially divisive past and an equally—if differently—divisive present.

The early plays of Suzan-Lori Parks, the subject of chapter 5, rely on different aspects of conjure. In her early plays, which are more directly engaged with the history of slavery than her recent work, Parks represents time as cyclical, cumulative, and repetitive and casts her role of playwright as that of a medium for spirit possession. In this manner, she makes manifest how the brutalities of slavery, specifically its genocide, shape the ideologies that govern our contemporary lives. Although her plays seem darker in tenor than the other work I discuss, Parks's experiments with language and dramatic forms are suffused with the energy of black humor. Mining what she calls the "strange relationship between theater and real-life," she serves as a channel for the dead of slavery, who reenter our contemporary world by "possessing" the actors on stage. Once conjured, the dead speak to the living (both on stage and in the audience) in a language that, while remembering the injustices of the past, simultaneously evokes the linguistic creativity of Black English (the spontaneity of jive; the ritual storytelling of the beauty parlor, juke joint, and barbershop).[72] Like Brown, Parks mocks the peculiar and creative aspects of minstrel speech, from its malapropisms and unorthodox orthography to its absurd dialect. Yet, in the process, she creates a humor that is as moving as it is fit to kill.

With these chapters I hope to make an intervention in the academy, where African American humor has been an underestimated realm of analysis. Many are the books that provide extensive compilations of tales, joke cycles, and folklore, but few are those that probe the depths of African American humor.[73] African American figures such as Langston Hughes, Zora Neale Hurston, Jessie Fauset, W. E. B. Du Bois, and James Weldon Johnson have acknowledged its power, but only Ralph Ellison has ventured far into the complexity of African American humor. In academic circles, perhaps the lack of this kind of exploration may be due to the challenges that humor in general presents for scholarly work, which tends for the most part to be woefully devoid of humor, as if to evidence the capacity or interest in laughter would make one appear less intelligent or not seriously committed to one's work. Thus theoretical excursions on humor in general are far from abundant; Freud, Bergson, and Pirandello are still some of the best in this regard, and I make use of them here. But perhaps the lack of deep explorations of African American humor is also due to the fact that, as Jeffrey Ferguson notes, for the "most part the American discourse on race has provided a stronghold for sincerity, melodrama, sentimentalism, and deep seriousness, but it has admitted the spirit of irony and humor only with the greatest of trepidations."[74]

Ferguson's fine book on the satirical writings of George Schuyler—a figure who, as Werner Sollors puts it, is the "godfather" of the black humorists in this book—is definitely a significant exception. As Ferguson shows in *The Sage of Sugar Hill: George Schuyler and the Harlem Renaissance* (2005), Schuyler debunked reified notions of blackness long before the postsoul generations and used his satiric wit to attack the foibles not only of whites and conservatives but also of blacks and radicals. "Although Schuyler understood well the need for protest and for compensatory rhetoric aimed at healing the injured consciousness of oppressed people," writes Ferguson, "he remained skeptical that an excessive focus on either would actually help to emancipate anyone."[75] In a rich journalistic career and in his brilliant *Black No More* (1931)—a novel that, among other things, anticipates Dave Chappelle's infamous black white supremacist skit on Comedy Central as it details the adventures of a black man who, through another's invention, appears white and masquerades as a white supremacist—Schuyler turned to humor to "encourage his readers," both black and white, to view race "complexly rather than dwell on it obsessively."[76] Like Schuyler, the black humorists that I examine are all too aware of the need to heal from slavery's lasting wounds, but they are also leery of identities built on victimhood. In their fictions of slavery, therefore, they use various forms of humor to expose not only white bigotry and tacit forms of racism but also how oppression can corrupt black folk, making them "want to imitate their oppressor, exploit their own people, invest in shallow materialism, revere fake symbols of exalted status," and "invest too heavily in an ideal of black peoplehood."[77] Of course, aside from Ferguson's book, there are other important exceptions.

Certainly Mel Watkins's *On the Real Side: A History of African American Comedy from Slavery to Chris Rock* (1994) has provided a much-needed corrective to the lack of sustained scholarship on African American humor. Watkins's extensive and incisive history of African American humor, in particular how it flourished within black communities and in other mediums (race records, vaudeville, the chittlin' circuit), its intricate relationship to minstrelsy, as well as its eventual convergence into mainstream culture in the 1970s, is invaluable not only for its meticulousness but also because it celebrates the spirit of African American humor. Unlike Watkins's work, and other more recent publications, *Laughing Fit to Kill* does not provide a historical account, either of African American humor or the development of a postsoul black humor.[78] Rather, I investigate the relationship between violence and humor and complicate distinctions between polite and popular representations of slavery in the past forty years. This has obvious ethical-political implications that I believe need to be addressed by close attention to formal and theoretical aspects. My hope is that readers will be persuaded by my case for a new understanding of the power, expansiveness, and the sheer raucousness of African American humor, of "laffin' fit ter kill."

"LAFFIN' FIT TER KILL"

Black Humor in the Fiction of William Wells Brown

and Charles W. Chesnutt

African American oral culture is rich in tales that use humor to represent the violence of slavery. The trickster animal tales featuring Brer Rabbit and Brer Fox, first popularized by Joel Chandler Harris in *Uncle Remus, His Songs and Sayings: The Folklore of the Old Plantation* (1880), are but one, albeit complicated, example. The tales, in which weaker animals like the Rabbit often outsmart stronger ones such as the Fox through wit and cunning, allegorize the great imbalance of power between master and slave and the ways that the enslaved found to sabotage it. As Mel Watkins notes, the tales "probably represent" the slaves' "most aggressive and cynical view of white America" short of physical rebellion.[1] Yet Harris, a white journalist who collected the tales (and therefore did help to preserve them), defused them of their critical edge by presenting them as amusing stories that Uncle Remus, a faithful retainer "who has nothing but pleasant memories of the discipline of slavery," would recount to a little white boy, the son of plantation owners, for entertainment.[2] While the tales depict anthropomorphized animals that kill and maim each other brutally, Harris claimed that the stories depict only the "roaring comedy" of animal life.[3] White southerners laughed, amused by the Rabbit's guile and cleverness. The enslaved laughed too, but for very different reasons. As scholarship has shown, slaves used the tales not only to release aggression but also as a medium for turning southern racial taboos on their head.[4] Thus, while they laughed at Rabbit's elaborate tricks, they made the Fox, usually the hero of European trickster stories, the dupe of the weak and repeatedly staged his violent death.[5]

The extensive cycle of tales involving John and Master represent another rich source of humor about slavery. Collected by folklorists such as Zora Neale Hurston and Julius Lester and circulated largely among the enslaved because of their unmasked aggression, these stories drop the symbolic disguise of the Rabbit versus the Fox and depict a clever slave, John (also called Nehemiah, Pompey, Jack, or Golias), who bests the Master in word and deed (although in a few stories the Master does trick John).[6] As the following example shows, the aggression in these tales is more direct than that of the animal tales but also less intense:

> Pompey, how do I look? the master asked.
> O, massa, mighty. You looks mighty.
> What do you mean "Mighty," Pompey?
> Why, massa, you looks noble.
> What do you mean by noble?
> Why, suh, you looks just like a lion.
> Why, Pompey, where have you ever seen a lion?
> I saw one down in yonder field the other day, massa.
> Pompey, you foolish fellow, that was a jackass.
> Was it, massa? Well, suh, you looks just like him.[7]

Examples of similar stories abound. A story about Nehemiah, a clever slave who had a reputation for avoiding work with his wit and humor, could easily be used to support the stereotype of the lazy slave, but it also illustrates the disarming power of laughter. Nehemiah is transferred from one master to another because of his ability to outwit his owners but is finally sold to David Wharton, the cruelest of slave masters in southwest Texas, who vows to "make the rascal work":

> The morning after Nehemiah was purchased, David Wharton approached him and said, "Now you are going to work, you understand. You are going to pick four hundred pounds of cotton today."
>
> "Wal, Massa, dat's aw right," answered Nehemiah, "but ef Ah meks you laff, won' yuh lemme off fo' terday?"
>
> "Well," said David Wharton, who had never been known to laugh, "if you make me laugh, I won't only let you off for today, but I'll give you your freedom."
>
> "Ah decla' Boss," said Nehemiah, "yuh sho' is uh good lookin' man."
>
> "I am sorry I can't say the same thing about you," retorted David Wharton.
>
> "Oh, yes, Boss, yuh could," Nehemiah laughed out, " yuh could if yuh tole ez big uh lie ez Ah did."
>
> David Wharton could not help laughing at this; he laughed before he thought. Nehemiah got his freedom.[8]

The outcome is hardly realistic, but the importance of the story is the way Nehemiah uses humor to outsmart his master.

Zora Neale Hurston suggested that the trickster hero John was closely associated with the magic and mystery of the conjuring root John de Conquer. "High John de Conquer came to be a man, and a mighty man at that," she wrote in 1943.

"Old Massa couldn't know, of course, but High John Conquer was there walking his plantation like a natural man."[9] Although there is no evidence in the tales or elsewhere for the connection that Hurston makes between the figure of John and that of the conjure root, her perhaps poetical association suggests that the tales did much more than express aggression. John, as the hero and trickster of a people, embodies an ancestral spirit and strength. "Old John, High John could beat the unbeatable," she writes. "He was top superior to the whole mess of sorrow. He could beat it all, and what made it so cool, finish it off with a laugh." So, while "Old Massa and Old Miss and their young ones laughed with and at Brer Rabbit," John de Conquer was "playing his tricks of making a way out of no-way. Hitting a straight lick with a crooked stick. Winning the jackpot with no other stake than a laugh."[10]

Slaves used forms other than the folktale to create humor about slavery. Parody, as John Lowe notes, was one of their favorite tools. While masters would have them believe that the Bible supported their oppression, the slaves would twist religious prayers and hymns. Hence the Lord's Prayer would become "Our Fader which art in Heaben! / White man owe me eleben and pay me seben / D'y kingdom come! D'y will be done! / If I hadn't tuck dat I woun't git none." "Reign, Master Jesus, Reign," would become "Oh rain! Oh rain! Oh rain, 'good' Mosser! / Rain, Mosser! Rain hard! / Rain flour an' lard an' a big hog head / Down in my back yard."[11] These and many other examples illustrate that humor about slavery flourished early in African American oral culture. The development of that humor among African American writers takes a different trajectory.

Racist assumptions regarding the "innate" relationship between gaiety and blackness not only supported arguments for slavery but also made it necessary for African American writers to maneuver carefully if and when they used humor until well into the twentieth century. This was especially true for antebellum African American authors who wrote primarily for the abolition of slavery (and thus largely to white audiences, for whom they needed to fashion selves that were "civilized") and after emancipation, against the violence of Jim Crow, causes that many considered too morally important and too earnest to be treated with humor. Often, they chose irony, satire, and parody—more sophisticated vehicles for humor than the slapstick and buffoonery with which blackness was often associated—to mockingly condemn slavery and racism. Very often, they hid their critique in sheep's clothing in order not to ostracize their audiences.[12] Yet readers, both in the past and now, have not always seen beyond the clothing. Nor have they seen that, despite the seriousness of the antislavery cause and the role of humor in the oppression of African Americans, black writers in the nineteenth century made intricate uses of humor, in its varied modalities, to critique slavery and racism.

In his well-known 1845 *Narrative*, Frederick Douglass maintains the moral seriousness of an antislavery crusader, but he employs a stinging satire toward the end of the text, one that is exemplary of the kind of humor that he often used as an antislavery lecturer. As Granville Ganter notes, along with his "formidable skills as a critic of slavery and racial prejudice, [Douglass] was widely remembered during the nineteenth century for being able to make his audiences laugh." Indeed, the source of Douglass's early success as an abolitionist lecturer was "his skill as a mimic—in particular, his burlesques of slaveholding consciousness."[13] Douglass's texts reflect his gifts for wit and satire, yet on the whole they do not seek to produce laughter. This is also true of the work of some of Douglass's peers. Harriet Jacobs, for instance, makes distinctive use of ridicule in *Incidents in the Life of a Slave Girl* (1861/1987), and David Walker employs a biting form of sarcasm in his *Appeal* (1829/2000), yet both authors retain the clear, moral earnestness of protest and thus produce a humor that is not conducive to laughter.[14] Perhaps because the humor in these texts remains relatively polite compared to the sometimes raucous humor of nineteenth-century African American oral culture, modern literary critics tend to ignore it. Instead, as Ganter rightly notes with respect to Douglass, critics tend to emphasize only the more "earnest passages" of their work.[15]

At issue here is the role of contemporary critics in framing nineteenth-century African American literature and, more specifically, that of representations of slavery by black authors. Take Henry Louis Gates's introduction to Wilson's *Our Nig* (1853/1983), the first known novel by an African American to be published in the United States. The full title of Wilson's novel, *Our Nig; or, Sketches from the Life of a Free Black, In a two-Story White House, North. Showing that Slavery's Shadows Fall Even There. By "Our Nig,"* signifies on the cruel humor that was used to humiliate slaves since colonial times. Noting the names that were imposed upon the enslaved, Joseph Boskin writes that there is "no question that one of the most insidious aspects of slavery was its oppressive humorous effects, names being one link in the larger design. . . . Black males were dubbed 'Fiscal,' 'Apollo,' 'Black Fat,' 'General Washington,' 'Nausea,' 'Limmerick.' Similarly, females were termed 'Fiscal Fanny,' 'Lies,' 'Paddle,' 'Present,' . . . 'Grief,' 'Chatt,' 'Icy' [even] 'Snowrilla.'"[16] While Gates does acknowledge Wilson's unprecedented and boldly ironic use of "Nig" in the title of her novel and as her pseudonym, he misses the satiric tone of Wilson's novel.[17] In the process of authenticating *Our Nig* as both a sentimental novel and an autobiography, Gates presents Wilson as someone who "preferred the pious, direct appeal to the subtle or the ambiguous" and who was able to create the first "black woman's novel" only by "adhering closely to the painful details" of her life and, as these did not fit the conventions of the "sentimental fiction produced by Wilson's white female contemporaries," inventing a suitable plot structure.[18] Thus, although Gates credits Wilson with creating "a new form of fiction," he places such an emphasis on the straightforwardness of her novel as to undermine its satiric aspects.[19]

Wilson employs satire both in its more conventionally perceived function, as a mode to inspire reform, and as a way to achieve some distance from her rage at the violence done to her. One must then wonder why a critic as astute as Gates, who has made possible our very reading of *Our Nig*—he recovered it from complete obscurity and republished it in 1983—does not acknowledge this aspect of Wilson's text. Elizabeth Breau suggests that "the ongoing pressure felt by African-American scholars to verify the claims made by slave narratives" led Gates to stress the seriousness of the novel. "A false or fictional autobiography," she rightly notes, "impugns the claims of black abolitionists to be truthful and undermines assertions about the horrific nature of slavery."[20] The implication is that the reliability of a black-authored account of slavery still depends, as it did in the nineteenth century, on its earnestness and seriousness.

Could this be the reason why critics have largely ignored William Wells Brown's strategic use of laughter and appropriation of racist stereotypes and assumptions? Is this why, until recently, Charles W. Chesnutt's powerful use of humor about and by African Americans has been relegated to critical obscurity? Unlike Douglass, Jacobs, Walker, and even Wilson, Brown and Chesnutt purposefully used more outlandish forms of satire while also appropriating racist portrayals of black Americans to critique slavery and racism. Yet, as late as 1969, William Edward Farrison published a biography of Brown that, while committed to highlighting the significance of the writer, grossly misreads his strategies. In part, Farrison's limited analysis is due to the challenge presented by Brown's hyperbolic use of minstrel conventions. Like Douglass, Brown turned the abolitionist platform into a stage where he lampooned racist stereotypes, slaveholders, myths about plantation slavery, and northern apathy.[21] As Richard Pryor would in *Black Ben, the Blacksmith* (1968), Brown wrote and performed one-man plays in which he assumed a range of voices across gender, racial, geographical, and political divisions. Of these plays, only one survives, *The Escape, or a Leap for Freedom* (1858), a play that satirizes what Harriet Jacobs called the "all pervading corruption" produced by slavery and that became the first African American play to be published in English.[22] In that play, Brown conjures, through mimicry, a whole array of demeaning characters, acts, and songs derived from plantation slavery and, in so doing, takes a risk that Douglass ultimately refused. As Ishmael Reed would in *Flight to Canada* (1976), Brown animates racial stereotypes, exaggerating their features in order to highlight their theatricality and their status as masks. Although he did so with the ultimate goal of critiquing their use to brand the "complex subject with the seal of reductive caricature and/or bad habit," he also got at the heart of what is *appealing* and powerful about them.[23] Stereotypes fascinated Brown. Although they were (and are) too often used to deny the humanity of his brethren, Brown knew that they could also be used as the means to freedom. He made special use of racial stereotypes, exploiting their performativity, what Emily Apter calls their "theatrical flare for striking a pose, assuming a guise, pretending an identity into existence."[24] It is this aspect of Brown's humor that critics like Farrison fail to address.

Probably first performed for audiences in Salem, Ohio, in February 1857, *The Escape* followed *Experience, or How to Give a Northern Man a Backbone*, a satire on a proslavery tract that, although not published, Brown read to audiences throughout 1856 with much success.[25] As one exemplary reviewer noted, "The drama is not only extremely amusing, but is really a very effective plea for the cause of anti-slavery."[26] In April of the same year, Brown read *The Escape* in Seneca Falls, New York, after which a reporter wrote, "If you want a good laugh, go and hear him. If you want instruction or information upon the most interesting question of the day, go and hear him."[27] Humor, as these comments suggest, enhanced not only instruction but also engagement.

Brown was so successful with his dramatic performances that, in 1856, the *Liberator* announced that he had "given up his agency" with the American Anti-Slavery Society to "devote his time to giving his lyceum lectures and the reading of his drama."[28] In 1858, writing to the head of the American Anti-Slavery Society in Ohio, Brown noted that his dramatic readings were more effective than his lectures, for people "who would not give a cent in an anti-slavery meeting . . . will pay to hear" *The Escape*.[29] Brown is best known as the author of *Clotel, or The President's Daughter*, a text that was long considered the first African American novel (it was published in England in 1853). Although it contains many humorous passages, *Clotel* has rarely been discussed as such and has, in fact, been widely misunderstood; one contemporary critic calls it "shamelessly hyperbolic," and another charges it with being "pornographic."[30] As John Ernest notes, the novel's "many sources and plots" and its intricate use of the conventions of several types of fiction, those of sentimental novels being one, have not only frustrated critics but also led to dismissive conclusions about the novel's artistic worth.[31] Critical dismissals of *Clotel* are also due, however, to the fact that, like *The Escape*, the novel is replete with racial stereotypes.

Brown, like Charles W. Chesnutt but unlike other nineteenth-century black writers, appropriated racial stereotypes and transformed them from vehicles of humor *against* African Americans to sources of humor *by* African Americans about racism. In Brown's case, the strategy was more successful in his dramatic readings than in his publications, largely because his audiences could more readily see the productive effect of a key strategy in his performances: the exaggeration of the already disturbing aspects of racial stereotypes for cathartic comic effect. Audiences could also appreciate the humor he created by contrasting his sophisticated persona with those of the buffoons he ridiculed.[32] In the private act of reading, especially over one hundred years after the public debut of Brown's plays, one might, instead of appreciating the hyperbolic edge in his work, give in to the critical tendency to ignore his use of minstrel tropes altogether or, worse, attempt to "explain" it as an "unfortunate symptom of the times."[33]

Brown knew that to critique slavery by using minstrel humor was to run the risk of affirming racist stereotypes, but he believed that the laughter it produced could be turned to social change. As Douglass did in the early years of his career, Brown capitalized on his audiences' "prejudiced habits of laughing at planta-tion stereotypes" by mimicking easily recognizable Negro characters. At the same time, he used the infectious good feeling of sharing and release that laughter can produce to make his audiences laugh at the bigoted whites that he also imper-sonated.[34] By the late 1840s, Douglass considered the risk implicit in minstrel humor too high; he "consciously sought to distance himself from the plantation burlesques he had practiced" in his early years and "became a vocal opponent of minstrel humor, performed by either blacks or whites."[35] Brown, by contrast, published *The Escape* nearly a decade after Douglass turned away from minstrel humor and left a record of a particularly risky but potent form of critiquing slavery.

But the challenge that Brown presents to critics today is also in his willing-ness to tackle unpalatable subjects straight on. He makes northern apathy and hypocrisy the main subject of his work, particularly in *The Escape*, treating both topics with a satire that is not hidden by sentimental rhetoric. He also does not shy away from presenting black subjects in unflattering lights. Witness, for ex-ample, his characterization of the pompous house slave Sam in *Clotel*. This is a crucial similarity his work bears to that of Wilson, who in *Our Nig* goes so far as to include a character who pretends to be a fugitive slave in order to profit as an antislavery lecturer.

Charles W. Chesnutt similarly addressed unpalatable topics, often in a style that makes use of racist stereotypes to humorous, but also socially progressive, ends. One of the first African American professional writers, and one with a tre-mendous command of his craft, Chesnutt was critically, if not commercially, suc-cessful when he first appeared in print at the end of the nineteenth century. Yet he lapsed into obscurity for most of the twentieth century, coming back into criti-cal attention in the late 1960s and into more thorough focus through William Andrews's comprehensive, but largely humorless, study of his work, published in 1980. Chesnutt's *The Conjure Woman* (1899), an intricately layered text that seemingly embraces demeaning racial stereotypes, was for a time dismissed as a set of stories of local color that pandered to white racism. Although the critical approach to Chesnutt's tales has changed radically—they are now appreciated for the "creative subversion" they effect—the richness of their humor has yet to be examined carefully.[36] The tragic aspects of the tales has faired better, with critics acknowledging Chesnutt's use of local color conventions and common stereotypes as masks for representing the "nightmare that the slaves inhabited."[37]

But Chesnutt's ability to represent the tragedy of slavery—especially in stories such as "Dave's Neckliss," a story that, although published independently, was originally part of the *Conjure Woman* tales—needs to be examined in relationship not only to the rich ironies of his work but also to the varied and powerful uses he makes of laughter.[38]

Repeated throughout the *Conjure Woman* and related stories are scenes of masters *and* slaves laughing to themselves, with each other, and even sometimes at each other, in what Uncle Julius, the ex-slave narrator in the tales, frequently describes as "laffin' fit ter kill." The phrase succinctly encompasses the extremes of humor and violence in the stories. In "Dave's Neckliss," a slave must enact the curse of Ham by tying a ham around his neck as punishment for a crime he did not commit. Dave looks absurd with his "necklace," and the slaves laugh "fit ter kill" when they see him not only because he looks silly but also because they are made to work harder when Dave is falsely convicted of stealing. But the necklace becomes a sign of death and destruction, as the spelling of the word in the vernacular suggests: neck-less. In "Mars Jeems' Nightmare," a master is temporarily transformed into a slave and subjected to the cruelty of his own overseer. When he is turned back into a master he laughs "fit to kill" as the overseer recounts the extensive violence he used to try to break a mysterious "noo nigger" who refused to submit to his cruelty. In "Hot Foot Hannibal" Chesnutt presents the reader with the hilarious spectacle of a slave who, having been "goophered" (bewitched) cannot control his hands and feet and therefore creates chaos in the house in which he is enslaved. Ultimately, however, the tale is one of revenge, as the goophered slave ends by laughing "fit ter kill" at those who conspired against him, while those who first victimized him end in tragedy and loss when the master sells one of them down the river.

In these and other tales, Chesnutt produces what Pirandello calls "the feeling of the opposite" at the heart of tragicomedy. Whereas mere comedy produces laughter from the "perception of the opposite" (via inversion, incongruity, and juxtaposition), tragicomedy produces laughter that is "troubled and obstructed" by the lingering eventuality of doom.[39] One is caught between a desire to laugh and the suspicion that, in doing so, one could be cruelly laughing at a tragedy that is about to unfold. One is caught, that is, between wanting and not wanting to laugh. Chesnutt's stories produce the "feeling of the opposite" at both the narrative and the metanarrative level. In "Dave's Neckliss," the slaves' mocking laughter is always troubled by the tragedy of Dave's predicament and by the fact that their fate too is tied to his punishment. In "Mars Jeems' Nightmare," the master's laughter at once recognizes the cruelty to which he is temporarily subjected and the fact that he subjects others to the same cruelty. But the reader experiences the feeling of the opposite not only through the characters but also through the tensions that Chesnutt creates between the ironic, comic, and tragicomic aspects of his tales. The *Conjure Woman* tales operate at two levels: that of the outer frame, which takes place in the postbellum South and involves John and his sickly wife, Annie, and that of Uncle Julius, whose tales are set in the antebellum years that constitute the stories' inner frame. The two levels of narration inform one another in intricate ways, sometimes interlacing and sometimes putting in tension a number of dichotomies: North and South, literate and illiterate, textual and oral, antebellum and postbellum. The various contrasts and parallels through which the story operates achieve rich levels of irony; it is this aspect of Chesnutt's work overall that has received the most sustained critical attention.[40]

The different levels of irony that Chesnutt creates through the structure of his tales and the comic aspects on which he relies—many of which engage with the racist images and ideologies of American popular culture—are often in conflict with the laughter that the stories represent, a laughter that, at its most powerful, suggests the violence and pain of slavery. That is, while the levels of irony and comedy in the tales refer to the power dynamics that inform interpretations of slavery and black culture, the laughter itself suggests that which is arguably beyond representation: the torture of bodies and psyches that the enslaved either endured or by which they perished.

In different ways Brown and Chesnutt use humor both as a distancing mechanism, making common racist stereotypes ironic or unfamiliar, and as the means of raising controversial and unpalatable aspects of slavery. Brown manipulates minstrel images to critique northern apathy and the racism underlying empty abolitionist rhetoric and sentiment. Chesnutt, focusing on what is paradoxically both a great source of comedy and a major principle underlying chattel slavery—the inability to control one's body—creates a tragicomedy that intensifies the tensions between the interpretation and the experience of slavery. Brown's play and Chesnutt's short fiction are representative of the strategies of humor employed by other African Americans in the nineteenth century. In the context of this study, however, these texts serve as specific models for writers and artists who take up the traumatic memories of slavery from a late twentieth-century and early twenty-first-century perspective.

The Escape; or, Brown's Shameless Hyperbole

Frederick Douglass called "Sentimental Abolitionism" the "effect of all antislavery effort," which, while filling "the whole North with sentiment opposed to slavery," produced "neither the will nor purpose to abolish slavery."[41] As John Ernest notes, "Many African American writers condemned anti-slavery sympathy as a kind of benevolent neglect that veiled an underlying racial prejudice.... The problem was not that antislavery sentiments were not being promoted, but rather that they *were* being both promoted and normalized among white northerners who supported the cause but resisted the implications of the message."[42] There were, of course, many white abolitionists who wrote passionately *and* effectively against slavery. As Ernest notes, *American Slavery As It Is* (1939) is a powerful collection of evidence against the evils of slavery written by white southerners and collected by Thomas Weld, Angelina Grimké, and her sister, Sarah Grimké. William Lloyd Garrison, Lydia Maria Child, and Harriet Beecher Stowe are among many other influential antislavery writers. While this list could be significantly expanded, African Americans "nevertheless understood that white writers were more likely to write strongly against slavery than to write knowingly against racism."[43]

Well aware of the fact that sentiment was not always conducive to action, that in fact it could deter action by purging people's energies in vicarious experience, Brown did not rely on sentimental tropes to critique slavery.[44] In *The Escape*, he operates through a piling-up method, mocking the mockery that the slaveholding class made of religion, marriage, love, and family, while exaggerating the already distorted qualities of the characters or types through which slavery was represented: the wicked mistress, the lascivious master, the ignorant field hands, the duplicitous house servant, the tragic mulatta, the heroic slave, the heartless and uncouth slave trader. In making both master and slave subject to his satiric hyperbole, Brown not only emphasizes the "all pervading corruption of slavery," but also highlights both the performativity of each role—especially since Brown assumed every one of them in his dramatic readings—and the ways such roles can be used to obscure "private motivations."[45] Perhaps more important for his immediate purposes, however, Brown also makes whites the subject of their own laughter.

Not surprisingly, one of the play's main objects of laughter is a man named Mr. White, who is the play's representative northerner. Strategically introduced at the end of the play, Mr. White serves Brown as a vehicle through which to satirize the inertia and self-congratulatory aspects of "Sentimental Abolitionism." Through *The Escape*, Brown tells an extended joke in which, as soon as the play opens and throughout, southerners are subjected to ridicule. But placing a sting at the end of the play, Brown introduces Mr. White, who is no more enlightened than any of the play's southern characters and is, arguably, worse than any of them. By the time Mr. White appears, Brown has built a comic atmosphere that ensnares his northern audiences in their own laughter. Operating through hyperbole, he sets a relationship between himself as writer and performer and his audience, in which everything is so exaggerated that normal expectations are suspended. Anything can become the subject of Brown's ridicule, including his northern white audiences, who become part of what John Ernest calls the "discomfiting cultural house of mirrors" that is Brown's play.[46] Northerners were used to seeing the South satirized, but the incongruity of seeing themselves as part of the charade created the potential for laughter that Brown masterfully capitalized upon.

The Escape opens with a scene not uncommon in the canon of Western art: a mistress sits looking at some drawings while a servant "stands behind the lady's chair" (*The Escape*, 5). The servant is always found in the corners and on the sides of drawings, paintings, and photographs representing white subjects, and is often black. In Brown's play, however, the servant, who is biracial, is described as a "white slave" since he is so light skinned and, in a later scene, is humorously "mistaken" for the master's son. At that point we learn through indirection that he is, in fact, the master's illegitimate son and slave. Such reference to the immorality of slaveholders was common enough in antislavery literature, but Brown, as he does throughout the play, presents the commonplace in a frenzied atmosphere in which what is ordinary becomes farcical. The play presents stereotypical settings and characters from sentimental abolitionist literature: Muddy Creek, a typical plantation where Mrs. Gaines, the evil mistress, unleashes her brutality on her slaves; a cottage in the woods where Dr. Gaines, the lascivious master, keeps Melinda, the tragic mulatta, prisoner; and Niagara Falls, the place where the heroic slave George, after reuniting with the mulatta, achieves a dramatic escape. But Brown exaggerates the qualities of these types to both undermine them and put them in the service of his extended joke.

The play's opening dialogue between Dr. and Mrs. Gaines takes on the tone of "shameless hyperbole" that critics have misunderstood in Brown's work. Hoping that the people in and near Muddy Creek may develop diseases and increase his number of patients and thus his income, Dr. Gaines begins a conversation with his wife, who responds to him in kind:

> Yes, I would be glad to see it more sickly here, so that your business might prosper. But we are always unfortunate. Everybody here seems to be in good health, and I am afraid that they'll keep so. However, we must hope for the best. We must trust in the Lord. Providence may possibly send some disease amongst us for our benefit. (*The Escape*, 5)

From the very start of the play, Brown sets a note of hyperbole that forecloses emotional engagement with the characters and situations. Instead, he presents the corruption of ideals in ridiculous relief and immediately burlesques one of the main vices supporting slavery: parasitic greed. He even puns on the name Gaines. Here and elsewhere, Brown takes up the discrepancy between assertions of piety and unethical actions in the lives of masters and mistresses—a well-covered topic in slave narratives and an important aspect of abolitionist rhetoric—but he spells it out in a language that, while quotidian in tone and diction, presents an outrageous image quite candidly: a supposedly pious doctor and his wife hoping that the Lord will make other people ill for their own benefit.

Brown thus quickly appeals to his northern audiences' sense of superiority, setting the South in dark contrast to the North. And, as if to indulge his audiences, he quickly piles up images of immoral southerners. As soon as the dialogue between Dr. and Mrs. Gaines ends, another slave owner enters the scene to deliver appalling lines with a straight face. Seeking the doctor's services because his previous physician made him lose "a valuable nigger," Mr. Campbell, the slave owner, reveals that he is in fact seeking a new doctor for all of his slaves because, "as [his] old mother used to say, 'change of pastures makes fat calves.'" Quoting his "old mother," no less, Mr. Campbell reveals his casual equation of people with animals. Purposefully refusing to set slaves at the opposite side of the spectrum—as Harriet Beecher Stowe does when she sets evil Simon Legree against pious Uncle Tom—Brown presents slaves that seem to fare no better than their masters; they too appear as grotesque images. Scene 2 opens with Cato, an overblown version of the house slave, who performs a classic minstrel scene when he dons his master's doctor's coat and attempts to perform his duties, to disastrous ends. Particularly through the dandy character, minstrelsy produced crude forms of humor by portraying African American men who dumbly attempt to mimic their masters, attempting to fulfill positions of authority but sorely lacking the intelligence to do so. In a version of this role, Cato dons the doctor's coat, claiming that he wants to look "suspectable," and yanks the wrong tooth from a poor, aching slave in a scene replete with minstrel antics and malapropisms (*The Escape*, 7). Cato straddles his patient while the latter screams, and they ultimately fight each other, creating chaos all around. When the master reenters, he scolds both slaves as if they were children, leaving Cato crying over the fact that "his" coat has been torn during the fight. In short, the slaves, especially Cato, are catty, silly buffoons who need the supervision of someone like Dr. Gaines.

Brown seems to give his northern audiences no more than familiar, albeit hyperbolic, images of slavery. But, as John Ernest suggests, one can well imagine Brown "reflecting on race in the American theater and wondering whether it might be possible to turn the tables and give white audiences more than they bargained for."[47] With each scene he exaggerates the stereotypes that he relies on to greater and greater degree, involving all figures in an increasingly complicated plot that moves forward as if on a sped-up, almost out-of-control cyclorama. Act 1 closes as Mrs. Gaines and Reverend Pinchen, another stereotypical figure, display the contrast between pious pretensions and unethical action even more shamelessly than the doctor and his wife do in the opening scene. Mrs. Gaines, who loves to "hear of Christ and Him crucified," listens to the Reverend tell of his "religious experiences," which, in one instance, turn out to be nothing more enlightened than using the mantle of religion to get his pony back from horse thieves, a story that Pinchen relates while Mrs. Gaines liberally threatens to whip her slave Hannah (12–13).[48]

As the play unfolds, Brown mocks the mockery that slave owners make not only of religion but also of marriage and family. In so doing, Brown shows, they confirm a view of humanity that the Reverend makes explicit to Mrs. Gaines and other characters in what becomes a refrain throughout the play:

> I've had great opportunities in my time to study the heart of man. I've attended a great many camp-meetings, revival meetings, protracted meetings, and death-bed scenes, and I am satisfied, sister Gaines, that the heart of man is full of sin, and desperately wicked. This is a wicked world, sister Gaines, a wicked world. (*The Escape*, 12)

Mrs. Gaines does nothing but confirm Pinchen's conviction. When she tells Hannah, "I've no doubt that I'll miss going to heaven on your account. But I will whip you before I leave this word, that I will," she recalls Stowe's Simon Legree in her wickedness (*The Escape*, 15). But whereas Legree is haunted into guilt by the image of his pious dead mother, Mrs. Gaines has no shame as such. Instead, she seems perversely interested in the passion of Christ—Brown repeats the fact that she loves to hear of "Christ and Him crucified" as a refrain throughout the play—because, as the sacrilegious mind of Ishmael Reed might put it, she *likes* suffering. Brown's characterization of Mrs. Gaines is, in fact, a paler version of Reed's sadomasochistic slave owner, Arthur Swille, who, as we will see in chapter 3, is a hyperbolic rendition of decadence and immorality.[49]

While the play's characters are farcical, its plot is frenzied. Most of it revolves around Glen and Melinda's struggle to stay together and achieve their flight to Canada in spite of Dr. Gaines's plans to have Glen sold down the river and have his way with Melinda. As he does in *Clotel*, Brown complicates this plot with subplots that destabilize the conventions and stereotypes on which he relies. Brown shadows Glen and Melinda's struggle with that of Hannah, who is forced to "jump the broom" with Cato when her husband, Sam, is sold away from her. When Hannah resists, Mrs. Gaines beats her violently and then stages a ridiculous ceremony that thoroughly mocks the institution of marriage. Brown thus suggests a more tragic and violent version of Melinda and Glen's story, but instead of detailing the beating, moves it offstage and crafts the comeuppance that Mrs. Gaines deserves in a comic mode befitting her character. When Mrs. Gaines realizes that the doctor is keeping Melinda captive in a cottage in the woods, she rides "ten miles bare-back" to beat her husband to the cottage and kill Melinda (*The Escape*, 30). Although scarcely able to walk when she arrives, Mrs. Gaines fights Melinda with a dagger but is defeated when Melinda takes a broom and "*sweeps off Mrs. Gaines*," who loses her "*cap, combs and curls*" (31). Defeated and humiliated (she ends on the floor, bald and powerless), the mistress meets her end in grand theatrical fashion.

Even as he creates the play's abundant hyperbole, Brown begins to dislocate the stereotypes of slavery, relying on a number of inversions and displacements that, by the end, build to an overhaul of his northern white audiences' expectations. He follows the buffoonery of Cato's minstrel antics with a scene that includes two soliloquies that conspicuously challenge stereotypes of black speech. Delivered by Glen and Melinda in scene 3 of act 1, the speeches should alert the astute reader to Brown's tongue-and-cheek use of theatrical conventions. Brown's biographer, William Edward Farrison, epitomizes the critics who miss the cue. He argues that Brown seems to have "vainly" patterned Glen and Melinda's language after that of Shakespearean characters, but while Farrison sees this as by "far the worst defect in the drama," it is, in fact, one of Brown's first attempts to turn the tables on his audience.[50]

Glen delivers a soliloquy that, though echoing Hamlet's first two soliloquies, is closer to the language of sentimental novels usually associated with female figures. Awaiting Melinda's arrival, he wonders out loud "what keeps her. . . . I waited long and late for her last night, and when she approached, I sprang to my feet, caught her in my arms, pressed her to my heart, and kissed away the tears from her moistened cheeks" (*The Escape*, 10). But when Melinda arrives, she promptly tells him, "Glen, you are always thinking I am in tears" and goes on to deliver her own soliloquy in a language usually reserved for male characters (10). "It is often said that the darkest hour of the night preceded the dawn," says Melinda. "It is ever thus with the vicissitudes of human suffering. . . . Oh, how I would that those who think the slave incapable of inner feelings, could only see our hearts, and learn out thoughts—thoughts that we dare not speak in the presence of out masters!" (11). Ostensibly elevating the two characters by patterning their language after Shakespeare, Brown actually regenders them, thus dislocating the normal associations between the stereotype of the heroic slave and the tragic mulatta while appropriating Shakespeare's language with a wink to the astute reader who, unlike Farrison, can see Brown's gesture as jest.

At the same time, Brown does not mock Glen and Melinda's heroism. They do, after all, achieve the leap for freedom in the title of the play. Nor does he unman Glen or transform Melinda into a manly figure, moves that would fit too easily with stereotypes of feminized male and masculinized female slaves. Rather, Brown highlights the ways "slave characters are always already rhetorical structures, bound by representational conventions," whether they are heroic or buffoonish.[51] He shows the seams of those conventions through the artificial language he assigns to Glen and Melinda and his inversion of gendered speech. In this respect it is significant that, although Brown appropriates many of the conventions of the minstrel stage, he does not reproduce the mock Shakespearean language popular on that stage, but offers a straightforward imitation of the poet.[52] This helps him set up a false contrast. Glen and Melinda seem to distinguish themselves from Cato, especially because they speak in an elevated language quite different from the malapropisms of Cato's minstrelsy. Yet Cato turns out not only to achieve his own leap for freedom on the same boat as the two heroic slaves, but also to deliver the songs that anchor the play.

As critics have often remarked, slaves like Cato used the mask of minstrelsy to "put on old massa." In *The Escape,* Brown not only sets up a dramatic contrast between mask and intent through Cato's minstrel antics and his songs, but also indirectly uses that contrast to comment on his own performance. Cato does not sing until act 3, up to which point he outlandishly fulfills the stereotype of the contented house slave. When he sings, however, he has this to say:

> Come all ye bondmen far and near,
> Let's put a song in massa's ear,
> It is a song for our poor race,
> Who're whipped and trampled with disgrace. . . .
>
> They take our wives, insult and mock,
> And sell out children on the block,
> They choke us if we say a word,
> And say that "niggers" shan't be heard [Chorus].
>
> Our preachers, too, with whip and cord,
> Command obedience in the Lord;
> They say they learn it from the big book,
> But for ourselves, we dare not look [Chorus]. (*The Escape,* 24)

What is immediately apparent is the straightforward language in which Cato delivers his indictment of slavery. His language is so far from that of the minstrel malapropisms that pepper his speech elsewhere that the word "niggers" is in quotation marks. At the same time, stage directions indicate that Cato sings his lines to the tune of "Dandy Jim from Caroline," a "deeply and mockingly racist" song common on the minstrel stage.[53] This move on Brown's part emphasizes the ironic contrast between how Cato is perceived and his true convictions. When Cato finishes his song, Mrs. Gaines reenters the stage, whereupon he immediately dons his minstrel mask, saying, "Yes, missis, I allers does what you and massa tells me, an' axes nobody" (*The Escape,* 25).

Later in the play, when Cato has made it to the North, he sings again, this time to critique the myth of northern deliverance, the idea that the North would welcome the enslaved to unqualified liberty, to the tune of "Dearest Mae." This composition, "more nearly bordering upon respectability" than other low-character minstrel songs and therefore arguably more suited for a critique of the more "respectable" North, is as mockingly racist a tune as "Dandy Jim."[54] The song concerns a submissive slave who works hard yet mirthfully so that he can get permission to see his beloved, Mae. But Cato appropriates the tune to expose the false notion of northern deliverance and thus underscores the difference between the true freedom he seeks, which he must seek in Canada due to the Fugitive Slave Law (a law that left runaway slaves in the North susceptible to capture and return to slavery), and the palliative freedom offered to the submissive slave.

Ultimately, Cato's songs underscore the fact that, despite his buffoonish minstrel antics, he is in tune with Glen's heroism. The two characters are among the most recognized performances of black manhood, on the minstrel and the abolitionist stage, respectively embodying notions of submission and resistance. Rather than privilege one role over the other or suggest a "true" manhood that the roles might obscure, Brown shows them for the performances they are even as he employs them in his critique of southerners and northerners alike.[55] Through Cato, he also suggests the instability of each role: submission may cloak resistance, and resistance may be delivered to the tune of submission.

Brown exaggerates the gap between perception and reality, one level of performance (minstrelsy) and another (antislavery protest), only to show their confluence in a single voice, that of Cato and indirectly his own, since he assumed Cato's persona when he performed readings of the play.[56] Such confluence not only mocks the mistress's ignorance of Cato's true design but also places Brown's northern audiences in a superior relationship to her since, in a case of dramatic irony, those audiences could see behind Cato's mask. At the same time, Brown also plays a joke on his northern audiences. Cato ultimately uses that mask to run away, just as Brown appropriates the tune of "Dandy Jim" to critique not only the hypocrisy of slave owners and that of religious types, as Cato does in his song, but also the inertia of his northern audiences.

Brown quietly introduces Mr. White in the fifth act of the play but quickly shows the role that the representative northern white man takes in relationship to the other types in the play. Mr. White makes his first appearance as he arrives in the South and bombastically begins to lecture his audience about the evils of slavery and the wonders of his own "free State" (*The Escape*, 35). Yet his performance earns him nothing but hostility: he must immediately take to a cellar, where he hides from an angry mob (including Dr. Gaines) that wants to lynch him (35–37). The next time he enters the stage, Mr. White is north of the Mason-Dixon line, glad to have escaped and never to have to go south again. Brown thus puns on the very concept of escape, suggesting not only the flight to Canada for which the enslaved fight but also the escape from responsibility that the Sentimental Abolitionist achieves in preaching, but not acting on, his word. In fact, we next find Mr. White merrily sketching the scenery of Niagara Falls on the border between the United States and Canada while two poor men beg him for money. Mr. White considers them a nuisance, exclaiming, "Will you stop your confounded talk, and let me alone? Don't you see that I am sketching? You have spoiled a beautiful scene for me, with your nonsense" (46). Romantic in his defense of liberty when he preaches to the southerners who run him off, Mr. White is unable to see misery when it stares him in the face.

Brown cleverly parallels Mr. White's escape with that of Cato, who arrives in the North at the same time. The two, fugitive slave and abolitionist, escape the evils of the South, but whereas the latter can forget the experience, the former must continue to flee onward, to Canada. "Oh! Shame upon your laws, dat drive me off to Canada," Cato sings, referring to the Fugitive Slave Law. "You loudly boast of liberty, an' say your State is free, / But ef I tarry in your midst, will you protect me?" (*The Escape*, 41). Staging another clever coincidence, Brown has Cato, Melinda, and Glen enter the beautiful scene that Mr. White is sketching as they run away from Dr. Gaines and the same gang of officers that chased Mr. White out of the South. "Why, bless me!" exclaims Mr. White when he sees them, "these are the slaveholding fellows. I'll fight for freedom!" And "*taking hold of his umbrella with both hands*," he does. Or, rather, he joins a scrambling fight in which several men fight each other until a ferryman enters and Cato and the heroic slaves achieve the leap for freedom of the play's title (47). Mr. White's valiant, although also comical, act (he fights with his umbrella, after all) is thus literally overwhelmed by the maelstrom of action of the last scene.

Brown further ridicules Mr. White's belated entry into the fight for freedom, a fight that the enslaved have long carried and might have achieved without him, by setting it against the backdrop of Niagara Falls. Elizabeth McKinsey has shown how Niagara Falls became a symbol for the promise, power, and grandeur of America and, as such, the object of numerous visual and textual patriotic odes. She notes that "the first truly American historical novel," James Fenimore Cooper's *The Spy* (1821), "reaches its climax at the Falls," as do numerous other American tales of heroic action.[57] Of course, Mr. White's fight pales in comparison to the heroism in those tales, while his relationship to the Falls, unlike that of the patriotic heroes to which McKinsey refers, is as an observer who merely paints their beauty but does not embrace their power. In fact, Mr. White trivializes the American grandeur symbolized by the Falls through his largely comical heroism.

Niagara Falls was also a conventional setting for climactic escapes by fugitive slaves in antislavery literature.[58] In some cases, especially in "The Fugitive Slave's Apostrophe to Niagara" (1841), the Falls were not only a dramatic setting but also a symbol, although not of American grandeur, but of its limits. In "The Fugitive Slave's Apostrophe" the Falls "are presented as a literal obstacle between the slave and freedom in Canada" and represent only a bastard form of freedom.[59] "The tumult of the Falls," writes McKinsey, "symbolizes the 'maddening passions in the bondsman's breast'; his voice joins with Niagara's thunder to shout a curse on slavery and a call for retribution that reads, to the retrospective eye, like a fiery prophecy of the Civil War."[60] As Chesnutt does in his story "The Passing of

Grandison," which also includes a farcically dramatic Niagara Falls scene, Brown juxtaposes both the patriotic symbolism of the Falls and their use by antislavery writers, suggesting that, in fighting for freedom, the enslaved fulfill the promise of America ironically by having to leave the country, while the Sentimental Abolitionist perverts it by preaching freedom but doing little to effect it.

Mr. White's lack of true conscience pales in comparison to Mrs. Gaines's cruelty, Reverend Pinchen's corruption, and Dr. Gaines's lasciviousness, yet Brown's satire reveals that, in remaining largely disengaged from the fight for freedom, Mr. White is complicit with the baser crimes committed by his fellow whites in the South. What is perhaps worse, he is not even aware of his own complicity and instead considers himself valiant and progressive. Such hypocrisy, Brown suggests, is as pernicious as the openly racist views of the southerners who, at the very least, do not claim to be friends of the downtrodden. Faced not only with the play's "shameless" hyperbole but also with the disparities of body and voice of Brown's multicharacter performance, one can well imagine audiences disarmed by a humor of incongruity. To be sure, some of Brown's audiences might have found only entertainment in his performance.[61] But setting his critique in the mode of entertainment also allowed him to change expectations and raise consciousness. One can imagine the surprise of those northerners who realized by the end of the play, an end that is conspicuously "happy," that far from being outside the extended farce it purports to present, they are its main attraction.

Transformation in Brown, Conjure in Chesnutt

Brown published *The Escape* during a decade in which the tensions that eventually led to the Civil War kept mounting. In fact, Brown, like Cato, Glen, and Melinda, had to flee the country (he went to England) as a result of the Fugitive Slave Law of 1850, a stricter version of a similar law previously passed. A year after his return in 1853 (after friends had purchased his freedom), Congress approved the Kansas-Nebraska Act of 1854 (an act that established the principle of popular sovereignty, allowing white males in new states to decide whether or not to enter the Union as slaveholding territories). Three years later, in the *Dred Scott v. Sanford* case of 1857, the Supreme Court declared that African Americans had no citizenship rights. Little wonder that by this time Frederick Douglass had no patience with burlesques. Why, then, did Brown? When Brown returned from exile to the United States, he returned not only to stricter laws protecting slavery but also to the flowering of minstrel shows, including the enormously popular "Uncle Tom" shows spawned from Stowe's blockbuster novel, *Uncle Tom's Cabin* (1852). As Eric Gardner notes, "Bigger cities, better presses, better theaters, and large-scale public debate over slavery and race" allowed "massive literary and performative production" of both abolitionist texts and minstrel shows.[62]

Seeking to capitalize on the power of mass production and consumption of both minstrelsy and abolitionism, Brown produced a play that, on the surface, seems to cater to market demands. He understood, as Paul Gilmore notes, how much slavery was mediated by "mass cultural representations." Hence the startling claim he often made: "Slavery has never been represented; Slavery never can be represented."[63] At the same time, Brown fervently believed in advocating for the enslaved, for speaking, as he put it, for "those who cannot speak for themselves," despite the challenges it presented. One such challenge was the fact that white readers expected and responded best to representations of slavery that made a spectacle of suffering and celebrated northern benevolence.[64] Rather than meet such expectations, Brown became a master at manipulating them while capitalizing on the power of entertainment.

Harry Elam notes that Brown performed his one-man play in the context of a highly charged "performative ex-slave oratory," in which he was susceptible to an objectifying abolitionist gaze.[65] Brown was that odd commodity: the ex-slave who could supposedly let a hungry public know what life was like "among the lowly" (to borrow the subtitle of Stowe's *Uncle Tom's Cabin*). A light-skinned man who, like Sampsey, the "white" slave in *The Escape*, was often mistaken for the master's son (he was, in reality, the son of his master's friend), Brown assumed the voice of each character in his play, becoming the "nexus" for the different ideological positions that the play's various stereotypes index.[66] One contemporary commentator noted that when Brown assumed Cato's voice, one could "lose sight of the speaker and instead of the educated Brown see the caricatured Cato."[67] While his audiences might have expected this kind of performance from an ex-slave, Brown delivered the less than expected, for just as easily as he assumed Cato's voice, he also assumed that of Dr. Gaines, of George, of Mrs. Gaines, of Melinda, and, perhaps most surprisingly, of the representative northerner embodied in Mr. White. *The Escape* is one instance of Brown's own creative leap for freedom Appropriating the mass cultural representations with which his audience was all too familiar, he assumed the "subject position of artist, playwright and performer" rather than that of an object to be gazed upon.[68]

It is in this context that Brown's choice for the epigraph of *The Escape* becomes clear. He quotes a simple line from Shakespeare's *Hamlet*, "Look on this picture, and on this," a line that Hamlet delivers while trying to convince his mother to repent for her complicity in the murder of Hamlet's father (*The Escape*, 1).[69] Hamlet shows his mother a picture of his dead father and contrasts it with a picture of his uncle, his father's brother and murderer. In using this line to open his play, Brown contrasts the "picture" of slavery that his audiences expected, one that would have been flattering, and the one he delivered, a play that does not pretend to be a "true" representation of slavery but that dislodges common expectations and stereotypes. Hamlet's line, delivered in the context of a crime between two brothers and of the complicity of a would-be ally (the queen), also implies the themes of Brown's play: the crime of slavery and the North's complicity.[70] Like Hamlet, who uses a play as part of his ploy to achieve justice, Brown used the growing power of mass entertainment to similar ends.

Transformation, appropriation, animation: these are the key terms in approaching Brown and the terms that help us better appreciate his narrative strategies overall and, more specifically, his use of humor with respect to slavery. They also illuminate his connection to a rather different writer, Charles W. Chesnutt.[71] Like Brown's, Chesnutt's humor arises from his ability to appropriate and transform stereotypes into something rich and strange. But whereas Brown works through mimicry and hyperbole, Chesnutt relies on a particular mode of storytelling to reclaim and transform the power of stereotypes. Much more so than Brown, Chesnutt made intricate use of African American folklore,[72] in particular of conjure, which involves not only the casting of spells and the summoning or warding off of spirits but also the transformation of people, often into things or animals. While Chesnutt publicly distanced himself from folk belief, he turned conjure into a powerful trope and a mode of storytelling, emphasizing its elements of transformation and metamorphosis to represent the violence of chattel slavery, its elision of people with animals and things.[73] Brown, who rarely invoked conjure explicitly, was also a conjurer in his own right. As it is clear in *The Escape*, he brought to life racial stereotypes through mimicry and hyperbole, strategies that were more obvious and arguably more potent in his dramatic readings (since these relied on his acting) than in his written work.

Conjure operates in Chesnutt's tales as a mode of narration in which to tell a tale is to cast a spell, a spell that has the capacity to "dissolve and rearrange the reader's historical sensibilities and racial assumptions."[74] The spell works its magic through Uncle Julius's language as well as through Chesnutt's ability to transliterate the power of African American oral culture. At the same time, through the relationship between Uncle Julius and his immediate audience, John and Annie, Chesnutt thematizes the limited extent to which that spell could work on subjects who remained cynical of the power of slave culture. To this end, Chesnutt relied on the double structure of his tales: the tension he created between the frame of the story and the story itself. In Chesnutt's stories the skepticism (of conjure, of the reality of Julius's stories) of the outer frame pivots against the reality (the cruelty of slavery) of the story within a story, producing "the exceptional originality and force" of Chesnutt's conjure tales.[75]

Writing after the Civil War, Chesnutt did not face the problem of Sentimental Abolitionism. Rather, he published during a time in which nostalgic stories about life before the war, rendered in what became known as the local color tradition, were the norm. Relying on dialect and stereotypes to give a sense of place, these stories increasingly became the means to fictively represent the reconciliation between North and South and the vehicles through which to create a myth of the South as the seat of a quaint, even picturesque slavery. Paternalistic masters, benevolent mistresses, and happy, loyal darkies were the principal characters of such stories as rendered by, among others, the "Old South's most romantic defender, Thomas Nelson Page."[76]

The challenge before Chesnutt, therefore, was the creation of a fiction that would counteract the myth of the Old South and represent slavery, its brutality, its complicated and strange intimacies, and, perhaps most of all, its deep, long, and violent impact on American culture after the war. To do so, Chesnutt made use of conjure at multiple levels. All of the tales in *The Conjure Woman* contain instances in which people are turned into objects, animals, or spirits. At times, conjure functions in the tales as possession does in voodoo—as a way to counteract the dispossession of slavery, turning people into spirits rather than objects. In most of these tales, conjure functions as a conduit for physical and psychic survival for the enslaved. But conjure can also reinforce the dispossession of slavery when used in the service of the depraved and selfish, as some of Chesnutt's tales demonstrate.[77] At another level, the stories also "appropriate the figurative power of conjure"; conjure becomes "the allegorical component that bridges the seeming discrepancy between" two "levels of temporality," antebellum and post-Reconstruction, "casting the two times in a simultaneous event."[78]

Through his rich use of conjure Chesnutt produced not only exceptionally original tales but also a powerful tragicomedy of slavery. The elements of conjure that he chose to emphasize, its metamorphic and spell-casting effects, signify on the violence of chattel slavery and the difficulties of representing it while simultaneously creating a humor of the body and a comedy that involves the thwarting of expectations, assumptions, and sensibilities (of Julius's immediate audience as well as of Chesnutt's readers). On a broader scale, Julius's tales suggest the qualities of dreams and what Freud called "joke work." Jokes, like dreams, Freud argued, are vehicles for the expression of fantasies, of wish fulfillments or repressed aggression. These are expressed through joke work, which, like dreams, involves condensation, multiple use of the same material, double meaning, "displacement, faulty reasoning, indirect representation, [and] representation by the opposite."[79] From John and Annie's perspective, Julius renders dreamlike tales (in which people are turned into mules, trees, wolves, etc.) in order to receive limited financial gain (slices of ham, a job for a relative, the use of a grape vine). But Julius's tales depend on a creative use of Black English that allows for a great deal of signifyin(g) and punning on John and Annie's limited perspective. Through Julius's tales, Chesnutt animates cultural fantasies as these are embodied in stereotypes, transforming the familiar by dislocating it from "normal" structures in ways similar to Freud's joke and dream-work. At times too, as for example in

"Mars Jeems' Nightmare," the tales effect certain levels of wish fulfillment from the perspective of the enslaved.

Like Brown, Chesnutt appropriated racial stereotypes, turning them to quite different purposes than those intended by local color writers like Page, and he did so without leveling their theatricality and their potential ambivalence. Julius manipulates and, at times, is complicit with the stereotype of the loyal retainer; John is the skeptical, rational listener who is all too ready to see only Julius's immediate economic motivations for telling his tales. Their performance plays out fictive versions of the confidence games that characterize Brown's work and life.[80] Annie, the representative sentimentalist, plays an essential role in the dynamic triangle of relationships she forms with John and Julius. Bound by the inequalities of gender, she often lends Julius a sympathetic ear, although like her husband, she too represents a negative model of listening. Much more attuned to the metaphorical levels and pathos of Julius's tales than her husband is, Annie also largely misses the way that the tales signify on post-Reconstruction race relations, in part because she listens selectively. Only those tales that seem to inform her own precarious position under patriarchy seem to impact her.

If Chesnutt animates the ideological perspectives that Julius, Annie, and John represent through their triangular relationship, he also appropriates and transforms minstrel stereotypes. Uncle Julius is Chesnutt's elaborate appropriation of Uncle Remus, and the triangular relationship that he sets between that character and the white couple is an extended parody of the teller-listener relationship that Joel Chandler Harris created between Uncle Remus, the little white boy, and, by extension, Harris's white audiences.[81] More specifically, Julius's tales include some of the most demeaning images of black subjectivity—chicken- and ham-loving thieves, naturally born lazy "niggers," and conniving house slaves, to name a few—in which they serve, ironically, as vehicles for an eviscerating critique of racism and typecasting. As Eric Sundquist argues, Chesnutt's transformation of racial stereotypes reveals another aspect of the writer's conjure, for, in fictively seizing upon demeaning images, Chesnutt effects acts of "cultural conjure," figuratively reclaiming and transforming their power.[82]

Since the recuperation of Chesnutt from critical obscurity, the best scholarship on his work has concentrated on the aspects of conjure to which I have thus far referred. In what follows, I offer an exploration of Chesnutt's short fiction, including not only the *Conjure Woman* tales but also other dialect and non-dialect stories, in which I focus on a less discussed topic: the role of laughter in Chesnutt's representation of slavery. I do so at the risk of sometimes understating the complicated dynamics of Julius's performance in the conjure tales, and the role of dialect more generally, but in the hopes that a shift from two well-covered topics in Chesnutt criticism can point us to domains yet to be explored.

The Tragicomedy of Chesnutt's Short Fiction

In Chesnutt's "The Passing of Grandison," a master asks his slave if he is happy with his lot, and the slave replies, "Yas, master," with all the obsequiousness that the master could hope for.[83] But Chesnutt expands the scene over the course of the story, exaggerating the slave's submissiveness while increasing the master's delight in it exponentially, so that, in the end, when the slave's submissiveness is revealed to be a well-performed charade, the master's foolishness lies fully exposed. In this and other stories Chesnutt makes an intricate use of the humor in the John and Master tales. Like *The Escape*, the story tells an extended joke in which the stereotypes and conventions of plantation fiction are satirized in a comic mode that includes not only hyperbole but also the humor of what-if games and inversions. The premise of the story is in itself ridiculous: Dick Owens, a well-educated but lazy young southerner, tries to win a lady's hand on a bet that he can match the heroism of an abolitionist who recently died in jail after aiding fugitive slaves. Drawing on the humor that results from the debasement of an ideal, Chesnutt has Owens set himself a comparatively easy and self-serving task: to take one of his father's slaves to the North and "free" him by leaving him there. But when Grandison, the slave, refuses to be set free, the story seems to engage in a what-if game: what if your slave were so loyal that you could not persuade him to leave you if your life depended on it?

As if winking at the reader, Chesnutt provides plenty of clues and humorous asides that allow the reader to anticipate Grandison's eventual "passing"—the fact that his submissiveness is simply a performance that allows him to free not only himself but his entire family. This has led at least one reader to consider the story "formulaic and predictable."[84] But if the story's plot has no surprises, it is because, rather than build suspense or any other element of realism, it relishes the absurdity of the stereotypes it sets in motion. In other words, the story delights in the how, and not the what, of its delivery. When Dick convinces his unsuspecting father that he needs to take Grandison with him on a trip north, Grandison indulges his master's paternalistic view of slavery and makes him laugh when he asks if he can hit any abolitionists that might come near him:

> "Certainly, Grandison," replies the colonel, chuckling, "hit 'em as hard as you can. I reckon they'd rather like that! Begad, I believe they would! It would serve 'em right to be hit by a nigger!"
>
> "Er ef I did n't hit 'em, suh," continued Grandison reflectively, "I'd tell Mars Dick, en he'd fix 'em. He'd smash de face off'n 'em, suh, I jes' knows he would."
>
> "Oh yes, Grandison, your young master will protect you." (*Stories*, 194)

The master then tries to scare Grandison, telling him that the abolitionists are a "desperate set of lunatics" and that he needs to stick close to his young master and "always remember that he is [his] best friend, and understands [his] real needs, and has [his] best interest at heart" (194). As the story unfolds, Grandison acts as if he had swallowed whole each of his master's words. Although young Owens gives him plenty of opportunity to run away—at one point even giving him the key to a drawer containing a hundred dollars and leaving him alone for a couple of days— Grandison loyally waits for his young master. Owens's repeated attempts to abandon Grandison, each more outrageous than the last, coupled with the consistency of Grandison's frustration of them, suggest a cartoon version of Sisyphean labor. The young master, who has never had to work for anything, makes great efforts to "free" his slave but is repeatedly vexed by the image of the loyal Grandison waiting for him at the end of each attempt. How "could he," the narrator comments, as if with a smirk, "find fault with one who so sensibly recognized his true place in the economy of civilization, and kept it with such touching fidelity?" (*Stories*, 198).

At the foot of Niagara Falls, where Owens takes Grandison on one last attempt, the story seems, if briefly, to come to the kind of dramatic resolution that Brown parodies at the end of *The Escape*. "I do not deserve to be an American citizen," Owens exclaims to a sleeping Grandison. "I ought not to possess the advantages that I possess over you," he adds, with more irony than he could ever fathom, "and I am certainly not worthy of Charity Lomax," referring to his beloved, whose first name puns on the pity that she eventually takes on his misguided self. But when Owens concludes his string of assertions to Grandison with "if I am not smart enough to get rid of you," the story quickly switches back to its comic mode, and Owens is finally successful in "freeing" Grandison (*Stories*, 200).

Three months later, when Grandison returns to the Owens plantation spinning a fabulous yarn, the story attains a higher level of comedy. Convincing the elder Owens that he was captured by the "infernal abolitionists" against his will and made to suffer unspeakable horrors, Grandison not only receives the welcome of a prodigal son but also manages to make his master his mouthpiece (*Stories*, 203–4). Repeating Grandison's tall tale to his wayward son, the master excitedly recounts how the abolitionist locked "the poor, faithful nigger up, beating him, kicking him, depriving him of his liberty, keeping him on bread and water for three long, lonesome weeks, and he all the time pining for the old plantation!" (204). Grandison escapes, as the master recounts, by "keeping his back steadily to the North Star" (203). The irony of this comical reversal becomes richer when Grandison eventually runs away with his entire family on a path well planned in advance and leaves the master in shock, "shaking his fists impotently" (205).

Through parody, Chesnutt reduces the stereotypes of "plantation fiction to shambles," thus clearing the path for his own representations of slavery, representations that mock the "false nostalgia" that plantation fiction invoked for "the prelapsarian black man who supposedly once labored in edenic bliss under the benign supervision of the southern white man."[85] In tales such as "A Victim of Heredity; or Why the Darkey Loves Chicken," Chesnutt adopts a different strategy to similar ends. Rather than negate common racial stereotypes, he presents them in all their absurdity with a straight face. The story sets out to answer the preposterous question suggested by the subtitle. But, like Brown's play, the story begins at the level of absurdity and then exaggerates that mode only to undermine it by subtly building another story underneath the surface, one that is far from absurd.[86]

Like *The Escape*, Chesnutt's story satirizes northerners who use seemingly progressive racial ideologies to mask their guilt and inertia. "A Victim of Heredity," one of Chesnutt's Uncle Julius tales, opens with a ridiculous image: John, a white northerner, is so besieged by guilt that he cannot find adequate punishment for a "midnight marauder" who had tried to steal one of his chickens. Chesnutt humorously allows his readers to track John's thoughts: he begins by wanting to give the thief five years in the penitentiary to give him "time to break the habit" and to "strike terror [in]to hearts of other thieves." The disproportion between crime and punishment (as well as the rhetoric with which it is expressed) is so outrageous that even John, who is often morally blind and deaf, can sense it, and he begins to reduce the punishment, first to two years, then to one year, then to six months, then to three months (all within the space of a few paragraphs). At each step, the individual circumstances of the thief interpose John's convictions, slowly breaking down the stereotype of the chicken thief and giving way to the individual behind it: a "very much frightened," "insignificant-looking fellow" with a "large family and a sickly wife."[87]

Despite the fact that John can sense the living human being behind the stereotype, he holds on to the image of the chicken thief and asks Julius "why is it that his people can't let chickens alone." "Is it in the blood?" (*Short Fiction*, 124–25). When Julius responds affirmatively, Annie indignantly retorts, "Why, Uncle Julius! . . . I am ashamed of you, to be slandering your race in that way" (125). If Annie thus voices the response that readers might have to Julius's affirmation of the stereotype, after she hears Julius's tale about an avaricious master, she lets the thief go unpunished, concluding, "If slaves did contract the habit of stealing chickens and other little things to eat, they were not without some excuse for their conduct; and we [she and John] ought not to be too severe with them because they haven't outgrown the habit in a few years" (131). Rather than take in the full force of Julius's tale, Annie is also besieged by guilt and, ironically, makes John's own guilt-produced elaborate deliberations come to naught.

Under the pretense of answering the mystery about chicken-loving darkies, Julius exposes a master's exploitation of and dependence on his slaves. He tells the story of a master who, having cheated his nephew of his inheritance, buys slaves and then, seeking to cut costs, pays Aunt Peggy, the local conjure woman, to devise a potion that will reduce his slaves' appetite and hence the rations he must provide for them. At first the slaves do not seem affected by the cut rations, but when the master's avarice gets the better of him and he applies a second dose, they become so weak that they cannot work, and the master risks losing not only his crops but also the investment that he has made in the slaves themselves. Just as the master's avarice doubles in on itself and creates a boomerang effect, the absurdity of the story doubles when the slaves, dying from starvation, eat vast amounts of food (the master's best hogs and cattle) but do not improve until the master begins to feed them chicken, upon which they require all the chicken in the county to recuperate.

In the end, Julius manages to answer the question that begins the tale—he claims that the slaves in the area now owned by John have genetically retained a taste for chicken—while contrasting the minor theft to the serious crime that the master commits in trying to cheat his slaves of one of the most basic forms of recompense they could receive for their labor. Exploiting another contrast, that between the response that Julius's tale merits and Annie's, Chesnutt reveals the inertia underneath both John's seemingly thoughtful consideration of the thief and Annie's paternalism. As Eric Sundquist notes, the master's successive reduction of rations in order to realize more profit can be taken "to represent the post-Reconstruction treatment of black labor through the inequities of sharecropping and convict lease." But rather than realize the connection between the exploitation of slaves and the exploitation of ex-slave employees like Julius, Annie is content to let people steal her "portable property" and John would rather punish the "victims of heredity" than examine his own complicity in perpetuating slavery (*Short Fiction*, 125).[88]

The strategy of appropriating racist caricatures in order to redefine their purpose is familiar to Chesnutt's readers, for it is a strategy that characterizes all of his tales of conjure and transformation. In "The Passing of Grandison," the strategy results in the explosion of a stereotype; in "A Victim of Heredity," it works as a screen for Julius's critique of exploitation. In the tales I examine hereafter, Chesnutt uses the strategy as part of a tragicomedy of slavery. In these tales, laughter is the sound of the tragic recognition of dispossession. Particularly in "Dave's Neckliss," laughter is uttered in the face of the cruelty of slavery, a cruelty that Chesnutt invokes not through sentimental or Gothic elements but through a comedy that highlights the slaves' lack of control over their own bodies.

Chesnutt sets such laughter in uneasy relationship not only to the comedy of the body, which he creates in part by appropriating aspects of minstrelsy, but also to the comic resolutions that he gives all, except the last, of these tales. Involving cases of wrongdoing facilitated by conjure, the tales end in light, comic fashion with the righting of wrongs and the punishment of guilty parties. Yet such resolutions are always ironic in light of the fact that the crimes of slavery, which Chesnutt so potently invokes through laughter, are never redressed. John and Annie miss such irony and listen to Julius's tales for amusement, entertainment, and at best edification, and consider his motives only at the simple level of material gain. Although theirs are negative examples of how to interpret Julius's tales, Chesnutt's critics replicated them for decades. But the reader who is attuned to Chesnutt's brilliant interposition of comedy, laughter, and tragedy can appreciate not only the irony that John and Annie miss but also the fact that Julius's tales, and by extension Chesnutt's work, could be so dismissively consumed.

Although it does not contain the potent laughter of the other tales here examined, "The Goophered Grapevine," is an excellent example of the ways Chesnutt used a comedy of the body to represent the tragedy of slavery. A master employs the conjure woman Aunt Peggy to cast a spell to prevent his slaves from eating his grapes. When a slave innocently eats some grapes, his vitality grows and diminishes according to the rhythm and cycle of the plant, making him young and strong when the vine flourishes and old and weak when it does not. As in "A Victim of Heredity," in which the slaves' bodies change drastically, almost to the point of death and then back again into life, Chesnutt suggests comic elements that are tinged with tragedy, mainly the vision of Henry, the goophered slave, as his appearance changes dramatically with the seasons. One of the most obvious changes is to his hair, which grows lustily as the vine becomes lush, thus invoking the image of woolly hair, a marker of racial difference, growing wild (as in an outlandish Afro) and diminishing with the seasons. Chesnutt uses nappy hair as he does the image of the chicken thief and chicken-loving darkies in "A Victim of Heredity," mainly as a trope from the minstrel stage that he makes deeply ironic in the context of his stories.

As Sundquist notes, Chesnutt here revises an African American folktale in which the "man who eats the goophered grapes finds that each season his penis gets larger" and argues that Chesnutt's revision has "an air of Victorian propriety."[89] But in shifting the focus away from the bawdy associations of the original tale, Chesnutt does much more than make the tale respectable: he emphasizes the tragic elements of Henry's predicament. Like a biblical Samson, Henry loses his strength each time he loses his hair, becoming not only weak and sickly but even more at the mercy of his master's will than any other slave. As in "A Victim of Heredity," the master in this tale is ruled by avarice; he schemes to sell Henry when he looks young and strong and buy him back when he withers. Again, Chesnutt borrows from the minstrel stage, as the ploy echoes the kind of antics performed there. But the allusion is ironic because he also hints at the tragedy of Henry's predicament. Henry must work for whomever his master wills, and eventually dies when the master unwittingly ruins the vine.

William Andrews reads Henry's death as less tragic than "curious and weird."[90] Indeed, Julius remarks that Henry simply goes out, "sorter like a cannel" (candle), showing no particular signs except for the usual rheumatism and lack of strength that he suffered when the vines withered (*Stories*, 17). But the fact that Chesnutt does not represent Henry's death as a dramatic event does not necessarily mean his death lacks tragedy. Rather, in focusing on the changes that Henry's body suffers, Chesnutt employs comedy in the service of tragedy. He highlights Henry's status as a thing that also grows and dies by tethering his fate to that of a plant, thus literalizing the common racist notion that the enslaved were closer to nature than were their masters and mistresses. But in focusing on the cyclical changes that both the plant and the human being undergo, Chesnutt does not stay within the realm of nature but invokes the kind of mechanical automatism that Henri Bergson identified as a key source of the comic.

Bergson argues that we "*laugh every time a person gives us the impression of being a thing*," especially in "coarser forms of the comic, in which the transformation of a person into a thing seems to be taking place before our eyes." Machines, unlike living creatures, are predictable; it is the interposition of the two opposites, the rigidity of the mechanical clashing with the suppleness of life, specifically when something "*mechanical [is] encrusted upon the living*," that produces laughter. Although Bergson could not have predicted it (he was capable of asking, in all seriousness, "[What] is there comic about a rubicund nose? And why does one laugh at a negro?"), his insights illuminate the kind of comedy that Chesnutt put to the service of tragedy.[91] Henry is subjected to the regularity of the seasons, and with them to changes between the suppleness of youth and the rigidity of old age. Although this would ostensibly bind him to nature and its cycles, Julius emphasizes the speed and regularity with which Henry undergoes such extremes, suggesting the image of a human being caught in a machine that accelerates the cycle of life and death. That Henry's master is ultimately responsible for such cycles and that he profits from them further emphasizes the unnaturalness of Henry's changes.

Ultimately, the tragedy is not Henry's death; rather, it is the fact that, like any other slave, Henry is subject not only to natural forces but also to the economy of chattel slavery, which, like a machine, could speed the cycle of life and death. Chesnutt thus moves the tragedy from Henry's particular case to the use and abuse of enslaved bodies in general.[92] Robert Bone also correlates Henry's story to that of field slaves who "were in fact, worth more in the spring, with the growing season still to come," and worth less in the fall, when "the owner was responsible for supporting" them through the "unproductive winter season." Such fluctuations, concludes Bone, "underscore the slave's status as *commodity*; his helpless dependence on the impersonal forces of the market."[93] In this context, it is not surprising that Chesnutt chose not to portray Henry's death in dramatic terms.

In letting his life go out like a candle, he highlights the tragedy that, under chattel slavery, such deaths occurred with regularity and insignificance.

"Hot-Foot Hannibal" reveals Chesnutt's intricate use of a comedy of the body and of laughter in the service of tragedy. In this tale, Chloe, Jeff, and Hannibal are caught in the same machinery that manipulates Henry's body, attacking each other in the process. Significantly, the tragedy takes root when a slave is denied the freedom to shape her own destiny and control her body. When Chloe's master decides that she should marry Hannibal instead of Jeff, the man she loves, she has Jeff appeal to Aunt Peggy for help. For a price, the conjure woman provides the couple with a baby doll in the image of Hannibal, and through the doll the couple begins a hilarious manipulation of Hannibal's body in a ploy to get Hannibal removed from his position as a house servant and, consequently, as Chloe's husband-to-be. Hannibal not only becomes "hot-footed" but also light-headed, thereby causing havoc everywhere he turns, and Chloe and Jeff essentially become complicit in a central ideology of chattel slavery: using someone else's body for personal gain.[94]

Chesnutt contrasts the humor of Hannibal's predicament to the tragedy that unfolds. When Hannibal learns that he has been goophered, he avenges himself by making Chloe believe that Jeff has been untrue. Telling Jeff that Chloe wants to meet him by a creek and Chloe that Jeff is meeting a lover, he disguises himself as a woman and then tricks both of them. Overcome by her jealousy, Chloe informs the master of the baby doll, whereupon the master decides to sell Jeff to a speculator in order to put fear into any slave who might want to fool "wid cunju'ation" (Stories, 92). It is then Hannibal's turn to laugh, and he does so "fittin' fer ter kill" (Stories, 92). He reveals to Chloe how he convinced her of Jeff's infidelity. Hannibal's cross-dressing revenge leads to the demise of the wrong-doers in a comic resolution of the story's inner frame. But Chloe's pathos against the background of Hannibal's boisterous laughter dislocates that resolution.

Ironically, when they challenge the master, the lovers lose not only whatever limited control of their bodies they had but also their will to live. Chloe's knees give out as soon as Hannibal reveals his trick, and she faints, staying unconscious for a half hour. Afterward, she can only creep and crawl about, "pale az a gos'" (Stories, 93). When she hears that Jeff was not only sold down the river by the speculator but also that he drowned on the way (in a possible suicide), Chloe goes mad, dies, and literally becomes a ghost, possessed by the terrible memory of utter loss, haunting the creek where Hannibal's charade unfolded. Interspersed throughout these tragic events is Hannibal's laughter, which seems as if literally fit to kill, and that of the master who, unwilling to believe that Chloe can't simply take up with someone else, laughs when he learns that she is pining for Jeff (93).

Chesnutt thus presents instances in which laughter is chillingly divorced from its associations with either joy or amusement. At the same time, he connects these two instances of laughter to the comedy of Hannibal, who, when hot-footed and light-headed, humorously fumbles about destroying the master's property and interrupting life on the plantation. Hannibal drops the master's dinner, pulls out expensive bulbs and feeds them to the hogs, can't use his time efficiently, and is so noisy that he wakes the mistress from her slumber. His actions recall the antics of the minstrel stage and play out the role of the trifling, dimwitted Negro. Chesnutt's juxtaposition of the chilling laughter of the tragedy and the light, amusing comedy of Hannibal's fumbling achieves the kind of "reciprocal interference" that Brown's use of racist tunes in an antislavery play produces.[95] The tragedy becomes a chilling version of the comedy and the comedy a debased form of the tragedy. But at their core, both the tragedy and the comedy reveal the enslaved in a struggle to take control of their bodies and destinies while living within a system that ultimately controls both.

Focusing almost entirely on the lovers' quarrel that frames Julius's tale and on the fact that in this story Julius takes on a more conservative role than he does in other tales, Henry B. Wonham misses the fact that the tragedy of Chloe and Jeff's love story is meant to contrast with the comparatively minor quarrel in the outer frame of the story, between Annie's sister, Mabel, and her fiancé, Malcolm. Chesnutt does not reveal the details of that quarrel and only hints that it has something to do with Mabel's "pride and independence" and with Malcolm's ability to say things that "no woman of any spirit could stand" (Stories, 84). In an otherwise sensitive account of the tale, Wonham argues that Julius sacrificially offers Chloe's tale in order to facilitate a symbolic reconciliation between North (represented by Mabel) and South (represented by Malcolm).[96] But the story is meant to achieve much more. It is meant to contrast the "pride, independence and spirit" with which Mabel and Malcolm can determine their destinies with the struggle of the enslaved, and their descendents, as evidenced by Julius's ambivalent performance throughout the Conjure Woman tales, to determine their destinies and, in some cases, take control of their bodies. Both Julius and the subjects of his stories do indeed evidence spirit, pride, and independence, despite their lack of freedom and rights, as Chloe's decisions demonstrate, but they do so often at great cost.[97]

Like "Hot-Foot Hannibal," "Mars Jeems' Nightmare" is a story that involves enslaved people trying to wrest control of their destinies from their master, but it does not have a similar tragic counterpoint. Instead, Chesnutt capitalizes on the comic resolution of the inner frame story to a greater degree and relies on the transformative aspects of conjure to produce a humorous reversal of roles. The cruelty of slavery, however, remains a key subject in the story, and laughter remains the most powerful conduit for its representation. The story within the story that Julius relates is in fact inspired by an act of cruelty that John and Annie witness. When they see a man beat his mare ruthlessly, the couple profess that "there is no worse sin and no more disgraceful thing than cruelty," which prompts Julius to relate a tale about Mars Jeems (*Stories*, 32). The man beating the mare is the grandson of Mars Jeems, who used to work his slaves to death, prohibited any form of expression outside of work, from singing to courting to marriage, and gave free rein to his brutal overseer. When Solomon, one of the slaves, is punished for courting and his girlfriend sold away, Aunt Peggy puts a spell on the master and gives him a taste of his own cruelty. In one of the few instances in Chesnutt's work in which a white character is conjured, Aunt Peggy temporarily transforms Mars Jeems into a slave who, after being subjected to the cruelty of his own overseer, is transformed yet again, this time into a more compassionate master (35).

The story's sentimental and conservative resolution (slavery is ameliorated, not ended) is misleading. At one level, Chesnutt seems to pander to racist arguments for slavery since the story plays out a what-if game. What if a white person had to endure the cruelties of slavery? How would that person act? When Jeems is temporarily turned into a slave, he meets every affront to his humanity with utter disbelief and resistance and cannot be broken by the overseer no matter how cruelly he is treated. Jeems is, in fact, sold because the overseer fears he will kill him before he can break him. The implication, of course, is that a white man could never withstand slavery. But the story's what-if game also plays out a wish fulfillment as the master is punished for his own cruelty and made to understand this fact explicitly, but only after he experiences his nightmare in complete darkness. Called the "noo nigger" throughout his transformation, Mars Jeems is not only "whipped and brutalized . . . he is also stripped of his name . . . and of any memory of where he has come from."[98] In short, he is made to experience the most disorienting and violent aspects of slavery without any recourse to kin or group knowledge.

The story suggests that Mars Jeems would have perished under slavery not because he is too strong to accept it, but because of his ignorance in how to survive under its brutality. Saved by Aunt Peggy, who transforms him back into a white man before he is sent away after he is sold, Mars Jeems returns to hear his unsuspecting overseer recount the details of his nightmare. It is then the master's turn to laugh "fit ter kill" (*Stories*, 41). Listening to the overseer, who grins "like a chessy-cat" as he recapitulates the brutal acts to which he subjected him, the master laughs in bitter recognition (42).

Mars Jeems's laughter in the face of the catalogue of cruelty that his overseer so callously delivers contrasts with and thus highlights the story's overtly facile resolution, one that even the usually insensitive John recognizes as such. When Jeems returns from his nightmare and realizes the effect of his cruelty, he immediately fires his overseer and allows his slaves enough leisure time not only to court and marry each other but also to do so with "fiddlin' en dancin' en funnin' en frolic'in fum sundown 'tel mawnin'" (*Stories*, 43). "'And they all lived happy ever after,'" John remarks when Julius's tale concludes (43). The resolution of Julius's story is indeed conspicuously neat. The master suddenly stops laughing, fires the evil overseer, and, on a hunch, rightly accuses him of stealing. The overseer, who, throughout the story, flashes his ugly "snaggle teef," making "de niggers 'low he look lack de ole debbil," disappears the next day, as if in a cloud of smoke (36). Meanwhile, Solomon, the slave who gets Aunt Peggy to put a spell on the master, ends by regaining his sweetheart, and the lady who had spurned the master because of his cruelty finally accepts him in marriage. The story's neat ending, however, highlights a deep irony. As a result of Jeems's transformation, his slaves are much more productive, producing capital gain. A master's moral edification thus results not in the end of slavery but in its perfection.

When read next to Chesnutt's masterpiece, "Dave's Neckliss," Jeems's nightmarish but temporary experience of slavery is light comedy compared to Dave's tragedy.[99] Not surprisingly, the role of laughter in this tale is more complex and the comedy of the body has darker overtones. There are two significant forms of laughter in the story, that of the slaves who mock Dave, and Dave's own laughter when he goes mad. The slaves' laughter is cruel. One woman "bus' out laffin' fit ter kill herse'f" when she describes to Dilsey, Dave's "junesey" (sweetheart), who deserts him once he is marked by the ham, what Dave looks like with his "neckliss." Other slaves continually make jokes about the ham and pester Dave so much that he takes to the "bushes w'eneber he seed anybody comin', en alluz kep' hiss'f shet up in his cabin atter he come in fum wuk" (*Stories*, 728). Their laughter drives him into isolation, which, along with his punishment and Dilsey's desertion, ultimately make him lose his mind. He begins to talk and sing to himself, to have visions of hams growing in trees, and finally, when it is clear that his punishment will cost the master and the ham is removed from him, to miss the ham. Secretly he substitutes the ham with a fat pine tied to a string to make a new "neckliss," eventually comes to believe that he has turned into a ham, and hangs himself over a fire in the smokehouse. In the midst of it all, Dave laughs "fit ter kill" (729).

If, as Sundquist notes, "minstrelsy and chattelism are joined in the ham, sign of labor, of stereotyped behaviors of consumption," laughter and horror are equally joined.[100] As the slaves witness Dave transform from upstanding community leader before his punishment to the outcast he becomes, they laugh in mockery and bitterness, but that laughter becomes shameful as they realize the madness to which the punishment drives Dave. Julius's description of the transformation also suggests an inwardly experienced dark comedy. At work and in his limited leisure, Dave is haunted by the ham: "W'enber he went ter lay down, dat ham would be in de way. Ef he turn ober in his sleep, dat ham would be tuggin' at his neck. It wuz the las' thing he seed at night, and de fus' thing he seed in the mawnin'" (*Stories*, 728). The inanimate object has a strange agency: *it haunts without actually doing anything.* Of course, the ham, as one of "the stereotypical foods of coon songs, which figuratively dehumanized blacks by making them into pathetic buffoons who are addicted to watermelon, hams, chickens, and the like," has been endowed with the power to haunt.[101]

In literalizing not only the curse of Ham but also the haunting power of stereotypes, Chesnutt brilliantly underscores both the burden of stereotype as experienced from within and its absurdity. The ham not only haunts Dave in his private moments, but it threatens to usurp his identity. "W'eneber [Dave] met a stranger," Julius recounts, "de ham would be de fus' thing de stranger would see" and the only thing the stranger would notice; most people "would 'mence ter laf, en whareber Dave went he could see folks p'intin' at him," telling jokes about the ham (*Stories*, 728). In "A Victim of Heredity" we see John briefly discover the human being behind the stereotype of the chicken thief; here we see how a similar symbol dehumanizes Dave even in front of those who should know better.

The story, especially Dave's self-inflicted lynching, dramatizes not only the life-destroying effects of racial stereotyping, but also how laughter facilitates the internalization of such effects by the victims of racism. The enslaved people who mock Dave see in him their own enslavement carried to a literal and thus absurd level. They laugh at a man who, tethered to a ham, walks the plantation where they labor, a place that is supported by more quotidian forms of dehumanization. In laughing they assert the distance between their own lot and Dave's, whose absurd punishment becomes the nadir of subjection against which other slaves measure theirs. Laughter thus operates as a defense mechanism, expressed in bitter recognition of a shared subjection to cruelty and as a way of asserting some distance from that cruelty.

If those who laugh at Dave laugh in self-defense, Dave's own laughter is that defense mechanism carried to the extreme. Describing Dave's descent into madness, Julius notes that with "dat ham eberlastin' en eternally draggin' roun' his neck" Dave took to "laffin' fit ter kill 'bout nuffin" (*Stories*, 729). Enslaved people, as most accounts of black humor claim, laughed in order not to go mad. Dave laughs *because* he has gone mad, but in so doing he makes laughter expressive not of the cruelty of slavery, but of madness. At the same time, as he escapes into that realm, he succumbs to the literalness of the joke foisted upon him, staging his own lynching in an act that is a revolt against his master, since he becomes worthless property, but also his own gruesome end.

J. L. Styan suggests that "the real climax of a dark comedy" is not "the place where the hero is pressed to a decision, the villain unmasked, the situation brought to a crux, but the place where the tensions are so unbearable that we crave for relief."[102] Surely the crux of this tale is the moment Julius finds Dave in the smokehouse, hanging over the fire. The moment contains no suspense. By this time, the villain has been found, or rather, the real thief has confessed, and the master is ready to make it up to Dave and the rest of the slaves by giving them extra cider. He offers Dave a public apology, regardless of the fact that Dave has gone missing, which ends with, "Now take ernudder drink er cider all roun', en den git at dat cotton" (*Stories*, 731). But the reader has been warned of Dave's descent into madness, and when we follow Julius retracing Dave's footsteps to the smokehouse, we do so with the foreboding that something terrible has happened.

By this time, too, the reader has been subjected to John's racist ruminations on the limits of black sentience in the outer frame of the tale. The contrast between John's callous observations and the tremendous tragedy of the story heighten at the moment of Dave's suicide, a moment that also underscores Julius's act of narration and echoes precisely at the moment when Julius finds Dave. When the tale opens, John is counting the number of slices of a Sunday ham that Julius is eating; with each slice the ex-slave consumes, John becomes more and more convinced of Julius's base nature. When, in the midst of his eating, Julius sheds a tear, however, John's interest is piqued. Later, he asks for an explanation, which results in the story of Dave's "neckliss." Before Julius can relate his tale, however, John delivers a dense paragraph expressing his suspicion that Julius, as representative ex-slave, is not sentient enough to understand the degradation he experienced:

> It was only now and then that we were able to study, through the medium of [Julius's] recollection, the simple but intensely human inner life of slavery. His way of looking at the past seemed very strange to us; his view of certain sides of life was essentially different from ours. He never indulged in any regrets for the Arcadian joyousness and irresponsibility which was a somewhat popular conception of slavery; his had not been the lot of the petted house-servant, but that of the toiling field-hand. While he mentioned with warm appreciation the acts of kindness which those in authority had shown to him and his people, he would speak of a cruel deed, not with the indignation of one accustomed to quick feelings and spontaneous expression, but with the furtive disapproval which suggested to us a doubt in his own mind as to whether he had a right to think or feel, and presented to us a curious psychological spectacle of a mind enslaved long after the shackles had been struck off from the limbs of its possessor. (*Stories*, 722)

Dave's story would seem to prove John's point, as it represents the plight of one whose mind remains "enslaved long after the shackles [have] been struck off." Julius's own relishing of the ham would seem to prove the point as well, for the ham, as Sundquist argues, is "transformed over the course of Chesnutt's narrative into . . . the body and blood of Dave," which Julius eats in "a ritual of remembrance in which comedy cloaks [Julius's] identification with a legacy of suffering."[103] Like Brown, however, Chesnutt fulfills the expectations of readers such as John only to create searing ironies. John doubts if Julius "even realized, except in a vague, uncertain way, his own degradation." But he finds evidence "in the simple human feeling, and still more in the undertone of sadness, which pervaded his stories," of a "spark which, fanned by favoring breezes and fed by the memories of the past, might become in his children's children a glowing flame of sensibility, alive to every thrill of human happiness or human woe" (722–23). Ironically, it is John who seems not to be "alive to every thrill of human happiness or human woe." While he thinks Julius is incapable of "speak[ing] of a cruel deed" with freedom of thought and feeling due to his continued mental enslavement, Julius in fact delivers a story of "human woe" with a complexity beyond John's comprehension.

No sensitive reading of "Dave's Neckliss" fails to comment on this irony. Yet the laughter in the story escapes notice. To ignore it, however, is to miss the intensity of Chesnutt's tragicomedy. In at least one contemporary instance, Dave's death becomes merely an act of sacrifice that Chesnutt symbolically carries out in the service of saving the master's soul. In a puzzling introduction to the 2001 Riverside edition of Chesnutt's major works, Sally Ann H. Ferguson reads "Dave's Neckliss" as one instance, among many, in which Chesnutt "exploits the Christian promise to save devils at the expense of angels and creates dark-skinned, Jesus-like innocents who lead, or at least try to lead, reprobate whites to truth and goodness." In her reading "Mars Dugal comes to regret that he wrongly accused and punished Dave" only after Dave becomes an "unheralded" symbol "of mortal suffering whose rewards await [him] after death."[104]

Ferguson misses not only the biting sarcasm with which Chesnutt mocks the master's "regret," but also the complexity with which Chesnutt makes Dave into a sacrificial symbol. The slaves' laughter not only has a role to play in Dave's grief, but is a major factor in his descent into madness. He bears the intensity of the slaves' abjection in ritual sacrifice but *not* for the master's profit. When Julius eats the Sunday ham, he eats the body and blood of Dave in the ritual remembrance of an ancestor who was made to carry the burden of the tribe, arguably to ensure its psychic survival. Dave's own laughter at the moment when he finds himself alone, bearing his burden, seems to mock the Christian paradigm of sacrifice to which Ferguson alludes. Dave dies looking for a "cure" or, in Julius's bitter pun, a "kyo," but a cure for what? For the madness of racism that has produced the suffering he bears? It is a desperate and ultimately tragic attempt, expressive neither of saintliness nor heroism. It is absurd and yet full of pathos. And it is to this peculiar mix that Dave's laughter, ostensibly a laughter about "nuffin'," gives a sound "fit to kill."

Aesthetic Legacies

Although Chesnutt's brilliant manipulation of stereotypes has not always been recognized, he has been lauded as a writer of singular gifts. In 1910 Benjamin

Brawley praised his overall aesthetic breakthrough and called *The House behind the Cedars* (1900), Chesnutt's first novel, "the best work of fiction yet written by a member of the race in America."[105] In Carl Van Vechten's novel *Nigger Heaven* (1926), a young aspiring black writer in Harlem wonders why Chesnutt is not better known among his peers given Chesnutt's "cool deliberation" of style, his "sense of form," and, most of all, his capacity for turning racial dilemmas into "living and artistic drama." The young writer admires most of all "A Matter of Principle," a story from Chesnutt's *The Wife of His Youth and Other Stories of the Color Line* (1899), a collection of stories that, like *The Conjure Woman* tales, received "rave reviews" upon publication from, among other influential critics, William Dean Howells.[106]

The young writer in Van Vechten's novel might have looked into the complicated nature of Howells's praise, which, like that of Walter Hines Page, Chesnutt's editor at Houghton Mifflin, partly resulted in Chesnutt's absence not only from the cultural atmosphere of the Harlem Renaissance but also from most of the twentieth century. Howells supported Chesnutt's local color fiction but found his more overtly political novel *The Marrow of Tradition* (1901) "bitter," while Page pressured Chesnutt to return to the style of *The Conjure Woman* tales long after the author had decided to abandon it. As would the late twentieth- and early twenty-first-century conjurers of racial stereotypes Richard Pryor and Dave Chappelle, Chesnutt became concerned with the potentially retrograde impact of his use of racial stereotypes.[107] Thus, early in his career, Chesnutt decided to drop Uncle Julius and the conjure trope altogether to focus instead on mixed-race characters and issues of the color line. In doing so he veered away from his powerful tragicomedy of slavery, but he maintained the satiric edge of the early tales and continued to address unpalatable subjects. "A Matter of Principle," like "The Wife of His Youth," for example, is a brilliant exposé of the Blue Vein Society, a fictional elite group of upper-class mulattos who have thoroughly incorporated notions of privilege according to skin color. Obsessed with his status as almost white, Cicero Clayton, the story's main character, not only protests "being called black," but also fervently believes that, since the "Anglo-Saxon race loves justice" and realizes it "where it does not conflict with their own interests," he will one day be accepted as white (*Stories*, 149). The story is a comedy of manners in which Clayton's obsessions have the boomerang effect of keeping him from one of his most cherished goals, marrying his daughter to another high-standing, light-skinned mulatto. As in the equally satirical "Uncle Wellington's Wives," which examines black obsession with whiteness from the perspective of a dark-skinned ex-slave, Chesnutt continues to pry the psychological effects of racism on black folk that he so effectively renders through "Dave's Neckliss."

Although in satirizing the Blue Veins Chesnutt lampooned a group to which he could easily have belonged given his own social standing and light skin, earlier critics such as Amiri Baraka saw him only as a "black parrot for white racist ideologies."[108] Writing in 1975, Robert Bone is an exception, for he not only appreciated Chesnutt's satire but also understood the literary tradition he founded. Calling *The Conjure Woman* tales "a tart confection of sly derision and purgatorial laughter" as well as the "most important product of the black imagination prior to the First World War," Bone rightly argues that Chesnutt's gift for satire is his "major contribution to Afro-American letters." "Drawing on the satirical resources of the black folktale," Bone writes, Chesnutt "founded a tradition that descends through Langston Hughes and George Schuyler to William Melvin Kelley and Ishmael Reed."[109]

As the rest of this study demonstrates, Chesnutt's contribution also includes the phenomenally powerful tragicomedy of the conjure tales, which resonates most clearly in the work of Richard Pryor, in particular in Pryor's ability to turn a comedy of the body into a powerful medium for representing black psychic pain. It resonates as well in Suzan-Lori Parks's use of laughter as a mode of mourning and in her experiments with language, which, like Uncle Julius's spell-binding tales, simultaneously relish the linguistic creativity of Black English and produce a distinctive grammar of terror, subjection, and survival. Likewise, Chesnutt's expert manipulation of racial stereotypes, which he shares with William Wells Brown despite their rather different styles, set a master template not only for Pryor and Reed, whose *Flight to Canada* echoes Brown's *The Escape* in its title alone and whose transliteration of conjure clearly improvises on Chesnutt's work, but also for Robert Colescott. Colescott's "blackening up" of famous modern European paintings through the use of racial stereotypes rearranges the historical sensibilities of viewers in ways similar to Chesnutt's "fictive seizure" and transformation of demeaning stereotypes.

The fact that critics have misinterpreted both Chesnutt's and Brown's manipulation of stereotypes, their gifts for conjuring them in the service of redefining their power, suggests a theme common in the critical reception of the writers in this chapter as well as the writers and artists examined in later chapters. Kara Walker's career, for example, has been shaped by the controversy produced by her ability to make vivid both the grotesque and the alluring aspects of stereotypes. A similar controversy has now put Dave Chappelle's career on hold. To trade in stereotypes is to play with fire, and these controversies highlight not only the potency of stereotypes but also the reach and limits of employing them, in particular in the often morally ambivalent terrain of humor.

How does gender further complicate the risk of trading in stereotypes? While exploring Brown's and Chesnutt's work, I have often wondered why there is not a nineteenth-century black female writer comparable to these writers in their use of humor to represent slavery. Certainly the fact that the stage and physical comedy have been off-limits to women plays a central role. As June Sochen notes, traditionally men have been able to assume the roles of "satirists and physical comics," whereas women have not. "If they ventured into this culturally forbidden land, they should only display restrained wit—sly humor, perhaps, but not [the] raucous, screaming demonstrative" kind.[110] Erika Kreger reminds us that, in the United States, it was not until the late nineteenth century that critics came to see wit and humor as incompatible with femininity. Indeed, she argues that "in the mid-1800s, women humorists were often popular and acclaimed." Yet the humor that they practiced was neither necessarily politically radical nor performed; it was largely textual.[111] Performing on stage was not an option for women, especially women of color, unless they joined vaudeville shows, where their place was decidedly ambivalent (the woman entertainer was included mainly "to make the place fit for decent women, yet everyone 'knew' that she could not be a decent woman herself"), or the minstrel troops of the late 1860s, which featured women as "giddy sex objects" and burlesqued their behavior "in much the same way as plantation blacks."[112] African American women such as Maria Stewart, Jarena Lee, and Sojourner Truth did take up public speaking, but they did so in the morally safer terrain of political activism or spiritualism. In the realm of comedy, women have been "regularly shunted into stereotypical roles as mannish or dumb, or as virtual harlots."[113] While early twentieth-century black women comics were able to find some audience acceptance and performance opportunities in forums that featured black artists performing for exclusively black audiences, such the chitlin' circuit, in general they still had to face public opprobrium as gendered *and* racialized subjects. Still, black female singers of the classic blues era, singers such as Ma Rainey, Bessie Smith, Ida Cox, Alberta Hunter, and others, often challenged injunctions against women's full range of expression, especially with regards to sexuality, by infusing humor and sass into their performance styles. And, in the mid-twentieth century Moms Mabley successfully created a comic persona that could directly address topics considered too edgy for the time, such as explicit critiques of racism or bawdy ruminations, but only because she presented herself as a nonthreatening, small, bedraggled woman in a house dress and an old lady's hat.

As writers, black women were able to use satire and wit to criticize slavery, yet critics routinely ignore this aspect of their texts. It bears repeating that much of the satire and wit in nineteenth-century texts by African American women is not conducive to laughter. But this should not lead us to dismiss a powerful aspect of their texts. In her slave narrative *Incidents in the Life of a Slave Girl* (1861), for instance, Harriet Jacobs uses ridicule to highlight the ironies of white power. She opens a chapter detailing the violent backlash against slaves following Nat Turner's rebellion, wryly noting the slave owner's fears and delusions, two main targets of early black humor. "Strange," she writes, quoting a popular myth about slavery, "that they should be alarmed when their slaves were so 'contented and happy'! But so it was." She then describes the extensive searches, violence, and vigilance to which slaves were subjected, noting that "low whites, who had no negroes of their own to scourge," saw the moment as a "grand chance to exercise a little brief authority, and show their subserviency [sic] to the slaveholders; not reflecting that the power which trampled on the colored people also kept themselves in poverty, ignorance, and moral degradation." Jacobs dedicates the chapter to lampooning the weaknesses of the "low whites," particularly their "ignorance," taking particular pleasure in instigating displays of it. "I knew nothing annoyed them so much as to see colored people living in comfort and respectability," she writes, "so I made arrangements for them with especial care. I arranged every thing in my grandmother's house as neatly as possible. I put white quilts on the beds, and decorated some of the rooms with flowers. When all was arranged, I sat down at the window to watch." For Jacobs, the ironies and limitations of white power seem almost amusing. What she sees out of her window are signs of terror: innocent black people are dragged out and threatened with death and rape. But inside her grandmother's house, which Jacobs knew would be protected by whites more powerful than the "low" ones, she watches a show that she has "arranged" so as to ensure the most outlandish display of white "poverty, ignorance and moral degradation."[114]

Not that Jacobs lacked the opportunity to witness such displays from powerful whites. Her mistress would rather spit on her food than have her slaves eat the remains of her meals, and Jacobs's epicurean master takes sadistic pleasure in force-feeding dog food to hungry slaves. Jacobs witnesses such displays of moral poverty and presents them with a satirist's detached sense of indignation. Later, however, when she "peeps" at her master's movements from the garret, she takes "satisfaction" in the fact that, even from her constrained position, she can "arrange" circumstances so as to taunt her master's deprived mind.[115] Jacobs's detachment from and her satisfaction in the scenes of degradation that she partly orchestrates suggest a more nuanced expression of protest than is generally accorded to her text.

As I have already noted, Harriet Wilson's *Our Nig* is a remarkably satiric text, yet scholarship on the novel has given "exclusive focus to the sentimental aspects of the narrative," in part because readers remain "uneasy with the rage that emanates from the center of Wilson's book."[116] Anger was and still is unbecoming in a woman, especially if she trades in unpalatable subjects such as northern racism and white women's complicity in the oppression of African Americans. Wilson had plenty of reason to be enraged. In her novel she details the painful experiences to which her protagonist and alter ego, Frado, who is also known as "Nig," is repeatedly subjected when, deserted by her white mother after her black father dies, she enters a long period of indentured servitude at the ripe age of six to a white family who treat her as a slave. Overworked and tortured by a cruel mistress and her equally mean-spirited daughter, Frado is sometimes comforted by the other members of the family, almost all of whom are men but who never rescue her despite their ability to do so. Critics have discovered that the Haywards (known in the text as the "Bellmonts"), the family that held Wilson as their servant, lived in Milford, New Hampshire, home of many prominent abolitionists who made Milford the site of huge antislavery rallies. The Haywards were intimately connected to another family, the Hutchinsons, famous abolitionist singers whose work was often praised as "unselfish and sublime."[117] Frederick Douglass credited them with having "sung the yokes from the necks and the fetters from the limbs of [his] race."[118] Yet, as P. Gabrielle Forman and Reginald H. Pitts note, placing *Our Nig* in the antislavery context of New Hampshire did little good for Wilson, who, like her fictional alter ego, was never aided by those around her. The irony "personalizes a central human contradiction and a particular American paradox: how can people who stand firmly against injustice ignore it—or enact it—in their own front yards?"[119]

Wilson exposes this contradiction and paradox with a particular edge, which is only sometimes hidden in the sheep's clothing of the sentimental novel, the autobiography, slave narrative, and other forms of which Wilson makes use.[120] Thus, while Henry Louis Gates Jr. presents the lack of attention that *Our Nig* received when it was first published in Boston as "one of the troubling enigmas of Afro-American literary history," one who is attuned to the novel's satiric mode can understand why the novel was ignored even in Boston, which at the time was "a veritable center of abolitionist reform and passion."[121] In the first chapter, for example, Wilson denigrates the tendency that "*professed* reformers" have for assuming a "holier-than-thou" attitude toward the downtrodden, and, as she ends her narrative, she writes that "enough has been enrolled to *demand* [the reader's] sympathy and aid."[122] Despite the brutality to which she was subjected and the callous indifference of those who simply watched, Wilson refused to plead, for to do so would have meant furthering her subjection. It would have meant the denial, or at least the taming, of the rage that she felt in response in favor of not disturbing the sensibilities of her all-too-complacent audience. Instead, she used satire to *demand* sympathy.

The novel repeatedly presents Frado bound, gagged, and receiving savage blows from Mrs. Bellmont, who positively enjoys her merciless cruelty (*Our Nig*, 37). Because Wilson delivers her narrative in the third person, Frado's beatings attain a level of abstraction (both from the author and the reader) that would have been impossible from a first-person point of view. Such abstraction, as Ronald Paulson notes, is typical of satire and has the effect of highlighting the violence of the scene through ironic understatement.[123] That is, although the violent scenes are based on Wilson's personal experience, she delivers them at a remove and without personal commentary (in one case literally announcing the omission), leaving the reader to face Mrs. Bellmont's naked cruelty (52).

As Elizabeth Breau argues, Wilson's satire "flatly contradicts the portrait of [white] women as angels of mercy and kindness," a portrait that was central to nineteenth-century notions of "True Womanhood."[124] Like other satirists, Wilson further abstracts the scenes of her oppression by working through character types. She purposefully subordinates the development of Mrs. Bellmont's character to a "two dimensional" type whose "primary sins are racism and cruelty."[125] Denying the mistress the humanity that racist discourse would refuse African Americans, Wilson figures Mrs. Bellmont as a "she-devil" capable of the most unspeakable horrors (*Our Nig*, 12). In one instance she orders Frado to eat out of her leftover dish, but Frado, confident that there is a witness nearby, defies her and orders her dog to lick the dish before she uses it (39). Although this makes Jack, son of the mistress and witness, "[boil] over with laughter," two paragraphs later we are told that Mrs. Bellmont threatens to cut out Frado's tongue if she tells of the "thorough beating" to which she is subjected as punishment (40). Often such beatings include Mrs. Bellmont wedging pieces of wood in Frado's mouth in order to literally but ironically silence her with her mouth open. In these scenes Wilson deftly intertwines scenes of laughter with scenes of subjection, leaving readers to feel sympathy for Frado but ultimately calling them to respond to Mrs. Bellmont's violence in ways not limited to sentiment.

Additionally, Wilson depicts the inertia of those who simply watched as complicit in her cruelty. When Jack watches Frado defy Mrs. Bellmont by ordering her dog to lick the mistress's dish before she uses it, he not only laughs heartily but gives Frado "a bright silver dollar," saying, "There take that, 't was worth paying for" (*Our Nig*, 40). Whereas the scene constitutes one of the few instances of victory for Frado, for Jack it is mere entertainment. The scene arguably signifies on the commodity value of slave narratives, which, unlike Wilson's novel, found an enthusiastic audience. It suggests that purportedly sympathetic subjects like Jack could read the trials and tribulations of slaves only as entertainment and so Wilson needed a strategy far fiercer than Frado's spirited defiance. She needed stinging satire rather than clever subversion to shock readers like Jack into action.

Judging from the lack of critical attention Wilson received, the strategy backfired. Ellen Pratofiorito argues that Wilson's contemporary audiences were not "ready, willing or able" to appreciate her message.[126] The novel received no critical response until Gates republished it in 1983. The reason for Wilson's failure, however, might also be in the risks implicit in employing satire as a form of social critique. As Michael Seidel argues, satire can contaminate the satirist. In "satiric invective," he writes, "the urge to reform is literally overwhelmed by the urge to annihilate," making the satirist so deeply implicated in the process of exposing degeneracy that he is "beside himself and beneath himself."[127] In other words, the satirist may forfeit the distance that satire affords depending on the force of the invective.

In *Our Nig*, Wilson is so intent on exposing Mrs. Bellmont's cruelty and the Bellmont men's callousness that she subsumes the narrative of her own desire under the weight of that purpose. The novel, as Julia Stern notes, represents Frado's own passion—her desire for freedom, for the Bellmont men, and for the man she eventually marries—only in terms of masochism, self-destructive yearnings, or passive aggressiveness.[128] To some extent, Wilson enacts in narrative form the silencing to which Mrs. Bellmont consistently subjects Frado. She silences the narrative of Frado's desire in favor of exposing the cruelty of her mistress. Such a singular purpose may have compromised Wilson's vision, but in refusing to handle her audience gingerly and giving voice to her rage, she achieved something remarkable. Rather than assume the supplicant tone of the conventional slave narrator, who sought to *prove* his or her humanity through writing, Wilson *asserts* her humanity through her satire.

To some extent, Brown and Chesnutt compromised in masking their true designs in performances and stories that, on a superficial level, appear to acquiesce to racist notions of blackness. Wilson was less willing to do so in part because she was overwhelmed by her anger against hypocritical abolitionists. Like Brown, she criticized those "who sustain[ed] interest" in the plight of the oppressed "only as long as it remain[ed] interesting and present" and those who claimed to feel sympathy but took "no concrete action."[129] But instead of operating through hyperbole and masquerade, Wilson turned to satire. She did so not only because satire lends itself to the criticism of social ills and the expression of anger but also because satire allowed her to create a crucial distance between her reader and the scenes of violence that she presents. This is a strategy that she shared with many other slave narrators, particularly women who wanted to testify to the sexual oppression they suffered without making their pain merely the object of empty pity, or worse, prurient interest. Enslaved women, much more so than enslaved men, had to guard against the always potential discursive consumption of their bodies. While Wilson was careful in representing the scenes of her subjection, preventing the commodification of her pain, she employed a particular brand of satire that ultimately alienated readers.

The silence that met her novel may also spring from a more general resistance to receiving and accepting black female satirical voices. In fact, even when women operate in a broader range of humor, as Zora Neale Hurston does in *Their Eyes Were Watching God* (1937), they are often met with harsh criticism. Richard Wright's review of Hurston's novel, for instance, chastises her for "voluntarily" continuing "the tradition which was forced upon the Negro," minstrelsy, and for keeping black characters "in that safe and narrow orbit in which America likes to see the Negro live: between laughter and tears."[130] Wilson's example, however, attests both to the resistance against accepting black female satire and the reach and limits of satire itself and thus suggests why the aesthetic legacy that I trace in this book does not rely on satire alone. Whereas satire can undermine the distance that humor affords, other forms of humor, such as hyperbole, burlesque, and, in particular, masquerade, can communicate intent through the indirect language of signifying. Indirectness, of course, carries its own risks, but it can also provide a necessary mask, one that can become intricately powerful when it makes use of popular and mass-consumed images. If, as Brown realized, slavery has always been mediated by mass cultural representations, to manipulate popular images, such as stereotypes of race and gender, opens up the possibility of turning the consumption of race upside down. By reappropriating commodified mass cultural images of slavery, Brown and Chesnutt, as do all the writers and artists in this study, turned stereotypes of race and gender into vehicles for the critique of their commoditization.

Wilson's anger limited the distance she had from her subject, which was due to the violence of racism that she suffered firsthand. As a slave, Brown suffered under conditions similar to Wilson's yet was able to turn his experiences into fodder for plays such as *The Escape* in great part because, as a man, the stage and physical comedy were not off-limits to him. Chesnutt, who was a more skillful writer than either Brown or Wilson, may have found ways to incorporate a wide range of humor forms with satire because of his literary gifts. But the distance afforded to him not only as a man, one light enough to pass, but also as someone who did not experience the brutality of slavery or indentured servitude firsthand was surely also a factor. The writers and artists I examine in the chapters that follow have a distance of over one hundred years from the historical experience of slavery and are thus poised to invoke the violence of slavery through comic modes that at times risk sacrilege. They take the risk in an effort to sustain a critical memory of slavery and an equally critical focus on its legacy.

Although Wilson turned to satire to represent abjection but prevent its commoditization, the force of her satire, fueled as it was by rage, alienated her readership. Late in the twentieth century Suzan-Lori Parks would also focus on the commoditization of abjection, but she would experiment with various forms of humor, from the kind of minstrelizing of minstrelsy that Brown offers in *The Escape* to Chesnutt's tragicomedy, thus avoiding the traps of satire. If Wilson fell prey to those traps, she, like Brown and Chesnutt, set in place an artistic legacy of profound power. In their distinctive styles, each of these writers walked a tightrope, using various forms of humor not only to thwart the expectations of their audiences, despite enormous risks, but also to face the challenge expressed in Brown's notion "Slavery has never been represented; Slavery never can be represented" and its implicit addendum: and yet, slavery must be represented.

THE CONJURER RECOILS

Slavery in Richard Pryor's Performances and Chappelle's Show

Bicentennial Nigger, Richard Pryor's 1976 album, is simply brilliant. It brims with a sharp, eviscerating humor through which Pryor highlights his country's founding contradiction: its profession of democratic principles despite its history of racial oppression. True to Pryor's style, none but the last track assumes the serious tone of that objective. The first track, in fact, features Pryor imitating a hillbilly screaming at the moment of orgasm, and the second depicts Pryor's varying degrees of success in satisfying the sexual appetites of both black and white women. Using his trademark ability to mimic cartoonish but clearly identifiable "white" and "black" voices, Pryor sets off a raunchy play of stereotypes. White women are docile: they consent to sex easily, don't complain if they do not reach orgasm, don't put up a fight when they are physically threatened, and are happy to stay at home when their man goes out in the evening. Black women, by contrast, are assertive and intractable: when their men announce that they are going out, they start getting ready too; they fight right back when their men threaten them with violence and refuse to give oral sex but complain when they do not achieve orgasm. After unsatisfactory sex one of them says (in Pryor's imitation of a sassy "black" woman), "Nigga, that's some *sad* dick!"[1]

Without Pryor's unmatched gift for delivery, his play with stereotypes could be seen as simply vulgar or even scandalous (especially since it involves his controversial use of the "N" word). However, he invariably grounds his outrageous humor in the harsh realities of American racism and reveals how it perpetuates the ideologies of slavery. Since transcriptions of his performances allow us to examine the design of his stand-up, in this chapter I first consider in detail particular tracks in the bicentennial album and the design of that album as a whole. I also examine his other major albums and film concerts, produced between 1968 and 1983, for they reveal how Pryor twists the tradition of the conjuror discussed in chapter 1. Invoking the past and seeking catharsis, Pryor uses his power as a conjurer to stage rituals of redress with respect to American slavery. At a crucial point in his career, however, Pryor recoils at his power as a conjurer and redirects it. Why he recoils and what it reveals about the power he taps into through his conjuring is the focus of later sections of this chapter.

Highlighting the ritualistic aspects of stand-up comedy, already a ritualized medium with its own codes and system of rites,[2] stand-up in Pryor's performances became not only a vehicle for catharsis—both for the release of racial tensions and for the purging of racist attitudes—but also a medium through which he symbolically redressed chattel slavery and its aftermath. Arising at the end of the civil rights and the beginning of the Black Power movements, Pryor's work, like Ishmael Reed's, is part of a larger movement toward redress, conceived as retribution, correction, and reparations for American slavery. At the same time, it expresses a conscious awareness of the impossibility of that redress given the enormity of the breach: the genocide caused by the slave trade and the institutionalized brutality of plantation slavery.

As I discussed in the introduction, what has remained in the aftermath of the tremendous crime against humanity that New World slavery constituted is what Stephen Best and Saidiya Hartman call the "limited scope of the possible in the face of the irreparable."[3] The result is a shuttling between grievance, the seeking of legal remedies to the crimes of slavery and the injustices perpetuated afterward, and grief, the expression of the deep sorrow occasioned not only by slavery itself but also by its long legacy. Pryor, as this chapter demonstrates, returns to the shuttling between grief and grievance that Best and Hartman locate, for instance, in Ottobah Cuguano's *Thoughts and Sentiments on the Evil of Slavery* (1787) by protesting against racist practices of his day while giving expression to the grief occasioned by slavery and its legacy. In so doing, he also gives sound to the "black noise" and "freedom dreams" left unrealized in the wake of slavery, Reconstruction, Jim Crow segregation, and the civil rights movement. In this shuttling, however, Pryor does not express grievance or grief in straightforward complaint, lament, or mourning but in comic modes of tremendous range, from outrageous, blasphemous humor to bitter satire and deep irony, to his own tragicomedy of slavery.

How does Pryor mobilize black humor to redress American slavery? In *Bicentennial Nigger* he does not exclude himself from the stereotyping play with which he opens the album, presenting himself as the kind of sexually insatiable black man who has inspired an uneasy mixture of fear, desire, and abhorrence in America. But he uses the stereotype to expose the contradictions of this mixture. Although, on other occasions, notably in *Wanted/Richard Pryor: Live in Concert* (1978), he parodies the idea of the macho man and laughs at the myth of black male genital superiority, in this performance he speaks of easily pleasing white women and in general about black men's exceptional sexual powers, thus playing with a taboo so potent that it had been criminalized only nine years before the bicentennial.[4] Pryor more than fulfills the fantasy that had upheld the law against miscegenation; he flagrantly flaunts it for white men who might, given the power of the taboo, imagine him as a sexual competitor with the upper hand as well as for white women who might imagine him as both a threat and an object of desire (depending on sexual orientation, white men might also see him as such). Knowing that black women in the audience will judge him for liking white women, he announces the fact that he has dated both black and white women in a mock confessional tone. Then, suggesting that these women might go so far as to refuse him sex after his disclosure ("Right on, motherfucker, *beg* me"), he declares the fact that he will sleep with white women nonetheless. In each case, he is an outlaw who exhibits his criminality with the gusto implied by the sexual satisfaction he provides, which he makes explicit by focusing on his performance of cunnilingus on both black and white women.

The audience quite audibly laughs, because, as Freud might have put it, Pryor has given voice to a taboo and allowed the energy involved in keeping it in place release through laughter. As in other performances, however, audience members—at the very least, blacks and whites—laugh from different perspectives and "in and out of symmetry." As John Limon notes, Pryor plays with stereotypes of "black lawlessness," "vulgarity," and "coolness" as against "white mechanicalness" and prudishness. In this and other performances, such as the opening act of *Live in Concert*, black folk "see themselves as whites see them," in the tradition of double consciousness articulated by W. E. B. Du Bois, "but they like what they see," and whites "now see themselves from the outside as well; but they are content, for the length of the occasion, to lend their mechanical bodies to the comic machinery." Blacks and whites "laugh from different positions that go in and out of symmetry," argues Limon, but "they all laugh."[5]

Aside from disrupting the possibility of passive spectatorship, Pryor thus creates communities that, while laughing "in and out of symmetry," find common ground, at least for the duration of his performance, in the volatile history of racial tensions that his self-transformations conjure. He also gives his performance a clear context. His flamboyant play on stereotypes in the skit about black and white women is rooted in the taboo against miscegenation, which, as the album makes clear, is itself rooted in the history of slavery. Even in "Hillbilly," the album's first track, Pryor suggests a historical context as he not only imitates a racist white man having an orgasm, but also adopts his voice to give an exaggerated version of America before its birth as a nation, as the heathen place that Europeans would civilize. The irony, of course, is that Pryor plays the white man's role as a civilizing agent with a crassness that betrays that role while making him the object of derisive laughter. *Bicentennial Nigger* ends with an eponymous track in which Pryor delivers a short but potent history of the Middle Passage and slavery, told from the perspective of a "two-hundred-year-old" "nigger in blackface . . . with stars and stripes on his forehead." Pryor thus couches his outrageous impersonations of stereotypes in between two tracks that provide clear historical referents even as he exaggerates the distortions that such stereotypes set in place.

Capitalizing on a humor of incongruity, the slender black man with an Afro "passes" both for a hillbilly at a moment of ecstasy and a frail white woman, even though he has no disguise other than his voice and gestures. He can also quickly transform into what, throughout the album, he places at the opposite end of the gender spectrum: a strong black woman. The performance, of course, risks ungendering black women and feminizing white women in the most misogynist sense of the word, while setting them against each other. But this is precisely the edge of Pryor's humor: it brings to life the most vulgar aspects of racism, often by flaunting stereotypes of race and gender while retaining a measure of transparency and belief. It is in the simultaneous gesture toward perfect imitation and toward transparency, a dual gesture that Pryor achieves by manipulating his voice as well as his long, bony frame, that conjure and humor coalesce.

Unlike Flip Wilson, who famously performed as his transvestite alter ego, Geraldine Jones, on his television show (1970–74) with the aid of elaborate costume and makeup, Pryor uses no such props, thus achieving both a productive equilibrium and a living contradiction. His audiences know that he is playing all the characters, and thus his persona is an element of each of them. Yet, by the same logic, even if only for the duration of the performance, each stereotype is an element of his body. His transformation, although virtuosic at the level of imitation, is not complete. Like William Wells Brown's performances, Pryor's transformations play an intricate what if game: what if one could see and hear a host of stereotypes come alive within one body? Audience members laugh not only at the ease with which they can recognize the stereotypes that Pryor imitates but also at the irony of both his accurate portrayal of distortion and the fact that he gives those distortions real referents.

Pryor claimed that when he was on stage he was "possessed" by the characters he portrayed.[6] Although one can hardly take this as evidence that possession in voodoo is analogous to Pryor's aesthetic practice, the transformations that he enacts suggest implicit connections, not necessarily to voodoo per se, but to conjure. Possession in voodoo is a passive state in which the devotee lends his or her body as a "horse," which the spirit of the dead, or loa, "mounts." Pryor takes on the much more active role of the conjurer who brings to life, not the spirit of the dead, but the most outrageous aspects of stereotypes, using an entire arsenal of rhetorical flourishes derived from black humor, from simple signifying to elaborate games of the dozens. In particular, he emphasizes the performative nature of black humor, the fact that it is primarily visual and attitudinal.[7] Unlike Charles

Chesnutt and later Ishmael Reed, Pryor does not transliterate conjure. Instead, he uses his own body as the means to make glaringly vivid the ideological fetishes embedded in stereotypes. Thus, rather than produce humor by emphasizing the mechanicalness of the body, as in Bergson's theory of humor, Pryor relies on the *elasticity* of his frame and voice to conjure stereotypes, a process that turns them into objects of laughter.

In the last track of the bicentennial album, Pryor again conjures a racial type and, as in other cases, highlights both its historicity and theatricality. But he takes on a radically different approach to mark the difference between his own acts of conjure and the minstrelsy expected of him. Instead of bringing to life the stereotype through sound and gesture, as he does in other instances, he first describes Bicentennial Nigger physically—he details the "big lips," the "little eyes" of the "two-hundred-year-old" "nigger"—and then pretends to don the masklike image. He does so to the sound of the drums from the "Star Spangled Banner" in what becomes a highly self-conscious ritual of turning a minstrel mask, a symbol of submission and effacement, into a tool for shamanistic purging of murderous anger and grief. When, having invoked the image of Bicentennial Nigger, Pryor assumes that figure's voice, he intermittently uses a disturbing laugh, one that parodies both the canned laughter of television sitcoms and that of the minstrel stage. The horn section of the "Star Spangled Banner" joins the drums as Bicentennial Nigger begins to speak:

> Ise sooo happy cause I been here 200 years. . . . I'm just thrilled to be here [with a chuckle that peppers the rest of the performance, a kind of "yak, yak, yak"]. . . . I'm so glad you took me out of Dahome [chuckle]. . . . I used to live to be a hundred and fifty. Now I dies of high blood pressure by the time I'm fifty-two. . . . That thrills me to death [chuckle]. I'm just so pleased America is gonna last. They brought me over here on a boat. There was 400 of us come over here [chuckles and snorts], 360 of us died on the way over here [chuckle]. I just love that . . . it just thrills me to death. . . . You white folks are just so good to us. . . . We got over here and another twenty of us died from disease . . . then they split us all up. . . . Took my momma over that way, took my wife that way, took my kids over yonder [chuckles]. . . . I'm just so happy [chuckles] I don't know what to do. I don't know what I'm gonna do if I don't get 200 more years of this. . . .
>
> Y'all probably done forgot about it. [Pause. And then, in Pryor's own voice] But I ain't never gonna forget.

Unlike the rest of the album, and Pryor's work overall, the monologue is not comic in the most basic sense; it is, instead, darkly satirical, even bitter. His laughter, mechanized and obviously constructed, is piercingly ironic, since far from expressing gaiety, it is from the start a laughter that kills. Bicentennial Nigger's often-repeated line "It thrills me to death" expresses such irony with a brutally angry undertone. But the minstrel mask, although richly elaborated, is ultimately only imagined. Pryor discards it easily when, at the end, he switches to his own voice to utter the most direct statement in the entire album and, arguably, of Pryor's entire oeuvre: "I ain't never gonna forget."

The track, which was recorded live at The Comedy Store in Hollywood on February 2, 1976, includes the laughter of the audience, a laughter that not only contrasts with the mechanized laughter of Pryor's character but that also begs the question: what kind of laughter is it, given the painful history to which Bicentennial Nigger testifies? Each time Bicentennial Nigger claims to be "happy" on the occasion of the bicentennial and then gives evidence to the contrary, the audience laughs in acknowledgment of the deep irony. They also laugh, perhaps uncomfortably, at a deeper irony: Pryor's superimposition of minstrel celebration onto mournful remembrance. In adopting the tone of celebration to recount a captive's survival through dispossession and enslavement, Pryor reenacts part of the violence of slavery, which entailed the forced performance of gaiety, while also restaging the impact of that violence on black performance. Ever since slave traders would "dance the slaves" on the upper decks of ships carrying human cargo—primarily to exercise the captives and thus ensure their survival and the capital invested in their bodies—black performance has been shadowed by racist associations between blackness and mirth.[8] Bicentennial Nigger's line "I'm so thrilled to be here" echoes the kind of statement with which comedians usually greet their audiences and serves as a satirical comment on black performance and the difference that Pryor insisted on (in his stand-up work if not in his work as a film actor) between minstrelsy and his unapologetically aggressive style.[9]

Declaring his commitment "never to forget" his country's history of genocide and enslavement precisely when bicentennial celebrations would obfuscate it, Pryor not only performs the previously segregated aspects of black humor— its aggressive, political, and nuanced aspects—but also roots the birth of that humor in slavery. "Y'all know how black humor started," Pryor tells his audience shortly before he begins "Bicentennial Nigger," "it started on the slave ships.[10] One cat was on his way over here rowing and another asks him, 'What you laughing about?' The dude says 'Yesterday, I was a king.'" Although born on the same ships in which slave traders danced their cargo, black humor, Pryor asserts, could not be more different from the gaiety forced out of his ancestors. Rather, for Pryor, black humor expresses the "tragicomic attitude"—captured so succinctly in the image of a dispossessed king, now a slave, laughing—that Ralph Ellison identified as a distinguishing characteristic of black Americans and, as such, is close in kind to the blues.[11] Indeed, when Ellison wrote his often-quoted because elegant definition of the blues, he could have been writing about black humor, for in both there is that "impulse to keep the painful details and episodes of a brutal experience alive in one's aching consciousness, to finger its jagged grain, and to transcend it, not by the consolation of philosophy but by squeezing from it a near-tragic, near-comic lyricism."[12]

Pryor used the power of black humor not only to remember the brutality of slavery, to "finger its jagged edge," but also to conjure the fantastic house of mirrors it produced. Although the most fertile ground for his stand-up performances was his own life—his upbringing, struggles with addiction, and violent behavior— he fulfilled his promise never to forget his country's history of genocide, enslavement, and persecution through near magical self-transformations that reveal the mutations undergone by slavery since emancipation. Bob Hickson, the artist who produced the painting used for the cover of *Bicentennial Nigger*, captures not only Pryor's gift for assuming diverse alter egos but also the role of slavery as a subtext throughout Pryor's work. The painting features Pryor as a cop, a pimp, a boxer, a preacher, a convict, a farmer, an aviator, a professional with suit and briefcase, a naked man with his back turned to the viewer (possibly a captive African since his hands are shackled), and an army man, each figure chained at the ankles, connecting them all. The painting also features on the lower left corner a black Uncle Sam, ambiguously attaching or releasing the chain, and on the upper right, another Pryor alter ego, a man in a military outfit bearing a rifle, presumably guarding the gang. The different versions of Pryor—each figure bears his features and the unmistakable Afro and mustache that the comedian sported after his transformative years in Berkeley—are placed in a semicircle (with the figures laid flat); a second semicircle is created by an elaborate Art Deco medal that includes the colors and eagle of the American flag.[13] The painting, like Pryor's comedy, places the various experiences indexed by Pryor's alter egos at the center of America by invoking the African American struggle for freedom, a struggle that, as the chain, the black Uncle Sam, and the rifle-bearing guard suggest, has been long as well as compromised from "within the circle," to borrow a phrase from Frederick Douglass. As the painting suggests, Pryor's comedy reveals the impact of slavery not only on figures from the ghetto like the pimp, but also on those on the other end of the economic scale.

Pryor also makes manifest the force of that impact on American culture by using his own body and life story to stage rituals of redress. Victor Turner, in his work on social dramas, defines redress as a period of "stock taking" and "plural self-scrutiny" that, while including elements of play in which meanings, codes, statuses, and social structures are set in a "subjunctive mood" and a "reflexive voice," can also include acts of sacrifice, "in which the tensions and animosities" of a community are discharged by the "immolation (real or in token form) of living subjects or valued objects."[14] Pryor enacts playful and symbolic forms of redress akin to those outlined by Turner through his rich use of signifying and his performances as the persona "Richard Pryor" whose self-immolation (a result of a freebasing accident)[15] can arguably be understood as an instance of ritual sacrifice. By effecting his redress of slavery through symbolic ritual, Pryor maintains the paradox that the breach of slavery presents—a breach that needs to be redressed but that *cannot* be redressed given its magnitude—while turning that paradox into a powerfully creative, though nearly self-destructive, source.

This paradox mirrors another: the fact that even as Pryor repeatedly invokes a divisive past he also works toward the creation of community. In "Bicentennial Prayer," a track placed strategically in the middle of the album, Pryor adopts a mode that specifically emphasizes community. Using the rhythms and accents of a black preacher, he becomes the minister of what he calls the "Church of Understanding and Unity" and engages in a call-and-response relationship with his audience:

> We are gathered here today to celebrate this year of bicentenniality, in the hope of freedom and dignity. We are celebrating 200 years of white folks kickin' ass. Now, white folks have had the essence of this understanding on their side for quite a while. . . . We offer this prayer and the prayer is: how long will this bullshit go on?! [loud applause] How long?! [an audience member repeats: "How long?"] How long?! [audience member: "Amen!"] How long will this bullshit go on?!

Even in its playfulness, the speech invokes the militant spirit of David Walker and Martin Delany. As the speech continues, Pryor connects the black liberation struggle to the human struggle for survival and dignity from the dawn of civilization, a strategy that Walker and other nineteenth-century orators employed. Pryor uses it with a characteristic mixture of jest and seriousness in a track that maintains the album's balance between his outrageous play on stereotypes and his almost bitter satire of minstrelsy. "How long?!" Pryor the preacher asks, his voice rising in a crescendo. "That is the eternal question man has always asked. When Man first got here, he asked, how long will these animals kick me in the ass? How long?! How long before I discover fire and stop freezin' to death?" Pryor connects the eternal struggle for freedom and dignity and its specific shape in the history of African Americans humorously, of course, but the gesture serves a much larger purpose: that of unearthing the core humanity of the fight for civil rights.

As he continues to preach, Pryor uses the richness of black humor to provide release while creating communion and instigating for change. "They say in the Bible that we will know how long [we will continue to suffer] when an angel come up out of the sea with seven heads and a face like a serpent and a body like a lion. I don't know about you, but I don't want to see no motherfucker looking like that. . . . If I see him, I'm gonna shoot him in the ass." He thus invokes but rejects both the Jeremiah tradition of prophecy that black writers and orators have appropriated to powerful ends (from Walker's *Appeal* through James Baldwin's

The Fire Next Time) and the notion of providential deliverance, a notion that, although central in black culture (from the self-fashioning of early slave narrators such as Olaudah Equiano through the civil rights movement), was also used to support slavery. Contrasting the otherworldly image of the seven-headed angel with his more earthly action ("I'm gonna shoot him in the ass"), Pryor's preacher suggests that deliverance must be achieved by the humans who are gathered around him. It must also be conceived by means other than the Bible, that Janus-faced source of oppression and liberation. "They say in the Bible," Pryor's preacher begins, only to render a fanciful image that seems to have no connection to the "bullshit" that black people have suffered as white folks "kicked ass." Apocalypse will come as "they," a dubious entity at best, "say in the Bible," and the imbalance of power will thus have a foreseeable end ("we will know how long"). But Pryor's preacher, speaking for a Black Power generation, would rather settle matters with his own hands (and gun).

The performance then morphs into a satire of black preaching, complete with a parody of an "old Negro spiritual," stories of scams involving the healing of the sick, the blind, and the mute, and petitions for large contributions for suspicious causes. In other words, Pryor turns the routine into a performance of classic black humor, which has made black preachers and religion in general its target since the early twentieth century, when "the sacred world view" of black folk declined.[16] In so doing, Pryor affirms a tradition that he knew well, not only creating with it recognition and affiliation for black members of the audience, much as Moms Mabley did before him, but also performing previously racially segregated aspects of black humor and therefore creating a greater community.[17]

As the example of *Bicentennial Nigger* shows, Pryor's symbolic redress of slavery takes on a wide range of modes and tones. The fact that his major albums, as well as his concert films, were recorded live allows us to appreciate not only the fullness of that range but also the vibrancy of Pryor's relationships with his audiences.[18] Aside from *Bicentennial Nigger*, Pryor's early albums, in particular *Richard Pryor* (1968) and *That Nigger's Crazy* (1974), as well as his early film, *Live and Smokin'* (1971), present Pryor as a powerful conjurer. In *Live on the Sunset Strip* (1982) and *Here and Now* (1983), he revises his early strategies, in particular, his use of the "N" word, and ultimately recoils from his power as conjurer. The causes and consequences of such changes reveal the reach and limit of redressing slavery via stereotypes. Like Chesnutt, whose Uncle Julius stories initially received a critical acclaim that overshadowed Chesnutt's other literary experiments, Pryor became temporarily caught, like a tar baby, by his ability to transform stereotypes into objects of laughter.

During the early stages of his career, Pryor conjured stereotypes of race and gender in such provocative ways that he would often leave audiences in open-jaw shock or send them into wild fits of laughter or both. By the early 1980s, when

Pryor had become a comic icon, the force of his conjuring was overshadowed by his fame. Audiences laughed almost as soon as he walked on stage and came to expect, even demand, certain acts from him. He then became concerned that his play on stereotypes, rather than lead people to question their habits of mind and action, had become another commodity to be consumed. Worse, he feared that through his play on stereotypes he was reaffirming rather than criticizing racist views. His embrace and subsequent rejection of the "N" word is but one example of this moment of crisis in his career. Before he renounced the "N" word and his host of stereotypical characters, however, he used both to stage rituals of redress that would have a profound impact on the popular treatment of slavery in American culture and black comedy more generally.

Witness *Chappelle's Show* (2003–5), a wildly successful television show on Comedy Central in which the contemporary comedian Dave Chappelle presents incendiary fantasies of redress: performances regarding reparations and retribution for slavery that play on racial stereotypes and fears with all the outrageousness of Pryor's early work. In one instance, Chappelle invokes the murderous anger of Bicentennial Nigger by staging the repeated shooting of a slave master in slow motion, like Abraham Zapruder's film of President Kennedy's assassination. Yet the performance also brims with the swagger of black humor. A conjurer of a different sort, Chappelle does not rely as much on a humor of the body (although he does manipulate his own long, bony frame in ways that recall Pryor), nor does he operate strictly through stand-up. Rather, relying primarily on the verbal creativity of signifying as well as on the conventions of comedic skits (costumes, makeup, stage design, etc.), Chappelle conjures realms of the fantastic. In one skit a white family bears the last name Niggar and is subject to common racist jokes involving the "N" word. Chappelle, who plays the family's milkman, delivers many such jokes with evident glee. In another, Chappelle plays a blind black man who becomes a white supremacist because he does not know he is black (a skit that is, remarkably enough, loosely based on Chappelle's own grandfather). In each of these skits, and most glaringly in the ones that directly address slavery, it is clear that Chappelle's power, like Pryor's, resides in his ability to give body and voice to racial and sexual taboos that Americans cherish and protect.

As we shall have occasion to examine in this chapter's coda, Chappelle, like Pryor, has had to recoil from this power. In a now much publicized dramatic exit, he unexpectedly left the set of *Chappelle's Show* despite the fact that he had a fifty-million-dollar contract with Comedy Central, allegedly because he is troubled by the possibility that his play on stereotypes reaffirms racist views, as some of his detractors have claimed. While much of the information surrounding Chappelle's departure is unreliable or conjectural, the fact that he has abandoned the show and has since produced *Chappelle's Block Party* (2006), a film that does not rely on stereotype-based humor, suggests a pattern whereby powerful conjurers that use stereotypes to redress slavery recoil at a moment of saturation. What, then, is the relationship between stereotypes of race and sexuality and the paradox that is so central to both Pryor's and Chappelle's work: the redressing of a crisis that *cannot* but that needs to be redressed?

Richard Pryor, Conjurer

In April 1968, Pryor performed and recorded a one-man play at The Troubadour in West Hollywood, a play that in many respects recalls William Wells Brown's *The Escape*. The play, a reenactment of a drama that Pryor witnessed while in prison, takes place in an antebellum setting, concerns an interracial romance, and consists of six different characters (all played by Pryor). *Black Ben, the Blacksmith*, as the play is called, is a tour de force.[19] Using only his voice and gestures as props, Pryor plays himself (as a prisoner witnessing the play), a white jail guard, the actor introducing the play to the inmates, and all of the characters in the play: a white planter, the planter's father and sister (a southern belle), and the title character. Like *The Escape*, *Black Ben* is a parody of minstrel shows. Like Brown in his dramatic readings, Pryor is the nexus for the different perspectives of each character across differences of gender and race. By setting the performance of the play in a prison where he is an inmate, however, Pryor also indirectly links three distinct time frames: the antebellum past; the early twentieth century, when minstrel shows were routinely performed in jails in America; and the late twentieth century of his performances in Hollywood. He also insinuates parallels between racism and homophobia, explicitly identifying the audience in the jail setting as including both gay and straight inmates and suggesting, albeit humorously, their common plight under the rule of a small-minded jail guard.

As a much more extended and elaborate instance of stereotype impersonation than the kind that Pryor performs in the opening skits of *Bicentennial Nigger*, *Black Ben* allows for greater access to Pryor's conjuring of the characters and to the obsessions, in particular that of miscegenation, that slavery produced. Like Brown, Pryor operates through hyperbole, piling exaggeration upon exaggeration while turning minstrelsy on its head. But unlike his predecessor, Pryor does not replicate the verbal and physical antics of the minstrel stage. Rather, he echoes but ultimately displaces the violence of that stage—its distortions of black speech and bodies—while creating a humor of incongruity that uncovers the sexual and scatological obsessions that fueled minstrelsy. Setting an impossible plot against a bizarre but strangely real background, he overly exaggerates racial and gender types that, more so than his black and white women, bring into the open difficult but significant features of American slavery and culture.

The plot of *Black Ben, the Blacksmith* is simple, but its delivery and implications are explosive. When an actor announces that the play is "about a southern girl who falls in love with a black," the jailer, a racist redneck whom Pryor conjures with sharp exactitude, quickly intervenes and orders everyone to leave, changing his mind only when the actor (another Pryor voice) tells him, "It's quite all right. The nigger gets killed." But Ben, the "nigger," does not; instead, he gets the girl and walks off arm in arm with his future brother-in-law (the white planter), who promises to help him establish his business. "We'll be the first family in the South to know true freedom and true love," the planter tells Ben. The plot is an outrageously embellished fantasy, out of which we are yanked when the jailer angrily yells, "Just a goddamn minute! . . . You said the nigger got killed! Well, nobody leave! I want a dead nigger here and if I don't get one, we gonna hang one of these homosexuals!"

The routine depends on Pryor's brilliant manipulation of voice, which is comparable only to that of his fellow comedians Lenny Bruce and Lily Tomlin, and, more recently, to that of the performer Anna Deavere Smith.[20] Like Pryor, these performers have enacted various characters across wide gaps of gender, race, sexuality, ethnicity, and age, using minimal props (various voices, mannerisms, temperaments, and emotions). Especially in the case of Tomlin and Smith, the ability to perform as such depends on a notion of identity as "radically theatrical and performative, constituted by repeated poses, postures, acts, and gestures."[21] Although Pryor often performs identity, especially in his Wino and Junkie characters, from a similar perspective, in *Black Ben, the Blacksmith* and much of his stand-up he performs characters who do not have identities, but embody stereotypes. The difference is crucial because what Pryor, unlike Tomlin and Smith, uncovers through his performance is not just the constructed nature of identity but also the performativity of stereotypes.

If, as one critic writes, "what interest[s] Anna Deavere Smith as an actor is a person's struggle within and against scripts,"[22] Pryor in his play is primarily interested in the opposite—in the ways that people *do not* struggle against pre-existing scripts but can so wholly give in to stereotype that they make reality out of ideological fetishes. Pryor's performance of the prison guard, for example, details through tone, diction, and syntax the perfect essence of the racist white man of limited but deadly power; not quite the master, he is poor, uneducated, and usually consigned to the role of slave auctioneer, overseer, patroller, and jailer. The story within a story of Pryor's routine highlights the persistence of this character across time. Conspicuously absent in the play itself, he quickly inserts himself when the rules by which he lives are threatened ("You said the nigger got killed!").

Pryor's voice so expertly becomes this white man's that, as one listens to the audio recording of the routine, Pryor seems to have transformed altogether, and one struggles to remember that it is Pryor's voice all along. A live performance would of course highlight the disconnection between body and voice, a fact that has other implications. Paired with Pryor's gift as a mimic, the disconnection would make emphatic the fact that stereotyped roles may be appropriated by anyone—including those against which the stereotype is created—because they are shared cultural fantasies. Once separated from the fact of their performativity, however, stereotyped roles can ossify into harsh, even brutal realities. Witness the guard's call for murder. Pryor's performance underscores both the transferability of the stereotype and its resolute fixity.

While Pryor performs the stereotype of the jailer with perfect accuracy, he exaggerates those he culls from the mythology of slavery: the planter, the southern belle, the Negro. Placing these stereotypes in a pastoral setting while making more grotesque their already vulgar aspects, he underscores the caricature status of the roles he plays. In this respect he anticipates the work of Ishmael Reed in *Flight to Canada* and of Kara Walker's silhouette work. He relies on the campiness of drag to play the role of the southern belle and on the conventions of minstrelsy to play Ben. While he thus emphasizes the clichéd status of such roles, he sets his figures in preposterous dialogues and impossible plots. Such incongruity produces a nervous but ultimately cathartic laughter.

Pryor begins by playing each role in easily recognizable ways but soon moves into the unexpected. As Ben he plays the part of the "coon" and as the master he plays the part of the bigot. Ben has been sent for by the master so that he can shoe his father's horse but spends much of the play asking, "Where is the hoss at, boss?" and doing a kind of slow verbal tap dance—constituting Pryor's echoing of minstrel speech—by sliding certain syllables and rhyming the words *shoe*, *hoss*, and *boss*. He enters the stage after the master's father says, "Here comes that black. Watch yourself, he's kinda smart. . . . Let's see what trickery he is up to now." But Ben's first words are a loud, happy-go-lucky "Hi y'all!" Obviously, he is the dimwitted but nevertheless suspicious minstrel "nigger." Initially, Pryor plays the role of the master in similarly unsurprising ways, complaining that "the acre's been down, the cotton is going bad, and I think my sister is in love with that coon." In the same breath, however, Pryor-as-master relates his plan to trap Ben: "I'll have her strip naked in the front room and, if he looks at her, then I'll know." Ridiculous as it is, the master actually enacts this ploy (we hear Pryor as the belle as she sits naked waiting for Ben, who of course, is also Pryor in another verbal disguise). But this ploy is only the beginning of the preposterous plot. One of the first things that the southern belle giggles to Ben is "My, you have some lovely biceps," to which Ben, in a serious and deep voice, answers.

> **Black Ben:** Thank you, Mam. Would you like to feel my ass? [loud laughter]
> **Southern Belle:** [In high pitch giggling] My, my . . . I just love to! Should I squeeze it or pinch it?
> **Black Ben:** Just help yourself.[23]

The southern belle then asks Ben if her invalid mother, who is "taking a little poo-poo," can take a pinch too, since it might "give her a little thrill." Ben responds by earnestly telling her, "I think I'm in love with you." The speed with which the characters move into lust and from lust into love against a scatological background creates an atmosphere in which anything and everything might be possible. Then the unbelievable does happen: the southern belle actually falls in love with Ben, who proposes instantly, and the master does not protest. In fact, he sees the marriage as an opportunity to know "true freedom and true love."

By making such an impossible ending the outcome of a preposterous scenario—involving lust, love, and shit—Pryor highlights a deep irony. While the scenario is an exaggerated version of the often imagined perversities of slavery—specifically through the taboo against miscegenation, played out by the southern belle as the secretly salacious "nigger lover" and the "coon" who is forever pining for her—the ending, which proposes "true freedom and true love," is deemed unimaginable from the jailer's perspective. The force with which Pryor highlights this irony could not be clearer and funnier than when he returns to the guard's perspective at the end of the play ("Wait just a goddamn minute!").

Everything, as in all good comedy, depends on timing. In the play within the skit, Pryor delays the movement of the plot so that, until the master decides to trick Ben, the only implied action is the shoeing of the horse. Once the master's zany plan begins to unfold, however, the play speeds up in ways that recall the madcap resolution of Brown's *The Escape*. Before yanking his audience out and back into the framing skit with the guard's call for murder, Pryor lets the conspicuously neat ending linger a bit. And so it is by manipulating comedic timing that Pryor gives the guard's demand added force.

The guard is just as much of a caricature as the antebellum figures that Pryor has just performed—in fact, he is a mutation of another stereotype, the plantation overseer—but he has no consciousness of it at all. Pryor's decision to conjure him with exactitude highlights the elision of stereotype with identity, the fact that a human being can act so much according to script that the script itself becomes the person's identity. The guard then guards not only the prisoners but also against any plot that would deviate from the often imagined, which in this case is interracial love—as romance and brotherhood—as opposed to miscegenation, which carries connotations of the forbidden or even the unnatural.

Pryor's one-man, multicharacter play makes explicit the sexual and scatological undertones that Eric Lott identifies as a subtext of minstrelsy. As Lott argues, the "vexing and unmeaning linguistic creativity" of stump speeches, which were characteristic of minstrel shows, called attention "to the grain of voices, the wagging of tongues, the fatness of painted lips." Through the speeches' "proliferation of huge, ungainly, and onomatopoetic words," argues Lott, "could be relived the forgotten liberties of infancy—the belly and the sucking of the breasts, a wallowing in shit."[24] While Pryor clearly references minstrelsy through his portrayal of Ben, he does not replicate the malapropisms of the minstrel stage. Rather, he connotes the sexual and scatological by naming it directly ("Would you like to feel my ass?") and through the campiness of his portrayal of the southern belle (whose mamma takes a "little poo-poo"). Lott also notes the aggressive emphasis on the sexuality of black bodies, particularly the black male body that characterized minstrel shows. He writes, "[The] body was always grotesquely contorted, even when sitting; stiffness and extension of the arms and legs announced themselves as unsuccessful sublimations of sexual desire."[25] In Pryor's play, there is also an emphatic focus on Ben's sexuality, yet his desire and others' desire for him are never sublimated, but are explicitly expressed, reciprocated, and rewarded.

As Suzan-Lori Parks would a few decades later, Pryor thus exposes, *without replicating,* key but sublimated features of the minstrel stage. That is, Pryor does *not* satirize the sexual and scatological underpinnings of minstrelsy by once again making black bodies and black speech carry the burden of contortion and distortion. Instead, in common English, albeit accented with echoes of minstrelsy and camp, his characters explicitly name, without acting, the unspoken subtext of minstrelsy. The fact that Pryor plays all of the roles, a fact that is difficult to keep in mind even when one listens to the performance—and more so when one reads about it, as in this chapter—emphasizes the transferability of stereotypes and therefore frees the black body from the clichés of sex and race to which it is so often bound.

In focusing his attention on stereotypes of race and sexuality, Pryor works within the tradition of black humor in which tendentious jokes regarding such stereotypes abound. Black Americans have not only created their own stereotypes of white Americans—of "peckerwoods" and "honkies"—but have also directed their laughter at the stereotypes with which they have been represented, appropriating those images in order to diffuse their power of humiliation. They have also used jokes about stereotypes of blackness to laugh at, and thus chastise, those who were complicit in perpetuating such images. By performing stereotypical roles rather than simply telling jokes about them, Pryor is able to expose the nature of the stereotype itself, showing what it masks and suggesting what people, across gender and race, have invested in it. The dramatic reenactment that is *Black Ben, the Blacksmith* also allows Pryor to make vivid the potency that stereotypes produced by slavery have had, and continue to have, across time.

This constitutes a major aspect of Pryor's conjure. Like Brown and Chesnutt, Pryor signifies on the conventions through which slavery has been mediated—since it was practice and law—by minstrelizing minstrelsy and lending his body to acts of transformation. His ability to conjure the ideological fetishes that slavery produced depends on a use of the body that recalls the transformations of Chesnutt's conjure tales without direct references to chattel slavery's transformation of people into objects or animals. At the same time, his power-ful use of imitation and hyperbole echoes Brown's dramatic readings of *The Escape*. Performing more than a century after Brown and nearly seventy years after Chesnutt, Pryor reveals the mutations undergone by the ideologies that supported slavery. Thus, while in *Black Ben* he conjures stereotypes of race and gender directly from the mythology of slavery, in the same routine, as well as in the opening tracks of *Bicentennial Nigger* and his work overall, he not only makes vivid how those stereotypes have attained new forms but also converts them into vehicles for catharsis.

As I noted in the introduction, catharsis in the Freudian model of humor occurs through the masking effects of jokes; in masking aggression, jokes allow the joker and his or her audience the release of energy used for the purposes of inhibition. Unlike the humor analyzed by Freud, however, Pryor's humor neither relies on jokes nor does it mask aggression or exposure; rather, it *relishes* both, following the tradition of signifying, of playing the dozens and toasting. Thus, Pryor's performance of stereotypes in *Black Ben* is propelled by the exposure of the simultaneously static and performative aspects of stereotypes. On the one hand, they are shared cultural fantasies that can be appropriated by anyone; on the other, they are scripts by which people live, die, and kill (as does the guard). In embodying both possibilities, Pryor produces a humor of incongruity in which one body holds mutually opposing ideologies. But whereas such tension might invoke Du Bois's sense of "two warring ideals in one dark body," in Pryor's performance the black body is not subject to the tension it performs. Instead it is a conduit for a laughter that releases that tension in a play that celebrates the body's freedom to *perform* rather than be defined by stereotypes.

"Niggerniggerniggerniggerniggerniggernigger"

> Look! Up in the sky!
>> It's a crow! [laughter, applause]
>> It's a bat! [laughter]
>> No, it's Super Nigger! [laughter as Pryor adds his version of "funky music" to introduce the black superhero]
>> Yes, friends, able to leap tall buildings with a single bound, faster than a bowl of chittlins . . .[26]

Black Ben is track four of Pryor's first major album, *Richard Pryor* (1968), an album that opens with "Super Nigger," a seemingly simple track in which Pryor creates a black superhero in part by turning the "N" word on its head. A closer look reveals how Pryor makes ironic the conventions of the comic book genre to give visual form to an aspect of African American popular culture, transforming the "N" word from one that has signified hatred and humiliation to one that invokes recognition and affiliation. In "Super Nigger," Pryor conjures a comic book hero without using any tangible visual markers. He does not, unlike other instances of conjure, use his body, relying instead only on his voice to bring into being a figure that highlights the invisibility of African Americans in 1960s mainstream American culture.[27]

"Super Nigger" is also an instance of Pryor's use of the "N" word as a prism through which to redress slavery. The word's power to invoke some of the most humiliating aspects of slavery and segregation has made it the "nuclear bomb of racial epithets," "the most obnoxious racial epithet in [the] contemporary American lexicon."[28] Yet throughout the 1970s, and especially in *That Nigger's Crazy*, Pryor capitalized on the ambiguity of the word, invoking it sometimes as he did curse words, as part of a "poetics of cursing,"[29] and at other times as the kind of code word that black folk use when signifying or toasting. He also used it in the way that racist whites have used it for centuries. The difference is always a matter of tone and context, two key, meaning-making elements in black street language that Pryor used to his creative advantage.

Not quite a curse word, "nigger" is in many ways more taboo than actual obscene words, which "derive principally from the malediction (*damn you*) or from bodily functions (*shit*)." The "N" word, however, does have important similarities to actual curse words. As Kate E. Brown and Howard I. Kushner argue, curse words derive their force from the fact that they absorb "the history of their past speaking," making them quasi-autonomous since their force "exceeds their immediate context." More so than other words, curse words "are not owned but are only *voiced* by the speaker." "Nigger" is the H-Bomb of racial epithets precisely because, like curses, it derives its force from the history of its past use.[30] My own euphemistic use of it as the "N" word throughout this chapter registers a personal discomfort, but I am also sensitive to the fact that banning the word would only add to its potency.

Randall Kennedy notes that the word "nigger" is "derived from the Latin word for the color black, *niger*. . . . [But no] one knows precisely when or how *niger* turned derisively into *nigger* and attained a pejorative meaning." We do know that "nigger" did not "originate as a slur but took on a derogatory connotation over time," becoming decidedly insulting by "the first third of the nineteenth century."[31] As Kennedy shows, the word is much more than a potent insult. Indeed, it is a word through which we can trace the racial history of America and one that has played important roles in major court decisions, the most famous of which is the O. J. Simpson trial, in which its repeated use by LAPD Detective Mark Fuhrman was essential in Simpson's acquittal. While the word has long been a staple in black humor, it remained off-limits, especially in mixed audiences, until Pryor's new self emerged in the 1970s. Amazingly, in a 1963 routine, Lenny Bruce attempted to purge the word of its hateful meanings through overuse—no doubt a bold move, especially from a white comedian. As Randall notes, however, Bruce "failed to inspire emulation." Pryor, by contrast, brought the word "to center stage."[32]

In repeating the word in front of mixed audiences, where it could simultaneously invoke all of its past and widely divergent meanings, Pryor created occasions for potentially productive tensions in which the pain and shame of slavery could be culled alongside black strength and anger as well as white guilt and defensiveness. Miraculously, he also made the word funny. In "Super Nigger" he makes the word connote the humor of the funny pages, of comic books—at once lighthearted and violent. And in most of *That Nigger's Crazy* (1974), but especially in track 4, he uses the word to flaunt racial difference at the expense of whites, a strategy that was revolutionary when he used it and one that, by the early twenty-first century, has become a cliché. White folks and "niggers" eat and have sex differently: white folk "eat quiet and shit . . . [using a serious tone]. 'Pass the potatoes. Thank you, darling. Could I have a bit of that sauce? How are the kids coming along with their studies? Think we'll be having sexual intercourse this evening? We are not? Well, what the heck?'" Black families have more fun when they eat: "[Imitating his father] 'Hey, bitch. Where the food? Goddamn mamma, come on! Shit. . . . Pass shit nigger, kiss my ass. Better get that meat on that bone motherfucker'." "I got an auntie," Pryor tells his audience, "can suck a neck bone. . . . It's a piece of art. . . . I mean she can *fuck* with a neck bone. Get that white stuff out [making sucking noises], throw it to the dog, the dog look at her, 'What am supposed to do with *that* motherfucker?'" In general, white folks don't play enough (when instigated to play the dozens they respond with, "My mom? She was a great old gal!") and they "fuck quiet." "Niggers" don't: "Oh you motherfucker! Goddamn baby! Don't move now, bitch. Ah, goddamn!" In the middle of these bits an audience member exuberantly yells out, "You crazy!"

As Mel Watkins argues, for many blacks, "[Pryor's] humor afforded a cathartic experience, a public purging of the embarrassments and frustrations built up over decades of concealing real attitudes and cultural preferences, suppressing customs that largely defined existence for them."[33] Of course, Pryor exaggerated such attitudes and cultural preferences, but he did so as a way of rejecting the pressure to sanitize black culture in the name of integration. If in most of *That Nigger's Crazy* Pryor produces cathartic laughter, in a few tracks in that album Pryor uses the "N" word as a way to underscore the connection between police brutality and the violence of slavery, producing instead a laughter fit to kill. Making the "N" word the bridge between a divisive past and an equally, if differently, divisive present, he intertwines the seemingly mutually exclusive terrains of outrage and humor.

Characteristically, Pryor does not assume the serious tone of his intent. In his imagination, Super Nigger is disguised as Clark Washington, a "mild-mannered custodian for the *Daily Planet*," who shuffles along, cleaning halls endlessly. Pryor invented the character out of a desire to fill a vacuum in television and film, media that, at the time (1968), never showed black heroes. But he carefully endowed the character with the abilities to "*see through everything except Whitey*" and, like the "Flying Fool" of African American folklore, to fly, although Super Nigger has to fly with one wing tied behind his back (*PC* 113).[34] The strategy is brilliant insofar as Pryor invokes black empowerment without denying the reality of racial oppression.

Clark Washington/Super Nigger signifies on one of the most visible comic book superheroes, Clark Kent/Superman. Like Robert Colescott, Pryor blackens an iconic figure and thus forges an ironic relationship between inside and outside, visible and invisible, and the hypermasculinity and emasculation implied by the perverse split man/"nigger." Superhero comic books rely on the dichotomy between strength and weakness to define masculinity and often correlate that binary with the identity of the superhero, which is usually split between a powerful secret self and a comparatively weak quotidian self. Yet the superhero's status and power is defined not only against his weak self but also in contrast to "those cultural identities represented as soft and vulnerable," including women and feminized men.[35] Employing the "N" word in this context, Pryor destabilizes the dichotomies of the genre while signifying on the role of superhero comic books in the dissemination of racial stereotypes. Ultimately, he takes a word loaded with the injustices of slavery and segregation and not only elevates it hyperbolically but also grafts it onto an exclusionary realm.

Aside from propagating demeaning images of nonwhites, the superhero comic book genre, as Marc Singer notes, has a "long history of excluding, trivializing, or 'tokenizing' minorities" and has also produced "numerous minority superheroes who are marked purely for their race: 'Black Lightning,' 'Black Panther' and so forth."[36] While the black superheroes to which Singer refers emerged as versions of characters in the briefly popular blaxploitation films of the mid-1970s, Pryor's Super Nigger not only anticipates such superheroes but also offers a radically different paradigm. Rather than fetishizing his character's physical powers and heroic disposition, Pryor simply and humorously tells us that he is faster than "a bowl of chittlins" and has him rescue his "secret stash" of marijuana. The humor allows Pryor to highlight the invisibility of black superheroes without replicating the limitations of the superhero genre. It also allows him to reinvigorate aspects of black folklore that are grounded in the history of slavery. Super Nigger, as my earlier allusion to the "Flying Fool" suggests, recalls the trickster figures of early African American folklore; like them, he is neither morally exemplary nor omnipotent yet remains an admirable figure of dissent that flies from drudgery and humiliation by using his secret identity. Even as Clark Washington, he refuses to conform. "Hey, man," he tells his employer, Mr. White, "I'm tired of doing them halls. Every time I finish . . . I got to do them over again. . . . I'm through" (*PC* 113).

Anticipating the use of comic book aesthetics in Ishmael Reed's *Flight to Canada*, Pryor conjures an ancestral sensibility using two key tropes in African American culture: the mask (secret identity) and flying ("Look up in the sky!"). He thus simultaneously reclaims a word of deep hatred, a word emblematic of slavery, and uses it to highlight African American invisibility in late 1960s mainstream America. In his 1974 album *That Nigger's Crazy*, recorded live in San Francisco, Pryor once again focuses on African American invisibility, this time by embracing the attitudes, lexicon, and perspectives of black figures least likely to be acknowledged in society, even by their African American brethren. Portraying winos and junkies, Pryor affirms ways of speaking and behaving in African American communities while reinvigorating another aspect of black folklore, the tradition of toasting. Extending that tradition, he redresses the violence that supported slavery by focusing on police brutality against African Americans in the late twentieth century.

Known also as jokes, toasts usually concern the life of the underworld—pimps, hustlers, whores, winos, and junkies—and are composed of long (some have over two hundred lines) and "complex metrical arrangements" that are "recited in a rhythmic, slightly musical 'rifting' style."[37] Toasts detail the "moral despair of a hero," usually a hustler or a pimp, who uses "verbal force to win" encounters and who is "bad" by virtue of the fact that he violates the "norms of white society in fighting, stealing, cursing, fornication, the illegal use of drugs and the excessive use of alcohol."[38] While he thus also violates the norms of the black middle class, he is considered a hero of the black lower classes, who view him as "ba-ad"—that is, admirable—in his ability to exploit a system that exploits black people. The redefinition of *bad* in this instance is part of a particular quality of the toast's lexicon, of the dozens and signifying in general, in which loaded words such as "nigger" or curse words such as "motherfucker"—both common in verbal dueling—are used in ways and contexts other than those normally intended.[39]

While Pryor does not replicate the length and rhyming of the toast, he employs its lexicon, in particular the word "nigger," its hyperbole, and its tropes for boasting, to make his most incisive critiques of police brutality. In several routines, some of which are his most often quoted, Pryor uses the "N" word to make implicit connections between that brutality and the humiliations of slavery and segregation. "Cops put a hurting on your ass, they really degrade you," starts Pryor in one such routine, "white folks don't believe that shit. . . . 'Oh c'mon, those people are resisting arrest.'" When the police directs a white driver to the side of the road, Pryor asserts, the driver can say, "Glad to be of help" and have a pleasant interaction. "A nigger," by contrast, has to enunciate every word of the following sentence: "I-AM-REACHING-INTO-MY-POCKET-FOR-MY-LICENSE [loud laughter and applause] 'cuz I don't want to be no motherfuckin' accident!'" "It's often you wonder why a nigger don't go completely mad," says Pryor later in the routine, and then creates the following scenario:

> You get your shit together, you work all week and then you get all dressed. . . . Say a cat makes $120 a week and gets $80 if he lucky. Right, and he go out . . . be drivin' with his old lady out to a club and the police pull over. 'Get out of the car! There was a robbery, a nigger look just like you! Alright, take your hands up, take your pants down, spread your cheeks!' Now, what nigger feel like having fun after that? . . . You go home and beat your kids. . . . Gonna take that shit out on somebody.

A "nigger," in Pryor's 1974 scenario, is someone whose life can be taken randomly, whose integrity and self-respect can also be taken—and in extreme ways, as the insinuation of sodomy suggests—despite his efforts to work (even at little pay) and to live according to the rules. In these essential ways, the meaning of "nigger" has not changed since the institution of slavery made the word ubiquitous. The police can "choke niggers to death," Pryor tells his audience in *Live in Concert*, and then contrasts black and white reactions: "Niggers be going yeaah, yeaah . . . white folks, 'I had no idea!'"

"Breaking a nigger" in the parlance of slave masters meant savagely beating a human being into submission; in Pryor's performance the phrase has its own brutal, literal meaning. Mimicking a policeman in the process of choking a black man to death, Pryor says, "Oh shit, he broke. Can you break a nigger? . . . Let's check the manual. . . . Yes, it says so on page eight, you can break a nigger." Police brutality is more than terror as usual; it is terror disguised as rules and procedures. Often, however, police brutality could not be more naked. In the same performance Pryor invokes the memory of bloodhounds running after fugitives when he talks about the dogs that the police "sic on you." Police dogs are fast, Pryor claims, but, while they can "catch the average white boy," they grow tired before catching "a nigger." Affording his audience relief from the associations between blackness and victimization that he has been drawing, Pryor imitates a young black man running so fast that he leaves a Doberman Pincer gasping for air. The performance is pure physical comedy as Pryor's lithe body assumes the gestures of speed and then freezes in a running pose.

The laughter comes at a necessary moment as Pryor maintains his attention on police brutality for quite a while, using the word "nigger" to signify black victimization and humiliation at the hands of whites. He begins by recounting one of his most publicized outbursts, his drunken shooting at his wife and friends on New Year's Day in 1978. Pryor characteristically turns the incident into hilarious comedy by editing the story so that instead of shooting at his wife, he uses his

Magnum to shoot his car. The car moans and writhes through Pryor's ability to give voice to inanimate objects. Even the vodka that he has been drinking speaks, telling him "Go ahead, shoot something else." The police arrive faster than a speeding bullet. "If you want the cops to respond quickly," writes Pryor in his account of the scenario in his autobiography, "all you have to say is, 'Hello officer, I want to report a black man with a gun.' It's like announcing the start of hunting season at an NRA convention" (*PC* 163). Just before the police arrive, Pryor goes inside his house because, as he puts it, "the police have Magnums too. And they don't kill cars. They kill *nig-gas*." Not even stardom, it would seem, can save a black man from being treated like a "nigger."

By culling humor out of racial violence, Pryor asserts what Freud called "the triumph of narcissism," using humor as black folk had throughout slavery and segregation, to signify "the victory of the ego which refuses to be hurt by the arrows of adversity and instead attempts to become impervious to the wounds dealt it by the outside world."[40] He also employs the boasting and hyperbole integral to toasts to assert strength in light of the violence against black Americans to which he testifies. The "N" word is in this respect instrumental.[41] "Niggers never get burnt up in buildings," Pryor claims. "They know how to get out of a motherfuckin' situation. They do. Whites folks just panic, run to the door, fall all over each other, choke to death and shit. Niggers get outside, *then* argue: 'I left my money in the motherfucker!'" In another routine, he suggests that "niggers" "know how to get out of a motherfuckin' situation" because, having survived centuries of oppression, they can do just about anything. "A lot of niggers ain't scared," he begins, going on to imitate an alarmed white voice recounting the landing of Martians on earth. By contrast, "Nothin' can scare a nigger, after four hundred years of this shit [laughter, loud applause]. I mean, right, a Martian ain't got a chance, boy. A nigger would warn the Martian. Better get your ass 'way from 'round here. You done landed on Mr. Gilmore's property" [lots of laughter, including Pryor's, and loud applause]. No one knows better, Pryor suggests, the violence with which property will be acquired and defended than a people who were once insidiously considered property.

Pryor also balances his use of "nigger" to signify humiliation with his use of it as a term signifying roughness and strength. His performances include many references to "bad-ass niggers"—athletes like Muhammad Ali, Leon Spinks, Joe Frazier, Jim Brown, or figures from his youth, such as his father—who exemplify a fighting spirit, a spirit he also invokes through repeated references to boxing. And he too embodies many of the qualities of "badness," including a slickness of character, plenty of mother wit, streets smarts, and, tragically, the kind of violence against women that is also characteristic of the heroes of toasts.[42] In *Live on the Sunset Strip* (1982), he dons a red suit and glittery shoes, assumes the smooth, dandy walk of Billy Dee Williams, and, as in many other performances, walks the length of the stage as if gliding through the fire of American racism. As we know from that same performance, among other sources, Pryor did not always keep such a cool distance from the fire; he literally burned and almost died in the fire. But Pryor never pretended otherwise. Instead, he walked a tightrope between badness and vulnerability, often remaining just balanced enough in that perilous position to manipulate it. As one critic puts it, Pryor plunged into the most disturbing aspects of American racism "fangs first, taking the skinny-boy license to draw blood and plead puniness."[43]

Pryor's vulnerability derived from his personal past, a traumatic and painful one, which would make him infinitely sensitive to the trauma of slavery and racism. Raised by his paternal grandmother, a domineering woman who ran a brothel, Pryor was coached to tell a judge he did not want to live with his mother when his parents divorced. He never quite recovered either from the loss of his mother or from the many scenes of violence and abuse that he witnessed and suffered. He was sexually molested as a child by a neighborhood bully and was exposed to his father's physical abuse of his mother and to the explicit sexual encounters between the men (many of whom were white) who frequented his grandmother's brothel and the prostitutes, one of whom was his mother. Peoria, Illinois, where Pryor grew up, was strictly segregated; his first encounter with whites was probably in the context of interracial prostitution. In *Live and Smokin'* and in his autobiography, Pryor recalls this time in his life, characteristically adding a commentary on racial dispossession and domination:

> Tricks used to come through our neighborhood. That's where I first met white people. They came down to our neighborhood and helped the economy. I could've been a bigot, you know what I mean? I could've been prejudiced. I met nice white men. They said, "Hello, little boy. Is your mother home? I'd like a blow job."
>
> I wonder what would happen if niggers went to white neighborhoods doing that shit. "Hey man, your mama home? Tell the bitch we want to fuck!" (*PC* 35)

The education that Pryor received at the brothel, where he was to meet black and white men of all walks of life ("Businessmen, Politicians, Junkies"), would ultimately empower him to critique stereotypes and to speak candidly about the racial politics of sexuality and the sexuality of racial politics (*PC* 35). In a routine from the 1970s, he observes that the futuristic movie *Logan's Run* does not have any black characters and concludes, "White folks aren't planning for us to be there." In the same breath he adds, "Whites know about pimping, because we are the biggest whores they got" [loud laughter, applause]. While the circumstances of his life were such that he experienced dispossession and domination intimately, Pryor incisively highlights the analogous relationship between his own experiences and those of African Americans more generally. It is through this analogy that he was able to transform his self-destructiveness, which he most dramatically manifested through his self-immolation, into a conduit for redressing slavery. How he came to disavow the "N" word and recoil from his conjuring of stereotypes reveals the intimacy of such analogy.

"No, there ain't no slavery today. Kiss my ass."

As Pryor recalls, he first used the word "nigger" in Berkeley while becoming "braver, more confident, and willing to tap into whatever provocative or controversial thoughts [he] had." He repeated the word throughout a good portion of his career, as if "saying it over and over again would numb [him] and everyone else of to its wretchedness." He repeated it, as he put it, "like a preacher singing hallelujah" (PC 116). But Pryor eventually concluded that even a shamanistic repetition of the word, one he came to consider "the most offensive, humiliating, disgraceful, ugly, and nasty word ever used in the context of black people," could never eradicate its power to invoke centuries of humiliation and pain. The change came in the wake of a freebasing accident and a trip to Africa, a trip that came to signify a rebirth for the comedian.

That Pryor ultimately considered his effort to purge significance from the "N" word a failure reveals how much it was bound by time and context. He claimed the word when to do so constituted a revolutionary stance on a par with the Black Power movement. Then, it allowed him to recall slavery in a condensed form while suggesting the vitality of African American culture, turning a word of insult and violence into one of recognition and affiliation. He renounced it in *Live on the Sunset Strip*, by which time the word had arguably been emptied of its revolutionary power. To his surprise, his decision made many of his fans angry: "People thought I'd gone soft, sold out, turned my back on the cause. . . . I received death threats. . . . [People] wanted my voice to be theirs. And they didn't want me to change" (PC 177). Ironically, his use of the word—revolutionary from some perspectives, scandalous from others—had made many black people angry when he started using it in front of mixed audiences, for while the word has had currency and a variety of meanings in private and in-group conversations among black folk for decades, it was rarely used when among whites. Some considered Pryor's use of the word a betrayal of trust; others felt pleasure at recognizing a standard aspect of black speech and humor used in an unexpected context. No black comedian as popular as Pryor had used it while performing for mixed audiences.

In *Here and Now* (1983), a concert performance delivered a year after he disavowed the "N" word, Pryor delivers his most direct address on slavery, employing an aggressive style that startlingly gives way to a posture of abjection.

The performance, which varies in minor although significant ways between the sound and film records, is called "The Weather" (in the video recording) and "Slavery" (in the audio version). It makes clear that, though he may have relinquished the "N" word, he never steered away from redressing slavery. Delivered through dynamic interchanges with his audience, the routine is a failure as a piece of comedy, but in and through that failure it becomes a stunning instance of ritual sacrifice as a form of redress.

"You can't tell what no motherfucker is down here," Pryor tells his audience at the beginning of "Slavery." "Motherfuckers look white and be black and the black ones talk that funny kinda shit." Miscegenation here is not something abstracted through stage drama, as in *Black Ben, the Blacksmith*, but the living reality of the audience in the room. Pryor goes on to mimic the "funny kinda shit" that black folk in New Orleans talk, creating a laughter of recognition, especially from the black women in the audience (who are visible in the film recording), while setting up the stage to address slavery and, then later, lynching.[44] Moving freely in and out of such charged topics through seemingly innocuous means, he suggests that miscegenation is a phenomenon particular to the Deep South, specifically to New Orleans. As it turns out, Pryor has singled out New Orleans only to praise it for its spirit of celebration, for its willingness to take to the streets in joyful parade "at the drop of a hat." He has now charmed the audience, making it laugh in recognition and applaud the praise that he lavishes on it. He continues on this innocent path by taking on the most quotidian of subjects: the weather. Yet he is only setting up his audience for the subject of slavery and implicitly circling back to the subject of miscegenation. "It get *hot* down here, boy," Pryor says and proceeds to mimic a man who is so bothered by the heat that he can hardly walk down the street, let alone talk to people. Then: "I don't know how you had no slavery down here 'cuz slaves would've quit. [Assuming the voice of slave who is speaking to his master] 'Hey man, fuck you. Shit, carry that shit yo'self'" [laughter, applause]. In the audio recording of the performance, Pryor continues, "No, there ain't no slavery today, kiss my ass. Fuck you" [much laughter and applause].

The audience still laughs and applauds because Pryor has yet to turn up the heat in the room. He does so when he pauses in wonder. "Slaves built all this shit or carried the shit that built it. Right, I looked at the Mississippi and said, motherfucker had to walk across that. [Then, assuming the voice of a master] 'Get your black ass down there and walk. Carry that tree. Don't start no shit.'" There is then a palpable silence from the audience which Pryor lets dangle only to laugh to himself and say, "You some cold motherfuckers, boy [pause]. Yo' ancestors" [laughter, applause]. The audience laughs nervously since Pryor has turned the tables quite fast—from praise to guilt. Immediately one hears the voices of hecklers, voices that will gain volume later in the performance.

In the performance recorded on video he does not let up; he quickly brings up lynching. In the audio recording, he does something just as significant: he follows the routine by talking about going "to Africa, back to the motherland."[45] In both instances, he continues to confront his audience with the memory of slavery. In the performance recorded on video, he follows the line "Yo' ancestors" with this accusation:

> You know, you guys didn't do nothing on holidays . . . or weekends . . . you motherfuckers just hanged black people. Right, be bored and shit . . . Saturday night. It's hot. Can't get no pussy. [Assuming the dopey voice of an ignorant hillbilly] 'What'cha wanna do? Huh, huh. Shoot, there ain't nothin' to do. . . . Go down to the jail and string one up, haa, haa. . . .' And black people be standing around watching talking about [assuming a stunned, silent, open-jaw facial expression, then assuming the position of the lynched man]. The guy be saying 'Fuck that! Help me!'" [laughter, applause].

Having created his own kind of heat, Pryor starts to speak of the cold weather to which he is accustomed in Illinois. While he thus circles out of the charged topics he has broached, he is soon confronted by the first of a number of hecklers in the audience who will not let go of the tension Pryor has provoked.

When Pryor suggests that the cold of Illinois is so bad that people suspend their prejudices until the summer, one heckler yells out, "Bullshit!" Although Pryor quickly retorts with "Bullshit, ma dick!" it is clear that the heckler has touched on something and that Pryor must resort to vulgarity to regain ground. Pryor's move, from lynching to suspended prejudices, does not ring true and provokes anger in an audience that has been subjected to images of slavery and lynching and that, more than anything else, has been held accountable ("Yo' ancestors," "You guys") for such crimes against humanity. Pryor's next move is to change the subject altogether: he speaks about having been sober for seven months and generally alludes to change and growth in his life. Soon, however, there is another heckler who yells, "I don't believe that!" and another who screams, "You're fucked up, Rich!" The audience will not let Pryor off; indeed, they seek to punish him even when he moves away from the subject of slavery and lynching to the turmoil of his own life.

As if to make amends for having brought forth such taboo subjects, Pryor returns to pleasing his audience, which wants "Rich" to play the role of the "fucked-up" comedian who drinks excessively, shoots cars (and wives), but makes everyone laugh. Thus, while he begins to talk about positive change in his life, he ends by playing the role of a drunk. Pryor becomes a drunk in a way that closely resembles his junkie character, a man so down and out that he cannot hide the deep pain that propels him toward self-destruction. The sequence ends as Pryor, dangling his long bony frame, bows his head, mumbles words about failure, and cries so convincingly that some audience members yell out in recognition of his talent. He has incorporated the pain to which he alludes in the routine, swallowing it whole so that his audience does not have to feel it after all. When he lifts his head, his eyes are glazed. But even such a performance does not calm the audience. Soon, another heckler yells out, hoping to get Pryor to play the dozens: "Hey Rich, how's your mamma?" Pryor, of course, knows the game well and answers with, "How's my mamma? I beg your pardon. I'll slap you in your mouth with ma dick."

It is possible that the last heckler wants to stop Pryor's self-abjection, to return him to the aggressive stance with which he started the routine by invoking the play of the dozens. But Pryor does not follow the lead. Instead, he carries his routine about being drunk to its extreme, literally giving up the posture of stand-up by falling on the ground while detailing the nausea and vomiting of drunkenness, perhaps in an effort to release what he has introjected for his audience. Only then can he return to the subject of race; when he does, he has to do it via the subject of marriage and divorce, two subjects that his audience shares regardless of race. Having married both black and white women (a significant fact in the context of his interracial audience), Pryor suggests that the only differences between the two kinds of women are minor. This is a far cry from the Pryor of *Bicentennial Nigger*, but the hecklers grow quiet as the comedian returns to safer ground, producing laughter that is based primarily on gender differences and only subtly on racial tensions.

As I have already suggested, the routine about slavery in *Here and Now* is a kind of failure: Pryor sets up the audience masterfully, making it self-conscious but lavishing it with praise, only to refuse to deliver material that creates cathartic laughter. Instead, he holds the audience accountable for crimes against humanity. The result, as evidenced by the hecklers, is tension rather than release, and Pryor must take the brunt of it. In symbolic sacrifice, he must incorporate the shame and guilt of a terrible past and act it out in terms of self-abjection.[46] Herein lies a great part of the power of Pryor's performances as a wino and a junkie and, for that matter, as the persona "Richard Pryor." Through such roles, he enacts the same process of introjection and self-abjection without first invoking slavery and the racism that perpetuates its ideologies. One might argue that this is essentially a conservative move insofar as it spares the audience a critical assessment of the past. But Pryor can summon the symptoms of racism so sensitively that he names the disease and its manifestations without naming them.

In a short but incisive commentary on Pryor's performance of the wino and junkie characters in *That Nigger's Crazy*, Eric Lott notes Pryor's "restrain[t]" even as he portrays the "ravages of black addiction and oppression." While the performance gives an "intimate" and intense rendition of black addiction, "rivaling anything in the more portentous undertakings of William Burroughs or Donald Goines," it never names white racism as the source, but rather "assumes it," provoking in the end "laughs of recognition" from audience members who know the unnamed source.[47] The performance, which Pryor first introduced in *Live and Smokin'* (1971), takes the form of a dialogue between a wino, a character Pryor culled from his memories of men in the streets of Peoria, but who is also a kind of type (the street preacher, street corner or stoop comedian), and a junkie, a younger version of the wino who is more open about his wounds in connection to his addiction. The latter arrives on the scene, which Pryor expertly invokes with few but poignant details, swaying in between street cars that swerve to avoid him, repeating the question "Wha's happenin'?!" in various stages of consciousness.

As Lott notes, Pryor sensitively performs the junkie's sickness and disconnection through the repetition of this question, which the junkie asks the world and himself, "as if repeating the greeting could bridge the two realities."[48] The wino, meanwhile, has assigned himself the role of traffic director; he is in no better shape but assumes a superior role with respect to the junkie, telling him that he is ashamed to see him in the state that he is in. In the full exchange between the characters, we learn that the junkie was some kind of street genius who "booked the numbers" without "paper or pencil" but who spent years in jail making license plates and is now in the streets without any prospects for employment:

> **Junkie:** Ashamed to see *me*? What about the shit out here?! Niggers is fuckin' with me, baby.... [Extended pause] Was I finished? I went to the unemployment bureau, baby.... I vomited and shit on the floor. I did, man—they'll make that nigger with that pistol down there clean it up! Nigger talkin' about, 'Clean up that vomit, motherfucker!' Ahahaha! I said, 'Fuck you, nigger, I ain't cleanin' that shit up.' He said, 'You don't clean that shit up I'll shoot yo' ass!' I said, 'Well who gon' clean up the blood, nigger?!' Ahahaha! That's the politics, baby. I'm sick, pops—boy, can you help me? My mind's thinkin' about shit I don't wanna think about—I can't stop the motherfucker, baby. Movin' too fast for the kid! Tell me some of that old lies o' yours to make me stop thinkin' about the truth. Would you help me?
>
> **Wino:** Yeah, I'mo help ya, boy, 'cos I believe ya got potential. That's right. You don't know how to deal with the white man, that's yo' problem. I know how to deal with him. That's right: that's why I'm in the position I'm in today.[49]

Steve Allen's 1995 *But—Seriously*, an excellent documentary about how comedians like Pryor satirize political and social ills, includes the junkie's monologue here quoted and splices it with images of real black men in the streets of America who, like him, sway in urban corners, barely avoiding traffic, and are just as sick and disconnected. The splicing reinforces Pryor's critique, which takes its most heart-wrenching tone when the junkie details his exchange with the black security guard who, ironically, must clean up after his sick brother but who also threatens to shoot him. The potentially spilled blood and the image of the guard cleaning it (and being punished for murder) suggest the truth that the junkie wants to quiet: self-destruction prompted by oppression. The irony of the wino's advice, and especially his last sentence, laughs it away, as Lott notes, at the expense of both characters.

I would not, as Herman Beavers does, read Pryor's burned body after his self-immolation as a symbol of "how hard it is to be a black man in America," for this risks pathologizing race. Pryor also took responsibility for his self-destructive and addictive nature and transformed himself into a better human being. And, while I partly agree with Beavers's claim that "Pryor's body is a text onto which the impact of racism is mapped," I strongly emphasize the active and conscious role that Pryor took in that endeavor. Pryor *lent* his body as a text on which that impact could be read. That is, Pryor's performances as any of his down-and-out characters (including the persona "Richard Pryor") enact the sacrificial aspect of redress to which Victor Turner refers. Such performances discharge "the animosities of the disturbed community" brought forth by the lasting effects of slavery to which Pryor's performances attest by making Pryor's body an effigy that is destroyed symbolically. In this respect, Beavers's large claim that there is "an unspoken confluence between [Pryor's burned body] and black men burned alive in the Jim Crow South" is intriguing for it suggests the aspects of ritual sacrifice that I wish to emphasize. Yet, rather than blame society for his shortcomings, as Beavers suggests, Pryor kept a fine but crucial balance between seeing "his addictions and other antisocial behavior" as "the results of the self-hatred precipitated in a racist society" and subjecting his behavior to "comedic critique."[50]

To this end, he used one of his most successful characters, Mudbone, an old man from Tupelo, Mississippi, from whose perspective Pryor often criticized himself. Mudbone, who remembers "back when there were no years, they just called it 'hard times,'" has the voice of an ancestor. Pryor describes it as a "muddy old voice that sounds somethin' between a preacher's Sunday mornin' sermonizin' and a grizzled seen-it-all coot sittin' at a bar drinkin' and spinnin' some wild bullshit" (*PC* 3). He is nothing like Uncle Remus since he tells the truth even if people look at him as though he were "askin' to fuck their mamma or something" (3). But he does bear an avuncular relationship to Pryor, and through Pryor, to audience members. Unlike Beavers, Mudbone identified the root of Pryor's trouble not in the racism that he surely faced in his life, but on the money he made as a star. In *Live on the Sunset Strip* (1982), for instance, Mudbone begins:

> You know, now I know that boy [referring to Pryor]. See, he fucked up. . . .
> That fire got on his ass and it fucked him up upstairs, fried up what little
> brains he had. 'Cuz I remember he could make a motherfucker laugh at

a funeral on Sunday, Christmas day. But you know what happened? He got money yeah that's what happened. . . . He said fuck it. Went all the way crazy.

By contrast, Mudbone says that he (and by association, a part of Pryor's consciousness) is "still hungry." Implicit, of course, is a view of Pryor's life and career as corrupted by fame and money. While he did indeed use his body to enact rituals of redress with respect to slavery, he was conscious of his weaknesses as a human being. "Don't let him get any of that powder," Mudbone goes on, because once he is on it, talking to him is like "trying to talk to a baboon's ass."

Given the balancing act that Pryor kept between his self-criticism and his use of his body as a medium to stage rituals of redress, it is significant that the soundtrack for his transformational years in Berkeley was Marvin Gaye's "What's Going On?"[51] On the album of which this song is the title track, Gaye sings in protest against the Vietnam War, the possibility of nuclear and ecological holocaust, the poverty of ghettos ("Inner City Blues"), what he calls "trigger happy policing," and the brutality with which the "picket lines and picket signs" against such conditions were met. It is also significant that even as Gaye sings of a "world in despair," he repeatedly invokes his faith in love. "For only love can conquer hate / You know we've got to find a way / To bring some lovin' here today." Poised amid songs about anger and despair and those invoking love and faith is one track that must have resonated deep within Pryor; in it, Gaye sings of "flyin' high" and away from such a world through drugs, through "self-destruction." Pryor must have listened carefully for he also carried on a balancing act—between his desire to vocalize (and in no uncertain terms) his own and black people's anger and despair and his desire to grow into a compassionate and loving self. In the middle of it all was also his intense desire to fly high and away from it all. His impersonation of his crack pipe goading him to cancel all his appointments and stay in his room with it forever is a post-fire testimony of the strength of such desire.[52]

Although he was to assume the character one more time in *Here and Now*, Pryor formally announced the end of Mudbone's stage career shortly before presenting the performance from *Live on the Sunset Strip* (film recording) that I have just quoted. This was yet another sign of the change that was occurring in his own career and, ultimately, in his method of redressing slavery. This is a moment in which, apart from renouncing the "N" word, Pryor wavers between Mudbone's warmth, his bluesman's sensibility and humor, and the aggressiveness and eventual ritual sacrifice of "Slavery." Listening to Pryor's early Mudbone routines is a process of meandering through stories of the old man's life in the South, his relationship with openly racist whites, his surreptitious acts of vengeance against them, and his work on the railroad, the depot, and, finally, on the sidelines in early Hollywood. To listen to him is to listen to the best aspects of American verbal art, as Mark Twain identified them in his 1895 essay,

"How to Tell a Story."[53] As Mudbone wanders from topic to topic without seeming to have a central point, he casually drops a studied remark (perhaps about seeing the making of *The Birth of a Nation*), pauses (having made himself laugh), and then takes off again, gathering the view of the landscape (late nineteenth- and early twentieth-century America) through the tenor of the blues. In one track, Mudbone actually breaks out into an improvised blues song.[54]

In *Live on the Sunset Strip* Pryor continues to work in the spirit of Mudbone rather than the adversarial mode of "Slavery." He performs the more indirect aspects of signifying, using slavery as a silent second text when discussing apparently unrelated subjects. Tracks 12 through 19 in *Live on the Sunset Strip* are particularly exemplary for it is there that he speaks of captivity and freedom but through stories of animals—those who are held in an American zoo and those who are free to roam in Africa. By anthropomorphizing the animals, making allusions to the Ku Klux Klan, prison life in America, and African liberation movements, he draws a number of charged implications which, when examined in relationship to one another, reveal racism, and more specifically slavery, as a subtext. Pryor masks his design with a conversational, as if casually improvised style, which recalls the meanderings of Mudbone. But in *Live on the Sunset Strip* he announces the end of Mudbone and, a year later, performs "Slavery," suggesting a critical shift from the catharsis and community-driven comedy of the 1970s. And, to some degree, that shift did occur.

As I noted earlier, by the time of *Live on the Sunset Strip* and *Here and Now*, Pryor did not have to do much to produce laughter from his audience. He had become such an icon that people laughed almost as soon as he appeared. He performs the Mudbone routine in *Live on the Sunset Strip* because his audience requests it but is visibly uncomfortable at having to fulfill the request. He grimaces and bends over in fake laughter before announcing the end of Mudbone and then performing in character. As the "Slavery" routine so amply demonstrates, Pryor did not want automatic laughter; he did not want his stand-up performances to become empty rituals. The denial of catharsis that he stages in that performance needs to be appreciated as his way of agitating against a facile consumption of his comedy. The tension he ignites in "Slavery" is palpable even in its recorded version (film and sound), but it is not Pryor's ultimate aim. True to the "never forget" promise he makes in the bicentennial album, his aim is to use black humor, or more specifically, his own brand of tragicomedy, to keep alive in his nation's aching consciousness "the painful details and episodes of a brutal experience." This aim is not due a pathological need to obsess about slavery, but because he sees plenty of evidence that his country is yet to transcend its effects. Late in *Here and Now* he again brings up his sobriety, observing that by the time he decided to become sober, the rest of the country had become addicted to drugs. He poignantly highlights the fact that, while African Americans (and one thinks of his Junkie character) had been battling addiction for a long time, it was only when large numbers of white people began getting high that drugs were recognized as an "epidemic." Calmly he adds, "Maybe next time you see black people in trouble you will help. Maybe." Like the miner's canary, Pryor suggests, black Americans have felt the ravages of addiction before many of their white compatriots.

In *Implicit Meanings*, Mary Douglas notes that for both Freud and Bergson, "the essence of a joke is that something formal is attacked by something informal, something organized and controlled by something vital, energetic, an upsurge for life in Bergson, of libido for Freud."[55] As we have seen, Pryor's comedy does not rely on the joke, as in Freud, or on the mechanical rigidity of the body, as in Bergson; it brilliantly exposes the ways that racial struggles in the United States, and not just in the white/black binary, have been struggles between "something organized, controlled," indeed institutionalized, legalized, against "something vital, energetic, an upsurge for life," for freedom and opportunity. But Pryor also employed his ability to assume other perspectives through voice and gesture to explore how such struggles achieve shape in other binaries, such as that between men and women, parent and child, and the self against itself—in a battle Pryor knew quite well, that between Eros and Thanatos. While Pryor masterfully locates the basic struggle between oppression and freedom in other relationships, he never trivializes the stunningly violent ways it has shaped race relations in America. In fact, one of the most significant achievements of his work is that it gives an extraordinary range of voices and gestures to the psychological and physical injury and pain that such violence has caused. In two of his most accomplished performances—one in which he enacts the pain of a heart attack (or, more precisely, the way that his heart attacks him) and one in which he performs the pain of his burned body in recovery—he simultaneously captures humanity in full vulnerability and the black body in the throes of pain. These performances, as well as the others we have examined, show that a great part of Pryor's brilliant legacy is precisely in his ability to symbolically redress slavery while speaking at many other frequencies.

The Conjurer's Revenge: Fantasies of Retribution in Chappelle's Show

> *Slavery is one of the most atrocious things ever. But it is part of our culture. There's only two ways you can deal with slavery: You can ignore it and hope it will go away, or you can address it. I choose to address most things with humor. You can't recover from a problem that you aren't willing to acknowledge you have.*—DAVE CHAPPELLE, quoted in "Repeat Offender," *Rolling Stone*, February 5, 2004, p. 27

The fact that Dave Chappelle speaks of slavery in the present tense, that he recognizes that it is "part of our culture," is only one of the various ways he distinguishes himself from Eddie Murphy, considered by some critics to be Richard Pryor's direct heir. Although Murphy is a talented comedian who was able to do the seemingly impossible—follow Pryor without becoming an imitator—he does not, as Herman Beavers notes, "exhibit Pryor's racial solidarity, nor is his work necessarily political." He also rarely invokes slavery in his stand-up and film work. There is, of course, nothing inherently wrong with that. From some perspectives, the fact that he generally adopts a stance that is, as Beavers puts it, "impenetrable" with respect to injury may work to promote a image of black masculine strength. Whereas "Pryor's comedy emanates from an articulation of injury, or the numerous ways that the black male body can be ruptured—either from within or without, Murphy's comedic presence is one that manifests itself as impenetrable surface."[56] It is not that Murphy avoids the subject of racism. Indeed, his numerous *Saturday Night Live* skits, among other performances, make incisive comedy about the injustice and absurdities produced by racism. His *Saturday Night Live* skit "White Like You" (1989), for example, in which he becomes white for a day, not only implicitly invokes George Schuyler's satirical novel *Black No More*, but also clearly takes off from Pryor's uncanny ability to mimic white voices and gestures. But Murphy's comedy, unlike Pryor's, is embedded in representations of a single, unfettered, black male figure who, when under attack, proves himself invincible.

When compared to Pryor's, Murphy's work reveals the extent that the mediums for black comedy in general changed in the late decades of the twentieth century. Pryor, as we have seen, was largely responsible for desegregating American humor. He even attempted to do so through the medium of television, which at the time of his attempt (1977) proved too constricting for his material, especially as he did not have the option of cable channels such as Comedy Central.[57] The opening skit in his series drew much criticism; it features Pryor as a television anchor reporting that he did not have to give up much to get his own show, while in the background we see an image of him in a body suit that makes him look naked and without genitals. By the time Murphy rose to prominence, in the early 1980s, television had become far more permissive, although, as many critics of black situation comedy argue, it continued to perpetuate minstrel stereotypes under the guise of more racially inclusive material.[58] Murphy was able to present *Saturday Night Live* skits such as the one in which he appears on stage dressed as a Rastafarian singing "Kill the White People" as he waves his hands and encourages his audience to join. But Murphy also knew how to appeal to audiences across racial lines, often drawing from "characters and processes" that are familiar largely because many of them are from television (Ricky Ricardo, Ralph Kramden, Buckwheat).[59]

Comedians Chris Rock and Dave Chappelle are much more political in their work, even if they don't admit it (as in the case of Chappelle), and often address slavery and its legacy. Again, comparing their work to Pryor's reveals the change in mediums for black comedy. By the time Rock published *Rock This!* (1997), a book that contains many of the routines he performed in his stand-up concerts, and Comedy Central began airing *Chappelle's Show*, much of what had been considered controversial or new in television and film during Pryor's time had become the stuff of mainstream. While the "N" word continues to generate heated arguments, in his first season Chappelle aired the now infamous skit about the black white supremacist in which the word "nigger" is said a total of seventeen times (as one disgruntled viewer noted), and in his second season he aired "The Niggar Family." The latter skit parodies the myth of American innocence deployed by 1950s family sitcoms through its music and setting, and although it is filmed in black and white (to be sure, this is also done to accent the skit's pseudo-nostalgic mode), it also suggests other paradigms of racial struggle when the "Wetbacks" visit the Niggar family. As the family's milkman, Chappelle, and presumably the audience, derives a great deal of pleasure from hearing common racist comments, such as one about a newborn who "has those Niggar lips" and about a member of the family described as "one lazy Niggar," displaced onto white subjects.

By contrast, Chris Rock has set out to critique the co-optation of the word "nigger." Far from being a term used to designate affiliation and recognition, as it was for Pryor in the 1970s, for Rock, "nigger" has become a way to fulfill and perpetuate negative stereotypes about black people; for him, it is a term drained of all its revolutionary potential and one that is now used to encourage black folk to glamorize their own debasement. "I love black people," Rock writes in *Rock This!* (1997), "but I hate niggers. I am tired of niggers." He then adds the sting characteristic of his stand-up: "I wish they would let me join the Ku Klux Klan. I'd do a drive-by from L.A. to Brooklyn."[60] This is a far cry from Pryor's "Super Nigger": "We find Super Nigger, with his X-ray vision that enables him to see through everything except Whitey" (PC 113). But Rock's critique of "niggers," like Pryor's valorization of them, is contextually bound. By the late 1990s, "nigger" had arguably become part of the commercialization of certain perceived aspects of black culture, a commercialization that is in line with images of "ghetto fabulous" stars and notions about "keeping it real" (that is, "authentically" black, which is too often equated with crime and lack of education). In this context, Rock's critique may be just as valuable as Pryor's earlier embrace of the term.[61]

Despite the changes that have occurred since Pryor's prime, changes that we can but glimpse through the different ways that Chappelle and Rock use the "N" word in their performances, the question of redressing slavery remains constant. In Rock's and Chappelle's comedy, in fact, the aggressive aspects of redress—reparation, retribution, correction—become more emphatic. The persistence and emphasis are surprising since both Rock and Chappelle express the distance that their generations feel with respect to the historical moment of slavery. Chappelle's comedy, for example, often comments not on slavery per se but on the representations of slavery produced in the late twentieth century. In one episode from his first series on Comedy Central, Chappelle presents his version of memorable scenes from the television miniseries *Roots* (1977), the moment in which Kunta Kinte's father names him and the scene in which a brutal overseer lashes Kunta because he refuses to accept his slave name. In Chappelle's version of the scenes, baby Kunta urinates on his father just as he has solemnly held him to a starry sky and uttered the words, "Behold, Kunta, the only thing greater than you." In a retake of the scene, the father accidentally drops the baby. The humor is classic in the sense that something high, something solemn is brought down to a quotidian plane where babies urinate and fathers fumble. In another scene, we witness Chappelle cast as Kunta Kinte; it is a move that in itself serves to dislodge Kunta from his place in popular imagination as the strapping heroic warrior forced into slavery, as we see him conjured in the body of a skinny comedian. We nevertheless see Chappelle in a familiar scene: as Kunta, he receives interminable lashes for refusing his new, slave name. But just as the lashing begins to become unbearable, Chappelle's Kunta suddenly frees himself from the post to which he is tied, runs to the overseer, and proceeds to beat him. "What did I tell you about getting out of hand!" yells Chappelle, turning his back to reveal the thick padding that protected him from the lashes all along.

Chappelle employs classic postmodern techniques to measure the distance from his subject. Not only are his scenes representations of representations, but they also flaunt their seams, thus bringing attention to the process of making fiction while commenting on the overt familiarity of the scenes they parody. Rock similarly employs humor to dislodge the images with which slavery is most commonly evoked. In an outrageous skit in which he pornotropes Aunt Jemima, he begins innocently enough by relating the story of his mother confiscating his porn magazines when he was a teenager. But then he tells of an instance in which, aroused, he was badly in need of an image but could not find anything but the box with Aunt Jemima's image:

> Get the box down. Look at her. Now she's looking at you. Your imagination kicks into gear and Aunt Jemima starts looking real good. She's young now. She takes the rag off her head, her hair touches the ground. Her big buttermilk breasts are hanging, she's got a big fat ass. And she starts talking to you in a real sexy voice.
>
> "Come on, baby, let your auntie suck it. Come on, baby, put some syrup on that bad boy."
>
> But right when you're ready to explode, Uncle Ben jumps off his box and says, "Leave her alone. That's my woman." (*RT* 23–24)

In another instance, Rock writes lovingly of his gay uncle, whose name happens to be Tom. "We call him Aunt Tom," he adds. "I love my Aunt Tom. I know that if I was in a fight, Aunt Tom would take off his pumps and whoop some ass" (*RT* 39). What does it mean to masturbate to the image of a sexy Aunt Jemima, to imagine Uncle Ben as her assertive lover, and to queer Uncle Tom? The libidinal force with which Rock reimagines such common icons of slavery suggests their continuing attraction even as he makes them wildly unfamiliar.

Rock's liberation of Aunt Jemima is certainly different from artist Betye Saar's *The Liberation of Aunt Jemima* (1972), which features a plastic figurine of the stereotypical domestic, a broom in one hand and a rifle in the other. Saar's intent was to transform a demeaning, racist image into a positive, revolutionary one. The image made a considerable impact when it first appeared, especially because it also featured the symbol of Black Power, a clenched fist. Yet similar work included in a recent show has been criticized for being dry and "didactic."[62] Renée Cox's more recent *The Liberation of Lady J and U.B.* (1998), a large cibachrome, comes closest to Rock's vision; it features Aunt Jemima and Uncle Ben transformed into "svelte, virile" figures who look more like superheroes than stereotypes, being led by Cox's alter ego, Rajé (also a kind of superhero) walking out of their respective prisons (the pancake and rice boxes).[63] Cox's *Liberation*, like Pryor's "Super Nigger," appropriates the visual tropes of comic books to transform a stereotype into a sign of power.

In a more controversial and arguably less humorous way than his contemporaries, Chappelle has also measured the distance he feels from the civil rights and Black Power generations. In a skit that parodies documentary reportage in the vein of *60 Minutes* (also the framework for the skit about Clayton Bigsby, the black white supremacist), Chappelle presents the story of the first black man to use a bathroom designated for whites only, an act precipitated by dire need more than courage but that nevertheless inspires a "shit-in," an obvious parody of the sit-ins that were common during the civil rights movement. The humor is classic in the sense that it associates the high (the courage of civil rights agitators) and the low (shit) and, in so doing, brings the struggles of the past down from the solemn realm in which they often ossify into exceptional figures and events. Of course, the skit also highlights both the absurdity of and degradations produced by segregation, especially when Chappelle is found in the whites-only bathroom sitting on a toilet, pants around his ankles, and is forced to leave by the police and their bloodhounds.

Despite the distance that Rock and Chappelle express in regard to the historical moment of slavery, and to the generations that returned to that enormous breach, each comedian recognizes the significant ways in which slavery is, in a real present tense, part of our culture. Rock humorously captures this simultaneous distance and closeness when he comments on his lack of knowledge about Africa. He writes, "The only thing I know about Africa is that it's far, far away. . . . A 35-hour flight. Imagine the boat ride. The boat ride's so long there's still slaves on their way here" (*RT* 26). Although the hyperbolic gesture is originally designed to connote a contemporary black man's estrangement from his "roots," it ultimately serves to ask us, once again, to "imagine the boat ride." Curiously, it also suggests that the impact of that boat ride is yet to be felt (since slaves are still "on their way here").

Both Rock's and Chappelle's comedy suggest that such impact entails rage. Like Pryor, Rock gives voice to that rage almost always in relationship to controversial contemporary topics, such as the current debate over reparations, while Chappelle plays it out through charged fantasies regarding slavery, involving not only reparation but also retribution. Comparing the Holocaust and slavery in terms of their tragic dimension, Rock writes that they are equal with one exception: the Holocaust was considered a crime punishable by law. Slavery, by contrast, was not only legal, but it never had the kind of closure that the Holocaust had through postwar trials. "No closure. Just over. As far as America is concerned, slavery and segregation were fads, just like pet rocks and disco" (*RT* 15). His performances, like Chappelle's, directly call for the need for rituals of redress and frequently enact them through fantasy-driven sketch comedy, as in most of Chappelle's work, or through observational monologues, as in Pryor's. On the purported disproportionate number of black people on welfare, Rock writes, "This whole welfare controversy makes it sound like black people just don't want to work. If I'm not mistaken, didn't black people work 200 years for free? They worked really hard, too. No breaks, no time off" (30). To emphasize his point, he imagines two slaves contemplating vacation:

> **Slave #1:** Massa gave me a vacation.
> **Slave #2:** Massa gave me one too. Where you gonna go?
> **Slave #1:** 'Round the back. Where are you gonna go?
> **Slave #2:** To the well. You should bring your kids. It's nice over there. (30)

The humor of the scenario is tame by Rock's standards, but it soon becomes more openly aggressive as the comedian considers the fact that "slavery *had* an up side" (30). "In the old days," he writes, "even if they were poor, at least white people had slavery to make them feel exalted":

> If there was one person in your life whose ass you could beat when you felt like shit, do you know how happy you would be? You could keep them locked in a room. . . . When you were mad, you could go in there and kick them. . . . Horny? That's right, you could mosey in there and fuck them. . . .
>
>   It was the same with segregation. . . . No matter how fucked up your life was, no matter how broke and dirty your house was, no matter how

ignorant you were, couldn't read, couldn't count, fucking your sister . . . you could rest your head on the pillow every night thinking, "I'm living better than a nigger." (30)

Rock's appeal to the human tendency to displace aggression in the opening question in this quote is particularly significant since it suggests that the abuses of power that characterized slavery were founded on instincts that anyone in his audience can recognize. Yet, as he gives a sense of those abuses, one can almost hear the grating of Rock's voice angrily testifying to the enormous imbalance of power between slaves, who could take a break only by going "'round the back," and people who could use them for physical and psychological profit. The fact that such inequality did not end with emancipation fuels Rock's quick and virulent reiteration of "white trash" stereotypes.

If Rock and Chappelle both signify on representations of slavery, it is Chappelle, more than any other contemporary comedian, who has inherited Pryor's conjuring powers. In fact, before his death in 2005, Pryor expressed his admiration for *Chappelle's Show* and stated that he had "passed the torch" to Chappelle.[64] Unlike Rock, but like all of the other artists and writers in this book, Chappelle is fascinated by stereotypes of race.[65] Although he is a talented stand-up performer, as a conjurer he works best through his character- and sketch-directed comedy, which thrives on bringing stereotypes to life in the tradition of William Wells Brown and Pryor.[66]

Moreover, Chappelle, as did Pryor, ultimately appeals to what Victor Turner would call *communitas*, a concept denoting intense feelings of social togetherness and belonging, often in connection with rituals. While Chappelle's communitas is decidedly infused with black solidarity, it is also interracial and often multicultural. Chappelle coauthored the skits for his show with his long-time partner, Neil Brennan, who is white. Together, with Chappelle acting the pivotal roles in each sketch, they have focused on how blackness *and* whiteness are performed in the American cultural landscape, modeling "comedic social discourse where the unspoken is spoken—and the absurdities and hypocrisies that often inform 'polite' conversations about race relations," and not only in the black/white binary, "are laid bare."[67] *Chappelle's Show* has a post–civil rights, hip-hop sensibility that, as Bambi Haggins notes, is rooted not "solely in racial affinity" but "as much—if not more so—in cultural savvy."[68] There are plenty of insider jokes involving, for instance, alternative or underground hip-hop culture, the use of black but still not (yet) mainstream slang, and, from some perspectives, "obscure" references to black cultural practices and ideologies. But the show's humor does not depend on particularized knowledge of black culture or racial identity but capitalizes on the fact that African American popular culture, for better or worse, has become representative of American popular culture more generally. The show has averaged "a viewership of 3.1 million" per episode on basic cable television, crossing racial and cultural boundaries in great part because there have been enormous changes in the American popular landscape since Pryor desegregated black humor in the late 1960s.[69]

Typically, Chappelle introduces each skit to a live audience framed as a reverie that he enacts and projects onto a screen in the studio and, by extension, into each viewer's habitat. Framing his reveries in this fashion allows him to stress the playfulness and constructed nature of his stereotype-derived humor and thus to counteract charges that his humor typecasts African Americans. The strategy has arguably not been entirely effective. In his first season at Comedy Central, he wonders out loud: what would happen if black Americans were paid reparations for slavery? Significantly, the skit begins with Chappelle relating a story to his live audience. He describes being invited to a talk show in which the topic "Angry White Men" is being discussed and shows them clips of the men talking and of himself, looking bored and alienated at the make-believe talk show. When one of the angry men complains that affirmative action forces people to act against their will (as when they have to hire people to fill quotas), Chappelle, who has nothing to say on the show, gets an idea for a skit which he then produces for his audience at Comedy Central. "Forced to act against your will?" Chappelle wonders silently. "You mean as in slavery?" The skit he consequently delivers, however, is not about slavery but about what would happen if black people were paid reparations for it.

As if taking the perspective of one of the angry white men, the skit performs a fantasy of pandemonium. Chappelle, smiling, shows his live audience a recording of that fantasy played out. Black people become so wealthy that one man from Harlem, known simply as Tron (played by Chappelle), topples Bill Gates from his position as the wealthiest man by winning a game of dice. In the guise of a white newscaster (donning a white face, fake facial hair, and a wig to transform), Chappelle reports that all the black players in the NBA have quit, millions of Cadillacs are sold immediately, FuBu (expensive street clothing favored in ghettos) and Kentucky Fried Chicken merge to become the world's largest corporation, and record companies are founded by the seconds. In short, black people quit work and spend their reparations money on expensive clothing, jewelry, cars, and music, all before "honkies change their minds." Donnell Rawlins, in the role of the stereotypical brother who "loves menthols," is interviewed by a white news reporter but can only yell out in joy, "I'm rich, bitch!" while pressing on his truck's horn. Rawlins echoes the logo for Chappelle's Pilot Boy Productions, which is shown at the end of every *Chappelle's Show* episode and features the image of Chappelle himself as a slave, hands shackled but full of money, with the sound of the horn and the statement, "I'm rich, bitch!" in the background.

While the skit mocks the kind of "ghetto" characters that would ultimately benefit white-dominated power structures by spending their reparation money on mindless pleasures, its images and sounds are so outrageous that it is hard, at least for this viewer, not to take the skit for what it is: a performance of a fantasy on a par with Pryor's *Black Ben, the Blacksmith* routine. Like Pryor's piece, Chappelle's skit plays a what-if game. What if we were to imagine reparations for slavery not from Chappelle's perspective but from that of an angry white man? Chappelle, as the dice champion that topples Bill Gates, embodies the result, since he plays the part with all the crassness (gold jewelry) and debauchery that one can imagine (he even asks a female interviewer for a lap dance).

Like Pryor, Chappelle plays multiple parts, but unlike Pryor, he uses all the props available to him (including video) to transform into various personas. In this skit, he is both Chuck Taylor, the "white" newscaster, and Tron, the craps master, switching parts in alternating frames so that we see one body occupying opposite ends of the color spectrum in the same way that Pryor's performance in *Black Ben, the Blacksmith* performs the transferability of the stereotype even as it underscores its fixity. As Taylor, Chappelle becomes an outraged white man, but he keeps a subtle grin that suggests he is having fun playing with a stereotype of whiteness, just as Pryor did in the opening of *Live in Concert*. As Tron, Chappelle's voice and mannerisms betray a jester's mischievousness as he embodies the "nigger" qualities that Pryor uses in his album *That Nigger's Crazy* to contrast white uptightness. Chappelle thus works in the tradition of African American humor, one that, as we know from Lawrence Levine, has frequently made art out of carrying out white fantasies about race to their most absurd levels.

In many ways the "Reparations" skit also makes possible the comic dynamism that Pryor created in *Live in Concert*, in which people laugh in and out of symmetry depending on race, gender, and ideological leanings, with the volatile history of race relations, specifically as produced by slavery, as common ground. The objects of ridicule in the skit include the stereotypically angry white men and their fantasies and the media's role, as represented by the skit's documentary frame, in not only parading the stereotypes of black lawlessness and vulgarity embodied by Tron, but also in passing them off as reality. The skit's satire of those whose behavior materializes stereotypes also brings to mind, albeit on a light register, Robin D. G. Kelley's warning regarding reparations for slavery in the context of capitalism. Without "even a rudimentary critique of the capitalist culture that consumes us," writes Kelley, "even reparations can have disastrous consequences. Imagine if reparations were treated as start-up capital for black entrepreneurs who merely want to mirror the dominant society. What would that really change?"[70] Kelley's imagined scenario is not absurd, whereas the one played out in the skit is, and yet both find common ground in their mutual critique of consumerist culture and their warning regarding reparations.

The skit's potential to create a community of viewers who can laugh at different registers and in and out of symmetry is complicated by the medium through which Chappelle works and by the comedian's, and his partner's, disavowal of the political aspect of their show. Unlike Pryor, who enacted rituals of redress in the already ritualized context of stand-up, Chappelle has worked through the confines of cable television, which, while much more permissive than the networks to which Pryor attempted to bring his comedy, has curtailed the comedian's autonomy and has not allowed him a clear sense of how his diverse public is reacting to his work. Is the "Reparations" skit a conduit for social and political introspection, as my analysis implies, or simply entertainment that makes light of racial stereotypes and the question of reparations for slavery? The potential for both is implicit in any work that mobilizes stereotypes, especially in a comic mode.

As we have seen, William Wells Brown was willing to take the risk in the name of abolition, whereas Frederick Douglass adamantly refused it. Chappelle's exit from his show suggests that he too came to consider the risk too high. His and his partner's repeated claim that their show's comedy is "cultural rather than political" has not helped matters.[71] As Haggins argues, although Chappelle and Brennan's disavowal of the political may have afforded their show "a greater degree of discursive freedom," that same disavowal might have facilitated a view of the show as one that neither endeavored nor aspired "to engage in more complex sociocultural critique."[72] By contrast, Pryor did not shy away from asserting the political import of his work. In *Wanted*, he asks for the lights in the house to be turned up to recognize the presence of Huey Newton in the audience and salutes him in solidarity.

Yet, for all of Chappelle's and Brennan's disclaimers, some of their skits have a decidedly political bent. In one sketch, which is, for the most part, performed in innocent fun, Chappelle plays a pimp who, along with a cohort called "The Player Haters," travels in time to "player hate" on villains from history. The group plays a rough version of the dozens, known as "player hating," and gathers solely to "hate" or cap on each other in outlandish ways. In one instance, a pimp (known as Beautiful and also as Jheri Curl Juice because he continually sprays his namesake hairdo) cuts another named Buc Nasty (played by Eddie Murphy's brother Charlie, who has a dark complexion) by saying, "Buc Nasty, you are so dark when you touch yourself [it] is like black on black crime." The haters, all decked out in capes, bright colors, over-the-top jewelry, sequins, fedoras, and gaiters, travel in a time machine (invented by the one Asian hater for the Player Haters' science fair—a humorous contradiction, of course) and player-hate on Hitler (they beat him up and call his momma names while Jheri Curl Juice douses him in hairspray). The premise is brilliant and thus far, the comedy light and fun.

At one point, however, they travel back to an antebellum plantation to hate on masters and free the slaves. The beginning of the sketch retains a light spirit. When the haters arrive on the plantation, which looks as if taken from a *Roots* episode, Buc Nasty caps on the horrible way the black slaves are dressed: "These lames ain't even got shoes, Jack. I could never go out that way." Silky, Chappelle's character, who is dressed in a pin-striped suit, a red shirt, hat, and shoes, rounded off with a voluminous black cape, tells Buc Nasty to be careful with his words, as one of the slaves could be his great-great-granddaddy. In a moment of brilliance the camera cuts to a slave (played by Charlie Murphy) looking tired and beat up, staring into the face of Buc Nasty (also Charlie Murphy) in his bright blue pimp suit, gold chains, and rings. The camera switches back and forth between the two faces and then cuts to the image of Murphy as the pimp, shaking his head in complete disbelief at the recognition of his ancestor.

Even when the sketch turns to a rough game of the dozens, it is funny and safe enough. But when the players decide to take action, the sketch could not be more controversial. When the master of the plantation comes out striking his whip at the sight of the slaves, who stopped work when the players arrived, and of the players themselves, a rough game of the dozens unfolds:

> **Master:** What are you niggers doing out here! [loudly cracks his whip]
> **Silky:** We have traveled though time to call you . . . a cracker!
> **Master:** You better watch your mouth! [loudly cracks his whip]
> **Buc Nasty:** Actually, you better watch your mouth, white boy, before I put these gaiters up your ass and show your insides some style.

Aware that the master is ready to use his whip, Silky pulls out a gun. The master holds his arms out as if about to be crucified, his long-sleeved white shirt extending out prominently. Behind him stand the slaves in tattered clothing watching their avengers with an awe that is broken when one of them asks Silky, "When is we gonna be free?" Silky responds, "How about now?" and shoots the master in the chest. The shooting is repeated, after the fashion of sensationalist news media, over and over again so that the master is killed a total of four times, his blood spurting over his bright white shirt. The violence is so potent that even the slaves look on in dismay as the master falls.

Chappelle showed the sketch in a venue that showcased pieces that were too controversial for television and had been edited from his regular show. The joke, of course, is that he is showing them nevertheless. Among other sketches is one that features a gay chapter of the Ku Klux Klan; its members wear pink rather than white hoods and politely ask black folk to move out rather than burn crosses in their yards. But Chappelle signals the slavery sketch as his favorite, even as he recognizes that not everyone thinks that "shooting a slave master is funny." "If I could," he adds, doubling over with laughter, "I would do it every show." The fantasy of return and of violent retribution that the sketch performs is as potent as anything in Pryor, if not more so. The element of sacrifice, which Pryor plays out through introjection and abjection, in Chappelle's sketch is transferred to the figure of the master.

This, of course, raises thorny issues. The fantasy of retribution finds violent, although also symbolic, outlet while the object of that violence is not, as in Pryor's scene of introjection, the black body. Yet its redirection to the white body of the master depends on simplified notions of retribution (and race) in which the crimes of slavery, enormous as they are, would find some kind of redress in the shooting of a white man. Still, the fact that the skit provides cathartic release—both in the form of the light humor that precedes the violent act and the violent act itself—is important given the need for the redress of slavery, even if only symbolically, that Pryor's, as well Rock's and Chappelle's, work make clear. In this case, the fact that Chappelle's and his supporting cast's deployment of stereotypes is not ambivalent helps to keep the political import of the skit in place. Thus, while the skit raises thorny issues, it invites social introspection rather than mere entertainment through its very thorniness.

The legacy of Pryor's raw edge is abundantly evident in Chappelle, especially Pryor's willingness to say the wrong thing in order to set the record straight or, as he might put it, to act the fool and flip the script. In fact, Chappelle's statement "If I could, I'd do it every show" echoes Pryor's "I ain't never gonna forget." The price that both artists have had to pay for being brave is also clear. Although Chappelle has not burned in ritual sacrifice, he has experienced a disorienting public withdrawal that has been understood as a nervous breakdown (caused, according to various sources, by pressure, paranoia, drugs, overwork, all of the above). One particularly hyperbolic explanation has its own website. Chappelle Theory (chappelletheory.com) is authored by an anonymous source who theorizes that the comedian's departure from Comedy Central was propelled by the pressure that six prominent African Americans exerted on Chappelle to quit. The six, allegedly Al Sharpton, Jessie Jackson, Louis Farrakhan, Bill Cosby, Whoopi Goldberg, Robert L. Johnson, and Oprah Winfrey, were purportedly motivated by their agreement that *Chappelle's Show* reinforces negative stereotypes of African Americans and so needs to be censored. The theory offers no concrete evidence and could be someone's zany joke on America's thirst for conspiracy theories (after all, the site claims that the group of prominent African Americans calls itself the "Dark Forces").

Nonetheless, in recent interviews (on *Inside the Actor's Studio* and Oprah's show) and stand-up shows, Chappelle has alluded to a certain discomfort in the wake of his success. The DVD of the first season of his show sold close to 3 million copies, making it the best-selling DVD of all time and a record for any television show.[73] Such popularity echoes Pryor's sales for *That Nigger's Crazy*, which earned a platinum record for selling 1 million albums in a matter of months, despite the fact that it had "no advertisement whatsoever," did not contain anything "a disc jockey could play on the radio," and made no special attempt at crossover appeal.[74] Pryor's album sold to both black and white audiences, a fact that surprised record executives who originally found the material too flamboyant to appeal to either. For Chappelle, success of this kind has meant an uncomfortable intrusion into his private life. People repeat funny but obscene lines from his show ("I'm Rick James, bitch!") in front of his children and expect him to act out his characters on request. More than anything, his experience with success has led him to express sentiments similar to those that artist Kara Walker has voiced in the aftermath of her success. In an interview with the philosopher Tommy Lott, Walker said, "I certainly didn't anticipate the level of support that I've gotten and it sometimes occurs to me that it's rather absurd. . . . The success that I've had in these past four or five years, necessitates that I be dead now by some dramatic overdose, suicide, something that would validate me and I decided not to do that."[75]

The question at hand is not merely about the difficulties of existing in the limelight but about the possibilities that such success presents for the co-optation of stereotype-driven art, especially when that art deals with slavery. Both Pryor and Chappelle have used their powers as conjurers to bring to life the fantasies created by the racist mind—their own, their audiences', their nation's—as a way of confronting the (im)possibility of redressing slavery. But is it possible, as one of Kara Walker's critics has asked, "to get inside the racist imagination without adding to its power?"[76]

Responding to Pryor's comment that he was passing the torch to him, Chappelle stated, "That's more pressure than [the] $50 million [Comedy Central offered him]. That's a lot of pressure. He was the best, man. For him to say that is, you know, that's something, I don't even know if I'll attempt to live up to that."[77] Chappelle's response is understandable. Pryor's trajectory suggests that, to get inside the racist imagination without adding to its power, arguably an impossible task, someone, specifically the comedian, must take the brunt. Like Walker, Chappelle does not want to be "dead of some dramatic overdose" or, as Pryor almost was, dead amid flames. Young as he is, however, it is still unclear if he will take up the challenge that Pryor's admiration for him implies. In a 2006 interview, he stated that he did not know whether he was going to be "a legend or some tragic [expletive] story but that [he] was going all the way."[78] What is clear is that the power that both Pryor and Chappelle have tapped into as conjurers who attempt to redress slavery is strong enough, as Ishmael Reed puts it in *Flight to Canada*, to "light a solar system." "Book titles tell the story," writes Reed:

The original subtitle for *Uncle Tom's Cabin* was "The Man Who Was a Thing." In 1910 appeared a book by Mary White Ovington called *Half a Man*. Over one hundred years after the appearance of the Stowe book, *The Man Who Cried I Am*, by John A. Williams, was published. Quickskill [the novel's main protagonist] thought of all the changes that would happen to make a "Thing" into an "I Am." Tons of paper. An Atlantic of blood. Repressed energy of anger that would form enough sun to light a solar system. A burnt-out black hole. A cosmic slave hole.[79]

It is also too early at this point to tell if Chappelle will be willing and able to give expression to the grief that Pryor was able to release, albeit at great personal expense, in his rituals of redress. Yet his most recent work, his stand-up performances after leaving *Chappelle's Show* and *Block Party*,[80] suggest that, like Pryor, Chappelle sees the crucial need to balance the two paradoxes with which we started: the need to redress a breach that cannot be redressed and the need to create community even while invoking a divisive past and an equally, if differently, divisive present.

CONJURING THE MYSTERIES OF SLAVERY

Voodoo, Fetishism, and Stereotype in Ishmael Reed's Flight to Canada

> *After* Uncle Tom's Cabin, *one needs a drink. Reed provides it.*
> —HORTENSE SPILLERS, "Changing the Letter," 33

In the late 1960s, when Richard Pryor temporarily abandoned the stage and his life in Hollywood for a period of introspection and reassessment in Berkeley, he met and befriended Ishmael Reed. Characteristically, this period was not in any sense monastic or sober for Pryor. Instead, it was a period in which, as jazz musicians put it, he "woodshed" his material in an atmosphere that was both inspiring and intoxicating.[1] Pryor found the drug culture of late 1960s Berkeley a haven for his fierce appetite for cocaine and other drugs. He also befriended a group of young black writers, among them Reed, Cecil Brown, Claude Brown, David Henderson, and Al Young, who were (and many of whom remain) deeply committed to racial equality and who, besides being tremendously talented, were known for using their acerbic but disarming humor to protest racial injustice. Pryor was then transforming himself from his original image—a slim, mild-mannered comedian with conked hair who had risen to some prominence with material patterned after Bill Cosby's—to the revolutionary comic performer who would bring the power of black street humor to mixed audiences and use it to critique his country's long history of racism. The young writers Pryor befriended in Berkeley would encourage and support his evolution, influencing his style and encouraging him to take the risks required for developing it.

It is not surprising, then, that during the year of the U.S. bicentennial celebration, both Reed and Pryor produced works that, through sharply eviscerating humor, address slavery and its legacy. Pryor produced the album *Bicentennial Nigger*, and Reed published *Flight to Canada*. Drawing on the connections between "the peculiar institution" and its legacy in the cultural landscape of 1970s

America, Reed's novel operates by anachronism. It maps the flight of three fugitive slaves within a fictional space that merges the past (antebellum and Civil War America) and the novel's present (the years after the civil rights movement), both of which intersect with our own present moment of reading. Through an aesthetic that blends history and fantasy, political reality and black humor, Reed parodies the slave narrative tradition, signifies on the nuances of the historiography of slavery more generally, and proposes an alternative lexicon for historical reconstruction.

In great satiric fashion, the novel corrupts the putative temporal boundaries between the historical past and the present. It freely juxtaposes antebellum figures such as Harriet Beecher Stowe and Edgar Allan Poe with references to such twentieth-century figures as T. S. Eliot and Ezra Pound and the phenomena of the "top forty, the best seller list and the Academy Awards."[2] In fact, it opens with a poem written by Raven Quickskill, fugitive slave lecturer and poet, who flees to Canada on a jumbo jet from a plantation where the mistress lies in bed watching *The Beecher Hour* on television and Abraham Lincoln, who pays the master a visit, waltzes through the slave quarters with the mammy figure to the tune of "Hello, Dolly." As Richard Walsh notes, this "casual use of props," along with the novel's references to "*Time* magazine, the *New York Review of Books* and all the paraphernalia of contemporary civilization," creates a "contemporary atmosphere" and "involves a fundamental disregard for the sequence of historical events."[3]

At the same time, the novel raises a number of thorny questions concerning the history and historiography of slavery. After the opening poem, the novel renders Raven Quickskill's meditations—in a section set off from the rest of the novel by italics—on the limits of the literature and historiography of slavery and the modes used to interpret them. In Raven's introductory commentary, history is mutable, flexible, and, to some degree, even incomprehensible. "Will we ever know," he asks, what is fact and what is fiction in the "strange" and "complicated" history of slavery? (*FC* 10). Invoking the gaps and contradictions in the records of slavery, Raven continues, "Will we ever know, since there are such few traces left of the civilization the planters called 'the fairest civilization the sun ever shown upon,' and the slaves called 'Satan's Kingdom'?" (10). The question requires both historical evidence and interpretation. How do we read a record that is split by the very violence it represents ("'the fairest civilization" versus "Satan's Kingdom")? And how do we account for the people and places for which there are only "few traces left"?

As Toni Morrison noted, "No slave society in the history of the world wrote more—or more thoughtfully—about its own enslavement" than did African Americans, despite the fact that it was illegal to teach a slave how to read and write. Yet it is also true, as Morrison has famously observed, that slave narrators "were silent about many things, and they 'forgot' many other things," since there was "a careful selection of the instances that they would record and a careful rendering of those that they chose to describe."[4] Between 1760 and 1947, more than two hundred book-length slave narratives were published in the United States and England, yet the abolitionist circuit that supported such publications limited the expressive possibilities of slave narrators.[5] Until the mid-1970s, when slavery assumed a central role in public discourses in America, slave narratives were dismissed as unreliable sources, and historical accounts of slavery were quite limited. As Raven notes, the "volumes by historians" of slavery and the Civil War leave much unsaid (*FC* 10).

As he highlights the gaps in the records of slavery, Reed also emphasizes how unnatural, even bizarre, history can appear when its contradictions and blindness are reflected upon. "Why does the perfectly rational, in its own time, often sound like mumbo-jumbo?" Raven wonders (*FC* 10). His question echoes throughout the novel, as when, for instance, Arthur Swille, the man who owns the novel's three fugitive slaves, claims that they are afflicted with *Dysaethesia Aethipica*, "a disease [that causes] Negroes to run away" (*FC* 18). Swille refers to a spurious nineteenth-century pseudo-scientific racial theory that was proposed as a viable hypothesis by the Louisiana physician Samuel Cartwright.[6]

Given the "strange" and "complicated" nature of slavery's textual records, Reed stages a self-reflective reconstitution of its history and fiction that at once signifies on its problematic nature and proposes an alternative. In *Flight to Canada* this means instigating a cathartic and interactive involvement with history through fiction. After Raven's introduction, the novel switches into the voice of an omniscient narrator through which Reed intermingles geographies and temporalities, mixes historical and cultural forms of knowledge such as rumor and myth, and merges poetry with narrative and drama with parody. He also tangles the novel's different narrative strands so that the stories of the fugitive slaves in the North mix not only with those of their fellow captives in the South but also with those of their master Swille and those of Lincoln, the "Great Emancipator." The narrative ends with another first-person meditation, that of Uncle Robin, a seemingly loyal but tacitly subversive slave, who reflects on the events of the novel. By bombarding readers with an intricate mix of characters, places, and genres, Reed keeps them alert to the process by which he reconstructs slavery, thus foreclosing the possibility of passively reading the history he represents.

Before rendering the full text of *Flight to Canada*, however, Reed invokes Guede, a mighty voodoo loa who has multiple powers and whose spirit infuses the novel. Guede is simultaneously the god of death and eroticism, the loa of history, and a "witty clown."[7] Guede is the lord of resurrection and therefore full of vitality and knowledge of the past; he is also a prankster and a satiric wit of the highest order and, as such, a most fitting loa for Reed to invoke. As *Flight to Canada* develops, it is clear that Guede is, in fact, its patron spirit.

Guede might indeed be the patron spirit of great tragic-comedians in the tradition of Pryor. Loa of Eros and Thanatos, one of Guede's principal characteristics is his laughter. Amused "by the eternal persistence of the erotic and by man's eternally persistent pretense that it is something else," he ridicules the sentimental, inventing variations on the theme of provocation, "ranging from suggestive mischief to lascivious aggression," to expose those who pretend "to piously heroic or refined immunity."[8] As Maya Deren observes, Guede's "greatest delight is to discover" a pretender, for he "will confront such a one and expose him savagely, imposing upon him the most lascivious gestures and the most extreme obscenities."[9] Yet Guede also serves as a constant reminder of the inevitability of death and, as such, elicits "nervous laughter" from those who hear him.[10] Known for his "rich repertoire of stories," which he narrates in a nasal voice that, as voodoo practitioners claim, suggests the sound that a corpse would make "if it were allowed to speak," Guede exposes all the secret affairs of a community, "omitting none of the lewd details."[11] If people "appear uncomfortable and embarrassed by his wantonness," Guede enjoys the opportunity to taunt them, displaying before them the most unrestrained and immoral mannerism," all the while subtly reminding them "of their eventual lot."[12] Yet, clown and trickster "though he be," Guede is "also history—the experience from which the living learn—and in this role he is as deeply responsible and trustworthy as he is bizarre in other aspects."[13]

In Guede's spirit, Reed assumes the role of a prankster with respect to the history of slavery. His conflation of time frames, his uses of anachronism, and his intermingling of different perspectives and forms of cultural knowledge are but a few concrete examples of how he playfully rearranges the familiar forms through which that history has been constructed. Yet Reed's pranks have as their ultimate goal a "deeply responsible" relationship to the history of slavery. Employing a sharp, sometimes dark satire, he exposes the extent to which the fetishistic notions of race and sexuality that slavery produced continue to shape our thoughts and actions. His satiric approach includes a punning, although also pointed, use of "black magic."

In *Flight to Canada*, he draws on the social, political, and artistic practices of voodoo, transliterating its ritual of spirit possession, or *crises de loa*, the moment in which the soul of an ancestor "mounts" the body of the devotee and attains physical presence. True to Guede's defiant spirit, Reed's use of voodoo challenges the most pervasive notions of the practice, one that is often equated in negative terms with black magic. As Deren notes, voodoo's concept of "religious possession is not only unfamiliar," it also "carries exotic and sensational overtones."[14] Joan Dayan suggests that for nonpractitioners, this unfamiliarity with "the demands and expectations" of the loa can turn the concept of possession into an abstract principle; voodoo then attains an aura of inaccessibility that some choose to associate with superstition.[15] Rather than a potent form of knowing and being, voodoo can become synonymous with superstition, evil, zombies, and black magic. Voodoo's negative reputation as an occult practice is exacerbated by the fact that a percentage of its practitioners use it as a form of sorcery. That is why the *houngan*, or voodoo ritual leader, distinguishes himself from the *boco*, who practices conjuring for witchcraft and uses it to create "zombies."[16]

Reed, however, takes what appear to be the strangest aspects of voodoo and explores them beyond their aura of superstition. "Zombification" as practice and concept, for example, provides Reed with metaphorical ways of remembering slavery. His views coincide with those of Dayan, who quotes Edward Rochester in Jean Rhys's *Wide Sargasso Sea*, when he finds this definition of zombie during his stay in the Caribbean: "'A zombi is a dead person who seems to be alive or a living person who is dead. A zombi can also be the spirit of a place.' Born out of the experience of slavery and the sea passage from Africa to the New World, the zombi tells the story of colonization: the reduction of human into thing for the ends of capital."[17] For Haitians, zombies are "those soulless husks deprived of freedom and forced to work as slaves, [who] remain the ultimate sign of loss and dispossession."[18] Deren also underscores the connection between the zombie and the slave: a zombie is "a soulless body . . . [whose soul] may have been removed by magic from a living person, or the body of someone recently deceased . . . brought up out of the grave after the soul [has] been separated from it by regular rites of death." The purpose, she notes, "is to make use of the body as a slave."[19] Because voodoo practitioners understand zombification as a "fantastic process of reification," Dayan suggests that their emphasis on possession should be understood as recognition of the material realities of reification and as sabotage against the powers of dispossession.[20]

But the zombie can also be the soul of an ancestor who, not having been properly mourned, is used by a boco for sorcery. According to Dayan, the elaborate burial rituals observed by Haitians who practice voodoo are in part a result of the need to protect the souls of ancestors, although the elaborateness of such rituals is also a consequence of slavery. "If the disposal of the dead slaves was a careless deed that marked irrevocable inhumanity," writes Dayan, "funeral rites in independent Haiti became central to both the living and the dead." Largely lacking such rites, the souls of the ancestors who perished during slavery are at greater peril than those recently departed. As Dayan puts it, the "landscape of Haiti is filled not only with spirits of the dead seeking rest and recognition but with other corporeal spirits who recall the terrors of slavery and the monstrous, institutionalized magic of turning humans into pieces of prized and sexualized matter."[21]

Reed transliterates voodoo's notion of zombification and belief in spirit possession while creating an aesthetic that also incorporates aspects of postmodernism. Such sampling or inventive assembling of diverse traditions is far from foreign in Reed's oeuvre; it constitutes what he calls his Neo-HooDoo aesthetics: a use of voodoo that intentionally dispenses with the notion of authenticity in favor of an open and fluid approach that enables him to use and mix the different traditions available to him as a writer of the African diaspora.[22] As he put it in his "Neo-HooDoo Manifesto," a piece that, aside from expressing the fluidity of his practice also satirizes the very concept of a modernist manifesto, "Neo-HooDoo borrows from Ancient Egyptians . . . from Haiti, Africa and South America. Neo-HooDoo comes in all styles and moods."[23]

In *Flight to Canada*, Reed uses his aesthetic to expose the connections between chattel slavery's reification of people and bodies—its "monstrous, institutional-ized magic of turning humans into pieces of prized and sexualized matter"—and the stereotypes of race and sexuality it produced. On the one hand, Reed uses his writing as a boco would his witchcraft, breathing life into stereotypes of re-sistance, submission, dominance, benevolence, brutality, and forbearance; by conjuring them as a group of embodied ideas, he creates zombie-like characters that represent humanity divested of its soul. On the other hand, he uses his writ-ing like a houngan would his conjuring powers, calling into being the ancestors or spirits—the historical as well as imaginative loa—of slavery. The word *loa* comes from the French word *loi*, meaning law, and refers to voodoo's concep-tion of the laws of creation. But as Sami Ludwig argues, what Reed means by loa are not only the historical ancestors from our past but also "the ideas that pre-structure our experiences as well as our interpretations, the principles [or laws] that govern our minds and our souls and the forces and institutions representing them."[24]

Through his conjure, Reed illustrates how slavery's stereotypes—as repre-sentations that embody fixed ideas, ideological fictions, and psychic fantasies—are inert in essence but alive in their effects. Like zombies, they are emblems of a "fantastic process of reification" that, through his fiction, assume the semblance of life. Reed's fictional power correlates to Guede's; as the loa that straddles "the great divide between the living and the dead," Guede has the power to animate the dead as zombies. In this "dark phase of his powers," writes Deren, "the trick-ster becomes a transformer." Guede can also change a person into an animal, recalling in this respect the metamorphoses that Chesnutt highlights in con-jure. Yet he is also "the greatest of healers" and can protect against the magic of malevolent *bocos* who would make "soulless husks" out of bodies.[25]

Reed thus assumes the powers of a postmodern "black magician," who inven-tively draws on voodoo belief and practice to stage his own ritual of redress with respect to slavery. Like Pryor, he shuttles between grief and grievance, commem-orating ancestral spirits while agitating against the past's hold on the present via his critique of stereotypes. Also like Pryor, and Pryor's and his predecessors Wil-liam Wells Brown and Charles W. Chesnutt, he improvises on the conventions of black humor to explore the theatricality of stereotypes. In *Flight to Canada*, zombie characters substitute stereotyped behavior for critical and conscious action. By contrast, characters that are able to repossess and manipulate stereotypes in order to realize personal and collective freedom figure as ancestors whose legacy Reed honors. The two kinds of characters are made to walk in each other's midst (as do the gods during crise de loa), often assuming similar manifestations and thus forcing the reader to wrestle with the hermeneutical challenges that the legacy of slavery presents. At the same time, Reed, like Brown and Pryor, operates through hyperbole, parodying zombie-like characters while endowing ancestor figures with an aura of mystery. In so doing, Reed seeks to resolve the dilemma facing any artist who uses stereotypes to critique the legacy of slavery; that is, how does one use such images without enlivening their baleful powers?

The Trickster Becomes a Transformer:
Neo-HooDoo in *Flight to Canada*

Reed patterns his main characters after easily recognizable historical figures or stereotypes. He conjures two of the fugitive slaves, for example, as figures of resistance: Raven Quickskill evokes the radical slave lecturer and author epitomized by Frederick Douglass, and another fugitive, simply named "40s," personifies the stereotype of the militant revolutionary most often associated with Nat Turner. The third fugitive slave, Stray Leechfield, suggests the more ambivalent figure of the minstrel performer. Meanwhile, the house slaves who do not escape, Uncle Robin and Mammy Barracuda, recall two central icons of forbearance and domesticity: Uncle Tom and Mammy. The master class is provocatively presented in a polarizing logic. Arthur Swille is draconian, sadomasochistic, and set against Abraham Lincoln, whose benevolent and heroic role as the Great Emancipator is exaggerated and parodied. While Reed employs most of these figures to unleash the power of zombie-like stereotypes, he also employs some of them—Raven and Robin, in particular—to evoke the spirits of slave ancestors.

Transforming voodoo's ritualistic practices into literary techniques, Reed is able to represent the zombies of slavery as unique entities whose effects we perceive through their actions. As a religion of the poor and uneducated (most devotees are illiterate), voodoo maintains its historical memory through rituals that include dance, music, incantations, oral stories, and, most prominently, *vévés*, or ground drawings.[26] Reed interprets and improvises these aspects of voodoo practice, using elements from popular culture to create his own particularized version of a literary voodoo ritual. He borrows from the content and style of visual art forms—especially comic strips, film, and photography—to create animated caricatures of slavery's zombies and the historical ideologies surrounding them. At the same time, he interlocks diverse time frames to show how the violence, lusts, and lures of the past—as these are embodied in stereotypes—manifest themselves across time.

Reed conjures the zombie-like qualities of slavery's stereotypes through an aggrandizing enterprise that relies on parody and highlights the distortions that such images promote, pushing them beyond their overtly familiar places in our imagination and exposing them as fetishistic forces. The fetish, Christian Metz argues, springs from a fear of what is perceived as absent in another (such as the absence of a phallus in women). The construction of the fetish, adds Metz, entails making the evidence one sees for this apparent lack "retrospectively unseen by a disavowal of the perception, and in stopping the look, once and for all, on an object . . . which was . . . near, just prior to, the place of the terrifying absence."[27] The stereotype, like the fetish, is a distorted image of all that seems "terrifyingly" different about another; it takes the place of actual understanding and acknowledgment of a common humanity. In the absence of that recognition, the fetishistic image or stereotype, at once generalized and specific, takes its place.

Reed defetishizes the stereotype by aggrandizing its distortions. In his hands, it comes alive, as if newly produced, and overwhelms the reader's senses. He makes it bigger, louder, more grotesque, and more insufferable than it already is in order to arrest our attention and induce us to explore the fears and fantasies that the stereotype, like the fetish, seeks to keep at bay. The ancients understood black humor as one of the four chief fluids or cardinal humors of the body—blood, phlegm, choler, and melancholy or black choler—all signifiers of the abject in Julia Kristeva's sense.[28] As if appropriating and redefining this definition, Reed exposes that which is normally excluded, even jettisoned, from polite representations of slavery and its legacy. As he parades the host of distortions produced by the institution of slavery, he creates a comic atmosphere with a cathartic and deconstructive effect, which allows him to conjure the difficult, hidden ideas and emotions that the stereotypes at once suggest and mask. He thus conjures mysteries in a dual sense: while he uses certain narrative techniques to evoke the ancestors or *mystères* of slavery, he aggrandizes the human distortions slavery produced to conjure the thoughts and emotions that the stereotype, as an obscuring phenomenon, renders mysterious.

The ritual of redress that Reed enacts through *Flight to Canada* takes form through the structure of the novel, which is patterned after a typical voodoo ritual. It begins, as all voodoo rituals do, with the chanting of the names of the ancestors, proceeds toward the crise de loa or possession stage, which is characterized by the novel's dynamic interplay between the past and the present, and ends when the novel fixes its focus on a more contemporary time frame. Raven's introduction is simultaneously a historiographic meditation and a literary incantation of the names of slavery's ancestors, an invocation that calls them into presence: "Lincoln. Harriet Beecher Stowe. Douglass. Jeff Davis and Lee. . . .

Stray Leechfield. Robin and Judy. . . . Mammy Barracuda" (*FC* 7). Some of the names are actual American ancestors; many are pure fantasies.

Reed establishes the shift from Raven's incantations to the possession stage of the novel through a change of narrative perspective. As Ashraf Rushdy argues, the fact that the novel begins with Raven's first-person meditation and then abruptly switches into the third-person account of an omniscient narrator suggests that the structure of *Flight to Canada* is Reed's enactment of voodoo's most basic practice, the act of spirit possession.[29] Shortly before the narrative adopts the third-person voice, Raven asks, "Do the lords still talk? Do the lords still walk? Are they writing this book?" (*FC* 10). Thereafter Raven's individual voice becomes "possessed" by a third-person narrator who connects the multiple manifestations of the loa and the zombies that Reed evokes. Although many critics recognize the ritualistic structure of Reed's novel, none has noted that the identity of the third-person narrative voice attains the qualities of a specific voodoo loa, Guede. "Guede is here," writes Raven as the novel begins. "Guede is in New Orleans. Guede got people to write parodies and minstrel shows about Harriet" (*FC* 9).[30] The only other time we come back "here" and to "New Orleans" is at the end of the novel, when we are told that "Raven is back" and the omniscient narrator signs off:

> 12:01 A.M.
> Tamanaca Hotel, Room 127
> Fat Tuesday
> March 2, 1976
> New Orleans (*FC* 179)

When Raven comes back, Guede's presence ends and the narrative returns to the present time of the novel (1976).

The allusion to New Orleans at the end of Raven's "possession" also returns us to a place known for its retention of conjure and, by implication, connects the wider world of the African diaspora (figured through voodoo) to the events of the novel. Reed draws out this connection through the novel's structure, which literally transliterates voodoo's ritualistic patterns. At the same time, he uses voodoo's metaphysical and epistemological aspects to create a memory of slavery that is functional, experiential, and nonlogocentric. Because voodoo belief and practice are neither centered on a single deity nor bound to a written text, its devotees locate meaning in flux, stressing flexibility, innovation, and improvisation in their forms of expression. This ideological approach finds a correlation in Reed's satiric, parodying reconstruction of history through fiction.

Reed's formal experimentation—his imaginative interpretation of voodoo and his development of a hybrid aesthetic that includes other forms of signification—reflects voodoo's improvisational mode. His research for *Flight to Canada* extended beyond rereading slave narratives to examining texts by Confederate apologists, reconsidering *Uncle Tom's Cabin* (seeing both its limitations and the "heart" in it), and listening to "common" people and the stories they tell about slavery.[31] Because Reed believes that historical consciousness is partly to be found in what he calls the "low-down and funky and homespun" of everyday reality, he also mined fields of popular culture such as "jazz, talk radio formats . . . television," and everyday dialogue. *Flight to Canada*, he claims, includes "overheard conversations."[32] Transforming his research into novelistic discourse, he points to those corners of slavery's archive that resist definition while opening the realms of historical possibility.

But his formal innovation also demonstrates his desire to perform a metaphorical rather than a naïvely authentic interpretation of voodoo's belief and practice. His zombie-like characters, for example, are as much a transliteration of voodoo practices as they are reference points to the blaxploitation films, particularly in the horror genre, that were popular shortly before the publication of *Flight to Canada*. Films such as *Scream Blacula Scream* (1973), *The House on Skull Mountain* (1974), and, in particular, *(The Zombies of) Sugar Hill* (1974), reappropriate monsters such as vampires and zombies as empowering black avengers who not only fight "against the dominant order—which is often explicitly coded as racist," but also stage vengeance in relationship to slavery. *Sugar Hill*, for instance, involves an eponymous heroine who raises zombies from the dead to avenge herself against a white gang that murders her lover.[33] The zombies "are explicitly marked as former slaves through both their dialogue and the prominent placement of their rusting shackles within the mise-en-scene."[34] Thus, while the movie details Sugar Hill's successful revenge, it also stages the return of the dead, who, as one critic noted, obliterate the white racists "in a dream of apocalypse out of Nat Turner."[35]

Reed invokes the redressive return of the dead through his imaginative conjuring of zombies but inflects that return with a humor that spoofs the comic black sitcoms that were popular in the mid-1970s, *Good Times* (1974–79), *Sanford and Son* (1972–77), and *The Jeffersons* (1975–85). In so doing, he satirizes Hollywood's commercial use of the language of redress—its blatant manipulation of phrases such as "orgy of *vengeance*" in ads for blaxploitation horror films—to simultaneously capitalize on fears of black retribution and empty the notion of redress of any real value.[36] Developed by Norman Lear and Bud Yorkin, television sitcoms featuring black casts constituted what J. Fred MacDonald calls "the Age of the New Minstrelsy":

> Here was the coon character, that rascalish, loud, pushy, and conniving stereotype, strongly achieved in types such as Sherman Hensley's boisterous George Jefferson, Jimmie Walker's grinning J. J. Evans on *Good Times*, and

Whitman Mayo's lethargic Grady Wilson on *Sanford and Son*. . . . Here, too, was the resurrection of the loud-but-lovable mammy, its roundest modern embodiment being Isabel Sanford's shrill Louise Jefferson, LaWanda Page's overbearing purse-swinging Aunt Esther on *Sanford and Son*, and Marla Gibbs' caustic character, Florence, the wisecracking maid on *The Jeffersons*.[37]

Like the blaxploitation films to which they were kin, the television sitcoms that featured these minstrel types paid lip service to pressing social issues and progressive agendas (and in this way differed from early shows such as *Amos 'n' Andy*), but they presented characters that were essentially no different from the servants or entertainers featured in Hollywood films of the 1930s and 1940s.[38] In these earlier films no other actor was more visible than Stepin Fetchit, who was often featured as the "lazy man with a soul," the house servant in intimate relations with a white master to whom he is a darling pet.[39] Uncle Robin is Reed's parody of such a character and America's obsession with resurrecting him.

Throughout *Flight to Canada* Reed conflates early representations of African Americans in film with those of the television sitcoms of the mid-1970s in the context of his fictional rendering of slavery, thus connecting the obsession with servants in film and television with the history of slavery. Characteristically, he operates through satire. He begins the novel's short chapters with visual descriptions that, as Matthew Davis notes, suggest stage directions and announce the framing of images that will be mobilized by overblown action and satirical dialogue.[40] The opening of chapter 3, for example, depicts the figure of the immoral and decadent southern master, made familiar most poignantly by Stowe's Simon Legree, with his pet servant, Uncle Robin:

> The Master's study. Arthur Swille has just completed the push-ups he does after his morning nourishment, two gallons of slave mothers' milk. Uncle Robin, his slave, is standing against the wall, arms folded. He is required to dress up as a Moorish slave to satisfy one of Swille's cravings. (*FC* 18)

The scene recalls Stowe's characterization of the master class as obscenely decadent and idiosyncratic, but here and throughout, Reed aggrandizes these excessive qualities and hyperbolizes their grotesque nature. He conjures Swille to discursively walk within the novel as a sadomasochist in love with his set of whips, his opium, his dead sister, Vivian, and the romance of an Arthurian South. Anachronistically, he is a corporate mogul whose money not only directs the course of the Civil War but also allows him to enact his private fantasies on a grand scale. Swille ravages the tomb of his dead sister while singing Edgar Allan Poe's "Annabel Lee," tries to buy a title ("Baron Swille . . . Sir Baron Swille? . . . Maybe the Marquis d'Swille"), and has Queen Victoria whipped for refusing to give him one (*FC* 109, 127–28).[41] Meanwhile, Uncle Robin plays the role of the loyal servant who satisfies his master's cravings.

What is fact and what is fiction in this exaggerated vision of mastery and servitude? Although Swille is quite obviously a farcical figure, he suggests real questions. How much, for example, does his image signify on a material reality of slavery in which the excessive power of masters could indeed be sado-masochistic? At the same time, while sexual licentiousness, miscegenation, and sexual oppression are painful parts of the history of slavery, how much are they also fetishistic images of the past?[42] Reed evokes these questions through "a multifocal point of view" that, as Norman Harris argues, provides a kind of "epistemological democracy" that "challenges the reader both to determine whom to believe and to question what is real."[43] Throughout the novel, the reader consistently returns to these questions: what is fact and what is fiction in the "strange" history of slavery? (*FC* 8). How are stereotypical notions both living and dead images of the past? How are they dynamically active forces of the here and now?

Reed's portrayal of Swille, after all, may be a spoof not only on notions of mastery produced by writers like Stowe, but also on the televisual embrace of white bigotry that the immensely popular show *All in the Family* (1971–79) represented. From 1972 to 1976 this show, which was also produced by Lear and Yorkin and inspired the pair to produce their black television sitcoms, ranked number one in the Nielsen ratings largely because it featured Archie Bunker, considered television's greatest character. Bunker, a racial bigot and "an obstreperous purveyor of intemperate [and reactionary] ideas" was, in fact, more a "diviner of the political temper and a harbinger of future politics in the United States."[44] Lear and Yorkin attempted to humanize the bigoted Bunker, a strategy many found troublesome. Reed, by contrast, takes a similar character and hyperbolizes his bigotry, endowing him with power and money so that he can outlandishly enact his fantasies. Patterned after the popular characters of the mid-1970s, Reed's zombies walk within the same fictional space as the ancestor spirits of slavery. How can the reader discern between the two?

By emphasizing the mysterious qualities of some characters while accenting the overbearing materiality and spiritual emptiness of others, Reed aids us in discerning between the loa and the zombies he conjures. As Matthew Davis notes, the minor character Pompey is known throughout *Flight to Canada* "simply as the slave who 'doesn't say much but is really fast.'" We know little else about him "until the end of the novel when it is revealed that Pompey, through his ability to impersonate 'the whole Swille family' . . . precipitates the demise of the Swille plantation." As Davis observes, Pompey masquerades as Mistress Swille's dead son, Mitchell, propelling her into madness, and impersonates Master Swille's sister, Vivian, causing Swille's death "when the spectre-like figure pushes him into the fireplace."[45] "He's a good voice-thrower too," Robin tells us, suggesting Pompey's trickster powers (*FC* 175). In the end, we know little else except the fact that he is the figure who appears "from out of nowhere" to announce Raven's return from possession (179). To Swille, however, Pompey is merely a good "bargain" because he does "the work of ten niggers . . . doesn't smoke, drink, cuss or wench, stays up in his room when he's not working, probably contemplating the Scriptures" (35). The joke, of course, is on Swille.

Like Guede, Pompey's presence suffuses the novel as a force whose effect is radical but not sharply defined. Does Pompey signify the indefatigable, creative, and amorphous power of resistance that made survival in slavery possible? According to Davis, Pompey is an allusion to William Wells Brown, who briefly appears in the novel to help Raven while he is on his way to Canada and whose autobiographical persona in *My Southern Home* was also named Pompey.[46] If so, Reed's Pompey is an evocation of Brown, an actual historical ancestor of slavery, whose artistic legacy has provided Reed with a model for his own work.[47] Reed's conjuring in this instance allows Brown's spirit to walk within the pages of his novel and to manifest itself in the novel's narrative present.

"Don't choo be sistering me"

Reed reserves the realm of mystery for the loa of slavery, emphasizing their power by showing their ability to escape classification. By contrast, he conjures the power of slavery's stereotypes through satire, overexposing their grotesque and limited nature. Through the overblown language and action with which he characterizes them, he also stresses the violence that the zombies of slavery perpetuate. His blatant parody of the mammy figure, for example, reveals how stereotypes are both obviously fictive and strangely real, part of both the past and the present. Mammy Barracuda is so clearly a stereotype that some have charged Reed with recirculating demeaning images of women under slavery. Though he has said that he "erred in giving her such an obvious name," I think it is precisely that obviousness that distinguishes her from the simple stereotype.[48] By overdrawing Barracuda's purportedly privileged position as a trusted house slave, Reed magnifies the distortions that the idea of the mammy has produced. When she enters the novel, he depicts her as the caricature of a caricature:

> Barracuda has a silk scarf tied about her head. A black velvet dress. She wears a diamond crucifix on her bosom. It's so heavy she walks with a stoop. Once she went into the fields and the sun reflected on her cross so, two slaves were blinded. (*FC* 20)

For Norman Harris, this description shows Barracuda's darkly humorous but violent and "determined attempts to make life static and predictable" for others.

As a stereotype, she not only preserves the status quo but also demands that others assume similar roles. Harris notes, for example, that when Mistress Swille rebels against the role of the southern belle, she "literally beats the woman back into the proper stereotype" just as harshly as she subjects the slaves under her power to perform their assigned roles.[49] What Reed stresses about Barracuda is not her historical accuracy but her role as a historically produced icon whose effect is neither uniform nor unreal. Like the diamond crucifix she bears, Barracuda looms large and heavy in our imagination, blinding us to the possible realities of women who were enslaved.[50]

Reed's emphasis on Barracuda's material privilege further suggests her commodity value as an ideological fiction.[51] There is something rich and alluring about evoking and circulating this character, Reed suggests, and something palpable in her effect. He creates this richness through the exaggerated language with which he represents Barracuda beating her mistress into the belle stereotype:

> Barracuda enters the Mistress' room. Surveys the scene. Puts her hand on her hips. The Mistress flutters her eyes. Turns her head toward the door where Barracuda is standing, tapping her foot.
>
> "Oh, Barracuda, there you are, my dusky companion, my comrade in Sisterhood, my Ethiopian suffragette."
>
> "Oooomph," Barracuda says. "Don't choo be sistering me, you lazy bourgeoise skunk."
>
> "Barracuda," Mistress says, raising up, "what's come over you?"
>
> "What's come ovah me? What's come ovah you, you she-thing? Got a good man. A good man. A powerful good man. And here you is—you won't arrange flowers when his guests come. You won't take care of the menu. You won't do nothing that a belle is raised to do."
>
> "But Barracuda, Ms. Stowe says . . ." (FC 111)

Barracuda so dramatically embodies the stereotype of the loyal slave that she praises the power of the man who keeps her enslaved. Her performance, however, amounts to a grotesque image of loyalty gone haywire. The interchange between her and Mistress Swille, therefore, climaxes in a darkly humorous swirl of violence and slapstick that satirizes the typical mistress-slave/black maid relations that Hollywood perpetuated throughout most of the twentieth century.[52] As Barracuda tries to force Mistress Swille to perform her belle duties, she yells:

> "Get out dat bed!"
>
> "Why . . . what? What's come over you, Barracuda?"
>
> Barracuda goes to the window and raises it. "This room needs to air out. Oooooomph. Whew!" Barracuda pinches her nose. "What kind of wimmen is you?"

Robert Colescott, *George Washington Carver Crossing the Delaware: A Page from American History* (1975). (Courtesy of Phyllis Kind Gallery)

Emanuel Leutze, *George Washington Crossing the Delaware* (1851). (Collection of the Metropolitan Museum of Art)

Robert Colescott, *I Gets a Thrill Too When I See De Koo* (1978). (Courtesy of Phyllis Kind Gallery)

Willem de Kooning, *Woman I* (1950–52). (Collection of the Museum of Modern Art)

Robert Colescott, *Sunday Afternoon with Joaquin Murietta* (1980). Collection of Arlene and Harold Schnitzer. (Cliff Edgington)

Robert Colescott, *Les Demoiselles d'Alabama: Dressed* (1985). (Courtesy of Phyllis Kind Gallery)

Kara Walker, *Presenting Negro Scenes Drawn Upon My Passage Through the South and Reconfigured for the Benefit of Enlightened Audiences, Wherever Such May Be Found, By Myself, Missus K. E. B. Walker, Colored* (1997). Installation at the Renaissance Society at the University of Chicago. Cut paper and adhesive on wall, 12 x 155 feet overall. (Photography by Tom Van Eynde)

Installation detail of Kara Walker, *Presenting Negro Scenes Drawn Upon My Passage Through the South and Reconfigured for the Benefit of Enlightened Audiences, Wherever Such May Be Found, By Myself, Missus K. E. B. Walker, Colored* (1997). Installation at the Renaissance Society at the University of Chicago. (Photography by Tom Van Eynde)

Kara Walker, *Queen Bee* (1998). Gouache and cut paper on paper, 62 x 42 inches. (Image courtesy of Sikkema Jenkins & Co.)

A. C. F. Edouart, *Mr. and Mrs. Josiah Quincy and Their Children* (1842). Cut paper and pencil. (Reprinted in *Shades of Our Ancestors* by Alice van Leer Carrick [Boston: Little Brown, 1928])

Installation detail of Kara Walker, *Presenting Negro Scenes Drawn Upon My Passage Through the South and Reconfigured for the Benefit of Enlightened Audiences, Wherever Such May Be Found, By Myself, Missus K. E. B. Walker, Colored* (1997). Installation at the Renaissance Society at the University of Chicago. (Photography by Tom Van Eynde)

Installation detail of Kara Walker, *Presenting Negro Scenes Drawn Upon My Passage Through the South and Reconfigured for the Benefit of Enlightened Audiences, Wherever Such May Be Found, By Myself, Missus K. E. B. Walker, Colored* (1997). Installation at the Renaissance Society at the University of Chicago. (Photography by Tom Van Eynde)

Kara Walker, *Consume* (1998). Cut paper and adhesive on wall, 69 x 32 inches. (Image courtesy of Sikkema Jenkins & Co.)

Installation detail of Kara Walker, *Slavery! Slavery! Presenting a GRAND and LIFELIKE Panoramic Journey...* at the Walker Art Center for the exhibition "no place (like home)," 1997. Cut paper and adhesive on wall, 12 x 85 feet. (Dan Dennehy for the Walker Art Center, Minneapolis)

Kara Walker, *Slavery, Slavery! Presenting a GRAND and LIFE-LIKE Panoramic Journey...* at the Walker Art Center for the exhibition "no place (like home)," 1997. Cut paper and adhesive on wall, 12 x 85 feet. (Dan Dennehy for the Walker Art Center, Minneapolis)

Kara Walker, *Virginia's Lynch Mob* (1998). Cut paper and adhesive on paper, 10 x 37 feet. (Image courtesy of Sikkema Jenkins & Co.)

"Why, I'm on strike, Barracuda. I refuse to budge from this bed till my husband treats me better than he treats the coloreds around here."

"Now, I'm gon tell you one mo time. Git out dat bed!"

"Barracuda! This has gone far enough." The Mistress brings back her frail alabaster arm as if to strike Barracuda. Barracuda grabs it and presses it against the bed. "Barracuda! Barracuda! You're hurting me. Oooooo."

Barracuda grabs her by the hair and yanks her to the floor.

"Barracuda, Barracuda, what on earth are you doing to my delicate frail body. Barracuda!"

Barracuda gives her a kind of football-punt kick to her naked hip, causing an immediate red welt. . . .

Barracuda pulls her razor, bends down and puts it to Ms. Swille's lily-white neck. "You see that, don't you? You know what that is now? Now do what I say."

"Anything you say, Barracuda," Ms. Swille says, sobbing softly.

"BANGALANG. BANGALLLLAAAANNNNG. YOUUUUUU. WHOOOOOO. BANGALANG." Barracuda, one black foot on Ms. Swille's chest, calls for her assistant. (*FC* 112)

This scene's verbal and physical vortex recalls the raucous interchanges common to the antebellum minstrel stage, but the scene attains yet another level of signification in Reed's hybrid style. Replicating the sounds, exaggerated gestures, and pace of an animated cartoon, Reed mixes fantasy, fact, and fiction as he forces into collision the image of the "delicate frail" mistress and that of the boisterous barracuda mammy. Although together these figures create a maelstrom of action, they repeat the same gestures: Barracuda attacks (screaming, kicking, and yanking) while the mistress lamely protests (sobbing as her "alabaster," "frail body" swoons). The scene thus creates the illusion of freeze frames of the characters turning speedily before the reader's eyes in slightly different postures, stopping only when Bangalang is called in by Barracuda's obnoxious, though eerily hilarious, command. Bangalang, like the mistress and the mammy, is a caricature of a caricature: a stereotyped "pickaninny," whose familiar characteristics and gestures Reed reemphasizes. She "rushes into the room, her pickaninny curls rising up, her hands thrown out at the red palms, her eyes growing big in their sockets at the sight" of Barracuda beating Mistress Swille (*FC* 112). Constituting the final freeze frame, Bangalang allows us to pause on the stereotype and examine its contradictions. It is as loud and obvious as Barracuda's language, yet empty of consciousness; it is violent in its effects—witness Barracuda's brutality—and yet it is as naïve as Bangalang and as infuriating as the seemingly innocent Mistress Swille.

While Reed shatters the rules of realism and verisimilitude, stressing instead the scene's cartoonlike qualities, he also shows that Mistress Swille, Bangalang, and Barracuda exist as powerful fictions whose strange and complicated natures are at once historical and mythical. He in fact constructs the interchange between Barracuda and Mistress Swille after an emblematic scene in David O. Selznick's film adaptation of *Gone with the Wind* (1939), where the mammy of Margaret Mitchell's imagination laces Scarlett O'Hara's corset and helps her get dressed for a social gathering. As in Reed's novel, the film's mammy is a figure of mythic proportions: physically enormous, desexualized, and heavily racialized, she is determined to help her overly pampered and delicate mistress officiate her position as a belle. As Maria St. John shows, the film's scene plays on this notion, showing Mammy as she forces Scarlett's tiny waist into the confines of an even smaller corset with a strength that so borders on violence that Scarlett must cling to her bedpost as Mammy tells her, "Hold on and suck in." Mammy, whose own physical size attests to how fully she fills the roles assigned to her, worries that if Scarlett does not eat before the party she might be "eatin' like a field hand" and not like the proper lady she (Mammy) has worked so hard to keep in line.[53] In the same scene, Mammy and Scarlett have a veritable tug-of-war over Scarlett's bust line, a tug-of-war Reed recalls but parodies by having Barracuda literally beat Mistress Swille.

In fact, Barracuda is so vociferous and demanding as the stereotype of race and gender she embodies that, in all respects, she outdoes the mammy of the screen. Reproducing the film's mammy-belle relationship but layering a cartoon style on it, Reed emphasizes the looming but fictive nature of the mammy and, at the same time, leads us to ask why it is that we persist in recreating and recirculating it. St. John notes that 90 percent "of the North American population has seen [Selznick's] film," and sales of Mitchell's original 1936 novel "have been rivaled only by the Bible."[54] Nevertheless, as late as 1998, Technicolor rereleased a digitally remastered version of Selznick's film. Why? Is it because we yearn to see Mammy force Scarlett into her corset time and time again? As the recent debate over Alice Randall's *The Wind Done Gone* (2001) would suggest, Mitchell's text continues to stir something in us. What is it? What fantasies do slavery's stereotypes, especially as rendered by Mitchell, embody? Why must we continually rehearse them? The image of the mammy of slavery in particular, St. John suggests, exists as "a dominant cultural fantasy" that is "reenacted with each new production of her image"; she exists as a "fantasied fugitive who escapes no matter how many times she is captured on celluloid or in print."[55]

Reed's conjure also suggests that the mammy stereotype, like that of the southern belle, works both as an index to the history of slavery and as a barrier against it. As such, its appeal rests in its power simultaneously to gesture to and obscure a difficult part of the national consciousness. As historical indexes, the mammy and belle stereotypes direct our attention to nineteenth-century ideologies of gender and alterity, specifically to the notion that white and black femininity mutually define and oppose one another. The battle that Reed stages between mistress and mammy not only dramatizes this point but also shows the violence necessary to uphold such a racialized notion of femininity.

But the battle also suggests that stereotypes of the mammy and the belle obscure the ways people in the nineteenth century questioned ideologies of race and gender. When Mistress Swille calls Barracuda her "Ethiopian suffragette," she whimsically alludes to the connection drawn by women such as Elizabeth Cady and Lucretia Mott at the 1838 Seneca Falls convention between the disenfranchised status of women and that of enslaved people in the nineteenth-century United States. Although the experiences of slaves and white women (particularly those from the upper classes) differed drastically, suffragists stressed that women's status aligned them with the enslaved population of the country because, like slaves, women could not control their own persons or property, vote, choose a profession, or hold public office. While African American figures like Sojourner Truth, Harriet Jacobs, Frederick Douglass, and other abolitionists appealed to women's sympathies in hopes of enlisting them in their cause, suffragists used the rhetoric of slavery to awaken white women's consciousness. In Reed's text, however, the mistress and the mammy are so consumed by the roles assigned to them that they cannot realize the promise implied by a union of the suffrage and abolitionist causes. Instead, Mistress Swille lamely calls out to Barracuda from her lair of leisure while Barracuda violently rejects her ("Don't choo be sistering me").

Reed's satirical conjuring moves us to explore how, as expressions of perceived racial difference, stereotypes can become violently obsessive fantasies. Yet his conjure is complicated and potentially problematic because it also shows the allure that stereotypes exert across racial divisions. Stereotypes can be used as tools by the master class to manipulate and oppress the dispossessed. But as David Mikics argues, for Reed, stereotypes "may also stem from, or be appropriated by, African-American counterculture," thereby becoming tools of empowerment.[56] Uncle Robin, for example, manipulates the stereotype of the faithful, childlike servant epitomized by Stowe's Uncle Tom in order to revolutionize the hierarchy of the Swille plantation. Swille, who suffers from dyslexia, comes to depend on Robin to care for his estate after his former secretary (Raven) escapes; Robin then uses the guise of the faithful servant to rewrite Swille's will so that upon Swille's death, Robin inherits the plantation and the right to free its slaves (FC 167–69). Once Swille dies—a death Pompey provokes but that would have occurred anyway since Robin has been surreptitiously poisoning the master's coffee for years—Robin frees Stray, 40s, and Raven and plans to transform the plantation into "something useful" for everyone (179). "Yeah, they get down on me an' Tom," Robin says, referring to Stowe's character. "But who's the fool?" (178).

Stereotype as Fetish, Conjure as Sabotage

Through Robin, Reed shows that the dispossessed can manipulate stereotypes, turning them into weapons with which to destroy those who impose them. Through Barracuda and Stray Leechfield, however, he demonstrates that the oppressed can be seduced into perpetuating the dehumanizing impact of stereotypes. Stray, whose name insinuates his deviant and parasitic characteristics, believes that the world the slave masters have created inescapably revolves around money and depends on the marketing of everything, including people. Unlike Robin, Stray does not believe he can redefine the power relations that render him property, insisting instead that the only possibility left for him is to manipulate the rules of the market. "If anybody is going to buy and sell me," he tells Raven, "it's going to be me" (73). Accordingly, he decides to purchase himself from Swille with the money he can earn in the pornography market by photographing himself and selling his image.

Stray's decision results from the illusion of mastery he creates by controlling the terms under which he is sold and from the monetary power he believes he garnishes. "I pull in more money in a day than you do in a whole year," he tells Raven. "You green, man. Brilliant but green" (*FC* 72). Raven, by contrast, will not accept his logic and vehemently argues against it. "We're not property," he tells Stray. "Why should we pay for ourselves?" (74). Unwilling to heed Raven, Stray continues with his plan. Along with his partner, Mel Leer, he develops a scheme that imitates nineteenth-century minstrel shows. Leer, who is white, pretends to be Leechfield's owner, dresses him in the exaggeratedly perfect image of a runaway slave ("black cloth pantaloons, black cloth cap, plaided sack coat, cotton check shirt and brogans"), and sells him, only to kidnap him back and "repeat the same routine to a different buyer the next day" (80). But soon they develop a more abstract form of this scheme. Leer takes photos of Stray performing the duties of a slave and sells them in a mail-order business they call "I'll Be Your Slave for One Day" (80). These photos feature Stray in compromising positions, as Raven finds out when he inadvertently walks into a session:

> Oh my God! My God! My God! Leechfield was lying naked, his rust-colored body must have been greased, because it was glistening, and . . . [a] naked New England girl was twisted about him, she had nothing on. . . . And then there was this huge bloodhound. He was licking, he was . . . [Leer] was underneath one of those Brady boxes—it was flashing. He . . . he was taking daguerreotypes, or "chemical pictures." (*FC* 71)

The switch from the actual scheme to its marketing through pornography elaborates Reed's connection between slavery as a market of bodies and the reification of its signs. At first, Leer and Leechfield restage the auction block as a profitable play act, but then they discover that its pornographic image sells just as well, if not better. Certain icons of slavery, Reed suggests, have quite a profitable market. "You'd be surprised," 40s tells Raven, "how many people enjoy having a slave for a day even when they can't touch them" (*FC* 80).

Through Stray and Leer's pornographic daguerreotypes, Reed suggests that, as vessels for cultural fantasies, stereotypes can embody sexual fetishes. Stray exhibits himself (at least in the photograph Raven describes) performing one of the most potent and obsessive visions born out of slavery: a hypersexualized black man in a naked embrace with a white woman. This image, like those created by Mitchell and Selznick and, for that matter, those created by blaxploitation directors and the television producers Lear and Yorkin, has a sizable market (Mel Leer's name satirically echoes Norman Lear's). It sells because it plays out a national taboo and thus satisfies a longing to see what has been historically prohibited. Black men have been killed for simply looking at white women, and they have constantly been imagined as raping them. Like Leer's flash, Reed's satire overexposes the outrageous proportions this fantasy has attained, showing us Stray's body, greased and glistening, while the New England girl writhes around it. The image of the huge bloodhound (licking Stray?) succinctly suggests that lynching is the violent result of this fantasy, by alluding to the chase just before the horror of blood and burning flesh.

Signifying on photography as a meaning-making medium, Reed uses the often imagined but impossible scenario of sex between black men and white women to suggest Stray's complicity in perpetuating a violent myth and promoting his own reification. He shows that although Stray believes he is purchasing his freedom through his scheme, he is in effect defining his own zombification. By choosing to sell himself in pornographic photographs, he turns himself into a material but spiritless image that replays a racial-sexual fantasy for somebody else's pleasure.

As Metz remarks, a photograph's signifiers seem bound to their referents through the image's contiguity with the world. Because mimetic photography retains the trace or index of actual living bodies and presents chemical images (or icons) that look like the objects the photographs represent, it creates a seductive illusionary pull. Spectators have a strange feeling of reality before a photograph, Metz argues, a desire to confound the signifier with the referent despite the fact that they know a photograph is only a representation.[57] The pictures that Leer takes of Stray suggest there is no gap between reality and the cultural fantasy of rape and sex associated with black men. Stray becomes the thing itself: the fantasy writ large. What is more, because photographs are small enough to be carried, handled, and touched, Stray and Leer produce a sexual fantasy that can be marketed as a fetishistic object. To paraphrase 40s, people might actually "enjoy having [Stray as] slave for a day" precisely because they can touch and pocket him.

Through the novel's historical transposition of time, Reed draws implicit connections between slavery as a market of bodies and its legacy in our contemporary world. When Raven and Stray argue over the question of purchasing themselves, they echo a dilemma that fugitive slaves faced in the nineteenth-century United States. Confronted with the difficult choice of purchasing freedom from their masters or remaining perpetually in flight, many fugitives bought themselves despite the implications of the gesture. In their slave narratives, Douglass, Jacobs, and Brown, among others, take up the nuances and difficulties of such a compromising position. Reed's Stray, by contrast, flaunts his decision and cynically argues that the act of buying oneself does not need to be as blatant as his own: "I don't see no difference between what I'm doing and what you're doing," he tells Raven (*FC* 72).

As Stray sees it, Raven, like Douglass and Brown, is an antislavery lecturer who also performs as a racialized being to market a consciously crafted image of himself. But whereas Stray's image brings in money, if not political power, Raven's brings insult. "You have to get evil-smelling eggs thrown at you," he tells Raven. Referring to events that actually occurred to Brown and Douglass, he continues: "I heard up at Buffalo they were gettin ready to throw some flour on William Wells Brown. Remember when those mobocrats beat up Douglass? Even Douglass, knocked on the ground like any old vagrant" (*FC* 72).[58] In contrast, Stray is rewarded for playing out stereotypes of black masculinity. At the end of the novel, he appears "dressed in a white Russian drill coat, ruby-red plush breeches, a beautiful cloth waistcoat . . . a splendid silk shirt and a rakish French hat from New Orleans . . . rings on all of his fingers, a diamond stickpin on a cravat and Wellington boots" (176). Like Barracuda, Stray is bedecked with items that, in their richness and materiality, suggest the commodity value he has as an ideological fiction. Reed implies that the fantasy of the black stud-rapist continues to seduce our imagination and that this seduction cuts across racial divisions. Exploiting his use of outlandish anachronisms—in which the past and present are conflated through glaring popular culture references or technological signifiers—Reed presents Stray as a version of a contemporary pimp daddy. As Swille tells us earlier in the novel, "the glistening rust-black Stray Leechfield" stole from him so methodically that at one point he became "big" enough to be seen

> over in the other country . . . dressed up like a gentleman, smoking a seegar and driving a carriage which featured factory climate-control air conditioning, vinyl top, AM/FM stereo radio, full leather interior, power-lock doors, six-way power seat, power windows, white-wall wheels, door-edge guards, bumper impact strips, rear defroster and soft-ray glass. (36)

His "carriage," like a pimp's car, is "full of beautiful women fanning themselves and filling the rose-tinted air with their gay laughter" (36). Reed's hilarious conjuring of Stray as a fugitive slave turned minstrel–porn star–pimp allows us to examine a potent and persistent stereotype in all its details. Like the carriage–pimp car Reed describes so carefully, Stray is an elaborate cultural fantasy, richly manufactured and infinitely marketable.

As a novelist, however, Reed is primarily concerned with how people are reified through words. In *Flight to Canada*, therefore, he presents us with a case of narrative zombification and enacts an imaginative sabotage against it. In the novel's first section, "Naughty Harriet," Reed humorously reiterates the charge commonly made against Stowe when she published *Uncle Tom's Cabin*: that she took her book's plot from the slave narrator Josiah Henson. In Reed's text, Harriet is "naughty" not only because she "stole" but also because she is said to have been inspired to write her novel by a petty desire ("Harriet only wanted enough money to buy a silk dress" [*FC* 8]). Strikingly, Reed suggests that Stowe's intentions and theft have something to do with "pornography" (8).[59]

According to Richard Walsh, Reed "freely acknowledges that his charge of plagiarism against Stowe is a tongue-in-cheek abuse of the scant evidence" behind Henson's rumored reputation as the real Uncle Tom. "I was having fun with Harriet Beecher Stowe," Reed tells Walsh, "saying that she took her plot in *Uncle Tom's Cabin* from Josiah Henson. You know, they did meet when she was four."[60] But the fiction provides Reed with a paradigm for exploring the debate, encapsulated in James Baldwin's well-known reading of *Uncle Tom's Cabin*, surrounding Stowe's discursive reification of African Americans. In "Everybody's Protest Novel," Baldwin praises Stowe for passionately critiquing the institution of slavery but derides her for declining to examine the internal and subjective experiences of the people who were enslaved. Stowe's novel became not only a best-seller but also the standard that shaped the subsequent production and reception of slave narratives and influenced the development of African American literature more generally. For Baldwin, however, Stowe's novel simultaneously established a paradigm for understanding slavery and represented those who were enslaved, without including their own stories. In his estimation, Stowe used slaves as signs to serve her own goals.[61]

Using the rumor regarding Stowe's theft of Henson's story, Reed correlates zombification with the reification of people through language. Henson, Reed suggests, is enslaved physically and reenslaved discursively when Stowe usurps his story, renames him Uncle Tom, and finally resells him on the literary market for her own economic profit and literary posterity. Stowe thus prostitutes Henson's story in a manner remarkably close to Leer's pornographic selling of Stray's body.[62] For Reed, discursive zombification occurs when people's stories are taken from their bodies, co-opted, and transformed to suit purposes other than those of the person to whom the story belongs. And what happens to those whose stories are stolen? According to Raven,

> People pine away. It baffles the doctors the way some people pine away for no reason. For no reason? Somebody has made off with their Etheric Double, has crept into the hideout of themselves and taken all they found there. Human hosts walk the streets of the cities, their eyes hollow, the spirit gone out of them. Somebody has taken their story. (*FC* 8)

What Raven refers to as a person's "Etheric Double" is also what he calls a person's "gris-gris," the "thing that is himself," and what in voodoo is known as one's "gros bon ange" (8). Voodoo practitioners in Haiti, notes Dayan, see individual identity as comprising three parts: the *petit bon ange* (a person's consciousness and affect), the *gros bon ange* ("the double of the material body—something like our idea of spiritus"), and the *corps cadavre* (or physical body). The gros bon ange can easily detach itself from the body and be "seized" by a sorcerer, never to return.[63] For Reed, our stories are synonymous with our gros bon ange: they are the double of our material body; they are our shadows. As Keith Byerman puts it, "Narrative [in *Flight to Canada*] is the self, the ordering of identity that gives body and voice through language."[64] Words are our gris-gris, or the charms that protect our shadows from co-optation. But sometimes words fail, and our stories are taken from us.

In the spirit of Guede, the loa with the power to animate the dead as zombies and to heal and protect against the possibility of being turned into one, Reed stages a case wherein the enslaved is saved from being discursively reified by the powers of conjure. Along with Raven's introduction-incantation, the novel begins with a key proposition: Robin asks Raven to write his life story. Given the example of Henson's narrative dispossession, Raven is to make sure he writes Robin's story in a way that prevents anyone from stealing it. "Now you be careful with my story," Robin tells him, requesting that he "put witchery on the word" (*FC* 13). This demand is, in fact, a localized case of Reed's own novelistic crux: the challenge of conjuring rather than zombifying the subjects of slavery. Raven, like Reed, must conjure Robin's story, and by extension, that of slavery, as a living text (even the alliteration of their names suggests their common purpose). Raven and Reed cannot, as Baldwin claimed Stowe did, present slavery through a litany of discursive characters and acts that repeat petrified images of enslaved people. Instead, Robin's story must be like Reed's maverick novel itself and call into being the ancestor spirits of the past.

At its close, the novel returns to the Stowe-Henson rumor to emphasize, finally and clearly, its difference from Stowe's narrative production. Robin, who delivers the novel's last reflective words, has not been zombified by the narrative. Thus, when Stowe reenters the novel to ask Robin if she can "do a book" on him, Robin promptly tells her that he already has an author (*FC* 174). He will not be reified. Circling back to its beginning, the novel leaves us as Raven returns to write Robin's story, a story that in the end is the account of slavery we hold in our hands.

Reed's formal innovation is thus crucial to the project against discursive zombification. It is also an element that sets his work apart from other contemporary representations of slavery. Although *Flight to Canada*, like other texts classified under the generic categorization of the neo-slave narrative, does signify on the form and conventions of the antebellum slave narrative, it is not limited to that enterprise.[65] It is driven by Reed's imaginative combination of voodoo and postmodern aesthetics, which allows him to provide "perspective by incongruity."[66] It allows him to show the underpinnings of the American racial mythology by returning us to the overtly familiar, overdetermined stereotypes of slavery with a grammar that gives way to concepts that might, at first glance, seem esoteric (such as discursive zombies) but that, through their uniqueness, serve to expose ideological fetishes at the heart of American history, literature, and popular culture. Like a number of other contemporary writers that focus their attention on New World slavery, Reed experiments with form to explore not only the disturbing contradictions in the discourses of slavery but also the ways such discourses continue to shape our own language and imagination.

"A COMEDY OF THE GROTESQUE"

Robert Colescott, Kara Walker, and the Iconography of Slavery

Brother, the blackness of Afro-American "black humor" is not black, it is tragically human and finds its source and object in the notion of "whiteness."—RALPH ELLISON, "An Extravagance of Laughter," 178

In 1936, when Ralph Ellison was new to the New York milieu in which he would eventually become a novelist, essayist, and critic, he was invited by Langston Hughes to see a Broadway production of Erskine Caldwell's *Tobacco Road*. The play, on whose white, poor, and rural characters Caldwell had satirically placed "the yokelike" stereotypes then commonly associated with African Americans, provoked such a wild fit of laughter in Ellison that at one point he, rather than the play, became the center of the audience's attention. Years later, in an essay appropriately titled "An Extravagance of Laughter," Ellison recalled the freedom the play unleashed in him—then freshly arrived from the South—to laugh at the stereotypes that had always signified the harsh realities of discrimination and the ever-present potential for crude violence in his life. For, in the world he had just left,

> Negroes were seen as ignorant, cowardly, thieving, lying, hypocritical and superstitious in their religious beliefs and practices, morally loose, drunken, filthy of personal habit, sexually animalistic, rude, crude, and disgusting in their public conduct, and aesthetically just plain unpleasant . . .
>
> [They] were considered guilty of all the deadly sins except pride, and were seen as sometimes the comic but nevertheless threatening negative image to the whites' idealized images of themselves.[1]

By placing such stereotypes in an unexpected scenario, Caldwell allowed Ellison to stare directly at the "wacky mirrors" of American racial discourse and to perceive ever more finely the conflicting emotions that stereotypes can elicit.[2] As he encountered the shock of recognizing racial stereotypes in a new incarnation, Ellison was beset by a trembling wave of "embarrassment, self-anger, ethnic scorn, and at last a feeling of comic relief" that burst out in a fit of laughter.[3] The essay ends with a note of gratitude toward Caldwell for having facilitated the catharsis of emotion out of which Ellison emerged with a sharper sense of why comedy is such an "indispensable agency for dealing with the American experience" and its "rampant incongruities." The "stress imposed by the extreme dislocations of American society," Ellison finally argues, calls "for a comedy of the grotesque," for the "greater the stress within society, the stronger the comic antidote required."[4]

In his comically trenchant *George Washington Carver Crossing the Delaware: Page from American History* (1975), the painter Robert Colescott renders visually not only the stereotypes Ellison enumerates, but also the connections he makes between these extremes of humor and violence (Figure 4.1). Reversing the incongruity of the scenes witnessed by Ellison, Colescott yokes stereotypes to an iconic scene of patriotic idealism and thereby provides a glimpse into the

FIGURE 4.1. Robert Colescott, *George Washington Carver Crossing the Delaware: A Page from American History* (1975). Courtesy of Phyllis Kind Gallery. [See color insert]

racial ideologies that form part of American culture. Colescott draws together Emanuel Leutze's *Washington Crossing the Delaware* (1851) and blackness as the "comic but nevertheless threatening negative image" of whiteness. Through this conceit, Colescott magnifies a host of familiar images—whisky-guzzling, happy darkies of plantation romances, the lazy banjo player and fisherman of racial folklore—and underscores both the distortions that racial stereotypes embody and the potent roles they play in the drama of American history and life.

Finished a year before the publication of *Flight to Canada*, the painting currently circulates in reproduction as the cover image for the latest edition of Reed's novel. The match is appropriate; like the novel, the painting caricatures stereotypes by emphasizing their most disturbing aspects and employing a satire that interweaves a wide range of associations. As we have seen, *Flight to Canada* signifies on the slave narrative genre and the work of prominent nineteenth-century authors such as Harriet Beecher Stowe and Edgar Allan Poe while incorporating myths about slavery, the Civil War, voodoo belief and practice, and aspects of popular culture. Colescott's aesthetic approach resonates with Reed's method for critiquing racial discourse. In what has become a trademark of his work, Colescott appropriates well-known images from the high art tradition of American and European painters, including, among others, Manet, Picasso, and de Kooning, in the process of conjuring a host of stereotypes of gender and sexuality. On the surface, Colescott's appropriations suggest the light humor of spoofing. Like Duchamp painting a mustache on the *Mona Lisa*, he seems to deface highbrow culture by superimposing crass stereotypes onto famous images. Yet his conceit produces layer upon layer of association, through which Colescott simultaneously signifies on the history of Western art and his country's history of racial oppression.

He shares with Caldwell, and the other artists and writers included in this book, a similar approach to stereotypes: he dislocates them from their habitual environments and places them in unexpected contexts drawn from a wide range of sources. Once removed from their customary places, the stereotypes he conjures become part of a hallucinatory drama that, despite its distorted nature, is also clearly embedded in the real and the historical. Fact and fiction refract in the "wacky mirrors" created by racial stereotypes producing the kind of "perspective by incongruity" that Caldwell afforded Ellison.[5] Colescott, like Ellison, sees the power that laughter has in the face of the absurd yet painful distortions produced by racism. "Ultimately, when you're dealing with supercharged issues," he told an interviewer, "you get down to dealing with them in terms of irony. . . . That's what the minstrels were about. Some of them were in black-face because they weren't black enough, and they were saying 'This is the way white people think we are supposed to act.' When the situation is ridiculous, you deal with it through silliness and irony."[6]

As is evident in *George Washington Carver Crossing the Delaware*, Colescott's satire, like Reed's, exploits the condensing logic of stereotypes and exaggerates their powers of distortion. Leutze's painting depicts the prelude to a battle considered to have been a psychological turning point in the Revolutionary War, a battle in which, without sufficient men or guns, American troops executed a successful sneak attack against the British by crossing the Delaware River in the middle of the night (Figure 4.2).[7] Dramatizing the image of revolution in action, Leutze portrays Washington standing in the prow of the boat as the "very personification of determination" and the troops as the embodiment of perseverance.[8] We see his men in their ragtag uniforms, struggling against the ice and pushing the flag in a strong diagonal. Others hunch in grim silence as their leader stands, powerfully counterbalancing the thrust of the flag. Pushing slightly left and forward, with the stolid contour of his profile isolated against the dull glow of dawn, Washington embodies courage and strength.

By contrast, Colescott's appropriation of the painting suggests every one of the stereotypes about African Americans listed by Ellison. Drunken, lascivious, lazy, reprehensible, and ignorant, George Washington Carver's troops do not push forward against the ice of a wintry Delaware; instead, in a state of mirth and sloth, they wade through what looks like tropical waters. The name Carver satirizes a certain strain of patriotism in African American naming practices, but it also suggests the crucial difference of color and all that it implies. Colescott's Washington Carver is a timid figure who stands looking out through his glasses

FIGURE 4.2. Emanuel Leutze, *George Washington Crossing the Delaware* (1851). Collection of the Metropolitan Museum of Art. [See color insert]

in a state of near complacency. Leading what looks more like a ship of fools than of rugged men of courage, he stands as an exception. And exceptional he was indeed. A revolutionary in his own right, Washington Carver was an agricultural chemist, botanist, researcher, and educator. He was born a slave sometime during the Civil War but persevered through its Jim Crow aftermath to become a distinguished scientist and teacher. His work redesigned southern agriculture and helped the lives of poor black farmers.

Colescott's painting suggests the warped logic of the stereotype according to which Washington Carver becomes the token exception amid a morally loose and aesthetically repellant throng. At the same time, the painting humorously signifies on the relative anonymity of a figure like Carver. Often known only as "the peanut guy" because he found hundreds of uses for the peanut, Carver's history as an ex-slave who became a pioneer scientist comes to the surface, if at all, as a brief blip during Black History Month.[9] In transposing "the peanut guy" and a host of characters derived from antebellum lore onto a famous scene of American patriotism, Colescott contrasts the legendary status of official history to the subaltern histories it displaces. He also evokes the nation's beginnings in connection with its most dramatic postrevolutionary crisis, the slavery debate and the Civil War. Thus, while Leutze's image glorifies the war by means of which the United States came into being as a nation, Colescott's suggests the one that threatened to destroy it: a war inextricable from the racial violence that also produced the images the painting represents.

As we shall see, however, Colescott has carefully selected the images he signifies on, drawing not only on their distinctive visual elements but also on their contexts. Leutze was a German who spent a considerable amount of time in the Unites States and created *Washington Crossing* in Germany (patterning the Delaware on the Rhine) at a time when the European democratic revolutions of 1848 were caught in a web of reaction and defeat; he hoped to call forth the American Revolution as a "historical symbol" and "brilliant metaphor for psychological encouragement."[10] Discussing the political context for the painting, Barbara Groseclose notes that the painting "represents the summit" in a body of work that "describes key episodes in Western man's search for religious and political freedom."[11] Leutze was, in fact, a great admirer of American notions of freedom, justice, and equality, even as he noted their limited application. As Karsten Fitz observes, when he died, he was working on a huge history painting on the emancipation of African Americans, and *Washington Crossing*, which includes a black figure (second from the far left), was used to raise money for the Union cause and the antislavery movement when the Civil War began.[12] Clearly, Colescott was attracted to *Washington Crossing* for the many ways it comments on American democracy. It is a painting that glorifies, even mythologizes American ideals and one that, through its context, shows the appeal of such ideals outside of the United States. At the same time, the painting's context also shows the extent to which, ironically, American ideals were compromised by slavery *within* the United States.

Expertly signifying on canonical works of art and their contexts, Colescott creates "a comedy of the grotesque" with a satire that, like Reed's, also employs popular cultural references and visual jokes that have been part of a long tradition in American racial discourse. In *George Washington Carver* he inserts two contemporary images, one from advertisements, that of Rastus, the Cream of Wheat chef (the second figure from the left), and another from urban life in America, the once ubiquitous shoe-shining "Negro" (the fourth figure from the left), into a scene that simultaneously signifies on the Revolutionary and Civil War eras. The result is a medley of temporal allusions that Colescott unites through a common denominator: a caricaturing style that highlights the most outrageous aspects of racial stereotypes. In this painting, he heightens that style through the intensity of his composition, including the use of bright colors, overly drawn features, and stylized postures. He also thrusts his figures forward toward the viewer (notice that Leutze, by contrast, places his figures midway through a vanishing perspective), thus forcing his audience to deal up close with the ridiculous yet destructive aspects of American racist ideology.

Like each of the other writers and artists in this book, Colescott runs the risk of being interpreted at face value. That is, his satirical play on stereotypes can be mistaken for unthinking and literal reproductions of demeaning images. In *George Washington Carver*, for example, we are presented with a mammy figure that recalls Reed's Barracuda: she is the only woman on the boat and she is shown baring her behind, protruding her belly, and performing fellatio. While it is obvious to some that such an outrageous image is satirical, unfortunately such is not the case for more conservative viewers. For those who take Colescott's depiction of this mammy or the banjo-playing, alcohol-guzzling, jolly figures as mimetic representations of reality, what could the painting be but a form of discursive violence?[13] Yet Colescott's images do not represent African Americans per se; rather, they signify on the racial and sexual stereotypes through which they are too often defined. It is clear that overly literal interpretations of Colescott miss the "comedy of the grotesque" that provoked Ellison's extravagant laughter.

In what ways does Ellison's phrase enhance our analyses of Colescott? The grotesque, as a notion and practice in the visual arts, has a long and largely undefined history of use, perhaps because, as Geoffrey Harpham notes, the word usually designates "a condition of being just outside of focus, just beyond the reach of language."[14] In common parlance, the term designates the horrible or the horribly exaggerated, but the term first appeared in the mid-sixteenth century to describe "fantastical figures" in Roman decorative art. It has since then been expanded to describe images that deform or decompose ideals and conventions or morph "unlike things in order to challenge established realities or construct new ones."[15] As expressions of the *comic* grotesque, Colescott's images do not evoke horror, but they do arise out of a grotesque sensibility, which tends toward entropy and transformation. In *George Washington Carver*, Colescott jokingly "deforms" an ideal image, using blackness as "the comic but nevertheless threatening negative image to the whites' idealized image of themselves" in order to mock the absurdity of such an enterprise. He also transforms both Leutze's image and the stereotypes that he conjures through the kind of "reciprocal interference" that William Wells Brown achieved by appropriating racist tunes for Cato's songs of protest.[16]

In the context of the patriotism that Leutze's image invokes, the motley crew that Carver heads seems to make a claim of national belonging and thus to threaten the nation's purported racial purity and sanctity. In this scenario, the mammy figure would take the lead role, and indeed, Colescott places her close to center. He also half turns her back away from the viewer and gives her sexual act a kind of visual ambiguity such that one must work a bit to realize what she is doing. Looking closely, we see that the penis she is holding is white, a realization that throws into question the racial categories by which we have been reading the painting. Are some of the figures white actors in blackface? The possibility, which is further suggested by the figures' exaggerated red lips and bright white teeth and eyes, redirects the purported threat to purity raised by these stereotypes to the interracial intimacies of the minstrel stage. Indeed, as Eric Lott, among others, has argued, the minstrel stage manifested the profound cross-racial love and theft at the core of American national identity. And, as W. T. Lhamon would argue, the process continues in minstrelsy's present-day manifestations.[17] Through his visual allusions to minstrelsy and his transformations of distinct time frames and images, Colescott mocks the very notion of purity that he both raises and nullifies. Racial purity, the painting suggests, is an absurd notion, especially in a country with a slave past that includes (the too often forced) interracial sexuality that the scene of fellatio so brazenly represents.

As we shall have occasion to explore in the second part of this chapter, Kara Walker enacts her own comedy of the grotesque. Like Colescott, Walker conjures the phantoms that haunt the American imagination, the cast of characters from its racially divisive history. But she does so in expansive installations of sharply cut black-paper silhouettes depicting stereotypes derived from plantation lore. Walker usually mounts her silhouettes onto white walls in panoramic friezes, but her figures seem to move as if propelled by a gleeful yet disturbing energy. Colescott's paintings are generally large in scale and enact a comedy of the grotesque that tends toward the carnival burlesque that Mikhail Bakhtin theorized. By contrast, Walker takes over entire rooms, producing a saturnine comedy of the grotesque more akin to that of Goya's etchings, *Los Caprichos* (1799). At first sight, Walker's images do not seem to be similar at all to Goya's monstrous images, which present portraits of human cruelty, perversion, and absurd and irrational behavior.[18] She creates formally simple but beautiful figures that draw the eye with their elegance and vitality and aligns these in what seem to be fairy-tale narratives.

But if Walker makes her images both beautiful and seductive, she also confronts the viewer with an array of shocks. Her work maintains an obsessive focus on incest, bestiality, cannibalism, miscegenation, sodomy, feces, and rape set against the historical and mythological landscape of slavery. If the initial lure of Walker's images is partly their embedded promise of narrative, their actual effect is to frustrate tale-telling, as, the more one looks, the more the fairy tales seem like gothic nightmares without coherent story lines. By this ruse Walker simultaneously suggests and denies the leisure of observation and contests any passive historical attitude toward her subjects. Creating a dynamic interplay between narrative and illusion, Walker, like Reed and Colescott, suggests the intertwining of fact and fiction, of myth and banality in the discourses of race in America.

Walker and Colescott produce two distinct forms of the comic grotesque, yet they both make intricate use of images from and allusions to the history of art while drawing on key elements of black humor. As Lawrence Levine notes, one of the principal objects of black laughter has been the ridiculous, absurdist, situations that white racist beliefs and practices have created. The laughing-barrel joke, a classic in the tradition of African American humor, captures well the absurdity of such situations. In "An Extravagance of Laughter," Ellison recounts the joke, which involves "some small Southern town in which Negro freedom of expression was so restricted that its public square was marked by a series of huge whitewashed barrels labeled FOR COLORED, and into which any Negro who felt a laugh coming on was forced—*pro bono publico*—to thrust his boisterous head." In the joke, the barrels were "considered a civic necessity and had been improvised as a means of protecting the sensibilities of whites from a peculiar form of insanity suffered exclusively by Negroes, who in light of their social status and past condition of servitude were regarded as having absolutely *nothing* in their daily experience which could possibly inspire *rational* laughter." In short, the barrels performed the important function of "providing whites a means of saving face before the confounding, persistent and embarrassing mystery of black laughter." While the joke showcases the ridiculous outcome through the image of "a bunch of negroes with their laughing heads stuck into the interiors of a batch of old whitewashed whiskey barrels," it also highlights the subversive power and contagiousness of black laughter, which needs to be contained and suppressed. "A Negro laughing in a laughing-barrel simply turned the world upside down and inside out," writes Ellison, "and in so doing, he *in*-verted (and thus *sub*-verted) tradition and thus the preordained and cherished scheme of Southern racial relationships was blasted asunder." When such reversals occurred, Ellison adds, "the whites assumed that in some mysterious fashion the Negro involved was not only laughing at *himself* laughing, but was also laughing at *them* laughing at his own laughing against their own most determined wills."[19] This is certainly as complex an order of humor as one might ask for since it entails self-mockery and, simultaneously, mockery of others' mockery as well as the ridiculing of their ignorance. Thus, even if only momentarily, black laughter disrupts power hierarchies in the most intricate ways.

For all of the power that Ellison rightly locates in black laughter, however, he also remains, in the essay and throughout his work, deeply aware of its limits. Laughter may momentarily turn the world upside down but it cannot achieve permanent change; it cannot eradicate the violence of racism. Colescott and Walker, like all of the black humorists in this book, have a similar view of black laughter; yet they also believe in the efficacy of transforming the conventions of black humor to critique racial violence in its various guises. Formal innovation is also key to their enterprise. Colescott's blackening of famous images provides an absurdist, topsy-turvy turn on notions of white privilege. Walker's use of the silhouette, traditionally an inexpensive form of portraiture that flourished in the polite culture of nineteenth-century parlors, achieves a similar end. While both Colescott and Walker lampoon fears associated with blackness, another traditional topic in black humor, they also expose how racial conflict can distort people's perspectives across racial and gender differences.

Like Reed and, as we shall see, Suzan-Lori Parks, Walker refers to her work as a mode of conjuring. While Colescott does not explicitly invoke conjure as part of his modus operandi, he too operates like a hougan and a boco, bringing to life the stereotypes of race and sexuality that flourished under slavery. As he transposes such stereotypes into familiar, more contemporary frames, he suggests how these stereotypes inform our ways of thinking and behaving and provides the carnivalesque thrill of seeing social codes and cultural values morphed and transformed.

I Gets a Thrill Too When I See De Koo

Viewing Colescott's *I Gets a Thrill Too When I See De Koo* (1978), one can almost hear Reed's question: What is fact and what is fiction in the strange and complicated history of racial discourse (Figure 4.3)? The painting presents us with a mammy figure that, unlike the one depicted in *George Washington Carver Crossing the Delaware*, is alone and immobile. Yet the usual details of her image are clear, for she is broad, big breasted, and eerily happy. Colescott gives her body a kind of boundlessness by filling the frame with it, using a combination of bright colors and broad brushstrokes. But he also isolates and details the features of

FIGURE 4.3. Robert Colescott, *I Gets a Thrill Too When I See De Koo* (1978). Courtesy of Phyllis Kind Gallery. [See color insert]

her face—its brown color, its red lips, its high cheeks, and its big black eyes—accentuating the markers of her race and gender by making them jump out of the frame.

Coupled with the irony and ambiguity of the painting's title, Colescott's emphasis on Mammy's features loudly calls attention to the racial ideologies on which the painting signifies. De Koo is, of course, short for Willem de Kooning, the painter whose image Colescott appropriates to make his own. The shortened name, however, insinuates that it is a "coon" that imparts a thrill. But who gets the thrill? On one hand, the painting echoes a racist notion: the mammy, as the "coon," gets a thrill "too" when she sees avant-garde art (de Kooning). In other words, she insists she is human and complex "too," despite stereotypes to the contrary. On the other hand, the painting suggests that it is the viewer who gets the thrill of seeing the mammy, the "coon" in her "proper" place (within a frame that cuts her up, spills and contorts her). Still more, one may get a thrill from seeing how Colescott appropriates and manipulates canonical works of art (like de Kooning's) to redefine how we interpret modern art as well as the roles played by slavery's stereotypes in our conception of race and sexuality.

Through *I Gets a Thrill* Colescott signifies on *Woman I* (1950–52), a painting in a series of images de Kooning produced in the late 1940s and 1950s and which he variously titled *Woman* (the titles are qualified by either roman numerals or dates; Figure 4.4).[20] Representing the human figure through a dynamic collage of abstractions, *Woman I*, like the other paintings in the series, is "packed to bursting with fragmentary, incoherent formal elements, scattered gestural color

FIGURE 4.4. Willem de Kooning, *Woman I*
(1950–52). Collection of the Museum of
Modern Art. [See color insert]

flecks, truncated brushstrokes, and unexpected reversals of direction" set against an indeterminate space.[21]

It is a painting in which abstraction and representation interlock to produce what Stephen Polcari calls "a figural embodiment of the cult, principles and experiences of [womanhood] in the 1940s."[22] As a commentary on femininity, the painting underscores the many associations projected onto the figure of woman. With such a general name and such a nonspecific look, Polcari argues, she can be all things at once: loving mother and lustful whore, pin-up model and high-art muse, girl next door and monstrous goddess. De Kooning highlights the mixture of myth and banality underlying these associations and suggests the contradictory feelings—the terror and lust, longing and repulsion, aggression and paralysis—they project. What is more, he uses the formal aspects of his work to show how such feelings can be sublimated into a single image all at once. He contains the spectrum of colors that dominates his canvas within one entity: the looming figure of womanness. He also divorces his colors from the need to designate real things, applying them to parts of the human form according to his own logic. This suggests an uneasy confluence of opposites; abstract fantasy becomes framed by recognizable and solid shapes. With this combination of figurative drawing and abstract brushwork, de Kooning retains, as Jörn Merkert puts it, "the image of the thing seen while simultaneously cutting free of it," recording "emotions felt in front of it" rather than merely representing an object in the world.[23]

In the paintings after *Woman I* de Kooning adds yet another layer of meaning. As before, he applies his paint with fury and draws his figures with jagged lines that suggest a raw sexuality. But he also gives the figures a sunny disposition.[24] Each one of the women, though huge and as ponderous as myth, bears a wide and harmless grin. Colescott capitalizes on de Kooning's strategy, making his mammy a giant with an empty smile, thereby underscoring the weighty mass of meanings assigned to one of slavery's central stereotypes while emphasizing her banality. He uses the formal aspects of de Kooning's work to show that Mammy personifies not only the various opposing concepts and ideologies projected onto women but also those projected onto racialized subjects. She is, on the one hand, an overtly familiar figure—the image of Aunt Jemima on syrup ads, the Mammy of *Gone with the Wind*—and, on the other hand, a stereotype of race and gender and, as such, "an organism let loose, a culture of limbs and labyrinths," of fragmented body parts made grotesque and utterly distorted.[25]

Colescott reproduces de Kooning's dynamic collage style and broad brush-work to suggest how a single stereotype can embody a variety of fantasies. As Michele Wallace has argued, in the discourse of slavery the mammy figure manifests in multiple and contradictory terms. She is a model of politeness, an advisor and confidante, a surrogate mistress and mother; she is also a figure who is both less and more than feminine, "a woman of inordinate strength, with an ability for tolerating an unusual amount of misery and heavy, distasteful work. [She] does have the same fears, weaknesses, and insecurities as other women, but believes herself to be, and is, in fact, stronger than most men. Less of a woman in that she is less 'feminine' and helpless, she is really *more* of a woman in that she is the embodiment of Mother Earth, the quintessential mother with infinite sexual, life-giving, and nurturing reserves."[26] In the proslavery literature of the antebellum period, Mammy appears as an older woman who is taken in by her white masters who kindly provide for her when she can no longer support herself. As Deborah Gray White demonstrates, her reality was far grimmer. She was often sexually persecuted in youth by her master's adolescent children and/or by the master himself; she was hounded in old age by jealous mistresses and eventually left without shelter. More recently, Mammy has often been represented as complicit with the master in the domination of captive peoples.[27]

Because Colescott, like Reed, superimposes his allusions to the past onto a contemporary frame and one form of expression (racial stereotyping) onto another (modernist painting), *I Gets a Thrill* signifies on both the antebellum culture of which Mammy is a symbol and on the context of de Kooning's painting. De Kooning started his *Woman* series shortly after World War II, an event that seemed to represent the darkest days of Western culture. The genocidal violence of the war was believed to be so unprecedented that many felt the destruction of civilization was at hand. Artists, de Kooning among them, responded by attempting to re-create a purpose and pattern to human life, exploring humans' relationship to the cosmic, sacred forces beyond their control and asserting the possibility of renewal and regeneration. Because the dramatic gestures of de Kooning's painting evoke a wide array of emotions, *Woman* suggests the psychic and physical violence inflicted on humanity by the war but also a vital instinct, a kind of life principle. One can see de Kooning's *Woman* emitting "the despairing cries of an oppressed existence" or the "quiet, open-eyed pleading" of an alienated subject. At the same time one can see her expressing the "hysterical laughter" and "unconstrained *joie de vivre*" of "a primordial earth goddess."[28] In his *Woman* series, de Kooning represents both the negative effects of the war on humanity and the forces of nature that allow for survival and regeneration.

Colescott's appropriation of de Kooning invites a reevaluation of modern painting's representation of historical violence and a critical exploration of the epistemic violence exerted through stereotypes. *I Gets a Thrill* suggests that, though extreme, the genocidal thrust of World War II was not unprecedented but alive and well centuries before, and not only in Europe but in the New World as well. As an icon of slavery, Mammy is an index to a history of brutality that includes the devastations of the Middle Passage and is preceded by the genocide of the native populations of the Americas. By inserting Mammy's well-known face in a frame that recalls de Kooning's fragmented brushwork, a painting technique that, in the immediate context of de Kooning's time, alludes to modernist notions of the human identity and psyche as fractured, Colescott signifies on the dehumanizing aspects of chattel slavery. In his figure's disjointed body parts he evokes the brutal punishments slaves were made to endure, punishments that disfigured and dismembered individuals and families and that certainly caused harm to the psyche.

Colescott gives the mammy icon a phantasmagoric quality that simultaneously speaks of past and present histories of persecution and destruction. Using lighter colors and a less frenetic mixture of lines and brushstrokes than de Kooning did, Colescott makes Mammy a mass of forms floating in a sea of color. In part, this is because Colescott substitutes de Kooning's use of black and muddled colors (especially the latter's gray-whites) for bright yellows, expansive, optic whites, and tropical blues, greens, and oranges. Like De Kooning, Colescott uses color expressionistically, liberating it from mimetic forms of representation. But he endows such an enterprise with an even greater, and continually more ironic joie de vivre than de Kooning's image suggests. Into this he inserts Mammy's face in stereotyped, figural form to recall how color as skin pigmentation has been subjected to an oppressive relationship to the body, and how such oppression has led to the kind of dismemberment of the body of which his figure is representative.

As Albert Boime and other art critics have noted, color categories (especially white and black) have been wedded to ideological biases in the semiotics of Western art for centuries. The antebellum period that gave birth to the mammy stereotype was no exception. Boime notes that throughout the "nineteenth century it was the idea of the opposition of black and white (and red and white in North America as well)" and the exclusionary political meaning of those oppositions "that fired the energies of painters and sculptors."[29] Placed in the liberated color scheme that Colescott takes from de Kooning, Mammy's face recalls the force with which ideologies of race and privilege have constricted the symbolic connection of color to skin pigmentation.

But Mammy's face in a work finished in 1978 also necessarily signifies on the racial politics that inform Colescott's work. The image evokes the ideologies that supported the exclusionary racial codes challenged by the civil rights movement in the decades immediately preceding its production. At the same time, it suggests the gender inequalities underlying the black nationalism of the 1970s. Central to black nationalism was a critique of matriarchy as obstructing healthy relationships between black women and men and destructive to the maintenance of the black family. As various critics have shown, this idea of matriarchy was based on a stereotype of black femininity that is rooted in the mammy image. To the predominantly male critical body of black nationalism, Mammy was not only an emasculating icon of superwomanhood (as well as a symbol of black complicity in the deployment of racial injustice), she was also a living legacy informing the matriarchal character of black families in the twentieth century. Black nationalists argued against a definition of black femininity informed by the purportedly male-threatening aspects of Mammy and insisted that black women concentrate instead on producing children for their revolution. This injunction, however, is based on a reproductive definition of black femininity, a definition that was also, ironically, at the core of American slavery's breeding system.[30]

Creating a deconstructive signifying fluidity between the legacy of slavery on the one hand and that of modern art on the other, Colescott transforms Mammy into a black nationalist nightmare. Like de Kooning, he highlights the fertility and nurturance of his figure while giving these qualities monstrous proportions. Her bosom and stomach (her womb) are enormous. Underscoring the connections between *Woman* and Mammy as Mother Earth figures, however, he also shows the irony in their similarities. While he conjures Mammy as the quintessential mother, he also emphasizes the aspects that make her an icon of slavery, reminding us that, as a black woman in America, she was denied, as a mere "breeder," the right to nurture her own children. In this context, Colescott's painting suggests that, in decrying the powers of black femininity as emasculating and constricting black female sexuality to reproduction, black nationalists upheld ideologies that contributed to the stereotype they so deplored.

Given the various and contradictory associations the mammy figure embodies, what do we see and feel when we see her in Colescott's 1978 painting? The painting's title and Colescott's appropriation of de Kooning's strategies suggest that one can experience both a representation of a familiar stereotype and the conflicting feelings evoked by it. Colescott's Mammy is both "de Koo" (the coon) and the disorientation (and, perhaps, the "thrill too") of being made to witness all she contains.

In other paintings, Colescott, like Reed, underscores the interpretative dilemmas created by the racial fantasies that American culture projects through stereotypes. In his *Sunday Afternoon with Joaquin Murietta* (1980), he presents us with a view of black femininity as lascivious and ambiguously powerful; the most striking figure in the painting is the black woman who, except for her red boots and painted lips, is naked (Figure 4.5). She is the only figure that stares at the viewers (and this, despite her nakedness) and the only woman who seems to share in the men's bounty: leisure, food, and drink. The painting, an appropriation of Manet's *Le Déjeuner sur l'herbe* (1863), exhibits the opposite extreme of the gender stereotype that the mammy icon embodies.

The black figure in Colescott's painting is hypersexualized (though, significantly, in a way that conjures the very absence of fertility) and is thus different

FIGURE 4.5. Robert Colescott, *Sunday Afternoon with Joaquin Murietta* (1980). Collection of Arlene and Harold Schnitzer. Photo credit: Cliff Edgington. [See color insert]

from Mammy and also from the raw, primordial exuberance of de Kooning's *Woman*. Assuming a complicit pose in relation to the men in the frame, she stands out against the (white) woman in the background. She also suggests the image of Jezebel, the biblical figure whom, as Deborah Gray White has shown, antebellum culture employed to designate a notion of black femininity as cunningly seductive. Circulated as one of two major stereotypes of black femininity, Jezebel functioned as the embodiment of corruption. Unlike Mammy, who was denied a sense of femininity in favor of maternal but masculinized attributes, Jezebel's femininity was connected to prostitution and to the purportedly bestial sexuality of blackness.

As Sander Gilman has shown, associations between femininity, prostitution, and blackness coalesced more generally in the iconography of the United States and Europe in the late nineteenth century.[31] They inform Manet's *Olympia* (1862–63), a painting connected to *Le Déjeuner sur l'herbe* by more than chronology, and to Colescott's painting by association. Gilman argues that notions of sexualized femininity crystallized around the image of the prostitute in nineteenth-century culture and intertwined with representations of blacks, particularly black servants, suggesting sexual similarities between blackness and prostitution.[32] The connection between prostitution, femininity, and blackness arose from pseudo-scientific theories on the supposedly primitive and wanton sexuality of black women. As Gilman shows, the physical attributes of black women, in particular the genitalia and buttocks of Hottentot women, were sublimated into visual representations of prostitution. In other cases, as in *Olympia*, the connection between blackness, femininity, and prostitution was only implied; the painting presents a prostitute staring boldly at the viewer as a black woman whose physical attributes recall Mammy's attends to her.[33]

Colescott echoes but reverses the categories and associations of *Olympia* in his appropriation of *Le Déjeuner*; the black woman seems to play the role of the prostitute and the white one in the background that of the servant. Here Colescott makes significant changes to the image he appropriates, since in *Le Déjeuner* there are no black figures and the central female figure is, though naked, not eroticized. Concerned with evoking and challenging stereotypical representations of the female nude (a time-honored theme in the history of art), Manet presents us with a woman whose nudity does not render her a figure of submission or of objectification but rather a source of discomfort. Like the prostitute in *Olympia*, she knows that her viewers are aware that she is naked, and yet she stares back at them brazenly. Her surroundings and identity are more uncertain, however, for, unlike the white woman in *Olympia*, the nude in *Le Déjeuner* shares the frame with people whose identities and purposes seem inscrutable. As Paul H. Tucker observes, rather than offering "clues as to what is occurring in [*Le Déjeuner*] or what our relationship is supposed to be to the scene as a whole," Manet provokes a series of questions: "[Have] we stumbled upon some kind of intimate encounter? Are we implicated in some way? Why does the woman look at us so unabashedly, and why are the men beside her so disengaged with her and each other?"[34]

Exploiting the ambiguity of Manet's image, Colescott uses the intensity of his composition to signify on particular versions of sexual and racial fantasies in American culture. While the deep brown of the naked woman's skin connects her to the tree trunks surrounding her, and hence to nature, it also connects her to the man sitting directly across from her, a man dressed in colors darker than her skin. Like the woman, this figure also wears red and seems powerful (notice the hand placed prominently on the gun). But he is also wearing a Mexican *charro* and seems to be "colored" by his dress. He is, in other words, the Joaquin Murietta of the title and hence a racially "shady" character. Is he white or brown? Murietta was in fact a Mexican outlaw in California who was provoked to murder when his wife was raped and killed by racist Anglo miners in the mid-nineteenth century. After he unleashed a furious revenge upon his wife's killers, Murietta became a Robin Hood hero who defended Latinos against violence and dispossession by haunting gold miners.[35] What connection could he have to the Jezebel figure who stares back at the viewer, and who is the man in the white shirt seated next to her? He too seems complicit in something obscure: he looks intently at Murietta and wears a bullet belt. Given this belt and his taupe hat, might he be a John Brown figure? How is he connected to the woman in the back who, like him, wears white? Like Manet's, Colescott's painting produces more questions than answers.

From one perspective, the three central figures in *Sunday* seem superimposed onto an idyllic scene of greenery and purity. The (brown) outlaw, the (black) Jezebel, and the complicit (white) man do not belong in the woods with the (virgin) maiden by the brook, for they are signifiers of race, sex, and violence. As such, one could see them as figures traditionally excluded from the high art tradition to which Manet belonged and as fantasies inserted into what is Colescott's appropriation of a white (art) master. Upon closer examination, however, one begins to see that Colescott, unlike Manet, has made the whole scene almost surreal, intensifying the hues with which he depicts the greenery of the woods, the darkness of the tree trunks, and the color of the brook. His figures are not superimposed onto a natural and pure landscape; rather, they form part of a scene that, as Colescott's colors suggest, is *all* fantasy. As such, the image suggests and denies all at once a scene that is often enacted in the paranoid mind of the master class. It seems to represent the socially dispossessed (the immigrant outlaw, the Jezebel, and the "darky lover") as involved in a dark and mysterious plot. Like Manet's figures, they evoke a discomforting sense that is further accentuated by Colescott's reference to the historical figure of Murietta. Are they plotting the kind of murderous revenge for which Murietta is known? But Colescott's color intensity also highlights the fabricated nature of this scene. Notice, for example, how he unifies the foliage and grass, applying a deep, dark green to both, giving the scene a hazy, almost surreal quality. By adding bursts of bright orange to objects near the front and a dull, mustard yellow to the trees in the back, he conveys an atmosphere of extreme heat, the kind that distorts perception. In other parts of the painting he uses color expressionistically, as when he makes the stream fuchsia, salmon pink, and pale blue.

Colescott's use of Manet illustrates a general tendency in his work: to make explicit and calculated references to the work of canonical painters in order to paint the psychic and social distances between people in a culture so dominated by ideologies of race. The strategy itself links him to Manet for, as Michael Fried has shown, Manet also made abundant use of other painters' work. But, whereas Manet referenced the work of other (European, predominantly French) painters to "secure or establish or guarantee the Frenchness of *his* own art," Colescott references European painters to unsettle the uniqueness of race as an ideology.[36] Most critics of Manet agree that the dynamic of his work rests in its "simultaneous assertion and betrayal of stereotypes," specifically those projecting middle-class fantasies; they argue that Manet puts stereotypes in his paintings "only to show them as such—not realistic."[37] In *Le Déjeuner*, he evokes the nude to suggest a breaking of Victorian sexual norms but sets up the scene so as to deny the fantasy of that transgression. Similarly, Colescott both invokes and deflates the possible plot of retribution in *Sunday*. In both cases the artist makes a spectacle of ideology, showing how social prohibitions (taboos against certain sexual behavior, against social intercourse across racial lines) produce fantasies charged with desire and, in Colescott's case, fear. In the sense that they are prohibitive in nature, racial ideologies are no different from Victorian sexual codes; they both produce fantasies that profane and threaten to destroy the society that the rules are, purportedly, meant to enable and protect.

Colescott uses other painters' work to underscore the self-ironic quality of racial prohibitions. Like de Kooning, he elucidates the mythical and the trite in the stereotypical imagery such prohibitions produce, while working, like Manet, through allusions to a high art tradition. In *Les Demoiselles d'Alabama: Dressed* (1985), his appropriation of Picasso's *Les Demoiselles d'Avignon* (1907), Colescott, like Manet in *Le Déjeuner*, offers a juxtaposition of classical elevation and contemporary banality (Figure 4.6). However, whereas Manet's is a straight-faced presentation, Colescott's is imbued with humor; in his hands, Picasso's world-renowned demoiselles become the stuff of kitsch.[38] It is this humor that allows Colescott to accentuate the deconstructive fluidity his work creates between the history of modern art and the discourse of race in the United States.

Colescott's *Les Demoiselles d'Alabama: Dressed* signifies on nearly every aspect of Picasso's work, from its gestation as the psychological explorations of

FIGURE 4.6. Robert Colescott, *Les Demoiselles d'Alabama: Dressed* (1985). Courtesy of Phyllis Kind Gallery. [See color insert]

a modernist painter to its relationship to Primitive art. Thus it is well worth exploring the context of *Les Demoiselles d'Avignon*. The painting has never been considered a humorous piece. Picasso's contemporaries found the picture anything but; they found it "disquieting, frightening, disappointing [even] inadmissible."[39] Now valued as a major turning point in the history of modern art, Picasso's painting is said to span "the polarity between Eros and Thanatos" and to have been central in changing the focus of modern painting from a primarily perceptual and illustrative mode to a conceptual and iconographic one.[40] Indeed, the painting addresses issues common to Manet and de Kooning, mainly the role of women in human sexuality and the challenges of representing the female form. Like Manet, Picasso suggests a connection between women, sexuality, and prostitution, though, unlike him, Picasso reveals aspects of his own psychology in the process. *Les Demoiselles d'Avignon*, as William Rubin argues, represents Picasso's "deep-seated fear and loathing of the female body—which existed side by side with his craving for an ecstatic idealization of it."[41]

As Rubin notes, Picasso's repulsion/attraction relationship to women is a common, even trite, aspect of male psychology. Yet the fact that he expressed it through the elevated medium of his art amplifies the topic and makes it all the "more universal for being so commonplace."[42] His revulsion toward the female body turned on the danger of venereal disease, a danger to which he exposed himself as a frequenter of bordellos (and to which he succumbed). Picasso feared and desired women (specifically prostitutes) because he saw them as the embodiments of contradictory impulses within him: thanatophobia on the one hand and eros on the other. While he expressed the latter of these two impulses through a ravenous sexuality, he also realized it through his art and his commitment to reinvigorating painting. One of the most remarkable aspects of Picasso's painting (and of Colescott's later appropriation) is how his desire to *evoke* rather than simply illustrate the feelings he associated with women led him directly to formal innovation.

To realize his vision in *Les Demoiselles d'Avignon,* Picasso turned to Primitive art (largely African and Oceanic),[43] and found in it the inspiration for transforming his work into a vehicle for the intercession of deep fears and desires. In *Les Demoiselles d'Avignon* he presents us with the results of this encounter. The painting depicts five prostitutes: one, to the far left of the canvas, stands alone and in profile, while two stand and face the viewer from the center, and two others (one seated, the other standing) strike poses to the far right. Originally drawn in what is known as Picasso's Iberian style, each of the women initially shared a similar physique and psychology. After seeing African tribal masks at the Musée d'Ethonographie du Trocadéro in Paris, however, Picasso changed the faces and postures of some of the women, particularly the two on the far right, giving them African plasticity and Oceanic coloring to evoke his horror of death.[44] With their monstrously distorted heads, the two prostitutes on the right seem to connote something akin to Joseph Conrad's heart of darkness, a savage sexuality and violence that, especially in the case of the seated prostitute, assume contorted physical and psychological attributes. The two figures at the center of the canvas, by contrast, retain the original Iberian style, which gives them a grace and beauty that the more sculptural figure on the far left is missing.

Colescott exploits the mixture of banality and elevation intrinsic to Picasso's innovative representation of a quotidian theme. He also captures the shift from perception to conception embodied by *Les Demoiselles d'Avignon.* In so doing, he engages with the connections implicit in Manet and Picasso between notions of femininity, sexuality, prostitution, and blackness while framing these in an American context. The most immediately noticeable aspect of Colescott's signifying is that his demoiselles are southern (from Alabama), clothed, and, in one crucial instance, whitened. The prostitute who in Picasso represents the most frightening and African-styled image becomes in Colescott the only white woman in the painting. Together, these shifts and reversals take us directly to the antebellum world on which *George Washington Carver, I Gets a Thrill,* and *Sunday* signify.

What struck Picasso most about the African masks he observed in Paris was their fetishistic function, the fact that they were "magical" objects "capable of deeply affecting" those viewing and using them.[45] When he painted the prostitute to the far right of his canvas, he invested her with the kind of fetishistic power he saw in the African masks, the power to invoke in her viewers the horror of death. The white woman Colescott paints in her stead is also a kind of fetish, but one whose origins are decidedly American. Arising from the same mythology that includes Mammy and Jezebel, the white woman in Colescott's painting evokes the southern belle and the cult of domesticity, a set of ideologies that, above all else, focused on the purity and sanctity of white women in a racialized society. From a black male perspective, the southern belle symbolizes a taboo sexuality. She cannot be coveted, never mind attained, since black men have been violently lynched for merely glancing at her. Colescott gives the belle in his painting an exaggerated, glossy prettiness, suggesting that she has been marked as off-limits and has thus become, paradoxically, an object of desire, a sexual fetish. At the same time, he makes her the substitute for the most horrific death figure in Picasso's painting, underscoring how the master class used the mythology surrounding this figure as an excuse to commit the murderous crime of lynching. Bringing forth the mixture of Eros and Thanatos projected onto stereotypes, Colescott elucidates how they evoke a particularly American heart of darkness.[46]

However, Colescott also underscores the banality of racial stereotypes by undermining the associations that Picasso's Primitive aesthetic suggests between blackness and sexuality. As before, he works through the intensity of his composition. He dresses and surrounds his demoiselles in such an array of loud colors that their mythical aspects attain clownish, bombastic proportions. The white woman, for instance, is larger than life in her symbolic status, yet Colescott gives her the aura of a caricature. Her hair is not so much blond as bright yellow, and her polka-dotted shirt and neatly drawn red lips suggest Roy Lichtenstein's pop art. The result is a figure containing a number of polarities: she is a signifier of purity and desire but also a blatantly fabricated image, a symbol of the unattainable but also a prostitute who turns coquettishly toward us and shows off her prominent blue behind. In contrast, the black woman standing behind her looks askew at the viewer in a threatening and almost malicious way. The second woman from the left shares the same psychology, turning her eyes scornfully upward as though posing awkwardly and reluctantly. Suggesting the kind of duplicity associated with Jezebel's deviousness, Mammy's masculinized femininity, and the illicit sexuality of both stereotypes, these two prostitutes, like the white woman, seem to loom within the frame. Yet one wears a bright yellow leopard-print bikini while the other, though broad and muscular, wears a pink prom dress that falls off her body.[47]

Between these two figures stands the darkest and most eroticized of all of Colescott's demoiselles. This figure frustrates any simple associations between her sexuality and race and thus signifies on the most "primitive" of Picasso's figures. Picasso styled his most frightening demoiselles after African masks that, to him, expressed a primitive "otherness, [a] savage sexuality . . . and . . . horror."[48]

The masks suggested a kind of barbarity he recognized in himself, but which he projected outward onto the prostitutes that he racialized via his allusion to Africa. Through them Picasso reinscribed the nineteenth-century connection between blackness and prostitution that Sander Gilman explores. In Colescott, the most "African" or darkest of the figures is eroticized, but not through the Primitive aesthetics that Picasso employed. Complete with her contemporary clothing and pink hair, she exudes a soft, bubble-gum sensuousness. Indeed, there is nothing savage about her. Colescott shifts the valence of the raised arms in the original image with details like her closed eyes, protruding red lips, bright green shorts, and open white shirt, which lend her all the garishness and brashness of American mall culture. She may be a black prostitute, but her sexuality has nothing to do with the savage primitivism Picasso saw in the masks at the Trocadéro.

Colescott similarly radicalizes the figure standing in profile on the far left. In Picasso's painting that figure shares the African and Iberian styles of the four other prostitutes and therefore contains both the Eros and Thanatos of the painting's theme. On Colescott's canvas she becomes a mirror image of the seated woman: she shares the white woman's attractiveness and, though she is racialized as black, also her skin pigmentation. In Picasso's painting the figure in profile is both African (savage) and European (Iberian and graceful); in Colescott's she is both black and white but neither savage nor graceful. Colescott's demoiselle retains the broad size and zombie-like vacancy of the original figure, but, unlike her, she does not merely contain polarities; rather, she refuses them outright. There is nothing extreme or excessive about her. Compared to the other women, she is neither provocatively dressed nor radically racialized. She has none of the original's sharp edges and oblique shades, sporting instead the only solid, dark colors of Colescott's composition. Her hair and facial features mark her as black, but a closer look reveals that she shares more similarities than differences with all of the demoiselles, even with those of different skin coloring. The southern belle prostitute with the bright yellow hair, for example, has a wide "African" nose, while the darker, more threatening figure to the upper far right has an aquiline, "white" profile. Colescott's painting thus suggests that, aside from giving us a mythology of race and gender that includes Mammy, Jezebel, and the southern belle, the institution of slavery also bequeathed to us a history of miscegenation that has always blurred the racial distinctions antebellum culture tried so hard to enforce.[49]

Colescott's send-up of Picasso's Les Demoiselles d'Avignon, like the original, is not based on perception; it is not what Colescott the artist sees in the world and then brings to life through his craft. Rather, it is the world, as it is conceived through a particular psychology, made manifest. Unlike Picasso, who used African art as a vehicle through which to exorcise the mysteries of his own soul,

Colescott is not concerned with an individual psyche but with the storehouse of fears and desires in a *national* psyche. The difference aligns him with Reed and Walker, with whom he shares not only a deep awareness of how slavery has shaped American culture but also similar strategies for exploring that culture. Like Picasso, Colescott reiterates the psychological and ritualistic aspects of African culture, but, like Reed, he does so in an American context. He employs a conjuring aesthetic that recalls Reed's voodoo-inspired Neo-Hoodoo, bringing to life the distortions and fantasies of the past into contemporary frames and showing how such distortions and desires possess our imagination. Like Picasso, he focuses on how we conceive rather than perceive the world; like Reed, he gives that focus a distinctly historical grounding. With Reed he asks, How do the myths, the people (the ancestors), the events, and the texts of slavery structure our modes of thinking, feeling, and acting?

Both Colescott and Reed use parody to resurrect the past, a bitter yet playful parody that depends as much on formal strategies as it does on outrageous revision of subject matter. While Reed shares such strategies with writers like William Wells Brown and Charles W. Chesnutt, Colescott shares them with artists like Kara Walker. Walker skyrocketed into prominence in the art world at a young age, creating a critical uproar with her "graceful but ferocious" silhouettes.[50] While some critics see her use of stereotypical images as retrograde, she implicitly agrees with Colescott, who has said that such images "are part of the American heritage" and that, as such, they need to be explored. "I had to come to terms with [this fact] for myself," Colescott admits, "ultimately controlling the images by making them say some things for me. First, I made these paintings and drawings as messages for myself to myself, getting in touch with my own fears, frustrations, and anger."[51]

Walker signifies on the stereotypical images that are part of the "American heritage" in the spirit of the comic grotesque with which Goya depicted the cruelty and barbarism of an age that believed itself rational and stable.[52] There are no moral certainties or judgments in her portraits of Confederate soldiers, mammies, pickaninnies, Sambos, Uncle Toms, masters, southern belles, and plantation "wenches" and "studs." Rather, Walker renders American slavery as if it were a dream in which almost anything is possible and meaning is nearly impossible to discern. As in Goya, human figures blend with beasts, are missing limbs or heads, but in Walker's work these associations take on added power by signifying on the objectification of and threat to the human body on which chattel slavery rested and which was certainly no dream at all.

"Miss K. Walker, a Free Negress of Noteworthy Talent"

Kara Walker creates what Baudelaire, with respect to Goya, called the "credible form of the monstrous."[53] Although she culls her subjects principally from the history of U.S. slavery, and thus evokes a particular time and place, her scenes are far from mimetic. Rather, they represent violent fantasies carried out without restraint. Like jokes and, as Freud might put it, dreams, Walker's silhouettes traffic in taboos.[54] But, whereas in the jokes Freud examines, taboos are addressed via the language of sublimation (condensation, displacement, projection), Walker's work, like Pryor's, relishes exposure; it evinces delight in visually spelling out American taboos regarding race and gender. Undoubtedly, Colescott achieves a similar effect. Yet Colescott gives free rein to those taboos in a carnivalesque spirit that seeks to turn convention on its head with regard to the place of African Americans in both American history and the history of art. His work appeals to the "ritually insurrectional laughter" of the lower classes, the laughter that Bakhtin emphasizes in his work on Rabelais.[55] Walker, by contrast, creates aesthetically beautiful but conceptually grotesque images that signal to, without claiming to represent, the cruel and bizarre intimacies of American slavery. More so than Colescott's images, Walker's produce the quintessential effect of the grotesque: they leave viewers somewhere between laughter, disgust, and astonishment.[56] They synthesize the ludicrous and the horrible as Walker combs the slapstick and debasing humor of minstrelsy for the violence, scatology, and sensuality underwriting it. The combination makes it difficult, as Walker has said of her own work, "to decide just how hard to laugh."[57] A set of images from her 1997 *Renaissance Society* show in Chicago makes evident the dynamism of Walker's work (Figure 4.7).

In this, as in other installations, Walker arranges her images in a sequence that, from afar, suggests a tale about music and dance, yet, upon closer look, reveals obscure and violent actions: bodies pierce each other, leap into impossible shapes, and engage in enigmatic rituals. With a few exceptions, Walker makes all of her figures black so that, while her contours suggest racial differences through hair texture, sharpness of feature, and stereotypes of demeanor and posture, she makes it difficult to discern separate identities and agents. Reading the images in the frieze according to the racial differences that Walker implies in her silhouettes, we witness something like a minstrel show carried to its most violent and absurd limits. A figure that looks like a (black) man struggles to play a banjo while spittle or blood dribbles from his eyes and mouth (here and elsewhere I use parentheses to acknowledge the racial identities that Walker at once suggests and denies by making all figures black). Behind him, a (black) girl rushes toward a keylike object that pierces the man's back. Is she about to turn it (and wind up the banjo player as one would a toy)? Or is she rushing to free him? The figure that leaps (or has been thrust up) resembles a rag doll as her limbs twist in every direction. But this limp figure threatens too: she holds a grenade. The trumpet that is stuck in or coming out of her genitals links her to the banjo player while adding a disorienting connection between musical performance and sex.

FIGURE 4.7. Kara Walker, *Presenting Negro Scenes Drawn Upon My Passage Through the South and Reconfigured for the Benefit of Enlightened Audiences, Wherever Such May Be Found, By Myself, Missus K. E. B. Walker, Colored* (1997). Installation at the Renaissance Society at the University of Chicago. Cut paper and adhesive on wall, 12 x 155 feet overall. Photography by Tom Van Eynde. [See color insert]

The next two sets of figures, the elegant pair of dancers and the three children, seem far tamer. Yet details suggest otherwise. Wild foxes wrap around or constitute the dancing woman's skirt. Meanwhile, a little (black) girl, who seems to be swallowing her own hand, directs a (black) boy with an impossibly big head to fill a (white) boy's behind with invisible contents; the latter appears to be missing a leg. The sequence ends with the image of a large (black) man in a Napoleonic hat leaping toward the gallery wall's edge (into what?) with a shovel held high.

Turning the corner to the left, we are greeted with more enigmas (Figure 4.8). We see isolated but busy characters; one looks like a white doctor and the other like a pickaninny. Again, the fact that the characters are all black destabilizes a racialized reading even as Walker's contours encourage it. The methodical and eerie play of shadows in the first sequence gives way, inexplicably, to the sparseness of the second.

Is the man with the shovel meant to signify Toussaint Louverture, a figure who came to symbolize both the dream of freedom for the enslaved and the nightmare of rebellion for the master? What does it mean that he seems to run senselessly toward the edge of the wall? Will he fall off the frieze into nothing,

FIGURE 4.8. Installation detail of Kara Walker, *Presenting Negro Scenes Drawn Upon My Passage Through the South and Reconfigured for the Benefit of Enlightened Audiences, Wherever Such May Be Found, By Myself, Missus K. E. B. Walker, Colored* (1997). Installation at the Renaissance Society at the University of Chicago. Photography by Tom Van Eynde. [See color insert]

or turn the corner and join the next frieze? The next set of shadows provides more questions than answers. Of what nature is the busy labor of its figures? In an implicit connection to the Louverture figure, the child frolics in a pile that seems freshly shoveled while the (white) man enigmatically loiters near it. However, despite all these details, it is still unclear of what the pile is composed, and what the figures' motivations may be. By maintaining an uneasy equilibrium between accessible reading, by suggesting the possibility of reading racial difference and a cohesive story line—and its opposite—by making every figure "black" and obfuscating causes, effects, and consequences, Walker blurs the line between fantasy and reality. The result is a play of shadows that seduces and disturbs all at once.

Walker produces this contradictory effect in ways reminiscent of Goya's strategies. Baudelaire praised Goya's *Los Caprichos* for masterfully fusing the real and the fantastic. The "line of suture, the point of juncture" between the real and the fantastic in *Los Caprichos*, claimed Baudelaire, is a "vague frontier," as Goya's monstrous images, his "bestial faces" and "diabolic grimaces" are always "impregnated with *humanity*."[58] The word *capricho* (caprice) circulated in Goya's time as a synonym for caricature, usually in political satires that were printed in Spanish newspapers. *Los Caprichos* are both morally more sober and more politically neutral than such caricatures. Goya's etchings obliquely refer to political figures and social ills of late eighteenth-century Spain and, more generally, of Enlightenment Europe, while giving free rein to the artist's imagination in depicting every deformity of human nature. In his *Caprichos*, outrageous hybrids, half-beast, half-human mutants with exaggerated or dwarfish features, sprout wings or fangs, producing what Frances S. Connelly calls a "savagely ironic" satire of Enlightenment rationalism.[59] Rejecting the idea that the monstrous, the cruel, and the irrational were inhuman, Goya did not provide a specific moral or physical point of view from which to judge these grotesques.

Because Walker employs similar strategies in her work, let us investigate further the particular character of *Los Caprichos*. In *Capricho* No. 42, Goya uses donkeys to represent the clergy and the rich; peasants bear these donkeys on their backs.[60] And yet the image does not read as didactic; Goya does not condescend to his viewers, does not instruct them on the oppression of the lower classes. This is because he maintains a position of neutral observation, which he manifests formally. As R. Stanley Johnson notes, Goya developed three crucial innovations by which he "plunged his viewers into a world in which normal terms of orientation" in the interpretation of art "simply no longer function[ed]": a reconfiguration of light, perspective, and background.

> In the history of Western art from the Renaissance to Goya light in a work of art originated from one single, clear source. That light, whether emanating from a candle or from God, was steady, unwavering and unchanging. Such light had illuminated art from the *Madonnas* of Botticelli to the *Fetes Champetres* of Watteau. In each of Goya's *Caprichos*, however, there was no single, steady or logical source of light; light here originated in the artist's mind, was "directionless," found its only use in clarifying and distorting an image and essentially followed the artist's whims, desires, exigencies. This breakdown in traditional artistic conventions, in which "the light of God" appeared to be replaced with "the light" of the individual artist, became a *fait accompli* with the publication of the *Caprichos* in 1799.

Goya rejected the idea of a "clear, predetermined, artistic universe," and thus, in most of his *Caprichos*, he does not employ "the normal up-down coordinates" of figure painting or "the one-point of view perspective present in Western art over the precedent centuries," leaving viewers with "no firm footing from which" to judge distances, motion, or backgrounds.[61] Goya's ability to fuse into fantastical form the monstrous aspects of his political, moral, and social milieu, to create a world of shifting perspectives, obscured backgrounds, and bizarre unions, led Baudelaire to conclude, "No one has ventured further than [Goya] in the direction of the *possible* absurd."[62]

Like Goya, Walker denies the viewer a firm footing to make meaning, and, as we have seen in the first sequences, she encourages certain readings and frustrates them at the same time. Manipulating perspective and background, she too withholds moral judgment and plunges viewers into worlds where the usual coordinates for orientation do not hold. The pieces in her work that most immediately resemble Goya's, however, are not the silhouettes for which she is best known. Walker works in other media, notably oil painting, printmaking (silkscreen, etching, aquatint), small, intimate drawings, Rorschach prints, and mixed-media collages that often incorporate text; she has also produced larger drawings on gouache, and these bear an obvious connection to Goya's version of the comic grotesque. Witness, for example, *Queen Bee* (1998; Figure 4.9), a work that also recalls Colescott and de Kooning. Here we have the mammy stereotype not only conjured in larger-than-life proportions but also made monstrous through a conjoining of human and animal parts. The frightening femininity of *I Gets a Thrill* appears in the enormous breasts, tipped with dark, protuberant nipples and set off by the impossibly small waist. That waist, in turn, sets up a stark contrast between the thick torso and neck and the feminine bustle-like bottom. The unruly hair, the mannish face with thick lips, big eyes and nose, and a hint of jowls contrast with the delicate wings behind. The title is meant to evoke the regal potency and fertility of a queen bee as well as the predatory instincts of the "welfare queen" and the emasculating power that the Moynihan Report assigned to black women. And yet the figure's distracted look makes her appear lifeless.

FIGURE 4.9. Kara Walker, *Queen Bee* (1998). Gouache and cut paper on paper, 62 x 42 inches. Image courtesy of Sikkema Jenkins & Co. [See color insert]

For all her thickness she also seems to float, not even fly. In fact, her little wings could hardly carry her weight. With the ludicrous contrast between her size and that of the other dainty bees, Walker caps a series of absurd contrasts.

In this drawing Walker uses techniques similar to Goya's to highlight the grotesque absurdity via a series of demeaning connotations associated with black femininity. Eric Lott argues that the most intense forms of vulgarity on the minstrel stage were expressed in blackface transvestism that aimed to mock and tame the purportedly "profane and murderous powers of women" in general and black women more specifically. White men's "contempt for white women," he writes, was "intermittently repressed through [their] 'protection' of them from savage black manhood" and "displaced or surcharged onto the 'grotesque' black woman."[63] This is the subtext that Walker's *Queen Bee*, like Colescott's *I Gets a Thrill*, makes explicit.

Queen Bee, like many of Walker's drawings and etchings, suggests that Walker studied Goya carefully. Yet it is in her silhouette work that she creates her own version of the "possible absurd." For, paradoxically, it is when Walker's work does not directly resemble Goya's that it is at its most powerful and most grotesque. Walker exploits what she sees as the fundamental connection between the silhouette and the stereotype, mainly that the former, like the latter, "says a lot with little information."[64] With this flattening technique, she refuses the humanity with which Goya endowed his monstrous figures. In fact, by choosing stereotypes and silhouettes as her principal forms, she seems to work in a distinctively opposite way. Ann Wagner notes that silhouettes "speak an economical language of substitution and erasure" so that what is shown is not "a body, but how a body blocks the light."[65] Stereotype works in a similarly reductive way, presenting not humanity but the ways that its distortions block it. Yet Walker grounds her reductive images in the historical, and she does so by "blending and bending" a medley of genres, including not only minstrelsy but also the slave narrative, pornography, Harlequin romances, posters of fugitive slaves, historical painting, and silhouette portraiture.[66] The result, as Mark Reinhardt argues, is that Walker's sequences are not only embedded in the antebellum era that her stereotypes index, but also suggest how the "iconography of that era has melded with other sources of popular culture to shape the imagery, consciousness, and political unconscious of race in the United States."[67] Thus, while Walker's silhouettes do not represent humans but rather the distortion of the human form, they clearly reference particular aspects of American culture and the human agents involved in its history of racial conflict.

Walker's images are in fact connected through a string of allusions to nineteenth-century culture, specifically to the history of visual art and racial science. Walker transforms the nineteenth-century genteel craft of silhouette portraiture into a vehicle for critical scrutiny. She has said that the silhouette works as "a side-long glance ... [a] little look ... full of suspicion, potential ill-will, or desire."[68] Historically, the silhouette was an art practiced by relative amateurs as a kind of middle-brow portraiture (silhouettes were known as "shadow portraits") that became popular in part because of its affordability at a time when the Unites States was still a struggling republic. As it had in Europe, the American silhouette portrayed ordered, rational, and distinctly middle-class society (Figure 4.10).

Walker describes the silhouette as an art that "speaks to purity of form, color, and, insidiously, of race and heritage." "I would think," she told an interviewer, "that this would appeal to an early America seeking to define itself against a flashy and uncomplicated Europe—a Europe . . . that went so far as to call shadow portraits 'silhouettes,' after the French finance minister whose policies were derided as cheap, and who also practiced the inexpensive little art. . . . The word is actually an insult."[69] In Walker's hands, shadow portraits still speak "insidiously" of race and "heritage," but with a sharp, even fierce, slant. She explicitly twists the silhouette's function in racial sciences and its emblematic quality as portraiture.

Silhouettes came to be associated with race through the work of Johann Caspar Lavater, a Zurich divine whose belief in physiognomy (or the ability to read character from people's faces) led him to use and promote the silhouette as a scientific tool.[70] Phrenologists also made extensive use of the silhouette, directing special attention to the shape, size, or character of the head as a record of individuality. Both branches of pseudo-science argued for the superiority of Caucasians and proposed that black people's physical attributes visually proved

FIGURE 4.10. A. C. F. Edouart, *Mr. and Mrs. Josiah Quincy and Their Children* (1842). Cut paper and pencil. Reprinted in *Shades of Our Ancestors* by Alice van Leer Carrick (Boston: Little Brown, 1928).

their inequality and even their inhumanity. Overturning the supposed racial certainties that the phrenological and physiognomic silhouette meant to convey, Walker uses the form to create portraits of intense ambiguity. She does so not only by exploiting these historical aspects of the silhouette but also by mining her own psyche.

One of the principal ways through which Walker achieves this recalls Ishmael Reed's Neo-Hoodoo practices. Walker often assumes the character of "Miss K. Walker, a Free Negress of Noteworthy Talent" (or a variation thereof), the persona who signs her work. Her 1997 show at the Renaissance Society in Chicago, for instance, bears the title *Presenting Negro Scenes Drawn Upon My Passage Through the South and Reconfigured for the Benefit of Enlightened Audiences, Wherever Such May Be Found, By Myself, Missus K. E. B. Walker, Colored*. The title is exemplary of Walker's work and serves as one of the many ways in which she signifies on nineteenth-century visual, literary, and scientific culture while troubling distinctions between past and present. Through her alter ego, the artist becomes the embodiment of a set of ideologies and desires; she becomes a body possessed by certain loa of slavery. This suggestion is perhaps most emphatically reinforced by her method of composition. Though she works partly from sketches, Walker claims not to plan the shape and composition of her silhouettes in her studio but to cut and compose according to the room; the process, she says, is like "cutting the shadows of the room in paper."[71] Recalling the process of creating her 1998 Wooster Gardens show, Walker speaks of her improvisatory style as a kind of possession: "There were all these little ghostly characters, these shadowy bits and pieces; bits of phraseology, the child-likeness, the tawdry vixen, the wicked; they all jumped into life—waking life—without my really controlling them."[72] She gives the "ghostly characters" and "shadowy bits" physical presence through her silhouettes, which she uses as vévés to conjure the mysterious or unknown (the voodoo) of her own psyche and that of her cultural heritage.[73] Her work, she claims, comes directly from a "play" between the conscious and unconscious, a play that manifests itself as a kind of "free association."[74] Her work entails an exploration of an internal and individual archive, which she insists is also part of a more general and collective national psyche. "Somehow," she told an interviewer, "there is just this enormous warehouse in the back of my brain filled with history and fiction and all kinds of things . . . bizarre levels of weird racist associations, jokes, or quotes, and . . . history, with everything mixed together in a jumble." The resulting images are so startling that Walker admits she is sometimes "afraid to make the work." But she also knows that in such cases, "the viewer is just as afraid to see [it]," and that the real "charge" of her scenarios come from these contradictory desires to conjure and not conjure, to see and not see.[75]

Walker began making her images in Atlanta, where she was raised, and continued when she moved to the Northeast, having decided to signify on the mythology of slavery despite her suspicion that the subject was overwrought. "I considered it almost a joke in itself to begin making work that employs characters from the culture of slavery and the ante-bellum South," she told Alexander Alberro, adding that the choice seemed "too expected" of her as an African American artist. To make the choice she decided to embrace an unsentimental, even irreverent attitude. "When I came up north, to freedom as it were, I was determined to expose all the injustices of being me," she told Alberro, satirically marking the distance between herself (a middle-class, well-educated, black artist centuries removed from slavery) and the subject she ultimately chose. "This strategy operated a little like the Slave Narrative tradition," she continued, "except that I was conscious that I played all the roles—Master, Mistress, and Abolitionist—and that the roles have been spoiled over time by Harlequin romances and pornographic genres."[76]

In a book simply titled *Kara Walker*, published in a limited edition (one thousand copies) by the Renaissance Society in Chicago the same year as her show there, Walker adopts her fictitious historical alter ego and writes a pornographic pseudo–slave narrative/blaxploitation book in which she does indeed play all of the roles. Including drawings by Walker, photographs from the show, writings by the "Negress," and images from distinct time periods (slavery, the 1970s blaxploitation era), and essays by Walker the artist from the early 1990s, the book, like Walker's work in general, makes visual the ways our shared "memory" of slavery is produced by the collusion of fact and fiction.

As Robert F. Reid-Pharr argues, one of the reasons why Walker's work resonates with American audiences is precisely because her images constantly point to this collusion. Walker, he writes, "challenges the idea that the portrayals of slavery that have captured the imaginations of contemporary Americans [one thinks here of "neo-slave narratives" like Toni Morrison's *Beloved*] can be either celebrated as realistic depictions of American history or easily discounted as particularly tacky—and thus particularly American—costume dramas." Instead, her work suggests that we tend to filter slavery through lenses colored by the "fantasies of interracial debauchery" that, for example, a film like Richard Fleischer's 1975 *Mandingo* makes vivid.[77] In an interview with Elizabeth Armstrong, Walker makes the point explicitly: "I am too aware of the role of my overzealous imagination interfering in the basic facts of history, so in a way my work is about the sincere attempt to write *Incidents in the Life of a Slave Girl* and winding up with *Mandingo* instead." There is, she concludes, a "collusion of fact and fiction" that has always informed her work.[78]

The scene in *Flight to Canada* in which Stray Leechfield poses naked with the New England girl for pornographic daguerreotypes and Colescott's image of fellatio in *George Washington Carver* similarly dramatize this point. Our cultural "memory" of slavery is made up as much by Hollywood's early roots in minstrelsy and its blaxploitation phase as by any collective knowledge we have based on slave testimony and history. Hence, claims that Walker's work represents the unspeakable horrors of slavery, that it visualizes the horrors that slave narrators like Jacobs could not represent due to censorship and the traumatic nature of sexual and racial oppression, miss the fact that Walker is also signifying on the ways that our own "overzealous" imaginations fill in those blanks.[79]

Similarly, those who decry Walker's work for circulating demeaning images of African Americans ignore the reasoning behind her aesthetic choices. Walker is drawn to racial and sexual stereotypes because, as she puts it, the "bawdy/body" associations on which these stereotypes depend are not simply "awful," they are also the means by which the "black body" is set off "jiggling around" to represent "everything but itself."[80] Much of the humor of the minstrel stage depended on this jiggling of the black body, and Walker signifies on that humor by exposing the violent fantasies it sublimated. Mark Reinhardt's point bears repeating: Walker is not only grounded in the past, for the medley of allusions that characterize her work suggests that the political unconscious of her country remains populated by those fantasies.

In her 1997 Renaissance Society show Walker included an image that exemplifies her preoccupation with stereotypes as repositories of fantasies. The image depicts a young (black) girl in the role of a nanny, holding a younger (white) boy, his naked behind held close to her big lips. In the figure, both the girl's lips and the child's behind protrude toward each other, exhibiting a mixture of desire (in the literal extension of body parts), pornography (mouth to anus), and immorality (nanny's mouth to boy's behind). The result is a preposterous incongruity of images and concepts that juxtaposes the past signified through icons of slavery with our present act of viewing, and the almost tangible contours of the silhouette with the illusionary effect of the image. Like any grotesque image, and much like Colescott's mammy in I Gets a Thrill, this silhouette awakens openly contradictory effects: surprise, perhaps discomfort, in the face of a resolutely unsentimental image of slavery and of childhood; delight at the complexity of associations produced by Walker's manipulation of a simple form; and laughter, albeit laughter "fit to kill," produced by her send-up of the pickaninny stereotype.

Context and scale make every difference. As can be seen in Figure 4.11, at the Renaissance Society show the image was originally mounted on the lower left side of a wall, somewhat dwarfed by the silhouette of a lone, mutilated foot. The foot is not mounted directly on the wall but on gouache. In a more radical way than Goya, Walker provides no firm basis from which to view her images. The foot, already a macabre image, gains potency by virtue of its senseless isolation, notwithstanding whatever unexpressed relation it might have to the children nearby. By the same logic, the pornographic associations of the latter also gain a measure of the macabre.

FIGURE 4.11. Installation detail of Kara Walker, *Presenting Negro Scenes Drawn Upon My Passage Through the South and Reconfigured for the Benefit of Enlightened Audiences, Wherever Such May Be Found, By Myself, Missus K. E. B. Walker, Colored* (1997). Installation at the Renaissance Society at the University of Chicago. Photography by Tom Van Eynde. [See color insert]

The nanny silhouette also points to what Eric Lott calls the intertwined pleasure and terror of the minstrel stage. Exploring this subtext might help explain, or at least suggest, what is haunting and strangely humorous about the more enigmatic presentation of the nanny silhouette in the installation. A good deal of the offensive humor of minstrelsy, its vulgarity, Lott notes, "approximated life in the nursery, whether in the nonsense in songs and puns or tirelessly absurd physical antics." He adds, "The minstrel show's 'black' body offered a terrible return to the gorging and mucus-mongering of early life," and this could be seen in the fetishistic importance that the minstrel show accorded to certain bodily zones—"lips, gaping mouths . . . big heels, huge noses, enormous bustles"—and can even be seen today in the "lingering resonance of the black mammy figure."[81] The mixture of desire and terror that this return afforded was one of the most important elements constituting the pleasure that the minstrel show provided. When Walker presents the nanny figure, she invokes but does not name the racial pleasure that Lott analyzes. The image's emphasis on infantile oral pleasures—one child's mouth to the other's anus—makes explicit what would have been distorted and disguised on the minstrel stage.

The silhouette of the children is reproduced in Walker's pseudo–slave narrative book, where it reaffirms these associations. In the book, the silhouette is presented alone and in larger form following a page bearing another lone but much more recognizable image, that of Topsy. Judging by her neat clothing, this is Topsy after she has been subjected to cousin Ophelia's civilizing magic (in Harriet Beecher Stowe's *Uncle Tom's Cabin*), although there is something of the wild child still evident. Bearing a big slice of watermelon and a grin, Topsy has managed to drop another big slice on the floor. Oblivious and smiling, she looks out from under a big hat, under which a few of her pickaninny dreadlocks protrude. In Walker's book, this image is presented so that when one turns the page, the image of the nanny-boy silhouette reveals itself as the image underneath, as in a pop-up book (Walker has actually produced a full-length pop-up book, about which more later). One turns the page and, exactly where Topsy would be, on the same side of the next page, one finds a (black) nanny, of Topsy's age and height, about to lick a (white) boy's behind (Figure 4.12).

The difference in these two versions of the nanny-boy silhouette exemplifies two different approaches in Walker's presentation of her work. In the first instance, she suspends direct references and clear connections, creating the kind of disconcerting effect that Goya created in his *Caprichos* and that has fueled much of the protest against Walker's work. At the same time, this disconcerting effect also establishes that a vital aspect of the value of her work is in keeping viewers on edge.[82] Her images haunt the imagination because they are often, in various degrees, partly familiar, partly bizarre. Sometimes too, as in the pop-up effect of the Topsy-nanny contrast, they are also disarmingly humorous.

FIGURE 4.12. Installation detail of Kara Walker, *Presenting Negro Scenes Drawn Upon My Passage Through the South and Reconfigured for the Benefit of Enlightened Audiences, Wherever Such May Be Found, By Myself, Missus K. E. B. Walker, Colored* (1997). Installation at the Renaissance Society at the University of Chicago. Photography by Tom Van Eynde.

In this sense, Walker liberates Topsy while presenting minstrelsy with its clothes off. She turns a medium she considered "too obvious" for her—"characters from the culture of slavery"—into fodder for her own aesthetic joke; she visually exposes the subtext of minstrelsy and suggests that, though Topsy may be gone, her shadow or silhouette remains. Walker thus implies a haunting, but rather than giving the ghost of minstrelsy gothic qualities, she gives it a mischievous agency instead. Still, her visual joke does not minimize the violence of minstrelsy's subtext. On the contrary, it highlights it. Withholding direct reference to the ghost of minstrelsy while making its acts so emphatically clear makes Walker's conjuring all the more powerful. I would wager that part of the discomfort the image provokes in the installation is precisely due to this dual act of withholding and specifying. In this discomforting context, the proximate image of the dismembered foot in Figure 4.11 connects one kind of violent act common to slavery, maiming, to another form of violence: the use and abuse of the black body as an object against which to project fantasies of abjection.

In the book that reproduces the image, the artist takes a different strategy: she withholds nothing, providing, in a pornographic narrative that runs through the pseudo–slave narrative *Kara Walker*, explicit details about a sexual triangle between a young master, a young black woman he sexually subjugates, and the male slave with whom she subsequently has sexual encounters. The eventual bloody revenge the master takes on the male slave, like the rest of the plot, is not surprising, especially to those familiar with the texts and images that Walker draws from: the anonymously published volume of racial-sexual fantasy called *The Master's Revenge* (Star Distributors, 1988) and blaxploitation films, parts of which she literally reproduces. She delivers this familiar plot in a style that creates a connection between racist pornography and the underlying principles of minstrel vulgarity. She operates through jarring temporal shifts, switches in narrative perspective (from first-, to second-, to third-person narration), and surprising changes in tone (from desire to lust to anger to shame and everything in between). Creating a narrative version of the grotesque, she shifts rapidly between these perspectives without warning, so that the narrator suddenly morphs from master to slave to a nameless third-person pornographer and back again. The reader occupies the role of the spectator only intermittently, as he or she can suddenly become the "you" accused of sexual enslavement or the "I" confessing both hatred and desire. The writing, although powerful in its sarcasm, is never as successful as Walker's images because it lacks the mixture of grace and comic glee that gives the imagery its haunting, paradoxical power.

In her silhouette work Walker also makes more effective use of allusion. She tantalizes her audiences with meanings that she does not make explicit. Again, her dual gesture toward specifying and withholding gives her work an energy that is largely missing in her sometimes too explicit written work. In *Consume*

FIGURE 4.13. Kara Walker, *Consume* (1998). Cut paper and adhesive on wall, 69 x 32 inches. Image courtesy of Sikkema Jenkins & Co.

(1998; Figure 4.13), Walker presents an image akin to the nanny-boy silhouette in that it makes explicit the libidinal fantasies of blackface minstrelsy. Everything in the image seems to be more than one thing at once: a young (black) woman who sucks on her own breast wears a Josephine Baker–style skirt of bananas, one of which a small (white) boy sucks so that, as David Frankel puts it, "fruit becomes penis, girl becomes boy, the body becomes food, and sex becomes both nurture and cannibalism."[83]

This image certainly contains the morphing of the comic grotesque, which produces a startling sense of the "possible absurd" through unstable meanings and perspectives in a far more immediate way than Walker's writing. By contrasting the long female figure, a graceful giant, with the rotund stubby boy, Walker creates visual humor out of bodily incongruity. Like Colescott's mammy in *George Washington Carver*, the young woman's belly protrudes and her buttocks extend, but she forms an elegant curve as she engages in her own pleasure. The skirt of bananas suggests something of the primitive even as details such as her neatly piled hair, her heeled shoes, her long fingers, and her delicate bracelet suggest a civilized, even elegant persona. If she is meant to signify blackness as savagery, in the traditional racist iconography that the skirt invokes, she is also not threatening but childlike in her sexual deviancy (she is, after all, literally linked to a child through the act of sucking). Similarly, if the boy is meant to signify the opposite—whiteness as civilization—he seems too puny for the role. In fact, Walker dwarfs him not only by placing him next to the female giant, but by placing him in the subservient, albeit impossible, role of performing fellatio on her. Characteristically, Walker has colored them both black and, unlike the nanny-boy figures, linked them in an act of comfort that is far from the lustful sex of Walker's writing and rather more like the pleasures of the nursery to which

Lott refers. Perhaps most important, the figures, like all of Walker's, seem perfectly content, as if they have been going about their business without our gaze and will continue to do so after we look away.

The allusion to Josephine Baker's skirt of bananas both indexes the colonial fetishization of the black female body and suggests a self-reflective commentary on Walker's part regarding the risks involved in using humor in her work. Baker, who combined sex appeal and comedy in her dance performances, used her skirt of bananas to flesh out but also to mock the primitive persona that she established in her debut in Paris in 1925. As critics have noted, Baker "sought to command some authority in her self-production" as the primitive sexualized Other, particularly by using "a form of feminine sexuality that when combined with her ethnic notions, or those projected onto her, made people laugh."[84] A beautiful and gifted dancer, Baker exaggerated stereotypes of black female sexuality by performing numbers such as the "Danse Sauvage" in minimal, "primitive" costume: bare breasted but with feathers, wings, and other such signifiers attached to her extremities. Often, she would be chased and captured on stage by white hunters.

She also infused her acts with a clownish disposition. As Susan Gubar puts it, "Throughout her career, Baker sauced her sexual numbers with comically exaggerated, antic gestures [she was known to cross her eyes in burlesque fun] that distanced her from the sexual frenzy she was putting on display."[85] Baker made it a point to contrast her on- and offstage personas to emphasize the artifice of her act. Offstage she was a sophisticated and glamorous beauty and, later in her career, a devoted civil rights promoter.

Yet Baker was so typecast by her stage role that she had a great deal of difficulty when she tried to "develop her singing and acting in pursuit of a more sophisticated persona in the 1930s."[86] In particular, she became almost synonymous with her skirt of bananas, which took on a life of its own. "Oh! How this idea has turned ridiculous!" Baker said of the costume. "How many drawings and caricatures it has inspired! Only the devil, apparently, could have invented something like that."[87] While the identity of the costume designer remains unknown, Baker's appeal in her primitive guise is all too clear. As Terri Francis argues, "Baker became the banana belt," thus inadvertently conflating two forms of colonialist consumption: that of a colonial product that, like sugar, tobacco, or coffee, has frequently been associated with pleasure, and that of black female bodies.[88] During the 1930s, she made overt efforts to work against her typecasting, especially by adding androgynous twists to her act. She also redefined her famous skirt. As Michael Borshuk notes, she turned the bananas into "absurd signifier[s] of black male phallic threat."[89] As early as 1927, the bananas had "become ever harder and more threatening," so that they looked more like spikes than bananas.[90]

In this context, Walker's *Consume* assumes even greater intensity of meaning. Who consumes? Like the nanny-boy silhouette and Baker's dance persona and performances, *Consume* is aesthetically beautiful in its contours and erotically suggestive in its content. At the same time, the bananas in Walker's skirt, like Baker's in 1927, look more like phallic spikes than bananas. Rather than simply expose or satirize the subtext of minstrelsy, Walker, through the formal qualities of her work, makes it alluring. This is arguably what makes her work so unnerving. Yet Walker also frees that subtext from the black body since, even as she uses black figures to represent it, all of her figures are black. In this sense, everyone consumes and is consumed. This was certainly not the case when Baker performed. Her public ultimately became captivated by "a bunch of bananas animated as a beautiful dancing girl, transformed by colonialist fantasy," and not by the burlesque that she, at least partly, intended.[91]

Unlike Baker, who burlesqued her performance as the consumable Other through self-mockery on stage, Walker dispenses with the spectator-performer relationship. Her silhouettes do not represent people performing for the voyeuristic consumption of others, but instead play out a shared political unconscious, though in different registers. Still, the fact that Baker was typecast by the fantasy that she tried to mock suggests some of the risks involved in Walker's work. While she deftly manipulates the economic visual language of the stereotype and the silhouette, she risks having that same language work for the facile consumption of her images. Walker's audiences may rather quickly register the libidinal pleasures that she exposes in connection to "black" imagery, without exploring the ironic ways she democratizes blackness and the urges that she exposes.

In Walker, then, there are higher stakes and greater risks than in Colescott. Colescott was originally drawn to stereotypical imagery culled from the culture of slavery in order to control it, to make it "say something" for him; Walker, by contrast, is interested in the imagery's mischievous agency. As I noted earlier, she claims that she lets her characters "jump into life without [her] really controlling them," making vivid the agency that stereotypes attain over time. How would they act if they could move on their own? her work implicitly asks. How would they behave without Harriet Beecher Stowe, Thomas Dixon (*The Clansman* inspired Walker to create her Negress alter ego), or even Kara Walker controlling them? They would, according to Walker's major conceit, take over entire rooms, melding history and psychology, social relations and internal identity, desire and nightmares.

Without the screen effect that the silhouette provides, however, and the comic glee with which Walker summons her characters, that mixture would be maddening. The silhouette form allows Walker to suggest human figures without actually claiming to represent them, and thus the viewer is not, as in an actual performance (such as Baker's), confronted with the human body carrying the burden of representation. Instead, Walker presents shadow plays in which the "actors" seem content to perform for themselves and, at best, for each other without an actual stage or the outside gaze of spectators. None of Walker's figures looks directly toward the viewer, and none of them seems to need or want a response. Instead, they are gleefully busy, carrying out their bizarre plots in pantomime. In a few cases, Walker presents her silhouettes with accompanying writing, but it is never directly identified as a description of, or the voice of, or even a footnote to the images. Instead, Walker depends on gesture to signify emotion and action. Strangely, those emotions very rarely include vulnerable ones such as pathos, shame, or surprise, even though the action often entails wild acts of cruelty or bizarre gestures of elation (as in Figure 4.3). The intensity of implied emotion coupled with the seeming silence of the figures suggests censorship, but it also leaves open the possibility that language is simply off limits.

In Walker's panoramic friezes, absurd humor attains the aura of the carnival or the circus in large part because they present several different scenes of busy action, often with no clear relation to each other, but with a common denominator: the playful yet sinister intertwining of fact and fiction that we have been examining. In *Slavery! Slavery!* (1997; Figure 4.14), for example, Walker once again uses the characters of her pseudo–slave narrative: we find the Negress at the center of a scene that seems to depict, among other things, a (white) master shackled to a (black) male slave. The title's repetition and exclamation marks (how could one *clamor* for slavery?) introduce a circus of absurdity.

FIGURE 4.14. Installation detail of Kara Walker, *Slavery! Slavery! Presenting a GRAND and LIFELIKE Panoramic Journey* . . . at the Walker Art Center for the exhibition "no place (like home)," 1997. Cut paper and adhesive on wall, 12 x 85 feet. Photography by Dan Dennehy for the Walker Art Center, Minneapolis. [See color insert]

The layout encourages a left-to-right reading: a child in circuslike wide pan-taloons and fez sprays something out of an old-fashioned perfume bottle at a (white) woman who is holding a comically simplified (black) mask with woolly hair and big hoop earrings. She walks toward a (white) man prostrating before the off-center "wench" (in penance? adoration?), facing in one direction even as he farts in the other. Meanwhile, the precariously balanced Negress oscil-lates between the ridiculous and the horrifying. Except for the mossy tree with its dangling ropes, there is nothing ominous about the image. And yet, when one looks closer, we see that the Negress is balancing on a skull that supports a monkey figure. It, in turn, supports the source or the remains of the liquid that spews out of nearly every one of the nude's orifices. The liquid could be any-thing from water to blood to breast milk. Still, she delicately holds what looks like a cotton flower in her right hand. On the other side of the fountain figure stand the master and slave, who we can now discern from each other—the slave, it turns out, is shackled to himself and labeled with a blank (read: black) rib-bon. Behind them are other barely distinguishable images engaged in their own, obscured dramas.

Walker conjures enigmatic rituals with these life-size entities, which she has freed from the dramas in which we are used to seeing them: Harriet Beecher Stowe's famous novel, the minstrel stage (where Stowe's book attained theatrical life), racist pornography, and blaxploitation films. In her pseudo–slave narrative, Walker includes an essay in which she refers to her figures as "stereotypes at-tempting to confront their own displacement."[92] Yet in the silhouettes we have ex-amined the figures seem too busy to be concerned with their displacement; many of them seem instead to rejoice in it. They have been let loose to perform, with total abandon, the fantasies that have been projected onto them for centuries.

In this sense, the busy sequences in Walker's installations approach the car-nivalesque spirit with which Colescott renders the comic grotesque of race in America. These sequences invoke the chaotic potential of circuses and suggest the freakishness of Walker's images. But if Walker's images are bizarre, it is not because they represent human anomalies but because they depict the "freakish psychological mutations" that have "flourish[ed] in the hothouse of racially divi-sive history."[93] Yet Walker does not set off her figures in a liminal realm, as if they were circus freaks, but displays them on the walls of art galleries and museums, thus making them part of public and official life. She also peppers her scenarios with historical markers (some obvious, as in the title *Slavery! Slavery!*; others subtle, as in the cotton flower) so that her figures cannot be dismissed as merely fantastical.

Walker envelops her viewers in the various contradictions on which her work turns. With the panoramic frieze, she intends to evoke the effect of the nineteenth-century cyclorama, a predecessor of film and an early method of mobilizing images. From "the moment that I started working on [the silhou-ettes]," she has said, "I imagined that some day they would be put together in a kind of cyclorama ... just like the Cyclorama in Atlanta that goes around and around in an endless cycle of *history locked up in a room.*"[94] The intended effect of the cyclorama is to make viewers feel as if they were standing in the center of a historic event or famous place, surrounded by a panoramic image. By contrast, Walker surrounds viewers with her intricate play between the factual and the fictional. An expanded version of *Slavery! Slavery!* gives a sense of the scale and depth of her work (Figure 4.15).

Walker can be quite open about her intent. "What I want to happen in my work," she told me in an interview, "the action I want to set in motion," is to have the viewer "go from a place of recognition, of the familiar, to a place of fic-tion, the make-believe, back into fact and then through a place of hyperreality, a place of the absurd, the 'too weird,' the 'too-out-there.'"[95] Even a brief history of the Cyclorama in Atlanta, Walker's frame of reference, suggests some of this dynamic action. Originally commissioned by John A. Logan, a vice presidential

FIGURE 4.15. Kara Walker, *Slavery! Slavery! Presenting a GRAND and LIFELIKE Pan-oramic Journey* ... at the Walker Art Center for the exhibition "no place (like home)," 1997. Cut paper and adhesive on wall, 12 x 85 feet. Photography by Dan Dennehy for the Walker Art Center, Minneapolis. [See color insert]

candidate who had commanded Union forces during the Civil War, the Cyclorama is a cylindrical painting (apparently the largest oil painting in the world) depicting the Battle of Atlanta, in which Confederate soldiers unsuccessfully defended their city on July 22, 1864. The painting was sold and ended up in the hands of a traveling circus, which eventually went bankrupt. The circus sold its animals to the Zoo Atlanta, and the painting was then housed next to the zoo. Today it still resides next to Zoo Atlanta but in a building designed to conserve it. Noting that the Cyclorama has been on display in Atlanta since 1893, the City of Atlanta Office of Cultural Affairs calls it "the longest running show in the United States."[96]

As if spoofing this description of the Cyclorama, Walker surrounds viewers with friezes that detail the drama of race in America, surely a likelier candidate for the longest running show in the country. This drama, whether expressive of the libidinal pleasures of infancy to which we have been referring or the cannibalism of race, is very often underwritten by the will to murder, as in the panoramic frieze *Virginia's Lynch Mob* (1998; Figure 4.16).[97] In this case, the layout of the silhouettes encourages a right-to-left reading, which renders, in a loose narrative, the energy, the excitement, generated by a lynching about to happen. The characters jump, march, and run while performing distinct acts, all absurd on their own, that together give a sense of ritual death in the making.

Starting on the right, the frieze presents two frightful figures running and leaping, one a dopey, gangly boy with a simian gait, the other a masked, one-legged human creature with a branch coming out of its anus. In front of them

FIGURE 4.16. Kara Walker, *Virginia's Lynch Mob* (1998). Cut paper and adhesive on paper, 10 x 37 feet. Image courtesy of Sikkema Jenkins & Co. [See color insert]

a large man twirls a lasso while a boy hangs from his neck. Then, as a girl holds a Klan mask at shoulder height, a man leads himself by a rope tied to his neck while dragging a boy who looks back at the girl with the Klan mask. A boy shoots his brains out, his bowl hat neatly flying away. A girl behind him looks away in horror. The sequence ends as a large man in a high hat, his head bent back and about to come off his neck, beats an enormous drum out of which a Negress flies, seemingly freed. But freed from what? As with the rest of the frieze, this image does not, cannot make sense. Still, for all of its absurdity, the frieze also contains enough familiar signifiers (the rope, the Klan mask) to suggest a possible narrative with a historical basis.

The only clearly ominous image in the frieze is off to the far right, above the figures. It is that of an eagle devouring another eagle, the symbolism of which cannot be missed. The image recalls the lyrics of one of the racist tunes that William Wells Brown appropriates in *The Escape*. In a song that is ostensibly an ode to the North Star, the slave Glen critiques the "burning lust / For gold" that enslaves him and his brethren:

> *This* nation to the Eagle cowers;
>> Fit ensign! she's a bird of spoil:—
> Like worships like! for each devours
>> The earnings of another's toil. (*The Escape*, 39)

In Walker's frieze, one eagle consumes the other while flying over a human ritual that is equally horrific but staged on a much grander scale. The image presents a more terrifying version of the appropriately titled *Consume* but with a greater sense of glee. Walker conjures racism as a cannibalistic force propelling its agents to destroy, to possess, to consume the Other, each other, themselves. She avoids the traps of victimization and guilt, which are so often filtered through the binary of black/white and, in the discourses of slavery, that of slave/master, by making all her figures black and difficult to distinguish as individual agents. In *Virginia's Lynch Mob*, everyone participates. In fact, the frieze is framed by two figures: a pickaninny on the right and a wench on the left, both beating sticks as if keeping the ritual's time. And yet, it is clear that the scene is a lynching in the making and that, as the title alone suggests, it is meant to invoke the brutal racial violence of American history.

I have, of course, chosen among Walker's large number of friezes and individual silhouettes the ones that contain both horror *and* glee. But I have made these choices because I find them more powerful than the ones that are more directly horrific and pornographic. The glee in Walker's work produces the quintessential distance of humor, but it heightens rather than dilutes or diverts the horror to which it signals. At the same time, the signifiers of horror make the glee sinister. The combination raises the seminal question of Reed's *Flight to Canada*: what is fact and what is fiction in the strange and complicated history of slavery? Walker intensifies this question by positioning her viewers inside her disorienting cycloramas, by denying them the usual coordinates for interpretation. In so doing, she keeps alive an aphorism common in slave narratives: in American slavery, truth may be stranger than fiction. Yet Walker also suggests that the fictions through which slavery is mediated may be stranger than fact.

Walker's intricate play of fact and fiction is surely a luxury afforded by time. As Teresa Goddu has shown, that fact could outdo fiction proved a great challenge to slave narrators. Harriet Jacobs, for instance, found that in attempting to represent the unspeakable acts that she suffered and witnessed as a slave, those acts resembled fiction because they were so outrageous. Like other slave narrators, she employed gothic conventions because they offered useful metaphors for representing experiences that, "written as a realist text," resembled "a gothic narrative." But gothic narrative constructions "could also empty history by turning [experience] into gothic tropes" that could be read as effect "rather than reality."[98] Hence Jacobs and other slave narrators used but revised the gothic to prevent history from being subsumed by the fictional conventions that were so useful for representing the horrors of slavery.

As we have seen, the gothic reappears in Walker's work as one of the many mediums through which slavery is mediated. Because her work is not mimetic or testimonial, she is not concerned about the validity of her visual narratives. Instead, she produces wonder. What were the terrors beyond what the gothic could and did represent? How do our overzealous imaginations fill in the gaps left by historical and fictional records? And how does the specter of the terror of slavery leave its traces on the political unconscious of the now? By raising these questions, indeed, by creating environments in which viewers experience the thoughts and emotions prompted by these questions, Walker, like Reed, keeps the discourses of slavery from being reified. At the same time, she keeps viewers wondering how and why our language and imagination may be shaped by those discourses.

Letter from a Black Girl, *or, a Postscript on the Risks of Co-optation*

Recently Kara Walker has been experimenting with more dramatic ways of taking over spaces by projecting onto darkened rooms great swathes of colored lights and black shadows to complement her silhouettes. The lights engulf the rooms, spilling onto the floor and ceiling. She thus creates environments in which the viewer becomes part of the work, since the viewer too casts a shadow, which mixes with the ones Walker has cut and mounted. This new development accentuates Walker's ability to link the past and the now, as the present act of viewing is literally intertwined with the iconography of slavery. It also makes palpable her conjuring of the "shadowy bits" that populate not only her own but also the national psyche.[99]

Though Walker has successfully seduced a great many through her dark humor, aesthetically pleasing drawings, and historically charged conjuring of slavery's legacy, she has also provoked a fury of resistance. Walker skyrocketed into prominence in the art world in the late 1990s, becoming the recipient of a MacArthur "genius" award (as did Reed, but at a much later point in his career) and a widely exhibited artist in the United States and abroad. However, because her strategies do not always engage viewers, she has also drawn fierce opposition from fellow artists, critics, curators, and viewers at large. For many, her explicit representation of racial stereotypes in blunt, bawdy, and carnivalesque scenarios are ultimately *only* repulsive and her instigating aesthetics nothing more than "sassy impudence."[100]

Walker's strongest detractors fixate determinedly on the stereotypes her images emphasize and decry her refusal to navigate her viewers in processing their effect. In the fall of 1999, Walker's *A Means to an End: A Shadow Drama in Five Acts* (1995) was pulled from a show at the Detroit Institute for the Arts because museum directors felt her images should be accompanied with "didactic material" that would help viewers "understand the work and the artist's intent."[101] Similarly, fellow visual artist Betye Saar has been leading the opposition against Walker's work and has publicly chastised her for irresponsibly recycling demeaning racial and sexual stereotypes.[102] For Saar, as for many who are insulted by her work, Walker not only endlessly repeats painful imagery but also makes it insufferable by making it "bigger than life" and mute.[103]

The fact that Walker is collected and circulated mainly among affluent white audiences, moreover, creates what Miles Unger calls an "uneasy alliance" between white privilege and black performance and fuels the tensions her works have produced.[104] Eerily recalling Reed's charge of "pornography" against Stowe and Leechfield's commodification of his "art," critics focus on the price collectors are willing to pay for Walker's work ($30,000 to $80,000 per silhouette). They claim that she has built a profitable career by literally banking on prurient fantasies that reaffirm stereotypes that people have struggled for centuries to annul, that she depends on shock to gain notoriety and market value. "What is it about our society that embraces [Walker's] imagery?" Saar wonders.[105]

Others object to the fact that Walker's projects, and similar work by other artists, notably Michael Ray Charles, are being exclusively selected by major art institutions (for example, the Whitney Museum in New York) as representative of contemporary African American art, thereby narrowing the exposure of all the other work now being produced. Added to this is the fact that, as young artists, Walker and Charles are separated by age from the generation of people who directly experienced the civil rights struggle (Saar included) and whose memories of it render them particularly sensitive to stereotypes. "How do young persons just a few years out of school get a show at a major art museum?" Saar asks. The issue is not just the generation gap, however; it also involves the muddied politics of representation and race. "The whole arts establishment picked their work up and put it at the head of the class," Saar continues. "This is the danger, not the artists themselves. This is the closet racism. It relieves them of the responsibility to show other artists."[106]

As the educational director of the Renaissance Society in Chicago suggests, older artists like Saar "want to protect" audiences from controversial imagery. "But can anyone ever control an image?"[107] In voodoo terms, one might similarly argue, as Reed does to some extent, that "mean-minded" readers and viewers might not "recognize" the conjure of Walker's work. The challenge of sifting through what is fact and what is fiction in the work of Reed, Colescott, and Walker is not easy, despite the magnified qualities of their satire. Walker's refusal to provide her viewers with explicit commentary or references for her work gives her conjure the ambivalence that exists between the voodoo houngan and the boco/"black magician." While Walker consciously signifies on this ambivalence, she operates without enough ritual codes that would make her conjure widely accessible. Her forms, the silhouette and stereotype, seem easy to read, yet ironically they are illegible to those viewers to whom the contexts and allusions she employs are obscure. This is not to say that Walker should provide "didactic" material, but rather that she might mediate more between her potentially dangerous zombielike images and her audience, which, at least in the United States, can be quite disengaged from slavery's history and grossly unconscious of its legacy.

This is perhaps why Walker has tried to make her concerns more explicit in her shows. In her 1998 Wooster Gardens project, for example, she included a shocking image with an empty caption floating above the shadows in a cloudlike formation. The image, titled *Successes*, presents a (white) master receiving fellatio from a (black) female slave. Both figures are missing limbs and have animal features (fur, paws, tails). While the empty caption suggests Walker's refusal to make her intent explicit, the image it accompanies was presented in obvious conjunction with two other images, each mounted on opposing walls on either side of it in a small room. One of them is a letter with which Walker covers a wall using large cut-out words that simulate the look of words on a page. *Letter from a Black Girl* angrily voices the denunciations of a girl who, like the woman in the first image, is subjected to her master's pleasures. Read as connected images, the letter and the figure ironically present the master as voiceless and bestial. They also suggest opposing views of the girl: whereas in the image she is animalized, in the letter she becomes an author with a vital voice, a voice with which she simultaneously denounces the master's crimes and leaves evidence of it for the future.[108]

As when we read Reed's outrageous portrayal of Master Swille, however, we are tempted to ask, What is fact and what is fiction in this horrible drama? Though the combined images at once evoke a more direct critique of slavery's injustices, they still leave room for ambiguity. The whole scenario is utterly exaggerated: from the figures' gross anatomies to the pornographic explicitness of the action, to the huge silhouette and letters of the girl's text and her seething, murderous anger. The result is an obscene shadow play of crime and rage which may accurately evoke the realities of the sexual oppression of captives but which attains notes of hyperbole in Walker's representation. Like Reed's narrative visions, Walker's silhouettes are poised not only between fact and fiction, but also between the past and the present, stasis and mobility. Like zombies, they are dead and thus inert and immobile (they are, after all, stuck on a wall) but also alive (in the emotions they evoke and the associations they produce).

But there is yet more ambiguity in these images. Through the "pounding rhythms" of her diction, the girl directs her loathing toward a slave owner but also, less clearly, toward a man who might, like her, be black.[109] The letter, which suggests a double oppression of black women under slavery and patriarchy, also uneasily evokes a connection to the third silhouette, which depicts a black woman's suicide.[110] Do Walker's apparent interventions help make this scene more accessible? Certainly the web of connections she suggests among all three images prevents one from reading any one of them in a literal or superficial way. The suicide suggests the girl's defeat, but the letter tells of her partial triumph in leaving evidence of the crime of which the master is apparently guilty. Also, because there is no way of telling which image is meant to be read first, the threads of narrative one can weave are many. Confronted by such quandaries, the viewer may actually opt for escape rather than engagement. As Walker herself suggests, sometimes her images actually provide the means to do just that since they can often be dainty enough to allow "the viewer an out" so that he or she doesn't "have to [really] see."[111] The delicacy of some of her drawings can soften the shock of her images and allow viewers to bypass the difficult questions they raise.

In fact, what makes Walker so provocative and problematic is that, unlike Reed and Colescott, she does not formally replay the ugliness of the grotesque. There is much that is beautiful in her drawings whereas beauty is largely absent in Reed's narrative and Colescott's paintings. Though there is much that is genius in *Flight to Canada*, it is not a work one savors for its poetic beauty. The pleasure it elicits comes mainly from its outlandish humor, its imaginative blend of styles, cultural references, and epistemological and hermeneutical propositions regarding slavery. Similarly, Colescott's paintings provide various forms of "thrills," whether through their spoofing of master works and stereotypes or through their elaborate reconfiguration of what we value when we see art. But their garish colors and cartoonish line forms do not please the eye. Walker's images, on the other hand, seek to trick the eye into seeing the brutal and horrific and to confront its libidinal pull. "I keep trying to make the work pretty enough that people's offenses won't pan out so thoroughly," Walker has said, "their sense of revulsion will sort of peter out at some point, as they're overwhelmed by a kind of desire."[112] This is what gives her work its charge, but it is also what makes it potentially dangerous.

For some, the fact that Walker's work has produced controversy makes it powerful and necessary since it opens collective discussion and debate about the meaning of stereotypes. Lowery Stokes Simms, the African American curator of twentieth-century art at the Metropolitan Museum of Art, has said that Walker's work encourages conversation about "our relationship to this imagery . . . about what is going on inside of us . . . [and our] concern with how the outside world is looking at these images."[113] At the Harvard University Conference on Racist Imagery, "Change the Joke and Slip the Yoke," held in conjunction with an exhibit of Walker's art at one of the university's museums, various African American panelists discussed the complex power of the relics of America's racist past. Henry Louis Gates Jr. publicly defended Walker's work but expressed "his horror of the anti-black imagery in toys, dolls and drawings that began to proliferate during the post-slavery era." The panel discussion revolved around the "strong and persistent attraction" that "black memorabilia" still has for us.[114] Julian Bond, the chairman of the NAACP, and Lowery Stokes Sims described their own collections of kitsch dolls, which pointedly depict racial stereotypes and speak to both heritage and pain. Sims suggested that her own attraction to the images has to do with the haunting visibility they have given African Americans: "in an odd sort of way," the fact that these images have had quotidian exposure in American households "kept black people at the center of American consciousness. We didn't disappear into a reservation, we didn't disappear into the fringes, we were everywhere."[115]

Although some of Walker's proponents are willing to entertain the idea that black memorabilia and associated imagery can have positive effects, they are concerned with the ways they can be co-opted and commodified. "Face it, we are in a society that commodifies everything," one has said. "We are not going to get away from that."[116] Of all the "strange" facts that could support this concern, none is more complicated than the Norton family's support of Walker's work. With a fortune made from a late twentieth-century computer invention, the Norton Anti-Virus software, Peter and Eileen Norton, an interracial couple with a high-profile cultural image in Los Angeles, commissioned Walker to make a Christmas pop-up book to be distributed among their many friends, including artists, curators, dealers, and critics. Produced in a print run of four thousand copies, Walker's book *Freedom: A Fable by Kara Elizabeth Walker—A Curious Interpretation of the Wit of a Negress in Troubled Times with Illustrations* depicts an ex-slave woman's dream of going to Liberia, "a land where brown skin means nothing," and where it will be "her duty to become a god."[117] The book includes text by Walker and four double-spread silhouette pop-ups that form a nonliteral illustration of the story. These remarkably detailed pop-ups depict an antebellum plantation, a desert isle with the dreaming protagonist, a scatological scene, and the protagonist giving birth while smoking a pipe. Cut entirely by laser beam, the images "were created at . . . one of only two firms in the country utilizing this technique, mostly applied to glitzy corporate publicity."[118] According to reviews, the recipients were fully seduced by Walker; indeed, they were "overwhelmed by desire." "I can't remember the last time I was so thoroughly delighted on opening a Christmas present," said one who found the book to be "an utterly splendid object."[119]

There is something eerily off about this story. Although the Nortons have a reputation for supporting many social organizations, especially those in the arts and with progressive agendas, their Christmas gift ironically makes Walker's work a high-value "glitzy" commodity.[120] One wonders, if Walker is paid $30,000 to $80,000 per silhouette, how much did she get paid for the book? Producing the gift entailed an enormous amount of work (and money) that was not Walker's. After the images were cut with laser beams, they were sent to a bookbinding firm, where twenty people in two teams took ten months to assemble the images by hand. Is it appropriate to give such an elaborate gift representing racial and sexual distortions, fantasies, and echoes of a difficult and painful history, especially during a religious holiday? Though the Nortons have explicitly stated their goal of supporting nonmoralistic art that is accessible to everyone and not just those specialized in the arts, we have to wonder exactly what kind of "delight" their recipients got from Walker's work. Were they seduced by the "glitzy" production the same way they might be seduced by "corporate publicity"? Did the seduction ever lead them to the deeper work of introspection Walker's work can elicit?

While those who object to Walker's work on the grounds that it is degrading to black people miss her powerful comedy of the grotesque, those who caution against its commodification are right to worry about the potential dispossession of its power. Walker's panoramic friezes of violence and perversity do not claim to mirror the realities of the black experience in America. What they do represent is the disturbing and "freakish psychological mutations" produced by slavery and its legacy. But as Walker signifies on the market of prurient fantasies slavery produced and questions their currency, she runs the danger of having her images co-opted for ambiguous and unexamined pleasures.

The higher risk, however, may be in not taking the risk at all. By obfuscating identities and agents, the real and the fantastic in her shadow plays, and by creating environments in which her viewers cannot be mere spectators, Walker explores the impolite, even crude desires and impulses produced by slavery *without* the usual language of victim and victimizer. I hasten to add: Walker does not minimize the importance of testifying to victimization or the clear need to identify victimizers, as a work such as *Letter from a Black Girl* shows. Yet her work, like Reed's, focuses on keeping the history of slavery from becoming ossified. Like Reed, she also proposes a new lexicon for examining the legacy of slavery in America. Being more leery of projects that turn her work into glitzy commodities may guard Walker's work from the dangers of co-optation; so would more use of the humor we have examined in her work. Aside from providing distance, such humor is a visceral, visual reminder that Walker's dramas are *shadow plays* and not mimetic representations of history or lived reality, however much her silhouettes index both. In *Successes*, together with *Letter from a Black Girl*, she mediates the nuances of her work by making more explicit the libidinal urges that she explores elsewhere, while highlighting the anger of the girl who is victimized by them. But these silhouettes lack the humor we have seen in her other installations and thus lack the power to keep us in the state of wonder that Walker can so masterfully produce.

In "An Extravagance of Laughter," Ellison recalls Charles Baudelaire's keen observation that "a wise man never laughs but that he trembles" and notes that watching Erskine Caldwell's incongruous juxtaposition of stereotypes of blackness superimposed onto white characters made him "tremble even *as* [he] laughed."[121] Walker's disarming ability to create images that are at once beautiful, grotesque, *and* comic produces the possible absurd, leaving us to tremble even as we laugh. The power of that intricate mixture—of the sublime and the absurd—lessens when Walker privileges the more explicitly grotesque or when she capitulates to the commoditization of her work. Judging from her most recent, major exhibitions, "Kara Walker at the Met: After the Deluge" and "Kara Walker: My Complement, My Enemy, My Oppressor, My Love" (at the Whitney Museum of Art), the crucial role that black humor plays in her work is abundantly clear and so is the fact that she will leave her viewers trembling *and* laughing for a long, long time to come.[122]

THE TRAGICOMEDY OF SLAVERY IN SUZAN-LORI PARKS'S
EARLY PLAYS

Judging by the subjects and titles of Suzan-Lori Parks's plays, particularly the early ones, one might conclude that the playwright has a somber imagination. Her first major play, *Imperceptible Mutabilities in the Third Kingdom* (first produced in 1989), concerns some of the most painful aspects of New World slavery. "Open House," the second section of this play, involves a dying slave whose teeth are extracted mercilessly as she recalls a life of dispossession. A character named Miss Faith extracts the slave's teeth while she remembers two children to whom she served as a primary guardian and who may or may not have been her own and a master who may or may not have been the father of the children; the play purposefully leaves this ambiguity open, as if to suggest the intimate levels of oppression in two intersecting and often interchangeable stories, that of the mammy and of the slave mother. Parks's second play, *The Death of the Last Black Man in the Whole Entire World* (1990), by title alone suggests a dark topic. Its titular figure vividly recounts his own death by lynching and electrocution. Similarly, her third major work, *The America Play* (also produced in 1990), presents the repeated shooting of a black man

One could argue that Parks's topics mirror the violence of American history, specifically violence against African Americans. Yet her plays do much more than simply mirror that violence: they underscore the traumatic repetition of New World and American history from the Middle Passage, slavery, and Reconstruction to Jim Crow and its aftermath. Particularly in her early plays, Parks also stages the return of those who perished in this history of genocide and persecution. The dead reinsert themselves among the living, seeking witnesses for their suffering. Both *The Death of the Last Black Man* and *The America Play* are interspersed with rites of burial and mourning, rites through which the dead can give testimony to an audience, and culminate when the main figure can finally rest. "His lonely death and lack of proper burial is our embarrassment," says a wife in *The America Play* about the death of a black father.[1]

Parks's approach to this material is refreshing for she does not depend on elements normally associated with ghosts and haunting, such as the uncanny or the gothic. Instead, she has developed a number of formal strategies to remember aspects of a painful past, including a combined use of the aesthetics of conjure and postmodernism as well as a nuanced and abstract use of the features of minstrelsy. Most important, Parks also experiments with language to produce a kind of humor that is sometimes derived from simple wordplay, as in punning, but that more often becomes part of a larger process of signifyin(g)—an intricate, intratextual and intertextual play of repetition with revision or, as Parks herself calls it, "Rep&Rev" (*AP* 9). In that intricate play, she signifies on the exploitive underpinnings of minstrelsy, underscoring how it continues to haunt the American stage, especially with regard to both black suffering and black laughter.

While minstrelsy's affect, its ghostliness, its residual impact, has preoccupied African American playwrights for decades, Parks distinguishes herself from her fellow dramatists in that, rather than merely parodying the features of minstrelsy, she signifies on such features so expertly that she turns them into vehicles for mourning. Parks develops a tragicomedy that both mocks the ghost of minstrelsy and summons it in order to mourn the dead. In taking up the work of mourning with respect to slavery, however, she undertakes a formidable challenge: how does one stage black suffering without making it into a commoditized spectacle? The challenge recalls Harriet Wilson's predicament in *Our Nig*. Since at least the emergence of gallows literature in America, black suffering has been forced into representational forms inspiring sensationalism and/or prurience. As has been well documented, slave narrators developed elaborate rhetorical strategies to represent the suffering they withstood and witnessed without catering to market demands for sensationalism. The struggle they faced persists in, for example, Saidiya Hartman's decision not to reproduce "one of the most well-known scenes of torture in the literature of slavery," the scene of Aunt Hester's beating in Frederick Douglass's *Narrative* (1845). In the opening pages of *Scenes of Subjection* (1997), Hartman writes that she does not reproduce Douglass's account because too often such scenes "immure us to pain by virtue of their familiarity . . . especially because they reinforce the spectacular character of black suffering."[2]

Each of Parks's plays evidences a finely tuned consciousness regarding the difficulties of representing black suffering, the casualness with which it is still evoked, the spectacle into which it is still made, and the indifference or narcissistic identification that it produces.[3] In *Venus* (1996), her fourth major play, Parks explicitly dramatizes the spectacularization of the black body and sets it against both a narrative of grief and a disarming, disorienting humor. Based on the historical figure of Saartjie Baartman, otherwise known as the Venus Hottentot, the play highlights the intersection of greed, voyeurism, and desire in the story of Baartman, who was exhibited as a circus freak because of her large bottom and distended labia, and whose body, in particular her genitalia, was macerated and shown in the Musée de l'Homme in Paris as late as 1994.

Like Kara Walker, Parks has elicited controversy because she creates a signifying fluidity between her historical subject (Baartman) and her fictional character (*Venus*) and because she refuses to demarcate clear lines between oppressor and oppressed.[4] Thus, rather than restage the story of the historical Baartman, Parks highlights the layers of mediation through which we perceive a figure whose very name, of Dutch origins, only dimly describes the Khoikhoi woman who became the Venus Hottentot. Specifically, Parks underscores how Baartman's stage name is in itself a kind of cruel joke since it yokes together the Roman goddess of love and Hottentot, a name first given to South Africans with cattle, which become a derogatory term (meaning "stutterer" or "stammerer") after Europeans settled in Cape Town.[5] Far from being Venus, object of adoration, Baartman was an object of prurient fetishization.

There are many facts about the historical figure that remain ambiguous or unknown, and Parks, rather than fill in the gaps, heightens them. As Harry Elam and Alice Rayner note, it is "not altogether clear, and was not even [in her lifetime] whether to consider Baartman a willing partner in her spectacle, or an exploited victim; whether to acknowledge her right to display herself or to try to save her from herself."[6] Indentured to the trader Hendrick Ceza Boer, who in 1810 took her from South Africa to England, she was exhibited for profit like an animal in a cage, jailed for prostitution and indecency, and subjected to medical inspection, eventually dying perhaps of alcoholism, pneumonia, tuberculosis, or syphilis.[7] Records indicate that Baartman testified in court, defending her rights to exhibit herself and thus leaving a vague mark on the official records of Europeans, who saw her people as nothing more than "stammerers." In 1996, her body once again became the subject of debate as descendants of the Khoikhoi petitioned the French government for the return of her remains to South Africa for burial; this petition was fulfilled in 2002. As Elam and Rayner note, however, it is not entirely clear that "Baartman was an actual member of the Khoikhoi, so possession of her body continues to beg questions of ownership and meaning of the body. Who has the right to her body?" Who has the right to represent it, view it, or possess it?[8]

Parks's play presents us with a figure known simply as The Girl and, later, The Venus Hottentot, who is pulled into, and is in some ways complicit with, the web of exploitation and greed underscoring colonialism. Yet, by constantly calling attention to the audience's role as spectators of the play, as well as that of the other actors on stage, Parks tempers Saartjie's complicity and calls into question the persistent desire to fetishize the black body. More important, Parks engineers a major reversal of expectations by showing how all those who turned Saartjie into a "freak" are freaks themselves. As Greg Miller argues, more than anything, the play explores how colonialism and later capitalism transform rituals of love into "narcissistic, parodic acts," freak shows, and spectacles of greedy voyeurism in which desire becomes a perverse form of oppression and need.[9]

Parks subjects all of the figures who greedily revolved (and still revolve) around Saartjie to a satire and parody that recalls William Wells Brown's in *The Escape*. She employs hyperbole and burlesque to mock the mockery that slavery and colonialism made of love, marriage, law, and scientific knowledge. Juxtaposed against the exploration of such vexed issues is a story of grief about a woman whose bewildering career as a freak leads to a slow but brutal death. In combining both humor and pathos, Parks, like Chesnutt, creates a distinctive tragicomedy of slavery. Through it Parks stages her own rituals of redress and, more than any of the other post–civil rights artists included in this book, mourns the death and destruction that slavery constituted.

In staging the work of mourning, Parks faces several challenges. While there is a widely disseminated discourse on mourning and notions regarding trauma, mourning today is generally depreciated as a type of melancholic obsession with the past. In this context, to mourn the losses of slavery seems, from certain perspectives, not only melancholic but also strangely belated, even retrograde. Worse yet, to carry on the work of mourning may seem complicit with a trend that Parks firmly criticizes, a myopic obsession in black theater with oppression. As *Venus* and Parks's earlier plays make clear, one of the ways we can have a more responsible and active relationship to the past is to challenge linear notions of time. "Could Time be tricky," Parks wonders in "Elements of Style," "like the world once was—looking flat from our place on it—and through looking at things beyond the world we found it round?" (*AP* 10). If we think of time not as linear but as cyclical, cumulative, repetitive, the act of looking back does not need to be a melancholic act.[10] Parks's early plays suggest that, even if one were to insist on the linearity of time, the monumental force of the Middle Passage and slavery have broken the barriers of time, leaving such experiences still unclaimed for collective consciousness.

Thus, in *Imperceptible Mutabilities*, as in *The Death of the Last Black Man*, time is cyclical. In *The America Play* time also transcends linear periodization, becoming "infinitely repeatable, as in a video."[11] The play takes place in a great hole, which is the "exact replica of the Great Hole of History," a kind of open grave for lost fragments of memory (*AP* 158). The copy of the hole, which is also described as a "chasm" and a "theme park" with historical parades and pageants, is a place where one can witness the repeated shooting of Abraham Lincoln (162). The part of Lincoln is played by a black man who is said to resemble Lincoln so well that he "ought to be shot," and indeed he does get shot, over and over again. As Joseph Roach puts it, it is as if "the Zapruder film ha[d] inspired a macabre Civil War enactment."[12] Assuming the Lincoln costume (the three-piece suit, the stovepipe hat, beard and warts), the impersonator repeatedly laughs at the same joke from *Our American Cousin* while different costumers, in the role of Booth, shoot him again and again and again. In this play, Parks suggests that history, like black suffering, is often made into a spectacle, one that is obsessively watched and consumed but not processed. The negative consequences of this are implicit in the fact that the play portrays the repeated shooting of a black man.

It is therefore imperative that we not only challenge linear notions of time, but also that we recognize the ethical necessity of mourning while criticizing the consumerism of grief. To this end, Parks has developed a metadiscourse on mourning, one that, as S. E. Wilmer notes, "insists on theatrical self-consciousness" in order to complicate the "role of the audience as spectators of real, represented, and revised versions of history."[13] In *The America Play*, for example, Parks features Brazil, a professional mourner, who learns from his father, the Lincoln impersonator, or, as he is referred to in the play, the Faker, parodic acts of mourning: "the Wail," "the Weep," "the Sob," and "the Moan" (*AP* 182). The father teaches the son how "to stand just so what to do with his hands and feet (to capitalize on what we in the business call 'the Mourning Moment')" because "'there is money init' [*sic*]" (182). In the play, Parks distinguishes the kind of mourning that her work dramatizes from the kind that the Faker teaches his son by insisting that her audience process rather than simply consume the mourning her plays enact.

Parks's experiments in language as well as her use of black humor are central to her project. At times referred to as a version of black vernacular, her language does not actually aim to reproduce that vernacular. Instead, as she told Alisa Solomon in an often quoted interview, she has chosen to signify on the varied layers of signification already inscribed in that vernacular. Parks reminds Solomon, "At one time in this country, the teaching of reading and writing to African-Americans was a criminal offense."

> So how do I adequately represent not merely the speech patterns of a people oppressed by language (which is the simple question) but the patterns of a people whose language use is so complex and varied and ephemeral that its daily use not only Signifies on the non-vernacular language forms, but on the construct of writing as well. If language is a construct and writing is a construct and Signifyin(g) on the double construct is the daily use, then I have chosen to Signify on the Signifyin(g).[14]

The result is a "word-sound choreography" that, while evoking the creativity of Black English, "the spontaneity of jive, the ritual storytelling of the beauty parlor, juke joint, or barbershop," incorporates what Parks calls her "foreign words & phrases," which are invented or improvised from spoken English (*AP* 17).[15] Her invented language ranges from scat sounds such as "do in diddly dip didded thuh drop," which she often uses as a "fancy 'yes!'" to sounds that "denote drowning or breathlessness" (17). In between there are more mundane sounds, such as "thuh," a variant of "the," and "iduhnt," a variant of "is not or isn't" (17). Yet even through these less dramatic sounds, Parks produces the musicality of her language.

Through "Rep&Rev" Parks arranges the various aspects of her language in a jazz framework that threads together disparate places and times. She writes, "'Repetition and Revision' is a concept integral to the Jazz esthetic in which the composer or performer will write or play a musical phrase once and again and again; etc.—with each revisit the phrase is slightly revised. . . . Through its use I'm working to create a dramatic text that departs from the traditional linear narrative style to look and sound more like a musical score" (AP 8–9).[16] *Imperceptible Mutabilities*, for example, is essentially four plays that Parks links through verbal riffs and repetitions into a whole. The first part concerns three black women in a contemporary time frame who are being bugged for observation by a doctor figure; the second concerns the Middle Passage; the third is loosely located in antebellum America; and the fourth concerns an African American family in the mid-twentieth century. In between the last two parts is a reprise of the second part so that the play moves backward even as it moves forward. The four different parts, which together give a sense of the African American experience from the Middle Passage through the late twentieth century, can be performed independently but are designed to signify on each other, thus creating intratextual, as well as intertextual, links. Each relates to the other via linguistic refrains that have the effect of evoking the presence of the dead in the language of the living.

Significantly, Parks does not evoke such presence with language that is out of the ordinary but with displaced echoes of simple phrases that change slightly in diction, intonation, spelling, or context. The first section of *Imperceptible Mutabilities* opens with a character named Molly considering suicide: "Should I jump should I jump or what?" (AP 26). In a later section concerning the Middle Passage, a captive on a slave ship repeats the phrase in a slightly modified way: "Should I jump? Should I jump? Shouldijumporwhut?" (55). In the continuous time of the play, the phrase comes back as an echo, even though on a historical linear time line it would have been spoken first by the captive on the slave ship. The result is a dislocation of time in which the audience experiences time as memory but out of sync with chronology.

Despite their multilayered nature, Parks's plays are nevertheless uncluttered; their plots are not convoluted and their landscapes, especially under the direction of Liz Diamond, Parks's longtime collaborator, are sparse. Parks relies on her verbal virtuosity rather than plot, character development, or setting to effect the temporal and spatial overlapping that characterizes her plays. On stage, her figures recall the coexistence of terror and amusement on the minstrel stage through various forms of laughter in a tragicomic mode reminiscent of Samuel Beckett's theater. While those forms of laughter include the satiric aspects of comedy, they are ultimately forms of laughter that evoke sorrow. In his novel *Watt* (1953), Beckett describes three varieties of such laughter:

> Of all the laughs that strictly speaking are not laughs, but modes of ululation, only three I think need detain us. . . . The bitter laugh laughs at that which is not good, it is the ethical laugh. The hollow laugh laughs at that which is not true, it is the intellectual laugh. . . . But the mirthless laugh is the dianoetic laugh, down the snout—Haw!—so. It is the laugh of laughs, the *risus purus*, the laugh laughing at the laugh, the beholding, saluting of the highest joke, in a word the laugh that laughs—silence, please!—at that which is unhappy.[17]

Laughter as ululation is arguably the defining characteristic of tragicomedy, which John Orr, among others, places in the historical context of modernism. For Orr, modern tragicomedy "starts with Pirandello and moves through Beckett and Genet to the plays of Pinter and Shepard"; it is initially a response to "the crisis in value and the collapse of order in European societies from 1910–1925 through war, revolution and economic catastrophe." Tragicomedy becomes the dominant dramatic form of the twentieth century, according to Orr, because it "forces us to question the certainty of self at the same time that it forces us in general to question the certainty of knowledge." Its challenge "echoes challenges in history to the security of the individual" provoked by "cyclical crises of corporate capitalism, the cataclysms of war, revolution and dictatorship." "Above all," writes Orr, tragicomedy "is a movement away from a sense of social experience anchored in tangible issues or moral right, of the good and the just and of their betrayal."[18]

Parks's use of the laughter of modern tragicomedy recalls Colescott's ironic take on famous modern paintings. Like Colescott, Parks shows how the movement to which Orr refers took place even earlier: in the context of New World slavery. The figures of *The Death of Last Black Man*, for example, affect the bitter, the hollow, and the mirthless laugh against the complete betrayal of justice that the slave trade represented; they howl at the consequences of racism, at the denigrating myths to which it has given birth and the tragic unalterable ends to which it has forced millions of people. But, while Parks's characters thus seemingly protest against that which is unethical, that which is not true, and that which is unhappy, theirs are not expressions of protest per se. Instead, their expressions are true ululations: loud, mournful, protracted, and rhythmical expressions of grief. They testify to a history of dispossession that, as Parks puts it, has been "unrecorded," "dismembered," "washed out," or, as in the historical trajectory that Orr implies, simply but savagely ignored (*AP* 4).

Thomas Mann argued that tragicomedy is like the comic grotesque in that the principle of "irreconcilable antithesis" is essential to both. Each simultaneously produces calamity and farce, the solemn and the ridiculous, such that it is "impossible to know whether to cry or laugh."[19] Thus, the comedy in tragicomedy, as in the comic grotesque, does not provide relief from the painful, horrible, or repressed, as in the Freudian model of humor. Rather, the comic highlights, through opposition, the solemn and the terrible. While Parks makes expert use of the "irreconcilable antithesis" of modern tragicomedy, she also maintains one of drama's most traditional effects: catharsis. Especially in *The Death of the Last Man*, she produces the release of anger and pathos through the actors on stage.

In some ways Parks's embrace of catharsis seems surprising, given Brecht's vilifying of Aristotelian catharsis, generally understood as the purging of emotions, especially pity and fear, produced by tragedy through vicarious experience. For Brecht, at least in the early part of his career, catharsis meant "the suppression of critical reason."[20] The function of catharsis, to which Aristotle devotes only a short and ambiguous passage in his *Poetics*, has in fact been endlessly elaborated. As Stephen Orgel notes, most critics assume that what Aristotle meant by catharsis applies to the audience and that it is "therefore the spectators who are purged through pity and fear." At the same time, exactly how "purgation works has been matter of endless debate."[21] What does purgation mean? Does it mean the ridding of pity and fear? Does it mean that these emotions are made more pure, distilled by drama? And what if purging does not occur in the audience but in "the structure of the drama" itself, or in the actors in the drama?[22] Since Aristotle wrote such a "compressed, elliptical and radically ambiguous passage about catharsis," argues Orgel, the meaning of catharsis in tragedy "has not only developed over time, [it] has changed with generations and inheres entirely in the history of its elucidation."[23]

I do not intend to solve the riddle of catharsis in order to discuss its function in Parks's tragicomedy of slavery.[24] Rather, I view catharsis in Parks as a purging of anger and pathos that occurs primarily among the actors on stage through the mirthless laugh. For Parks, this purging does not mean the ridding of pity and fear but constitutes a ritualistic release of the cosmic rage and grief produced by slavery and its legacy. This purging does not occur in front of a passive audience since Parks's formal experimentation constantly challenges audiences to participate in what may be understood as a kind of "cognitive catharsis."[25] Drawing on a denotation of catharsis meaning "clarification," recent scholarship has emphasized the "intellectual insight" that spectators gain through vicarious experience of the pitiable and the fearful. "The audience's understanding," or clarification, writes R. Darren Gobert, "derives not from intellectual argumentation . . . but rather from an emotionally engaged spectatorship that leads spectators to a judgment about the causes of the protagonist's suffering."[26] In Parks's dramaturgy, the intellectual insights we gain are not so much related to the causes of suffering, for these are clear, but how such suffering inheres in the world we live in now.[27]

Central to both the purging of anger and pathos that the actors experience on stage and the clarification that the audience experiences is the mirthless laugh that we have seen with particular power in Chesnutt's tragicomedy of slavery. Chesnutt's use of conjure signifies on chattel slavery's transformation of people into objects and produces a comedy of the body that highlights the pain of that transformation. And laughter, as disassociated from mirth, signals to the ineffability of that pain. Nearly seventy years later, Richard Pryor would dramatize the lingering effects of slavery through his own conjuring and tragicomedy. His performance as the Wino and Junkie in *Live and Smokin'*, to name one example, prefigures Parks's use of the stage to represent the ways that slavery has mutated. But whereas Pryor capitalized on the richness of Black English to conjure his characters, Parks "signifies on the signifyin'," thereby producing absurdist forms of humor against which she sets the pathos of mourning. In what follows, I explore Parks's experiments with language and with notions of time in *Imperceptible Mutabilities* to lay the ground for an extensive meditation of how those experiments result in a tragicomedy of slavery in *The Death of the Last Black Man*. In the chapter's concluding section I return to *Venus*, specifically to how the play constitutes a significant shift in Parks's tragicomedy of slavery.

Suzan-Lori Parks's Neo-Hoodoo

Although Parks's plays are grounded in history, she does not restage or reinterpret the past. Rather, through a creative process that is based on what Ishmael Reed would call Neo-Hoodoo principles, she *conjures* the structures of feeling produced by the past.[28] In "Possession," the first of three essays published in *The America Play and Other Works*, Parks consciously refers to her creative process in terms of conjure: "One of my tasks as a playwright [is to use] literature and the special strange relationship between theatre and real-life [to] locate the ancestral burial ground, dig for bones, hear the bones sing, write it down" (*AP* 4). As if she were a *mambo*, or voodoo priestess, Parks serves as a medium for ancestors who enter the contemporary world, in this case by "possessing" the actors on stage, in order to commune with the living (both on stage and in the audience). Hence, rather than transliterating voodoo's concept of possession, as Reed does in *Flight to Canada*, Parks mines the "strange relationship between theatre and real-life" to make the plays themselves into rituals of possession.[29]

Joseph Roach's notion of "surrogation" as well as his attention to the nuanced meanings and uses of the "effigy" suggest fruitful ways of distinguishing Parks's particular form of conjure from Reed's. In chapter 3, I argued that Reed animates the ideological obsessions and taboos embodied in racial stereotypes through an aesthetics that borrows from the traditions of voodoo, as well as film and caricature. Reed thus illuminates the fetishistic power that the racial and sexual stereotypes produced under slavery have had across time. While Reed also employs his aesthetic to call ancestral spirits into being, his conjure is a purely textual performance. In Parks's work, actors are surrogates for the bodies of the ancestors and, in this sense, become living effigies in the rituals of mourning and burial that Parks's early plays effect.

With respect to the various uses of effigy, Roach notes that the word is normally used "as a noun meaning a sculpted or pictured likeness" and that in more particular uses the word suggests "a crudely fabricated image of a person, commonly one that is destroyed in his or her stead, as in hanging or burning *in effigy*." He notes, however, that "effigy" can also be used as a verb to designate the act of evoking an absence, of *bodying* something forth, "especially something in the distant past." In this rare usage, he argues, the effigy becomes not only more "elusive" but also more "powerful" because it suggests a process of embodiment in what Roach calls performed effigies.[30] Turning back to Reed, we see that he effigies forth that which is obsessively present, that which is fetishized rather than examined, and that he aesthetically highlights both the overwhelming presence of the fetish and its appeal. Parks, by contrast, effigies the *dead*, she "bodies forth" the *absent figures of the past*, but she does so in a manner that suggests that the dead are never wholly absent.

In "Elements of Style," another essay in the collection, Parks refers to the people "[from] time immemorial, from . . . PastLand, from somewhere back there," who visit her and to whom she gives shape, as "figures, figments, ghosts, roles" (*AP* 12). She insists that they are not "characters," that to call them so "could be an injustice" because her writing is not an act of mimesis but of conjure. "The state of possession and mediumship," she writes, quoting from John S. Mbiti's *African Religions and Philosophy*, "is one of contemporizing the past, bringing into human history the beings essentially beyond the horizon of the present time" (8). For Parks, writing is not the means through which to *recreate* history; it is, instead, the means to *create* "history where it is and always was but has not yet been divined" (5). In *The Death of the Last Black Man* and *The America Play*, writing is a way of bodying forth the absent, the dead, through surrogation in effigy. In *Imperceptible Mutabilities*, Parks brings forth the dead in more subtle ways, making the sounds of the dead audible in the language of the living. She creates echoes that sound and resound, marking the movement of time with each repetition while circling back to the lonely deaths of those who died without witness or ceremony.

Parks, like Reed, "divines" the past through an aesthetics that is clearly informed by voodoo; like Reed, she also clearly rejects any essentialist or nostalgic evocation of the practice by incorporating aspects of postmodernism. It is in this sense that her work is not merely Hoodoo on stage, but *Neo*-Hoodoo, a particularized way of using an African tradition. She consistently calls attention to the artifice of the theater, principally to impede passive spectatorship, but also to highlight the constructs and biases through which we arrive at a sense of history. These seemingly disparate realms of culture, voodoo and postmodernism, coalesce in Parks's notion of time, which is circular, repetitive, and cumulative and which forms the basis for two simultaneous movements in her work: the underscoring of the distance that separates us from slavery and the staging of the often imperceptible ways through which slavery has mutated. Hence the title of her play, *Imperceptible Mutabilities in the Third Kingdom*, in which the Third Kingdom designates a space between an ancestral home, from which the figures of the Middle Passage have been expunged and to which they cannot return, and a new home, where the figures of the more contemporary frames do not fully belong. The figures in contemporary frames connect to those from the Middle Passage and slavery through the verbal riffs that underscore the mutations that slavery has taken.

Like her predecessor Adrienne Kennedy, Parks capitalizes on the way dramatic time can intertwine past, present, and future tenses. Yet she also highlights what Gertrude Stein called the theater's "continuous present," the specific moment of staging and watching a play and the experiences that occur therein.[31] In *Imperceptible Mutabilities* a slave ship becomes a hospital room, which then becomes a desirable co-op apartment. The mutations to which the title refers recall the transformations in Kennedy's stage directions for *The Owl Answers* (1963) with what at first seems like a higher degree of absurdity.[32] As Alisa Solomon notes, Parks never literally equates slavery and gentrification, the two experiences underwriting this particular association in the play. Rather, through a "whirl of visual and verbal riffs, [Parks] evokes them as spokes all spinning around the same historical hub."[33] Gentrification echoes slavery as a form of dispossession based on racism, which is, simultaneously, the cumulative result of the history of that form of dispossession. Parks also presents more recognizable associations—in the play, a white man is a possible father, possible owner, possible lover/rapist—suggesting that these possible relations are no less outrageous, only more familiar.

In the first production of *Imperceptible Mutabilities*, directed by Liz Diamond, the same actors play multiple characters, a fact that reinforces the potential interchangeability of such roles. It also underscores Parks's use of theater as a medium for expressing her Neo-Hoodoo principles since the same body can be possessed by diverse "spirits" or subjectivities. In the play, Molly, later reintroduced on stage as Mona (they are the same character, played by the same actor), is confined by poverty and unemployment and lives in a Kafkaesque world in which she is watched from all angles. In fact, she and her roommates are wiretapped for observation by a character known as both The Naturalist and Dr. Lutsky. Recalling the cold racism and pseudo-science of Schoolteacher in Toni Morrison's *Beloved*, The Naturalist/Doctor has made Mona and her roommates Chona and Verona his objects of observation in order to monitor what he calls the women's "mundus primitivus" and has renamed them Molly, Charlene, and Veronica (*AP* 29). Parks

tempers the darkness of The Naturalist/Doctor's design, which has as its ultimate goal the annihilation of the women, with comic absurdity. Not only do we
have the implausible rhyming of the women's names, but there is also an improb-
ably large cockroach (reminiscent of Kafka's own bug) on stage, meant to literal-
ize both the bugging of the women and the fact that they live in a roach-infested
apartment. In this context, Mona's despair at her predicament, reinvoked through
the captive's question in the second section, "Should I jump? Should I jump?
Shouldijumporwhut?," becomes retrospectively linked (but not equated) to that
of the captives in a slave ship, in the same way that Parks suggests gentrification as
a form of dispossession linked to slavery.

The cycle of time that Parks makes audible through linguistic repetition is
not, as Linda Ben-Zvi rightly argues, a cynical admission of the "cultural inevitability of the African American experience. Yet the cycle, and in particular
the linguistic repetitions, are also more than just signs of a "societal need to address modes of thinking and speaking that have been encoded" in language."[34]
The repetitions are expressions of a "ghostly power" that Joseph Roach identifies
in African American rhythm and blues:

> The voice of African-American rhythm and blues carries awesomely over
> time and distance, through its cadences, its intonations, it accompaniment,
> and even its gestures. . . . The degree to which this voice haunts American
> memory, the degree to which it promotes obsessive attempts at simulation,
> impersonation, derives from its ghostly power to *insinuate memory* between
> the lines, in the spaces between the words, in the intonation and placement
> by which they are shaped, in the silences by which they are deepened or
> contradicted. By such means, the dead remain among the living.[35]

Through repetition with revision, Parks creates a linguistic musicality that also
insinuates memory: in the spaces between each reiteration, in the intonation and
placement by which each reiteration changes. As Louise Bernard argues, Parks's
language "mirrors" the "blues idea of 'worrying the line,' including 'changes in
stress and pitch, the addition of exclamatory phrases, changes in word order,
repetitions of phrases within the line itself, and the wordless blues cries which
often punctuate the performance of songs.'" Parks also creates "the multi-layered
equivalents" of jazz compositions: repetition and difference "within a given tune,"
"the intertextual dynamic between a (European) standard and a jazz riff," and the
jazz "musician's riff on another jazz musician's 'standard.'"[36] Parks's music insinuates the memory of the cultural and linguistic uprooting that was the Middle
Passage and suggests the ways that such uprooting has mutated across time.

In section 3 of *Imperceptible Mutabilities*, Aretha, the mammy/slave mother,
wonders, "How many kin kin I hold. Whole hold full" (*AP* 43), echoing the voice
of an ancestor in the Middle Passage who in part 2 says, "How many kin kin

I hold. Whole hull full" (39). The repetition, with the subtle shift from "hold" to "hull," marks both the distance and the connections between slave ship and plantation. Although this is more evident in the text than in the performance of the play, in both cases, the spelling of "can" as "kin" clearly evokes notions of kinship, as do the names of the ancestors in the Middle Passage, names that Ben-Zvi notes are "homonymic parodies: Kin-seer, Us-seer, Shark-seer, and Soul-seer, which signify on the last line: Over-seer" (193). Aretha's dual role as mammy and slave mother requires her to "hold"—birth and care for—various kin. Yet at the time of the play, which is loosely set at the onset of Reconstruction, she is being uprooted (signified by the extraction of her teeth) like the ancestors in the Middle Passage. She is told, "The book says you expire. No options to renew," and that she must leave the children and her "place" (45).

Aretha's repetition of the ancestors' words is set in the context of "footnotes," which Miss Faith recites while she extracts Aretha's teeth. These footnotes refer to facts about the slave ship, the *Brookes*, to the number of captives that were forced into its dungeons, and to more general facts about slavery, but they are not actual textual footnotes since they are included in the body of the text and are announced as such by Miss Faith: "Footnote #1: The human cargo capacity of the English slaver, the *Brookes*" (*AP* 43).[37] In this context, the echo not only sonically suggests that Aretha's inability to "hold" on to kin is a repetition (with a difference) of the Seer's rupture from culture, but it also directs us back to the previous section of the play, a section that opens starkly with each Seer simply calling out his or her name.[38] The looping back via Aretha's echo intertwines parts 2 and 3 while highlighting the contrasts between them. Part 3 is explicit in its representation of violence, both in terms of Aretha's individual suffering—her bleeding gums, her dispossession of kin and rights—and in terms of the number of people that suffered under slavery, details of which the footnotes provide. By contrast, part 2 positions the Seers in the midst of the Middle Passage and gives a sense of the painful existential unmooring that was the journey, but represents the violence of that experience in abstract language. Aretha's echo of the Seers' voices in part 3 underscores the absence of the ancestral voices in the factual descriptions of the *Brookes*—the "human cargo capacity of the English slaver, the *Brookes*, was about 3,250 square feet" (43)—and the other related historical documents to which Parks refers. By the same logic, Aretha's repetition-with-a-difference of the ancestral voices of part 2 in part 3 highlights the dearth of individual and detailed accounts of the Middle Passage by captive Africans. Aretha's name too, evocative as it is of Aretha Franklin's (who is often referred to by first name alone), links the distinct time frames of the play to the ghostly power that Roach identifies in the awesome sound of African American rhythm and blues, a sound to which Aretha's voice would give thunderous power.

The central recurring echo in the play repeats and revises what Ben-Zvi calls "the cultural and linguistic expunging—from home, from self, from language and from history—" that the Seers experience during the Middle Passage.[39] This expulsion is expressed in the image of a split self.[40] In the first part of the play, for example, we repeatedly hear Molly/Mona speaking in the third person, expressing a sense of self-exile: "Once there was uh me named Mona who wondered what she'd be like if no one was watchin" (27). Parks often renders such meditations in an absurdist comic mode that serves to highlight the painful history that her verbal riffs interweave. At one point, Mona identifies herself as "Lucky" in an interchange that, like the name she chooses, alludes to Beckett's *Waiting for Godot* (1953):

> Mona: "S-K" IS /SK/ AS IN "AXE" Oh dear. I'm Lucky, Dr. Lutsky.
> Lutsky: Call me "Wipe-em out." Both of you. All of you.
> Chona: Wipe-em out. Dr. Wipe-em out.
> Lutsky: And you're "Lucky"?
> Verona: He got uh gun!
> Mona: MeMona.
> Lutsky: Mona? (*AP* 33)

Through these stark phrases so reminiscent of Beckett's in their seeming absurdity, Parks not only returns to the beginning of the play but also further interlaces the play's various parts. When the play opens, Mona contemplates suicide because she can no longer cope with the bizarre world in which she lives. She has been sent to school by her job to learn "basic skills," under the threat "Speak correctly or you'll be dismissed!" (25). At school she is subjected to lessons meant to correct her habit of saying "ax" instead of "ask," in an obvious reference to debates about the validity of Ebonics. The lessons are meant to teach her "correct" English through rote repetition of phrases such as "The little-lamb-follows-closely-behind-at-Mary's-heels-as-Mary-boards-the train." While she counteracts the sheer absurdity of such schooling by repeating the phrase in mocking tones and adding stings such as "Ain't never seen no woman on no train with no lamb," she finally becomes overwhelmed by the pressure to reform (25). By contrast, her roommate Chona encourages her to redefine the language to which she is subjected by signifying on it. Chona rewrites the fairy-tale phrase: "Once there was uh little lamb who followed Mary good n put uh hex on Mary. When Mary dropped dead, thuh lamb was in thuh lead" (27).

Chona's signifying is a localized version of Parks's own signifying, which not only refuses the subject position suggested by the name Lucky but also puts a "hex" on the language of subjection. Lucky in Beckett's play is the symbol of the exploited; as a slave to Pozzo, he lives in a world of "illusion and is convinced that he was 'made to suffer.'" But he is also fortunate (as his name implies) because he has opted out of "the panic that life is." As he reveals in his "schizophrenic oratory," however, he has become free of the illusions that bind Pozzo only by surrendering to his "knowledge that man is doomed to 'waste and pine and waste and pine . . . for reasons unknown,'" and by "becoming Pozzo's unquestioning slave."[41] Just as Lucky eventually becomes mute, Mona too loses all control of language and is only able to identify herself as "MeMona." By contrast, Chona so embellishes the absurdity that undoes her roommate that she explodes its script and creates a new one, one that mocks servitude and humility.

The satire of Chona's signifying, which engages with the violence of which Mona is a victim by dramatizing it in reverse (a dead Mary, a usurping lamb), is emblematic of the comic aspects of Parks's work. In *Imperceptible Mutabilities*, and even more so in *The Death of the Last Black Man*, Parks puts a "hex" on the conventions of minstrelsy, mocking its demeaning laughter while producing a tragicomedy that sets at tension the pathos of mourning and the satiric edge with which she signifies on the violence of the minstrel stage.

The "laugh laughing at the laugh": Conjuring the Ghost of Minstrelsy

Parks's use of minstrelsy at times suggests a straightforward sense of the comic since it relies on incongruity, juxtaposition, and inversion. Aretha of *Imperceptible Mutabilities*, for example, has a peculiar last name, although because she is a slave, it is most likely her owner's: Saxon. Her wards are even more peculiarly named Anglor Saxon and Blanca Saxon. In the play, they mutate from nineteenth-century children in antebellum America to a twentieth-century couple shopping for a co-op apartment and performing in whiteface. The humor is simple—it derives from their obvious names—but through it Parks comments on miscegenation in a comic form that recalls the conjure tales of Chesnutt, the interracial humor of Twain's *Pudd'nhead Wilson*, some of Faulkner's work (as in the lighter tone of his short story "Was" in *Go Down, Moses*), and certainly the satiric edge of George Schuyler's *Black No More*. As nineteenth-century figures, Anglor and Blanca Saxon are siblings and at least partly black, although, in their historical context, they would simply be black, given the one-drop rule. When they mutate into twentieth-century figures, it is difficult, if not impossible, to suspend their previous associations, despite the perceptible whiteface they wear. Viewed from the continuous present in which the audience experiences their performances, they are a white husband and wife who are actually siblings and, though visibly white, actually black. There is, as Parks suggests, "a nigger in the woodpile" in Anglor Saxon's family, and incest to boot.

Parks's use of whiteface in this instance is clearly an inversion of blackface minstrelsy and a playful rearrangement of taxonomies and hierarchies, both of which reveal how permeable and fluid these are. She similarly invokes other conventions of the minstrel stage, particularly its manipulations of language. Ostensibly, her preoccupation with minstrelsy places her in line with

playwrights who, from the late 1970s through the early 1990s, have been employing comedy as a social corrective and a means of providing release from
the tension created by the evils of minstrelsy and its continuing effects. Take
Ntozake Shange's *Spell #7* (1979). The prologue to the play constitutes a short
but pungent minstrel show: actors in blackface masks (with exaggerated white
lips and eye sockets) wear shabby overalls, dance to the rhythm of washboards
and kazoos, and sign and chant in typical minstrel fashion. At the end of the
prologue, the actors vanish, leaving a giant replica of the masks they wear hanging over the stage. This mask, which disappears as the play unfolds and provides
the stories of the prologue's actors (and, in particular, the obstacles they face *as*
actors in the shadow of minstrelsy), reappears at the end of the play. As Shawn-
Marie Garrett observes, Shange's prologue attempts to "exorcise the demon" of
minstrelsy "once and for all," yet the play as a whole suggests that, despite these
efforts, the demon continues to haunt the stage in specter fashion.[42]

Seven years after Shange's play, another black dramatist, George C. Wolfe, in-
augurated a trend in contemporary black theater that attempted once again to
exorcise that demon. Kim Euell identifies Wolfe's *The Colored Museum* (1986) as
the precursor to plays premiering in the late 1980s and early 1990s that signify
on the prominent features of minstrelsy in order to decrease their power.[43] Euell
argues that "these works ask the audience to participate in [a] ritual of adjudication, either actively or as witnesses," a ritual whose goal is the exorcizing of
stereotypes and the assessment of what, if any, aspects of their legacy should
be maintained.[44] Unlike the playwrights Euell discusses, Parks neither replicates
the features of minstrelsy, nor does she create rituals of adjudication. Rather, she
evokes minstrelsy's stereotypical naming, innovative wordplay, and unorthodox
spelling (much of which translates phonetically in the sound of her invented
words) to underscore the ways that the very medium in which she works has been
complicit in making black suffering into spectacle. At the same time, she makes
those minstrel features abstract and unfamiliar and turns them into vehicles for
remembering and honoring the dead. Thus, while Parks creates comedy by in-
verting, juxtaposing, and otherwise de-familiarizing the features of minstrelsy,
she uses that comedy as a counterpoint to highlight the tragic aspects of her
drama. In *The Death of the Last Black Man* especially, she appropriates minstrel
tropes to open the possibility of "witnessing" the deaths of those who died without ceremony. Her plays make use of the humorous and pathetic aberrations of
black speech and sentiment that minstrelsy produced and include contemporary
references to suggest the persistence of minstrelsy's effects.

But her powerful dramas do not conjure the ghost of minstrelsy simply to
exorcise the shame and anger that it still elicits. As she makes clear in the essay
"An Equation for Black People on Stage," Parks refuses to produce the kind of
drama that obsessively focuses on "the representation of Blacks as oppressed,"

the kind of drama that forfeits the exploration of black life in all its richness and variety (*AP* 20). Rather, Parks argues for an art that can both attest to the reality of oppression and explore the many "ways of defining Blackness on stage." "We have for so long been an 'oppressed' people," she writes, "but are Black people only blue?" (*AP* 19). Although Parks does not discuss specific plays, the works to which Euell refers fall within the parameters of her critique in their adjudicating mode and their replication of minstrel features. Robert Alexander's *I Ain't Yo' Uncle*, for instance, features the characters of *Uncle Tom's Cabin* transformed into contemporary figures (Topsy, for example, is a hip-hop artist) who have gathered around Stowe, who is also a character, to take her to task for the limited ways she imaged their subjectivities. Although its tone is humorous, Alexander's play nevertheless falls within a category of work that, as Parks observes, ultimately dramatizes "a series of reactions and responses to the White ruling class," in this case embodied in the Stowe figure (17). Alexander's use of minstrel speech is also problematic. He and other dramatists like him (Breena Clarke and Glenda Dickerson, for instance, in their play *Re/membering Aunt Jemima: A Menstrual Show*) aim to burlesque minstrel speech by exaggerating its features, yet often they merely replicate its inanity.

Parks, by contrast, rejects the posture of "response" and "reaction" by creating her own language to signify on minstrelsy. The names she chose for the characters of *The Death of the Last Black Man*, for example, clearly echo the racist antics and language of the minstrel stage: Black Man with Watermelon, Black Woman with Fried Drumstick, Lots of Grease and Lots of Pork. Obviously these names "comment directly on deleterious 'soul food' stereotypes, historically associated with African Americans."[46] Yet they also constitute evidence of Parks's playful but pointed use of black vernacular culture. She names one of her figures Yes and Greens Black-Eyed Peas Cornbread, clearly pushing language to absurdist limits and thereby highlighting the absurdity inherent in historically inscribed stereotypes. She also uses these names, in particular that of Black Man and Woman, for figures that, as Alisa Solomon notes, stand as allegories for "universal themes of human survival and reach," making deeply ironic the dehumanizing implications of racist naming.[47]

On one level, *The Death of the Last Black Man* simply concerns the separation of a wife and husband through death and, as such, adopts the elegiac mode of tragic love poetry (in particular the passages in Dante's *Divine Comedy* regarding the separation of lovers through death). At another level, however, the play presents the death of an ancestral figure, his interactions with other dead ancestors and his wife, to whom he pays ghostly visits. We are told that he died "yesterday today next summer tomorrow just uh moment uhgoh in 1317" and understand that his ghostly visits are motivated by his need for witness and testimony (*AP* 111). Organized in panels rather than scenes and acts, the play opens with an overture and then alternates between panels that present Black Man and Black Woman alone in an intimate setting—the porch of the house they used to share—and panels that present a chorus of nine spirits, some historical, others imaginary or mythical.

The panels featuring Black Man and Black Woman recall Beckett's *Godot* in that they present a sparse landscape inhabited by two figures struggling with existential questions in an absurd world. Black Man is stuck, without burial rites and thus dead but not yet properly of the dead. Parks makes literal his existential quandary by showing him sitting on his porch chair unable to move his hands because a large watermelon holds them in place. Black Man thinks that the watermelon has been "planted" on him, a comic turn on the notion of stigmatization: an overt literalization of a conspiracy against a black man through one of the ultimate symbols for stereotyping black folk. His wife, meanwhile, tries to act normal in the face of the abnormal (another classically humorous setup). She is profoundly perplexed by her husband's return from the dead but seeks to normalize the situation by feeding and comforting him—by acting the part of a wife—and by convincing herself that he is not really dead: "You comed back. Comin backs somethin in itself. You comed back" (*AP* 105). Her feminine care goes haywire, however, and she ends up acting stranger than her ghostly husband—that is, outdoing the absurdity of her situation with nurturing acts that turn violent.

Unlike the panels featuring the couple, the choral panels are quite busy since they bring all eleven figures on stage. In them, Parks interweaves time and space modalities such that, as S. E. Wilmer notes, the "stage space is simultaneously historical, contemporary, and imaginary," a place where "mythical and stereotypical figures" can co-exist and "engage with more realistic figures, both living and dead."[48] The choral figures are "kin" to Black Man, in the sense that, like him, they are ancestral voices seeking testimony and witness. The play's main concerns, the need for Black Man's resting peace and for testimony, are encapsulated in two refrains that are modified via Rep&Rev: "This is the death of the last black man in the whole entire world" and "You should write that down and you should hide it under a rock . . . because if you dont write it down then they will come along and tell the future that we did not exist" (*AP* 102, 104).

Yet, as the iconic names that Parks chose for some of them suggest, the figures also speak of the need to guard against the misrepresentation of history and the distortion of testimony, both past and present. The most obvious name in this respect is Voice on Thuh Tee V. Assuming the voice of a newscaster, this figure reports the "death of the last living Negro man in the whole entire known world" and gives that man a name and a history: "Gamble Major born a slave rose to become a spearhead in the Civil Rights Movement. He was 38 years old. The Civil Rights Movement. He was 38 years old" (*AP* 110). This figure suggests that one way of interpreting the name of Parks's play is as a marking and mourning of the death of the civil rights movement and the hope for change that it represented.

After all, the movement's most acclaimed leaders, Malcolm X and Martin Luther King, were both assassinated at the age of thirty-nine. But Parks loosely suggests this interpretation in the context of a play that highlights questions about the reliability of historical representation.

As Elam and Rayner observe, the characters Queen-Then Pharaoh Hatshepsut, Before Columbus, And Bigger and Bigger and Bigger, and Ham all make reference to historical, literary, and religious instances of textual erasure, distortion, and manipulation.[48] Queen Hatshepsut, one of the earliest women to rule in ancient Egypt, was essentially erased from historical records by a son who was jealous of her rule. The name Before Columbus refers to a controversial but little discussed study documenting African travel from Mali to North America before Columbus. The name could also simply refer to the peoples who inhabited the Americas before Columbus arrived and whose cultures were decimated. And Bigger and Bigger and Bigger recalls Richard Wright's character from *Native Son* and suggests that the angry young black man Wright created has grown "too big for [his] own name" (*AP* 115). He has become an overembellished stereotype or, as Elam and Rayner put it, the "prototypical, angry, savage and dangerous black brute."[49] But though he is the strongest voice of anger in the play, he is not violent. Like Black Man, he is stuck, unable to move his hands. His name thus also implies that the frustrations of being bound grow bigger and bigger with the generations, often exploding into violence, as in Wright's novel. Finally, Ham indicates a story of manipulation since his name and the biblical story attached to it were used to validate the actions of those who profited from the African slave trade.

The figures gather onstage to express their grievances, to each other and to the living, and experience a catharsis of anger and shame. The dead, Parks suggests, do not forget the deep evil done to them but carry the memory of it beyond life. However, the play does not dwell on pathology. One of its most important refrains, "Where is he gonna go now that he done dieded?" constantly brings the audience back to the ritual purposes of the play. The refrain circles back to the fact that beyond questions of evidence, blame, and consequence is the need to give the dead rituals of burial and mourning. The play answers the question of the refrain as it unfolds, becoming the "place" where Black Man can indeed rest. In fact, at a reading at Harvard in 2003, Parks referred to the play as Black Man's grave and headstone.

The ritual of burial, however, cannot happen until testimony has been given and anger and shame have been exorcised. As a group, the figures of *The Death of the Last Black Man* perform this exorcism through the laughter of tragicomedy and in Parks's particularized language. This play mixes her "signifying on the signifyin'" with the peculiar and creative aspects of minstrel speech, including its malapropisms and absurd dialect. Among the foreign words and phrases in

Parks's language are exclamatory sounds, often simple ones such as "ha," which become vehicles for deeply felt ululations. In *Death of the Last Black Man*, the exclamation is usually spoken in a rising volume, at first by a singular figure and then collectively, in a manner that combines anger and mockery and recalls Beckett's description of "the laugh laughing at the laugh":

Queen-Then-Pharaoh Hatshepsut:	I saw Columbus comin. / I saw Columbus comin goin over tuh visit you. "To borrow a cup of sugar," so he said. I waved my hands in warnin. You waved back. I aint seen you since.
Lots of Grease and Lots of Pork:	In the future when they came along I meeting them. On thuh coast. Uh! Thuh Coast! I—was—so—polite. But in thuh dirt, I wrote: "Ha. Ha. Ha."
All:	Ha. Ha. Ha Ha. Ha. Ha. Ha. Ha. Ha. Ha. Ha. Ha. Ha. Ha. Ha. Ha. HHHHHHHHHHHHHHHH. (*AP* 104)

Here the figures effect a catharsis of emotion, which, in a manner characteristic of Parks's theater, is both self-consciously fictive and ritualistic. The Queen speaks in quotidian language that Parks, as in other instances, makes ironic by underlining its connection to the history of colonialism ("Columbus comin going . . . 'To borrow a cup of sugar'"). Lots of Grease and Lots of Pork meanwhile voices a fantasy of retribution that Parks accents through typography and staccato pronunciation ("I—was—so—polite") and a painstaking spelling out of what the colonized both writes (in the imaginary space of "the future when they came along") and speaks out (in the actual stage space where all echo and multiply the imaginary, vengeful message). In the 1990 Brooklyn Academy of Contemporary Art (BACA) production, the actors emphasized the mixture of mockery and anger in the statement by infusing it with a laughter that increased in both tempo and volume. The laugh, a mirthless one indeed, changed as it escalated from bitterness to high-pitched anger, finally ending in a loud sigh signifying release.

Significantly, Parks shows that such anger can turn inward. The kin express their anger at Black Man for not having used communal wisdom to escape persecution and death in a moment that recalls the passage about Sandy's root in Frederick Douglass's *Narrative*. They also express anger at each other for the injustices to which they give voice. Throughout the play the kin ask, "Whose fault is it?" (referring both to the death of Black Man and to their own losses), to which at various times each one answers, "Aint Mines," "I cant remember back that far," "And besides, I wasnt even there." The disavowal of the self that characterizes the responses suggests the inaccessibility of memory and an implicit, though ironic, assumption of guilt even as the group seeks to adjudicate blame. Having turned inward, the kin's rage can be directed at anyone.[50]

At one point, for instance, the kin force Ham to explain their genealogy since, using the story in the Bible, they blame him for slavery. Parks suggests that the Bible story can be used against Ham within his own community. Ham shows, however, that the genealogical tree is so convoluted that the blame cannot be traced easily to any one ancestor. In a long speech he delivers at the beginning of panel 4, he testifies to the violence of slavery, the destruction of families, the impossibility of clear genealogies, and the shame that the people who were subjected to such a fate felt as a consequence. In this way his speech recalls the monologue "Bicentennial Nigger" in which Pryor details the devastation of the Middle Passage from the perspective of a two-hundred-year-old "nigger in blackface." Yet Parks's Ham delivers his speech in a mode that so expertly signifies on the language of the minstrel stage that it turns that language inside out. If the language of minstrelsy was meant to mock the ways that black folk spoke, Parks creates a laughter that mocks the laughter of minstrelsy:

> Ham: Ham's Begotten Tree (catching up to um *in medias res* that is takin off from where we stopped up last time). Huh. NOW: She goned begotten One who in turn begotten Ours. Ours laughed one day uhloud in from thuh sound hittin thuh air smakity sprung up I, you, n He, She, It. They turned in engaged in simple multiplication thus tuh spawn of theirselves one We one You and one called They (They in certain conversation known as "Them" and in other certain conversations a.k.a. "Us"). Now very simply: Wassername she finally gave intuh It and together they brought forth uh wildish one called simply Yo. Yo gone be wentin much too long without hisself uh comb in from thuh frizzly that resulted comed one called You (polite form). You (polite) birthed herself Mister, Miss, Maam and Sir who in his later years with That brought forth Yuh Fathuh. Thuh fact that That was uh mother tuh Yuh Father didnt stop them 2 relations from havin relations. Those strange relations between That thuh mother and Yuh Father thuh son brought forth uh odd lot: called: Yes Massuh, Yes Missy, Yes Maam n Yes Suh Mistuh Suh which goes tuh show that relations with your relations produces complications. Thuh children of That and Yuh Fathuh aside from being plain peculiar was all crosseyed. This defect enhanced their multiplicative

possibilities, for example. Yes Suh Mistuh Suh breeded with hisself n gived us Wassername (thuh 2nd), and Wassernickname (2 twins in birth joinded at thuh lip). Thuh 2 twins lived next door tuh one called Uhnother bringing forth Themuhns, She (thuh 2nd), Auntie, Cousin, and Bro who makeshifted continuous compensations for his loud and oderiferous bodily emissions by all thuh time saying excuse me n though his graciousness brought forth They (polite) who had mixed feelins with She (thuh 2nd) thus bringin forth Ussin who then went on tuh have MeMines.

Yes and Greens
Black-eyed Peas
and Cornbread: Thuh list goes on in on.

Ham: MeMines gived out 2 offspring one she called Mines after herself thuh uther called Themuhms named after all them who comed before. Themuhms married outside thuh tribe joinin herself with uh man they called Who-Dat. Themuhms in WhoDat brought forth only one child called WhoDatDere. Mines joined up with Wasshiname and from that union come AllYall. (*AP* 121)

As Parks told her audience at Harvard in 2003 after reading Ham's speech, the idea of using pronouns to make up an ancestral tree came as she faced a supremely difficult question: how does one create a genealogy when the ancestral names have been violently erased? Parks's strategy is at once richly innovative and satirical. Her playful use of basic grammatical terms, as well as her inclusion of slang, other linguistic codes, and her "foreign words & phrases," emphasize rather than fill the gaps of history. At the same time, her linguistic creativity pinpoints the acts of historical violence that created those gaps.

Parks begins her genealogy in the most innocent way. Echoing the sense of mystery and the miracle of creation myths, she first presents She, who appears out of the blue to birth One, a pronoun that connotes a sense of the divine, who in turn births Ours, a pronoun that suggests a sense of a people. The playwright thus evokes a prelapsarian time in which, significantly, it is laughter that becomes the source of fecundity. Laughter emanates from Ours, and its "sound hittin thuh air smakity" gives birth to the multiplicity of beings who in turn create the world of the play. Laughter, as in Parks's own work, is life-affirming.

The genealogy that Ham's tree traces, however, like the book of Genesis, suggests that strife among the ancestors began quite early (They can be Them or Us, depending on the conversation). Although ambiguously, it also locates the blame that the ancestors on stage are trying to account for in a revised version of the fall from Eden: "Wassername she finally gave intuh It and together they brought forth uh wildish one called simply Yo." Parks's use of a slang term commonly associated with Black English subtly racializes the strange relation between Wassername and It, while her clever use of the impersonal pronoun It deftly evokes the transformation of people into objects, on which chattel slavery rested. She similarly employs the pronoun That as the genealogy continues: "You (polite) birthed herself Mister, Miss, Maam and Sir who in his later years with That brought forth Yuh Fathuh. Thuh fact that That was uh mother tuh Yuh Father didnt stop them 2 relations from havin relations." Both instances suggest a fall from grace, but in both cases it is not just sexual (as in Eden) but perverse: subjects copulate with objects and mothers mate with sons in what is merely the start of a litany of incest.

Yet Ham's speech is also strikingly funny. At the 1990 BACA production of the play, at the reading Parks gave of the speech, and watching the video of it that I presented at a lecture, audiences erupted at the sound of Ham's account of the "strange relations between That thuh mother and Yuh Father," which, as he so humorously tells us, "brought forth uh odd lot: called: Yes Massuh, Yes Missy, Yes Maam n Yes Suh Mistuh Suh." Unlike the moments in the play when the figures enact a catharsis of emotion among themselves through the "laugh of laughs," the "mirthless laugh," the laughter that Ham's speech provokes is shared among audience members in the same fashion that Pryor's audience shares laughter. People laugh from different positions, depending on their gender, race, age, class, and politics, in ways that modulate between symmetry and asymmetry. As in any tragicomedy, however, such laughter depends on this kind of perplexity. On the one hand, the speech operates as a kind of in-joke for Americans familiar with black slang (in particular when Ham speaks of WhoDat and WhoDatDere), but it also includes references to the denigrations of the minstrel stage (especially when Ham describes Bro's obsequiousness). The speech exemplifies Parks's bountiful creativity at the same time that it evokes a past in which such creativity would have been ruthlessly denied. Parks distills that past, the birth of a nation through the "strange relations" between master and slave, into a quick progression of increasingly more outrageous satiric images, peaking at one point with "Wassername (thuh 2nd) and Wassernickname (2 twins in birth joined at thuh lip)." Throughout, Parks produces the "feeling of opposite" at the heart of tragicomedy in which easy recognition turns into the desire for disavowal and pleasure turns to pain.

The humor of the speech derives its fire from the unpalatable suggestions it makes. Ham implicitly locates the origin of the tribe, and by allegorical extension the nation, in two taboos, incest and miscegenation, both of which produce oddities and deformities. Yet he does not designate any clear victims and villains. Rather, he ambiguously locates the beginning of the fall from grace in the moment when "Wassername finally [gives into] It." With this short phrase Ham touches upon one of the major contradictions of the slave trade and the myths surrounding it: the fact that masters repeatedly dehumanized slaves and yet inadvertently affirmed their humanity by having sexual relations with them. The phrase also implies two notions simultaneously: that masters actually dehumanized themselves by "[giving into] It," by consorting with those they considered primitive subhumans, and that slaves somehow "chose" to give into the lasciviousness of masters.

Parks's linguistic creativity recalls Hortense Spillers's brilliant discussion of the peculiar "grammar book" that the slave trade produced. Like Spillers, Parks emphasizes not only the "stunning contradiction" in which the "captive body" is reduced to "a thing," one that is, nonetheless, the source of an "irresistible, destructive sensuality" for the captor, but also how the "incestuous, interracial genealogy" of slavery gave way to a dizzying "confusion of consanguinity." Spillers carefully explores how the "dynamics of naming and valuation" of the slave trade, the way captive bodies were branded as property irrespective of personhood, gender, or kinship, "remains grounded" in the grammar of American culture. She argues that the "project of liberation for African-Americans has found urgency in two passionate motivations that are intertwined—1) to break apart, to rupture violently the laws of American behavior that make [possible] a *syntax* [in which people and things are equated] 2) to introduce a new *semantic* field/fold more appropriate to his/her own historic movement."[51]

Parks's mixture of historical and contemporary language acknowledges the persistence of the syntax to which Spillers refers, while her formal innovation produces a purposefully peculiar grammar that seeks to break free from it. As Elam and Rayner have observed, the structure of Ham's speech "parodies a 'stump speech' from the olio section of a nineteenth century minstrel show."[52] At the same time, it includes a mixture of allusions to historical moments preceding the minstrel stage and to contemporary popular culture, thus underscoring the connections that Parks makes across distinct time frames. Parks gives the various associations that she condenses a maddening hilarity through the litany of made-up names that constitute the bulk of Ham's long speech, a litany that in both the BACA production and Parks's reading at Harvard was delivered with a speed that is difficult, if not impossible, to appreciate on the printed page.

In fact, in both the BACA production and Parks's reading, the repeated break of kinship ties and the "confusion of consanguinity" that slavery produced, the consequences of which are the focus of Spillers's essay, become a cacophony of sound. It hits the air "smackity," like the laughter emanating from Ours. Unlike Ours's life-affirming laughter, however, the laughter that Ham's speech incites affirms life through irony: it satirizes the corruption of an ideal, the integrity of personhood, and it recognizes the repeated loss of kinship.[53]

The speed of the speech increases ever more rapidly with each instance of that loss and becomes most obvious when Ham relates the eventual fate of the ancestors whom he introduces at the beginning of the speech. In a section that, as Elam and Rayner note, replicates the "staccato rhythms" of the "auctioneer at the slave auction block," Ham highlights the ease with which relations of kinship were broken in the market of bodies.[54] Significantly, the grammar of the speech becomes more convoluted and abstract as Parks includes what appear to be random numbers, placed as superscripts over the invented ancestral names:

> **Ham:** SOLD! allyall^{9} not thuh be confused w/allus^{12} joined w/ allthem^{3} in from that union comed forth wasshisname^{21} SOLD wassername^{19} still by thuh reputation uh thistree one uh thuh 2 twins loses her sight through fiddlin n falls w/ugly old yuh fathuh^{4} given she^{8} SOLD whodat^{33} pairs w/you^{23} (still polite) of which nothinmuch comes nothinmuch now nothinmuch^{6} pairs with ycssuhmistuhsuh^{17} tuh drop one called yo$^{9-0}$ now yo still who gone be wentin now w/elle gived us el SOLD let us not forget ye^{1-2-5} w/ thee^{3} givin us thou$^{9-2}$ who w/thuh they who switches their designation in certain conversation yes they^{10} broughted forth onemore^{2} at thuh same time in thuh same row right next door we have datone^{12} w/disone^{14} droppin off duhtherone$^{4-4}$ SOLD let us not forget du and sie let us not forgetyessuhmastersuh^{38} w/thou^{8} who gived up memines$^{3-0}$ SOLD we are now rollin through thuh long division gimmie uh gimmie uh gimmie uh squared-off route round it off round it off n round it out w/sistuh$^{4-3}$ who lives with one called saintmines^{9} givin forth one uh year how it got there callin it jessgrew callin it saintmines calling it whatdat whatdat whatdat SOLD.
>
> **Black Man with Watermelon:** Thuh list goes on and on. Dont it. (*AP* 124)

"If in no other way," writes Spillers, "the destruction of the African name, of kin, of linguistic, and ritual connections is so obvious in the vital stats that we tend to overlook it."[55] The almost bizarre mathematical constructions that Parks includes in Ham's speech, which are evident only in the written script, call attention to the number of ancestors who were sold, particularly as the numbers and the word "SOLD" stand out on the printed page. Yet they also suggest that the cold statistics that make the destruction of the African name and kinship so "obvious" still do not give a true account of the total loss.[56] Even after Ham has delivered his elaborate "long division," Black Man resignedly reminds us that

the "list goes on and on. Dont it." Similarly, the impetus to remember the ancestors, evoked repeatedly in the phrase "let us not forget," is at odds with the lack
of names, a lack Parks highlights with her foreign and invented words—"callin
it jessgrew callin it saintmines callin it whatdat whatdat whatdat SOLD"—and
with the desire, born perhaps of shame, to forget some of the ancestors who
can be named (as in the double meaning of "let us not forgetyessuhmaster-
suh"). The fact that the numbers in superscript are apparent only typographically also suggests that the numbers of ancestors who perished can be ignored
depending on the kind of representation, oral or textual, in which their fate is
represented.

The pull between naming/numbering and lack/disavowal, a double gesture
best expressed with Parks's invented word "saintmines," a phonetic elision of the
words "this ain't mines," creates a perplexity that, unlike the kind that permeates
the early part of the speech, does *not* produce laughter. Instead, it evokes the
humor of the minstrel stump speech in order to signify on it. As several critics
have observed, the humor of the stump speech derived significantly from the
speaker's use and misuse of language. That linguistic distortion was connected to
what made the minstrel show so popular: the fact that it made black bodies into
fetishes and commodities through sexuality. With respect to the malapropisms
typical of the minstrel stage, Eric Lott writes that, while the speeches figured as
a kind of "witless orality signifying nothing beyond itself," their subtexts usually betrayed sexual fantasies and pointed to a "vexing and unmeaning linguistic
creativity" that produced "huge, ungainly, and onomatopoetic words" that called
attention to "the grain of voices, the wagging of tongues, the fatness of painted
lips."[57]

Parks does not reproduce such vulgarity but, in signifying on the stump
speech, she conjures it and sets it at odds with her own linguistic creativity. Far
from performing the "witless orality" of the minstrel stage, her linguistic dexterity measures the enormous distance between the way African Americans were
represented, the way they were perceived, and the experiences that shaped their
lives. As Alisa Solomon observes, through her "stage imagery and experiments
with language," Parks "pulls taut" the tensions between "inner and outer life,
between black and white worlds, between reality and appearance."[58] In Ham's
speech, for instance, "saintmines" is conspicuously close to "jessgrew," Parks's
take on Stowe's figuring of Topsy as someone who, as an orphaned and enslaved
child, miraculously "just grew," like a weed. Like Ishmael Reed who, in his novel
Mumbo Jumbo (1972), also signifies on Stowe's phrase, Parks contrasts Stowe's
callous representation of natal alienation with her own, intimately more nuanced
rendering of it.[59] Juxtaposing the often bewildering gaps between the binaries
that Solomon specifies, Parks embellishes the absurdity of the absurd, thereby
provoking forms of laughter that mock and satirize. At the same time, she elicits

the kind of laughter that creates tension between opposite feelings. On the one hand, we feel the desire to reject and disavow the specter of minstrelsy that she conjures. On the other, we are compelled to look and listen to that specter, which speaks and moves as though possessed by Parks's words.

Rites of Mourning

Parks thus maintains the most traditional function of theater, the production of catharsis, even as she experiments with almost all other aspects of the medium. Comparing the catharsis that *The Death of the Last Black Man* creates to that of voodoo rituals devoted to the Petro loa, one of the three main families or groups of spirits in voodoo as well as the spirits of the ancestors who experienced the Middle Passage and slavery, we can see that her reasons for doing so are rooted in the history of the African diaspora. As Joan Dayan notes, some practitioners claim that the Petro loa do not let the descendants of African slaves "forget the tribulations of slavery ... [that the] story [is] passed on through generations ... who remember the gods and ancestors left out of books, who bear witness to what the standard histories would never tell."[60] When the Petro loa are summoned, argues Maya Deren, they manifest the rage "against the evil fate which the African suffered, the brutality of his displacement and his enslavement" in the New World.[61] Their rituals are known to be fierce, aggressive, and angry and to entail upheaval and fire.[62] The loa's rage is, as Deren puts it, "the crack of the slave/whip sounding constantly, a never/to/be forgotten ghost." But the Petro rage is not wicked. Rather, it commemorates the violence suffered by the enslaved by repeating it in the present. When the Petro loa Erzuline Ge-Rouge possesses a devotee, for instance, the person mounted experiences a "terrible paralysis of frustration." Deren describes the encounter: "The neck is rigid and the tears stream from the tightly shut eyes, while through the locked jaw and the grinding teeth there issues a sound that is half groan, half scream, the inarticulate song of in/turned cosmic rage."[63]

As the medium through which the ancestors speak, Parks makes this rage intelligible to us, who are separated from the experiences of the dead by centuries. She makes it articulate by crafting it in a language that is, by turns, otherworldly and piercingly intimate and recognizable. She also emphasizes that the expression of such rage must have as one of its goals the possibility of honoring those who died anonymously. Hence, she highlights the ritual elements of her plays.

In the production of *The Death of the Last Black Man* directed by Liz Diamond, the ritual elements were noticeable even before the actors emerged. Aside from showing the façade of a log cabin and the couple's porch, all under dim lights, Diamond displayed a peculiar altar nestled in an aperture of the cabin: a large watermelon placed on top of a television set that projected a warm yellow light and, under it, slices of watermelon displayed as offerings. Serving as a visual reminder of the past, of its stereotypical imagery and the ancestors once stigmatized by it, the altar pointed to the way that contemporary media continue to disseminate stereotypes. It also suggested the Neo-Hoodoo aspects of Parks's work. On the one hand, it recalled the altars that are central to voodoo rituals, which include vévés, or ground drawings, iconographic symbols of ancestors, and food offerings placed to win their favor. On the other hand, the altar was abstract and kitsch and thus in keeping with the self-referential mode with which Parks reinforces the artificiality of the theater.

The altar was also in keeping with other ritualistic elements, such as the tolling of bells, which sound at various points to signal changes in the motion of the play. The movement, as I have been suggesting, is, first, toward the release of anger and pathos through testifying and witnessing, and, second, toward rest for the dead and mourning and acceptance for the living. While such description implies a straightforward procedure, the play actually moves between announcing the "death of the last black man in the whole entire world" and suspending it, creating in the process ever deepening circles of collective and individual testimony. The last panel, which is called "In Thuh Garden of Hoodoo It," a title that riffs on the question of blame raised by the play while literally spelling out the word hoodoo, shows us Black Woman preparing Black Man for burial. She cleanses and dresses his body while the two figures repeat "Miss me," "Remember me," after the fashion of blues stanzas.

The process through which Black Man and Black Woman arrive at the moment of burial depends on the collective remembrance and testifying of the kin. It depends also on Parks's audiences, who are simultaneously involved in the play's rites of mourning by virtue of their presence, and prevented from being mere spectators by Parks's absurdist humor. The intimate scenes between Black Man and Black Woman further demonstrate this point. Their scenes are marked by the quick shifts in mood that are characteristic of tragicomedy; the scenes turn from deep grief to absurdist humor, or from humorous though violent descriptions to deeply sobering images, or from mournful moments to ironic ones. Parks produces these shifts and tensions by contrasting the narratives of the man and wife, who speak at cross-purposes throughout and thus seem not to communicate at all. Yet the two share a narrative of grief, one that Parks builds precisely by accentuating their separation through language. She also progressively integrates their stories as Black Woman slowly accepts her husband's death and Black Man finishes the account of his multiple deaths. Only at such a point can Black Woman begin to ready her husband for burial.

As Black Man sits on his porch immobilized by a watermelon, he tries to take inventory of his body, which has been variously dismembered and destroyed. In the meantime, his wife tries to feed him a meal that she went to great lengths to prepare. In a passage that underscores the mixture of anger and grief with which

Black Woman bears witness, she tells the ghost of her husband how she prepared the meal:

> Strutted down up thuh road with my axe. By-my-self-with-my-axe. Got tuh thuh street top 93 dyin hen din hand. Dropped thuh axe. Tooked tuh strangling. 93 dyin hen din hand with no heads let em loose tuh run down tuh towards home infront of me. Flipped thuh necks of thuh next 23 more off. Slinged um over my shoulders. . . . Awe on that. Hen? You got uhway. Knew you would. (*AP* 106)

The absurdity of the imagery against the background of a domestic scene—the cabin, the porch—produces a heightened surrealism, which signals the figures' struggle without either sentimentalizing it or making it simply fantastical. Black Woman chops the heads off ninety-three chickens and wrings the necks of twenty-three more to keep up the illusion that she can comfort her husband back from his painful deaths. In the midst of a swirl of action in which she is strutting, flipping, strangling, and slinging, she lets the headless animals loose "tuh run down tuh towards home" in front of her.

While Black Woman makes us imagine the chickens she has beheaded and let loose, Black Man tells the story of his own death, explicitly detailing the physical and psychic pain he endures. The switch between the two perspectives—from the ridiculous to the tragic—has the effect not only of disarming the viewer but also of making him or her more cautious. As J. L. Styan argues, at such moments in a tragicomedy, the audience member is "charged with a tension as a result of which he is more alert and therefore a responsive participant."[64] Parks employs this tension to guard against a passive witnessing of Black Man's account of his deaths. In part, she achieves this by giving him control of how to represent his own death in an ironic allusion to the slave narrative tradition, in which the writer controlled the manner of representing his or her life, and by allowing the audience to become his witness through an empathetic connection to Black Woman.

But Parks also heightens the tragedy of his accounts by rendering them in the same abstract language with which Black Woman paints her absurd domestic vision. In one passage Black Man tells of being electrocuted:

> Thuh straps they have on me are leathern. See thuh cord wagging full with uh jump-juice try me tuh giggle from thuh waggin but belt leathern straps: width thickly. One around each forearm. Forearm mines? 2 cross thuh chest. Chest mines: and it explodin. One for my left hand fingers left strapped too. Right was done thuh same. Jump-juice meets me mine juices I do uh slow softshoe like on water. Town crier cries uh moan. Felt my nappy head go frizzly. (*AP* 108)

As Yvette Louis argues, Parks's "disruption of logical structure and discontinuity of language" in passages such as this one "seems to free up the emotive potential of words."[65] The attention to detail in the passage is surprising given its schematic nature: different limbs are accounted for as the electric power, the juice, meets the man's own energy, what he calls "me mine juices," leaving us with a vivid picture of his electrocution. Some of the details connote a piercing irony. When Black Man tells of being on the electric chair he notes, "Closer to thuh power I never been," suggesting both his literal destruction by electric power and the fact that in that moment he could not have been closer to the power others have to kill (108).

The reactions that Black Man has to the "jump-juice" recall minstrel antics, from wagging, wiggling, and jumping to slow "softshoe." This has the effect of yoking one form of violence to another: the theater and the spectacle of electrocution. Significantly, this connection is not made explicit in Black Man's account of his lynching. Instead, Parks aims our focus almost myopically on details that we perceive from the point of view of Black Man:

> Swingin from front tuh back uhgain. . . . Chin on my chest hangin down restin eyes each on eyein my 2 feets. Left on thuh right one right one thuh left. Crossed eyin. It was difficult tuh breathe. Toes uncrossin then crossin for good luck. With my eyes. Gaw. It began tuh rain. Oh. Gaw. Ever so lightly. Blood came on up. You know tough. Like riggamartins-stifly only— isolated. They some of em pointed they summoned uh laughed they some looked quick in an then they looked uhway. It had began to rain. . . . Ever so lightly gaw gaw. (*AP* 119)

The emphasis on eyes and vision places us alongside his perspective such that we become witnesses to the process of his dying, as if we were dying along with him. The fact that we look from his dropped chin all the way to his feet suggests an image of crucifixion viewed from the perspective of the crucified. Contrasting with such a dramatic image is the simple sentence "It was difficult tuh breathe," rendered mostly in Standard English amid Parks's idiosyncratic language, and therefore achieving a quiet but forceful impact. The tender irony of his statement "Toes uncrossin then crossin for good luck" produces a quick "feeling of the opposite": one wants to laugh at Black Man's act of superstition in the face of death but ultimately feels sympathy and sorrow. The impulse to laugh makes one implicitly complicit with those who, witnessing the lynching, can summon a laugh as they point to Black Man, a realization of which further deepens the compassion that one finally feels for him.

And then there is the sound "gaw," which is interspersed throughout Black Man's account. The sound both heightens the pathos of the speech and undercuts the possibility of empty sentimentalism. One of Parks's "foreign words & phrases," "gaw" is a "glottal stop" which requires that the "root of the tongue" snap, or click "in the back of the throat," to create "a strangulated articulation of the word *Gaw!*" (*AP* 17–18). It is similar to the "foreign" word "uh! or uuh!" which Parks suggests should be said with a "deep quick breath" to denote "drowning or breathlessness" and which resounds predominantly in the "Third Kingdom" parts of *Imperceptible Mutabilities* describing the victims of the Middle Passage. "Gaw," as Black Man says it in his account of his deaths, has the effect of disorienting the audience in the same way as do Parks's quick shifts in mood. In the 1990 BACA production of the play, the actor portraying Black Man added a quick sideways thrust of the head, vividly evoking an effort to speak through strangulation.

Throughout the play, And Bigger and Bigger and Bigger echoes both Black Man's "gaw" and his desire to "move his hands," a phrase that becomes synonymous with his wish to be finally free to rest in peace. As in *Imperceptible Mutabilities,* these echoes connect Black Man, mythical-historical figure of slavery and Jim Crow persecution, and And Bigger and Bigger and Bigger, in many ways his twentieth-century counterpart. However, And Bigger echoes both the sound and the phrase in angry protest. He channels the rage of the Petro loa, a rage that in this context is expressive of the need for resolution to the central crux of the play, the fate of Black Man. In the final chorus, the play's figures announce the death of the last black man as if declaring the end of a vicious cycle and all together repeat the mirthless laugh "Ha. Ha. Ha. HHHHIIIIIIHHHHH-HHH," this time adding a final "HA!" (*AP* 131). It is then that Black Man can at last move his hands. As the play's title and major refrain suggest, however, the end of the vicious cycle could also be understood as genocide since the last black man in the *whole entire world* is free at last, but freed unto death. The resolution that And Bigger demands is thus both dream and nightmare, and the ritual catharsis of emotion that the play enacts is suspended between both.

As we saw in chapter 2, Richard Pryor stages the paradox that the breach of slavery presents, a breach that needs to be redressed but that *cannot* be redressed Parks stages a similar paradox: the need to commemorate, celebrate, and lay to rest the ancestors who perished while acknowledging the threat to genocide that still threatens their descendants. Thus, the end of the play is indeed a "celebration," as Louise Bernard concludes, and a resolution, as Elam and Rayner claim, for Black Man has "successfully crossed over the land of the dead"; he has been "connected to the history of the figures that have passed on before him."[66] Yet the end of the play is also an acknowledgment that the terror to which the ancestors were subjected cannot be forgotten. As Dayan notes, the ancestors demand that it never be forgotten. In many ways also, the terror has mutated into forms of institutionalized racism that cannot be ignored. Black Man, after all, dies "yesterday, tuhday next summer, tuhmorrow just uh moment ago."

The play ends with all figures saying, "Hold it. Hold it. Hold it. Hold it. Hold it. Hold it. Hold it," as if charging audiences to "hold" the contradiction between celebration and acknowledgment of terror (*AP* 131). Formally, the play holds this contradiction through Parks's tragicomedy while offering itself as the document that will testify to the plight of the ancestors and to the plight of their descendants. Hence, while the play begins with the statement "You should write it down . . . you should hide it under a rock," it ends with "You will write down thuh past and you will write down thuh present in what in thuh future. . . . You will carve it all out of a rock so that in the future when we come along we will know that the rock does yet exist" (*AP* 131). As a performance, the play maintains the coexistence of opposites, the solemn and the absurd, the horrible and the comic, the celebration of linguistic creativity and humor and the memory of degradation, but when the performance is over, the viewer must come to a cathartic resolution on his or her own.

If we take catharsis to mean clarification, in what ways do the tensions that Parks maintains clarify the connections between past and present? How might such clarification lead to ethical judgment and action? If such catharsis is cognitive in nature, it is facilitated by an emotionally engaging spectatorship that is also balanced by Parks's abstract language and absurd humor, which resists the passive consumption of grief. The viewer has the choice not to engage at all, of course, especially as Parks's topics and experimental style can prove alienating. As Shawn-Marie Garrett notes, Parks's "methods make some in the African-American theatre community uncomfortable," and others find her too abstract, thus "Parks' plays are rarely produced at theatres exclusively devoted to the production of African-American drama." Her "tendency to attract predominantly white audiences and directors sparks further questions in some minds about whether she is speaking to or for the African-American experience."[67] Still, Garrett, who has followed and observed Parks's plays for a number of years in different cities and who has informally interviewed spectators, concludes that "the only consistency in audience reaction to Parks's plays" is that "it cannot be broken down by race, age, education, income or any of the other usual 'predictors.'" Garrett rightly argues that Parks takes the "unpredictable assortment of theatre artists, audiences and critics" who follow her work "through double- (and triple-) takes, asks them to observe what changes and what stays the same over the span of historical and performance time, and to take nothing at face value—particularly not the language through which history exerts its force."[68] It is a testament to Parks's virtuosity as a playwright, and to her immense capacity to render the beautiful and the comic alongside the ugly and the painful, that her audiences repeatedly choose to engage with the challenges and pleasures of her plays. Attendance for the production of *365 Days/365 Plays* at the Public Theater in New York City (from November 13, 2006 to November 12, 2007) has been remarkable both for the quantity of people attending and for its diversity.

Parks also depends on silence to deepen the tensions she builds. Her plays are interspersed with what she calls "spells," or "elongated and heightened" rests. As she describes them in "Elements of Style," spells are "denoted by the repetition of figures' names with no dialogue"; on the printed page they have an "architectural look" (*AP* 16). In a scene from *The America Play*, for example, Lucy, a "Confidence" (or someone who can hear the voices of the dead), and her son Brazil, the professional mourner, speak of their deceased husband and father, but the dialogue breaks into a spell:

> Brazil
> Lucy
> Brazil
> Lucy
> Brazil
> Lucy (178)

A spell "is the place where the figures experience their pure simple state," writes Parks. It "is a place of great (unspoken) emotion," the experience of which she compares to looking at planets aligning while trying to imagine the "music of their spheres" (17). Joseph Roach calls such deep silences "liturgical," and argues that, while they are "a feature common to modern drama," such silences are particularly "conspicuous in [Parks's] plays." Parks seeks the theater and the "special, strange relationship" it has to "real-life" because, as Roach argues, "it is the place where deep silences can either follow significant revelations or create the emotional space into which revelation can enter."[69] The silences in Parks's plays arrive with the same surprising effect that her shifts achieve; they provide, not relief, but a space where the tension heightens. Within the play, the release comes as her figures affect the "laughs of laughs," the laugh that laughs "at that which is unhappy." Within the audience, the catharsis comes as we gain clarity about our relationship to the past. For the past in Parks's work "is still and always with us—all of us . . . in our collective memories, in our gestures, in our genes, in our rituals and habits, and most of all . . . in our words."[70]

In *Venus*, Parks's tragicomedy takes a different turn. In this play Parks refuses to provide the kind of catharsis she provides in *The Death of the Last Black Man* and, instead, heightens the juxtapositions of her tragicomedy to new, agonizing levels. The result is a play that is more politically strident than her earlier work but also one in which the very absence of catharsis argues for its need. The humor of the play does not provide the mixture of distance from and intimacy with the past that characterize her earlier work. Rather, it consistently highlights the ways the black female body has been and continues to be an object of sexual fetishization. The Venus of the play, as the embodiment of such objectification, does not emit the mirthless laugh, although the audience is well aware of her deep suffering. Instead, we are left aching for its sound.

"She'd Make a Splendid Freak": Venus, or a Coda on Black Humor and the Black Body

In 1996, when the descendants of the Khoikhoi petitioned the French government for the return of Saartjie Baartman's remains, *Venus* opened to the public for the first time at Yale Repertory Theatre. For Tony Kushner, "*Venus* expresses a global empathy, a mourning for all of suffering humanity, and at the same time an anger at oppression and oppressors, an indictment of wrongs yet to be righted."[71] Indeed, *Venus* is a play that, like all of the rituals of redress examined in this study, shuttles between grief and grievance. Yet, unlike *The Death of the Last Black Man*, the play does not operate through Parks's abstract language but adopts the more straightforward style that has come to characterize her recent plays, her two revisions of Nathaniel Hawthorne's *The Scarlet Letter*, *In the Blood* (1999) and (the hilariously titled) *Fucking A* (2000), her Pulitzer Prize–winning *Topdog/Underdog* (2001), and *365 Days/365 Plays* (2006). The difference with respect to the humor in her fictions of slavery is significant, for, while her plays continue to mix humor and pathos, often in the context of the legacy of slavery and colonialism, the humor in those plays does not depend on the kind of defamiliarizing language that Parks employs in Ham's speech in *The Death of the Last Black Man*. In some ways the departure makes her plays more accessible, and thus implicitly responsive to the criticism that her work has received. But the shift also makes her design more apparent and therefore denies the shield, or escape, that her formal experimentation might provide for some. In *Venus*, specifically, the departure also entails another significant shift: from using an abstract language as the primary means of producing a tragicomedy of slavery, to using the black body to invoke a historical narrative of grief and pain, a narrative that Parks juxtaposes with a hyperbolic satire of voyeurism and exploitation.

· Parks risks much with this play. Despite the fact that it maintains a signifying fluidity between the historical Baartman and the figure of Saartjie, and that it emphasizes the fact that the historical Baartman, like her stage alter ego, was a "theatrically created sign of desire" for the Other, it risks repeating the original violation inflicted on the body of a real historical figure through the surrogate relation that the actress in Saartjie's role bares to Baartman.[72] Parks mitigates this risk in multiple ways. As Elam and Rayner note, *Venus* has two contrasting kinds of structure. On the one hand, the play provides a narrative based on the real historical story of Baartman, a story that, though presented in reverse, starting with the death of the Venus, chronicles Baartman's life in a way that provides the comforting distance of history, of a whole story distanced and sealed by time. On the other hand, the play interweaves a series of scenes that connect the display of Baartman's body to the "exploitation of strangeness in freak shows, sideshows, novelty, and circus acts" through the story of Mother-Showman, a character based on the various keepers who exhibited Baartman, and her "9 Human Wonders," a group of human "anomalies" in which Saartjie becomes the main attraction.[73] In these sections, Parks, who continues to use Rep&Rev as a central conceit, plays on the homonymic relation between "wonder" and "wander" to invoke the relationship between Otherness and exile in the same way that she interlaces sonic links between the concept of "God's Great Chain of Being," with the racist implications that it would come to have, and the simple word chain, which of course signals to the objects used to tether captives. She even invokes the chorus in Aretha Franklin's "Chain of Fools" through a simple repetition of the word, "Chain Chain Chain."[74] Clearly, Parks still makes language do a great deal of work in her plays, even as she makes it sparser. Just as Saartjie joins the Human Wonders, they, speaking in chorus, declare, "Chain. / We wander thuh world: Here is the Reason: / Our funny looks read as High Treason" (*Venus* 33).

As Elam and Rayner note, the Human Wonders scenes clearly foreground theatrical artifice and, as such, continuously disrupt the comforting distance invoked by the narrative of Baartman's life. Mother-Showman constantly demands that her Human Wonders "Pull out all thuh stops!" and provide a "Big Finish!" for the show she puts on (*Venus* 34). The narrative of Baartman's life is also interrupted by the series of historical footnotes (recalling those Parks uses in *Imperceptible Mutabilities*) read by the Negro Resurrectionist, a kind of emcee who announces the title of each scene. Another series of interruptions is provided by a play within the play, called "For the Love of the Venus," in which a young man's obsession with a Hottentot woman threatens his impending marriage. Parks intersperses portions of this play throughout *Venus*, clearly replicating the main issues of the larger play in both the content and the staging. Watching the play within the play is the Baron Docteur, a French physician who invokes the historical figures of Georges Cuvier and Henri Blainville, the two anatomists who performed autopsies on Baartman. The Baron Docteur, like the young husband in the play within the play, is infatuated with a Hottentot, with Saartjie, to be precise; his infatuation is a potent mixture of desire, disgust, and lust for her and ambition for his scientific career. Watching the Docteur, however, is the Venus, and watching it all, of course, is the audience, who is implicated in Parks's complex resurrection of the Venus.

Parks has thus put her maverick formal innovation to the service of reconstituting (as opposed to merely representing) the thorny questions of voyeurism and exploitation that were raised by the display of Baartman's body during her life. In addition, she constantly connects the past and the present, sometimes in obvious, anachronistic ways, such as when one of the 9 Human Wonders complains of having jet lag, but more extensively through her satiric treatment of those who exploit or consume difference out of greed, be it monetary, sexual, or otherwise. While the two kinds of structure that constitute the play—the narrative and the Human Wonders sections—contrast in elaborate ways, each scene has a common denominator: a hyperbolic, satiric tone that seems to cap on the hideous yet absurd excitement and fear implicit in the interpellation "Look, a Negro!" famously addressed by Frantz Fanon. The play turns that interpellation around as if to imply a different statement: "Look, Colonizers!" This reversal is apparent visually when Saartjie watches the Baron who is watching the play within the play, his gaze redirected away from Saartjie and toward those obsessed with Hottentots. Parks sustains the artificial and eerie excitement of sideshows and circuses ("Step right up come on come in") that the Human Wonders sections make emphatic when she turns our attention to the various institutions that are corrupted by the potent mixture of desire and disgust underwriting the obsession with the Venus. Thus, in courtroom scenes, scenes of courting and marriage, scenes of scientific and colonial exploration and exploitation, the play highlights the corruption of ideals through a satire that, though sharp, never quite vilifies its subjects. Instead, Parks presents people whose lusts, prejudices, and superstitions turn them into parasites and freaks. When, during a courtroom scene, a widow testifies that her "dear man," who "was fond of sights," saw "The Venus H." and received "a feather from her head." The widow includes the dead man's testimony and her conversations with him about the Venus:

> They [the feathers] are said to bring good luck.
> "A fight ensued. 3 men died. Uh little boy went mad. Uh
>   woman lost her child."
> My man escaped with thuh feather intact.
> "Poor Creature."
> "Very extraordinary indeed!"
> "This is a sight which makes me melancholy!"
> My husbands words exactly.
> He was home standing by the window. I can see him now.
> And then he walked away from me, in deep thought,
>   and then, totally forgetting his compassion, shouted loud:
> "Good God what butts!"
> (Rest)
> Thuh shock of her killed him, I think,
>   cause 2 days later he was dead.
> Ive thrown away the feather. (*Venus* 69)

The man's prurient fascination with the Venus is more pathetic than evil, as is the scrambling and mayhem that ensue when the crowd fights for the feather.

Still, Parks does not let one forget the violent repercussions of the event, silly as it might be. When the man "forgets" his compassion, dramatically shouts his "admiration" for the Venus's posterior, and then falls dead, apparently killed by the "shock of her," Parks's hyperbolic style clearly and mockingly highlights how people's obsessions can get the better of them. By contrasting this satiric mode to the display of Saartjie's body, which is painfully, disturbingly reconstituted by the play itself, Parks gives her satire dark, piercing tones. Preceding the widow's account of her husband's death, for instance, we are told that the Venus "was surrounded by many persons":

> One pinched her, another walked round her;
> one gentleman *poked* her with his cane
> uh *lady* used her parasol to see if all was, as she called it
>   "*natural.*"
> Through all of this the creature didnt speak.
> Maybe uh sigh or 2 maybe when she seemed inclined to
>   protest the pawing. (*Venus* 69)

In this instance we are only given a description of the egregious humiliation to which the Venus was subjected; in other scenes we are witnesses to the humiliation itself as the Venus poses for other characters in the play and, by extension, for the audience of the play. The contrast between the pathetic spectacle of people gawking and poking at the Venus and the tragedy of the caged Venus produces the effect of a disturbing, haunting, and sickening funhouse.

As I have been suggesting, Parks extends her critique of past abuses of spectatorship to those of the present, most poignantly by reinstantiating the display of the Venus's body. But, as Elam and Rayner argue, most of the play's responses, both approving and not, focus on the historical instance of voyeurism, spectatorship, and violence of Baartman's story rather than on its reinstantiation, because it is easier to condemn the past than to come to terms with the "fact that even in a re-production we, the contemporary audience members, are still viewing the Hottentot Venus with an assumption of superiority over those earlier spectators, thus ignoring our own complicity in the sight." Not that Parks makes it easy. In fact, she re-creates the moments in which the Venus poses for the inspection of others, with all of the "vulnerability, shamefulness, and the shame of her exhibition" fully exposed.[75] In fact, in at least two productions of the play, the New York Public Theater's (1996) and Harvard's Loeb Experimental Theater's (2004), the actress in the role of Saartjie was literally exposed, wearing a costume that, while consisting of an enormous fake behind, gave the semblance of nudity. In this costume the actresses posed for inspection, a feat that proved consistently challenging, as evidenced by the trouble Harvard's production had in keeping the same actress in the lead role (during the rehearsal period two lead actresses quit the play). A great deal of the challenge lies, of course, in being exposed. But the role also calls for posing without introjecting the shame of the exhibition. "The display of the Venus is shameful," as Elam and Rayner put it, "but the shame belongs more to the spectators than to her," and the actress is meant to gaze back at the spectators in much the same way that the Venus watches the Baron Docteur watching the play within the play. She is meant to gaze back, deflecting and mirroring the potent mixture of lust and greed that made her a spectacle in the first place. In this posing and gazing lies the potential for a complicated form of resistance since the "pose is an act that paradoxically accepts and refracts the gaze of the spectator."[76]

This is a tall order for any actress and any audience. It is easier to judge the wrongs of the original audiences for Baartman's posing, just as it is easier to think about the ways that the play indicts contemporary culture for its obsession with "bootylicious" black women's bodies than to recognize how, in the moment of performance, the terribleness of the past is resurrected *and* reinstantiated. These are the moments in which at least this audience member craves the distance and catharsis that black humor can provide. Yet, unlike her previous plays, Parks's *Venus* does not provide cathartic release. Instead, its satiric humor is directed at the spectators, past and present, of the Venus Hottentot, while the black body is made, once again, to carry an enormous burden. The denial of catharsis is meant to make uncomfortably clear the urgent need to interrogate not only the past history of abuses of spectatorship and voyeurism but also their material legacy in the moment of performance. In the sense that catharsis means, at least in part, the production of clarity, the play does provide plenty of opportunity to achieve it *in the audience*. But it does not stage the release of anger and pathos of the Venus. This is not to say that Parks represents the Venus as a mute victim. On the contrary, as Elam and Rayner argue, through the figure of the Venus she "recuperates Baartman as a complex subject, not a symbolic or figurative body."[77] In one of her most significant soliloquies, the Venus details the history of chocolate, and through it expresses with understated but deep pathos the parallels between her own twisted commoditization and that of chocolate (*Venus* 155–56). As in other instances, Parks mixes opposites—the seemingly insignificant history of chocolate and the tragedy of human exploitation—and thus makes poignantly clear, from the Venus's perspective, the sorrow of the colonized. Still, in most of the play, we witness a Venus who poses for others, for us, alone among her spectators without recourse to the mirthless laugh. The denial of her own catharsis leaves the black body to suffer with no guarantee that the ritual of reinstantiation will lead audiences to deep exploration and change. And even if such suffering could produce revelation and change, is the cost, the reinstantiation of black suffering, too high? This is the greatest risk that Parks takes in *Venus*.

The same can be said of Richard Pryor's performance in New Orleans, when he introjects the shame and guilt of slavery while denying his audience catharsis through laughter. Kara Walker's more strident work, especially the silhouettes and written pieces that express anger without the comic glee of some of her best pieces, also denies catharsis. By contrast, the other fictions of slavery that we have examined all provide, through formal innovation, the distancing and cathartic release of humor. More specifically, they make intricate use of the rich tradition of African American vernacular culture, especially of conjure, to represent a painful past without making a spectacle of black pain. Thus, William Wells Brown minstrels minstrelsy and satirizes Sentimental Abolitionists but moves the scenes of black suffering offstage. Although Charles Chesnutt does represent black suffering, he also gives it a sound fit to kill through a tragicomic laughter of enormous, resounding impact. And, as we have seen, in many of his stand-up performances, Pryor manipulates his voice and long, bony frame to show the theatricality of stereotypes and thus frees the black body, at least performatively, from being typecast by them. Similarly, Ishmael Reed uses his Neo-Hoodoo aesthetic, expertly mixing voodoo belief and practice with aspects of postmodern and popular culture, as a way to defetishize stereotypes. In much of their work Robert Colescott and Kara Walker use familiar images from the history of European painting and the tradition of silhouette portraiture as distancing mechanisms. While Colescott uses his spoofing of master paintings to expose the comic grotesque of America's racial imagination, Walker capitalizes on the silhouette form, which never shows bodies but how bodies block light, to dispense with the spectator-performer relationship; her silhouettes do not represent people performing for the voyeuristic consumption of others but instead expose the freakish psychological mutations produced by racial obsessions. The expert signifying on the signifyin(g) of Parks's early plays achieves a similar distancing goal. Signifying, Parks ruptures the American grammar that still, at times imperceptibly, equates people with things while introducing a new lexicon for historical remembrance.

The fictions of slavery in this study highlight not only the difficulty of representing black pain, particularly when the black body is physically present on stage, but also the challenge of creating an embodied, physical comedy given the lasting power of the specter of minstrelsy. In different ways, the writers and artists here examined have conjured and manipulated that ghost, turning its language and conventions inside out so that, instead of being a vehicle for humor against African Americans, the ghost expresses an idiosyncratic and sharp black humor, one that can provide the catharsis of emotion necessary to face the persistent legacy of slavery. Still, even in the performances of the most gifted, there are considerable risks. First and foremost is the issue of animating racial stereotypes. If the different conjurers I have examined enliven the ghost of minstrelsy in order to manipulate it, there is always the possibility that to enliven it is to do just that: to give it life and therefore power. Much of the controversy involving Kara Walker's and Dave Chappelle's work, for instance, speaks to the issue of how much their exploration of the racist imagination fuels rather than critiques its fire. Richard Pryor's burned body also reminds us that to get close to that fire can mean, quite literally, self-sacrifice. His was arguably a burning in effigy, a ritual purging of the shame and anger of a painful past through the body of a powerful conjurer. The danger that he tapped into suggests the fine line between the houngan, the voodoo ritual leader, and the boco, the sorcerer. Both can tap into a terrible past of dispossession, both can bring into life the spiritual world and the dead through rituals of possession, and yet one can heal and another destroy. The conjurers I have gathered here walk a tightrope over a burning fire as they invoke the brutality and murder of slavery and the cosmic rage that it produced. The fire and the risk of walking over it are all the more potent because they have accumulated power with each pernicious permutation of the original catastrophe. As Saidiya Hartman writes, we live in "the afterlife of slavery," a life in which black lives have been and still are "imperiled and devalued by a racial calculus and political arithmetic that were entrenched centuries ago."[78] To invoke slavery in the present is to invoke not only a terrible past but also its lasting and devastating impact.

Black humorists in the tradition I have examined also run the arguably less perilous risks of being misread or ignored. Brown, Chesnutt, and Harriet Wilson all suffered such fates. It seems impossible, from my perspective, to read Chesnutt as Amiri Baraka once did, as a "black parrot for white racist ideologies," or to label Brown a "pornographer," or to ignore Wilson's satire. And yet these misreadings are fairly recent. Perhaps a less pernicious risk may be to be taken solely as entertainment, especially if their intent is to be taken otherwise. Brown's *The Escape* certainly ran this risk. Yet by using modes of entertainment, black humorists have tapped into the immense power of popular culture and capitalized on it. Brown understood how much slavery was mediated by the mass cultural representations produced by, among other sources, the minstrel stage and the sentimental novel and, rather than dispute their reliability, manipulated them for his own ends. Walker has followed his lead, highlighting how much America's popular memory of slavery is constituted by images produced by entertainment industries.

The risks involved in creating black humor that addresses slavery and its legacy are formidable indeed, but the possibilities that such humor engenders are more formidable still. Contemporary black humorists maintain and improvise on a rich tradition of freedom, a wrested freedom that was born, as Richard Pryor put it, on the very same slave ships that held millions captive. African American humor has been, for centuries, a humor of survival. It has been a safety valve, a mode of minimizing pain and defeat, as well as a medium capable of expressing grievance and grief in the most artful and incisive ways. It has been a way of asserting one's humanity in the face of pulverization and mass murder. The importance of the physical in this tradition—of the artful control of the body in the name of humor—is no doubt a manifestation of the dispossession of the body that slavery entailed. Devalued as it has been by those who have misunderstood it or felt threatened by it, African American humor has also been a mode of laughing at the laugh created by the minstrel stage. Most important, although this aspect is certainly less recognized, it has been and remains a tremendously creative medium of artistic and political expression.

The black humorists in this book improvise on the arsenal of African American humor conventions—from the verbal rituals of insult and the indirection of signifying, to the elaborate tall tales or "lies" of stoops, kitchens, barbershops, pool halls, beauty shops, and street corners, to the swagger of toasts, the triumph of the trickster tale ("born and bread in the briar patch!"), and the blues-infused laugh of defeat—to mourn the losses of the past without spectacularizing black pain or colluding with a consumerism of grief. Perhaps most pressingly, the black humorists whose work we have examined keep us in tune with the imperceptible mutations of slavery and its systems. As if rephrasing the title of Countee Cullen's poem "What Is Africa to Me?" they ask, "What is slavery to me? To all of us living in its aftermath?" Through their manipulation of time they make clear both the distance and the layers of mediation through which we invoke slavery *and* the nearness of its legacy. In this double bind of distance and nearness we need not only the ethical, the hollow, and the mirthless laugh. We need also a laughter that's fit to kill.

NOTES

Introduction

1. See Michael K. Brown et al., *Whitewashing Race.*
2. Stephen Steinberg, "The Liberal Retreat from Race during the Post–Civil Rights Era," in Lubiano, *House That Race Built,* 22.
3. Virtanen and Huddy, "Old-Fashioned Racism and New Forms of Racial Prejudice," 313.
4. Robin D. G. Kelley, "Into the Fire 1970 to the Present," in Kelley and Lewis, *To Make Our World Anew,* 575.
5. Howard Winant, "Racial Dualism at Century's End," in Lubiano, *House That Race Built,* 105.
6. As quoted in Levine, *Black Culture and Black Consciousness,* 309.
7. Ibid.
8. Watkins, *On the Real Side,* 32.
9. This folk saying appears in numerous sources, including slave songs and blues lyrics. It is reprinted in ibid., 52.
10. Dollard, *Caste and Class in a Southern Town,* 309–10, as quoted in Levine, *Black Culture and Black Consciousness,* 313.
11. As quoted in Watkins, *On the Real Side,* 79.
12. As quoted in Levine, *Black Culture and Black Consciousness,* 342.
13. Freud, "Humour."
14. Ellison, *Going to the Territory,* 193–94.
15. Darryl Dickinson-Carr makes a similar distinction in his book on African American satirical novels with respect to contemporary representations of racial conflict in America. See Dickinson-Carr, *African American Satire,* 166.
16. Arguing that "racial segregation is crucial to explaining the emergence of the urban underclass of the 1970s," Douglas S. Massey writes, "By any measure, the character of American poverty changed significantly during the 1970s. The poor became poorer relative to the rest of society, and income levels increased. . . . Poverty also became

geographically concentrated within inner-city neighborhoods. . . . These trends were specially acute for blacks and Puerto Ricans." Massey, "American Apartheid," 329.

17. W. Solomon, "Secret Integrations," 471. See also Winston, "Humour noire and Black Humor."

18. Spillers, "Changing the Letter," 28–29.

19. Turner, *Drama, Fields and Metaphors*, 37–41.

20. Richard Schechner summarizes Turner's four-part scheme in *Performance Theory*, 215.

21. Ibid.

22. This is why the psychological paradigm of "working through" a trauma is not adequate with regard to slavery. There is no cure for that wound; there is only ritual remembrance. Some of that remembrance may indeed take the form of traumatic repetition, but in this book I am largely concerned with redressive remembrance.

23. Best and Hartman, "Fugitive Justice," 1.

24. Ibid., 9.

25. Winant, "Racial Dualism at Century's End," 94–95.

26. Kelley, *Freedom Dreams*, 62–63.

27. Hence, when Martin Luther King turned his attention to poverty and other chronic evils not resolved by civil rights legislation, he began to be hounded by the FBI. The Black Panther Party and other militant black organizations, such as the Revolutionary Action Movement, were subjected to outright violent measures.

28. Winant, "Racial Dualism at Century's End," 94–95.

29. Patterson, *Ordeal of Integration*, 61.

30. Kelley, "Into the Fire: 1970 to the Present," in Kelley and Lewis, *To Make Our World Anew*, 574–75.

31. See Kelley, " 'A Day of Reckoning': Dreams of Reparations," in *Freedom Dreams*, 110–34.

32. Spillers, "Mama's Baby, Papa's Maybe," 67.

33. See Rushdy, *Neo-Slave Narratives Studies*, 38. Between 1968 and 1970, slave narratives became popularly available, as six different anthologies were published. Soon after, the Works Project Administration interviewed former slaves and compiled *The American Slave: A Composite Autobiography* (1972). During the same year, the first two books to systematically employ slave testimony to produce a historical portrait of slavery—John Blassingame's *The Slave Community* and George Rawick's *From Sundown to Sunup*—were published, signaling the first practical results of the restoration of slave testimony as historical evidence.

34. Rushdy, *Neo-Slave Narratives Studies*, 3.

35. Reichardt, "Time and the African American Experience," 479.

36. Omi and Winant, *Racial Formation in the United States*, 63.

37. Virtanen and Huddy, "Old-Fashioned Racism," 313.

38. Norma Miriam Schulman, "Laughing across the Color Barrier: *In Living Color*," in Dines and Humez, *Gender, Race and Class in Media*, 439.

39. Reprinted in DeCosta-Willis, Martin, and Bell, *Erotique Noire*, xxxi.

40. In all likelihood, this version of the tale has been cleaned up, perhaps for mixed audiences, as the word "black" rather than "nigger" is used. The word is more likely

to have been uttered by the master and is common in in-group African American humor. As I note in my discussion of Pryor, African Americans have turned a word that, like curse words, immediately invokes the history of its terrible past use into a word that signifies affiliation. At the same time, it can summon the degradations of slavery and segregation instantly and thus, unlike curse words, cannot be used by just anyone.

41. Dayan, *Haiti, History and the Gods*, 40.

42. My treatment of voodoo and conjure is *not* a way of grounding the work in an "exotic" or "authentic" folk tradition. Rather, my approach is inspired by Joan Dayan who, especially in *Haiti, History and the Gods*, fruitfully challenges popular notions of voodoo as occult while showing the social and political power of a practice that is in constant flux. Driven underground for being a "pagan" practice, voodoo had to incorporate not only other belief systems to survive but also the imagery of mass culture, imagery that it both mimics and, through its mimicry, resists. Voodoo, as Dayan observes, "does not oppose what we might called 'Western' or 'Christian' [culture] but freely associates seemingly irreconcilable elements, taking in materials from the dominant culture even as it resists or coexists with it." Ibid., 51.

43. See George, *Hip-Hop America*, xi. See also his humorously titled *Post-Soul Nation: The Explosive, Contradictory, Triumphant, and Tragic 1980s as Experienced by African Americans (Previously Known as Blacks and before That Negroes)*.

44. This is Mark Anthony Neal's periodization. See his *Soul Babies*, 3. The Bakke case successfully imposed limitations on affirmative action by challenging the use of quota systems in university admissions.

45. Hartman, *Lose Your Mother*, 39–40.

46. Steinberg, "Liberal Retreat from Race," 15.

47. Dalfiume, "Forgotten Years of Negro Revolution," 106.

48. See ibid., 106.

49. West, *Cornel West Reader*, 135.

50. Kelley, *Freedom Dreams*, 7.

51. Neal, *Soul Babies*, 3.

52. Fuller, "Towards a Black Aesthetic," 204.

53. T. Ellis, "New Black Aesthetic," 235.

54. Ibid., 237.

55. Ibid., 239–40.

56. See Boskin, *Sambo*, 208–24.

57. For an extended discussion, see M. D. Harris, *Colored Pictured*, 84–124. The stereotype figure-turned-revolutionary also appeared in writings during the Black Arts Movement. In Amiri Baraka's play *J-E-L-L-O*, for instance, the Jack Benny–show retainer Rochester (Eddie Anderson) becomes militant.

58. Watkins, *On the Real Side*, 519.

59. George Houston Bass, introduction to *Mule Bone*, 3.

60. Boskin, *Sambo*, 224.

61. There was also an investment from segments of the black community in promoting the virile characters of blaxploitation films. As Mark Anthony Neal writes, although

the portrayals of black men in these films are "rife with many problematic elements, including unchallenged expressions of patriarchy, queer bashing, misogyny, and crude political ideas," blaxploitation films such as Marion Van Peebles's *Sweetback's Baadasss Song* (1971) "did help usher in a cultural moment in which African American male identity was presented in broadened ways." Neal, *Soul Babies*, 24.

62. Garrett, "Return of the Repressed." On the question of the colorblind casting that became popular and controversial with Joseph Papp's "Shakespeare in the Park," see A. Thompson, *Colorblind Shakespeare*.

63. Ibid., 30, 32.

64. Ibid., 32.

65. Ibid., 35.

66. Lhamon, *Raising Cain*.

67. Garrett, "Return of the Repressed," 36. See Lott, *Love and Theft*, 136–68.

68. Lott, *Love and Theft*, 149, 150.

69. Ibid., 162–63.

70. Gilmore, "'De Genewine Artekil,'" 744–45.

71. Ault, "Latest Chappelle DVD Is Selling Like Crazy."

72. Bernard, "Musicality of Language," 692.

73. Aside from the titles already mentioned in this introduction, there is also Dickson-Carr's *African American Satire: The Sacred and the Profane Novel* (2001), which examines how, by transgressing boundaries of taste, propriety, and decorum, satirical African American novels critique oppressive ideologies. Dickson-Carr provides a historical overview of the role of satire in African American novels; I focus on slavery specifically, but also extend the focus across disciplines and various forms of humor. For recent compilations of African American humor see Cumber Dance, *Honey Hush! An Anthology of African American Women's Humor* (1998); Watkins, *African-American Humor* (2002); and Beatty, *Hokum* (2006).

74. J. B. Ferguson, *Sage of Sugar Hill*, vii.

75. Ibid., 103.

76. Ibid., 216.

77. Ibid., 44.

78. For the latter, see Haggins, *Laughing Mad*.

Chapter 1

1. Watkins, *On the Real Side*, 70.

2. Joel Chandler Harris, *Introduction to Uncle Remus, His Songs and His Sayings* [1980] in *The Complete Tales of Uncle Remus*, xxvii.

3. As quoted in Bernard Wolfe, "Uncle Remus and the Malevolent Rabbit," in Dundes, *Mother Wit*, 528.

4. Wolfe, "Uncle Remus and the Malevolent Rabbit," 529.

5. See Dundes's introduction to Wolfe's essay in *Mother Wit*, 525.

6. Watkins, *On the Real Side*, 75.

7. As quoted in ibid., 67. The tale is also quoted in Charles H. Nichols, "Comic Modes in Black America (A Ramble through Afro-American Humor)," in Cohen, *Comic Relief*,

107. Nichols attributes the tale to Peter Randolph, the slave narrator of *From Slave Cabin to Pulpit* (1893).

8. Anonymous, "The Laugh that Meant Freedom," reprinted in Watkins, *African-American Humor*, 24.

9. Zora Neale Hurston, "High John de Conquer," in Dundes, *Mother Wit*, 543.

10. Ibid. Hurston claimed that "John de Conquer had come from Africa." As Alan Dundes notes, in a sense he did, especially if we take into account Hurston's efforts to portray John de Conquer as an ancestral spirit that followed the slave ships across the Middle Passage (543). But many of the tales, as Dundes notes, are "undeniably European" in origin. See *Mother Wit*, 541.

11. Both satirical prayers are anonymous and reprinted in Talley, *Negro Folk Rhymes*, 122.

12. "Historically, the satirist has often had to be on his guard and hide his satires beneath the sheep's clothing of a commonly accepted form." Paulson, *Fictions of Satire*, 5.

13. Ganter, "'He Made Us Laugh Some,'" 535–36. Scholars have noted the satire in early slave narratives, especially the "sting" at the end of seemingly pious or self-effacing chapters in Gustavus Vassa's (Olaudah Equiano's) narrative and other texts by his contemporaries. See Carretta, *Unchained Voices*.

14. Jacobs repeatedly draws attention to the deliberate calculations through which she sabotages her master's power, to her co-optation of his weapons (literacy), and to her use of cunning and wit in battling him (she even titles one of her chapters "Competition in Cunning"). Perhaps because of this, critics have noted her resourceful "tricksterism," her manipulation of her master from the confines of the small garret where she hides for seven years. See Randle, "Between the Rock and the Hard Place"; Beardslee, "Through Slave Culture's Lens Comes the Abundant Source."

15. Ganter, "'He Made Us Laugh Some,'" 535.

16. Boskin, *Sambo*, 32–33.

17. Appropriating the most anonymous yet most familiar name for an American slave, the pronoun "our" plainly signifying on that national familiarity, Wilson, as Gates notes, "reverse[d] the power relation implicit in re-naming rituals." Gates, introduction, li.

18. Ibid., xl, xxiii, xlvi; Breau, "Identifying Satire," 455–56.

19. Breau, "Identifying Satire," 456. See also C. Davis, "Speaking the Body's Pain: Harriet Wilson's *Our Nig*," for another reading that misses the satire in the novel. While Davis carefully examines Wilson's representation of pain in relationship to the overt sexualization of the black body and myths about its lack of sentience, she focuses so narrowly on Wilson's account of her painful experiences as to obscure other aspects of the text.

20. Breau, "Identifying Satire," 458.

21. Farrison, *William Wells Brown*; Ganter, "He Made Us Laugh Some," 535. For a detailed reading of Douglass's use of irony in his 1845 *Narrative*, see M. K. Burns, "A Slave in Form but Not in Fact."

22. Jacobs, *Incidents in the Life of a Slave Girl*, 51. The African American writer and French expatriate Victor Séjour wrote *The Jew of Seville* in French in 1844. For additional information regarding Brown, see Ernest, introduction to *The Escape; or, A Leap for Freedom: A Drama in Five Acts* (1858/2001), x. Subsequent references are cited parenthetically. See also Ernest, "Reconstruction of Whiteness," 1110.

23. Apter, "Acting Out Orientalism," 17.
24. Ibid., 18.
25. See Fisher Fishkin, "Bondswoman's *Escape*," 118.
26. Quoted in Farrison, *William Wells Brown*, 281.
27. *Seneca Falls Courier*, April 30, 1857, quoted in *National Anti-Slavery Standard*, May 9, 1857, p. 2, quoted in ibid., 285.
28. Henry C. Wright, "William Wells Brown—His Drama—Their Power for Good," *Liberator*, October 8, 1858, 163, quoted in Ernest, introduction, x.
29. As quoted in Farrison, *William Wells Brown*, 294.
30. For claims regarding the "shamelessly hyperbolic" aspect of *Clotel*, see R. J. Ellis, "Body Politics and the Body Politic," 108. For a rather bizarre interpretation of Brown's novel, one that claims the novel is an expression of Brown's "pornography of self," see Alis, introduction, xix. For a much more sensitive reading of *Clotel*, see du Cille's "Where in the World Is William Wells Brown?" especially 454–60.
31. Most critics have considered *Clotel* a deeply flawed text, important only because it is one of first novels written by an African American. See Ernest, *Resistance and Reformation in Nineteenth Century African-American Literature*, 20–21.
32. As Ganter notes, when Douglass used conventions of minstrelsy in his lectures, he also used his "strong personal charisma as a lively refutation of racist theories of the inferiorities of blacks" and was such an intelligent and powerful orator that when he "put on the mask of a buffoon," as in satires that he did of bigoted preachers, "it was so unlike" him that "it made the performance funnier." A similar phenomenon must have occurred during Brown's performances. Ganter, "He Made Us Laugh Some," 540.
33. Robert F. Reid-Pharr makes this point about Brown's use of minstrel conventions in an article about Kara Walker, "Black Girl Lost," 31.
34. Ganter, "He Made Us Laugh Some," 537.
35. Ibid., 539.
36. Wonham, " 'Curious Psychological Spectacle,' " 55.
37. For an exemplary essay, see J. S. White, "Baring Slavery's Darkest Secrets."
38. "Dave's Neckliss" originally appeared in *Atlantic Monthly* in October 1889.
39. Pirandello, *On Humor*, 118.
40. For an excellent example, see Eric Sundquist's "Charles Chesnutt's Cakewalk," in *To Wake the Nations*, especially 323–92.
41. Douglass wrote, "Sentimental Abolitionism is abundant. It may well be met with in the pulpit, sometimes in religious newspapers, and more frequently still we meet it in the meetings of the Republican party; yet among them all there is neither the will nor purpose to abolish slavery." Frederick Douglass, "The Abolition Movement Re-Organized," in Foner, *Life and Writings of Frederick Douglass*, 2: 522.
42. Ernest, introduction, xxxix.
43. Ibid., xxxii–xxxiii.
44. As I have already noted, Brown did use sentimental tropes, particularly in *Clotel*, but he also used burlesque, hyperbole, parody, and satire, refusing to rely solely on sentiment.
45. Ernest, "Reconstruction of Whiteness," 1110.

46. Ernest, introduction, xxxv.

47. Ibid., xxxvi–xxxvii.

48. In another scene, we learn that Pinchen participates in the slave trade, excusing his acts by claiming that he only does it to "pay for [his] traveling expenses" (*The Escape*, 20). He also considers himself successful in converting a slave trader when the latter decides to stop selling "a man from his wife, if he can get one to buy both of them together" (20, 17). "I tell you, sir," Pinchen tells another slave trader, "religion has done a wonderful work for him" (17).

49. In fact, in a 1972 interview with Al Young, Reed remarked on the similarities between Brown's work, specifically *The Escape*, and his own work: "And I was very surprised, after I wrote *Yellow Back Radio Broke-Down* I read William Wells Brown's play . . . *The Escape; or, A Leap for Freedom*, and I found out some of the same satirical thrusts there I used myself." Dick and Singh, *Conversations with Ishmael Reed*, 46.

50. Farrison, *William Wells Brown*, 303.

51. R. J. Ellis, "Body Politics and the Body Politic," 107.

52. See Lott, *Love and Theft*, 73; Levine, *Highbrow/Lowbrow*, 11–82.

53. Ernest, introduction, xxxv.

54. Anonymous, "Obituary, Not Eulogistic," in *Dwight's Journal of Music*, unsigned reprint, Boston, July 10, 1858. Available at www.iath.virginia.edu/utc/minstrel/misohp.html.

55. Paul Gilmore makes a similar argument with respect to Brown's presentation of black manhood in *Clotel*, 749. See Gilmore, "De Genewine Artekil."

56. For an excellent reading of Brown's linking of antislavery and minstrelsy, see ibid.

57. Elizabeth McKinsley, "An American Icon," in Adamson, *Niagara*, 90. See also McKinsley, *Niagara Falls*.

58. Farrison, *William Wells Brown*, 302.

59. H.E.D., "The Fugitive Slave's Apostrophe," *Boston Courier*, November 1, 1841, reprinted in Joseph T. Buckingham, *Personal Memoirs and Recollections of Editorial Life*, 2 vols. (Boston, 1852), 2:192–94, quoted in McKinsley, "An American Icon," 95.

60. McKinsley, "American Icon," 95.

61. "To say that *The Escape* is a commentary on identity as a social performance," notes John Ernest, "is not to say that Brown's audiences necessarily recognized the implications of the drama or that they emerged from the performance with a newly raised collective consciousness and a determination to rethink the concept of race." Ernest, "Reconstruction of Whiteness," 1116.

62. Eric Gardner, "Introduction," in *Major Voices*, xxx.

63. As quoted in Gilmore, "De Genewine Artekil," 750.

64. Ernest, introduction, xxxii.

65. Elam, "Black Performer and the Performance of Blackness," 293.

66. Ernest, "Reconstruction of Whiteness," 1100.

67. Gilmore, "De Genewine Artekil," 744.

68. Elam, "Black Performer and the Performance of Blackness," 293.

69. William Shakespeare, *Hamlet*, act 3, scene 4, lines 2435–36.

70. The line Brown quotes from *Hamlet* also suggests that, despite the fact that *The Escape* has none of the anger that so motivates *Our Nig*, the play is framed by a hint of

Brown's own urgent indignation. When Hamlet shows his mother the contrasting pictures, one of a slain noble soul and the other of a murderer, he is commanding her to come to her senses and refuse complicity in crime. Using a verbal force that comes close to physical violence, Hamlet seeks to enlist his mother on his side to achieve justice by avenging his father. Brown, of course, seeks to do the same with respect to his audience.

71. Chesnutt would probably resent the comparison to Brown, for he criticized his work, calling Brown's books "mere compilations" that are "beneath the dignity of criticism." With respect to Brown's *The Negro in the American Rebellion; His Heroism and His Fidelity* (1867), Chesnutt wrote, "The book reminds me of a gentleman in a dirty shirt. You are rather apt to doubt his gentility under such circumstances." Always a careful stylist and a rather proper Victorian gentleman, Chesnutt probably did not take to Brown's "shameless hyperbole." See Brodhead, *Journals of Charles Chesnutt*, 164. "The Passing of Grandison" in this respect could be seen as a much better crafted rewriting of *The Escape*.

72. As Eric Sundquist notes, Chesnutt also made extensive use of animal trickster and other folktales (such as those belonging to the Master-John cycle). The rich relationship between Chesnutt and Joel Chandler Harris is also worth noting. See Sundquist, "Charles Chesnutt's Cakewalk," in *To Wake the Nations*, 323–47.

73. In 1901, Chesnutt published "Superstition and Folklore of the South," an essay in which he calls conjure a relic of "ancestral barbarism," and claims that it thrives on "delusion" and "ignorance." As Eric Sundquist notes, given Chesnutt's "precarious position straddling the color line, and given his clear aspirations to middle-class professional respectability, it is not surprising that Chesnutt would detach himself from the irrationality of conjure." Sundquist, "Charles Chesnutt's Cakewalk," in *To Wake the Nations*, 295.

74. Sundquist, "Charles Chesnutt's Cakewalk," in *To Wake the Nations*, 359.

75. Ibid., 368.

76. Andrews, *Literary Career of Charles W. Chesnutt*, 48.

77. Ibid., 59–60.

78. Sundquist, "Charles Chesnutt's Cakewalk," in *To Wake the Nations*, 358–59.

79. Freud, *Jokes*, 104–105.

80. Brown was able to transform much of his lived experience into fiction, often recontextualizing materials from his various texts—poems, the various versions of his novel *Clotel*, travel narrative, plays, autobiographies, historical studies—appropriating (in some cases lifting) aspects of other people's texts. He had a keen eye and ear for what made "truth stranger than fiction" and often revealed it with exceptional wit. He created and shifted across different versions of the identities that he assumed in his autobiographies, in the various genres in which he wrote, and in the performances he delivered as an antislavery lecturer. Among other things, he was also a conductor on the Underground Railroad, a doctor of questionable skills, and a barber. Performing and shifting across the different selves he created allowed Brown to escape, or at the very least challenge, the branding violence of the stereotype to which he was susceptible. See Ernest, *Resistance and Reformation*, 21–22.

81. Sundquist devotes a large portion of his chapter on Chesnutt to exploring the relationship. See Sundquist, "Uncle Remus, Uncle Julius, and the New Negro," in *To Wake the Nations*, 323–47.

82. Ibid., 381.

83. Chesnutt, *Stories, Novels and Essays*, 193. Subsequent references are cited parenthetically as *Stories*.

84. Wonham, *Charles W. Chesnutt*, 64.

85. Andrews, *Literary Career of Charles W. Chesnutt*, 95.

86. Like Brown, Chesnutt makes ironic use of popular racist tunes. As Sundquist notes, the tale's subtitle echoes popular "coon songs" such as "Who Dat Say Chicken in Dis Crowd?" See Sundquist, "Charles Chesnutt's Cakewalk," in *To Wake the Nations*, 380.

87. Chesnutt, *Short Fiction of Charles W. Chesnutt*, 123–24. Subsequent references are cited parenthetically as *Short Fiction*.

88. Sundquist, "Charles Chesnutt's Cakewalk," in *To Wake the Nations*, 380.

89. Ibid., 362.

90. Andrews, *Literary Career of Charles W. Chesnutt*, 61.

91. Bergson, *Laughter*, 58, 61, 37, 40.

92. As many critics have noted, the grapevine serves Chesnutt as a symbol with which to represent the ways individual circumstances are tied to the fates of others in the system of slavery as well as to those in the postbellum period. See Andrews, *Literary Career of Charles W. Chesnutt*, 61.

93. Bone, *Down Home*, 85.

94. William Andrews, like other critics, notes that Chesnutt refused to "combat subhuman plantation fiction stereotypes with superhuman counter-stereotypes." Instead, Chesnutt renders slaves as "no better and no worse" than their masters, as capable of committing morally reprehensible acts as being "saintly." Most of the slaves in Julius's stories "belong in the realistic middle ground of representative humanity." Andrews, *Literary Career of Charles W. Chesnutt*, 59. Aunt Peggy's act of conjuration has a role to play in Henry's death, of course; as such, it is one of the few instances in Chesnutt's stories in which conjure functions against the enslaved. Significantly, it is also an instance in which conjure is purchased for an individual's selfish purposes.

95. Bergson defines reciprocal interference thus: "*A situation is invariably comic when it belongs simultaneously to two altogether independent series of events and is capable of being interpreted in two entirely different meanings at the same time*" (italics in the original). Bergson, *Laughter*, 96.

96. Wonham, "'Curious Psychological Spectacle,'" 43, 40. Quoting from Chesnutt's journals, Wonham argues that Chesnutt chose "Hot-Foot Hannibal" as the last story for *The Conjure Woman* collection because he wanted to leave "'a good taste in the mouth' of his predominantly white readership." But reading the tale as Wonham does only replicates the callousness toward Chloe and Jeff's tragedy that Chesnutt expected of his white readership.

97. "Po' Sandy" is a remarkable instance of both the spirit and independence with which slaves sought to control their destinies and the awful price they paid, often with their bodies. Like Henry in "The Goophered Grapevine," Sandy must work for multiple

masters when his owner hires him out, repeatedly yanking him away from whatever personal attachments Sandy is able to make. When, tired of being separated from his loved ones, Sandy asks his wife, Tenie, a conjure woman, to turn him into something more permanent, tragedy ensues. Tenie turns Sandy into a tree and, while she is sent away to take care of his master's son's wife, the tree is chopped down. She returns just in time to see Sandy's limbs, now logs, being carried to the sawmill and, like Chloe, first loses her mind to grief and then her life. Ultimately, she too becomes a grief-ridden ghost.

98. Sundquist, "Charles Chesnutt's Cakewalk," in *To Wake the Nations*, 371.

99. As originally conceived, *The Conjure Woman* tales included both stories. But when the collection finally appeared, "Dave's Neckliss" had been dropped, perhaps because "conjure as such is not present—but perhaps because it was simply too unsettling." Sundquist, "Charles Chesnutt's Cakewalk," in *To Wake the Nations*, 379.

100. Ibid.

101. Ibid.

102. Styan, *Dark Comedy*, 252.

103. Sundquist, "Charles Chesnutt's Cakewalk," in *To Wake the Nations*, 382.

104. S. A. H. Ferguson, introduction, 7–8.

105. Brawley, *Negro in Literature and Art*, 48.

106. Van Vechten, *Nigger Heaven*, 176–79; Andrews, *Literary Career of Charles W. Chesnutt*, 46.

107. Wonham, "'Curious Psychological Spectacle,'" paragraph 16, available through Academic Search Primer.

108. Wonham, "'Curious Psychological Spectacle,'" paragraph 2. See also Baraka, *Blues People*, 131–32.

109. Bone, *Down Home*, 75.

110. Sochen, *Women's Comic Visions*, 13.

111. As Kreger notes, the "oft-repeated claim that in the nineteenth century humor was perceived as masculine assertiveness" has led to the "assumption that female authored humor is therefore always subversive," whereas much "nineteenth century women's comic-ironic writing could affirm—rather than subvert—conventional views, aligning some women humorists with the non-radical progressive optimism of much male-authored American humor." Kreger, "Nineteenth-Century Female Humorist," 5.

112. Gray, *Women and Laughter*, 119; Watkins, *On the Real Side*, 97–98.

113. Watkins, *On the Real Side*, 390.

114. Jacobs, *Incidents in the Life of a Slave Girl*, 63.

115. Jacobs, *Incidents in the Life of a Slave Girl*, 115–16.

116. Stern, "Excavating Genre in *Our Nig*," 441, 446.

117. Ramsdell, *History of Milford*, 522.

118. As quoted in Forman and Pitts, introduction, xxxvi.

119. Ibid., xxxvii.

120. As Julia Stern argues in "Excavating Genre in *Our Nig*," Wilson made extensive use of the conventions of Gothic fiction to represent the brutality to which she was subjected.

121. Gates, introduction, xxx. For Ellen Pratofiorito the fact that *Our Nig* was ignored upon publication is not "the anomaly that it first appears to be" ("To Demand Your Sympathy and Aid," 42). Pratofiorito considers the reception of novels by Wilson's contemporaries (Martin Delaney and Frank Webb, for example) and argues that only when authors limited their attention to slavery and the evils of the South and did not, for example, examine the racism practiced in the North and "issues facing black Americans which were not solved by emancipation" were they able to receive critical attention (37). *Our Nig*, as a novel that offers what Barbara White calls "an unconventional treatment of racism in the North," was thus poised for obscurity ("*Our Nig* and the She-Devil," 19). Also, although Wilson addresses her story specifically to her "colored brethren," she includes topics that may have been unpalatable to them. As I noted earlier, in her novel she identifies a fake fugitive who used his assumed identity for profit on the abolitionist circuit.

122. Wilson, *Our Nig*, 6, 72, emphasis added. Subsequent references are cited parenthetically as *Our Nig*. With respect to Wilson's critique of northern apathy, Pratofiorito concludes that *Our Nig* presents a paradox: the novel is "essentially a text with a 'purpose'[:] to be a commodity in the marketplace but with a 'message' that few were ready, able or willing to buy in its time." Pratofiorito, "To Demand Your Sympathy and Aid," 46.

123. Wilson sought to shock her readers into action by employing satire, a form through which she could represent the terror of slavery without allowing readers to lose themselves in that terror. As Ronald Paulson notes, a "determining factor in the effect [of] the satiric [image or scene] is the distance maintained between the reader (and the author) and the satiric fiction that is being presented. . . . The distancing, or the remove at which we witness the act . . . keeps us from losing ourselves in the horror." Paulson, *Fictions of Satire*, 14–15.

124. Breau, "Identifying Satire," 461.

125. Ibid., 460.

126. Pratofiorito, "To Demand Your Sympathy and Aid," 46.

127. Seidel, *Satiric Inheritance*, 3–4.

128. Stern, "Excavating Genre in *Our Nig*," 451.

129. Breau, "Identifying Satire," 461.

130. R. Wright, "Between Laughter and Tears." Alain Locke had similar complaints; see review of *Their Eyes Were Watching God*, by Zora Neale Hurston, *Opportunity*, June 1, 1938.

Chapter 2

1. Pryor, *Richard Pryor . . . and It's Deep Too.* Unless otherwise noted, all further references to audio recordings of Pryor's performances will be made to this collection.

2. Rituals and jokes may at first seem disconnected for, as Mary Douglas observes, a ritual distinguishes itself from a joke in that the former "imposes order and harmony" and "creates unity in experience," while the latter destroys "hierarchy and order." But if in joke telling, or in what Douglas calls "ritual joking," the joke "devalues

social structure, perhaps it celebrates something else instead." It can, for example, present the "value of individuals as against the value of the social relations in which they are organized. Or it could be saying something about different levels of social structure; the irrelevance of one obvious level and the relevance of a submerged and unappreciated one." Similarly, ritual joking can celebrate community without emphasizing hierarchy and order, producing instead the positive aspects of community: "fellowship, spontaneity, warm contact." Ritual joking, in other words, creates a unity of experience but within "unhierarchised, undifferentiated social relations." Mary Douglas, "Jokes," in *Implicit Meanings*, 155–56.

3. Best and Hartman, "Fugitive Justice," 1.

4. Marriage between blacks and whites, which was illegal in many states, became legal in the United States in 1967 with the *Loving vs. Commonwealth of Virginia* case. Pryor released *Bicentennial Nigger* in the fall of 1976.

5. Limon, *Stand-up Comedy in Theory*, 84–85.

6. Rovin, *Richard Pryor*, 85.

7. Watkins, *On the Real Side*, 551.

8. As Joseph Boskin notes, it was "common practice to force Africans to the upper deck to jump, sing, dance, and generally move about as often as the weather permitted" in order make their survival more possible as well as to dissipate hostility and the possibility of uprising. The first episode of the television miniseries *Roots* includes a scene of "dancing the slaves," as the ritual became known, but the slaves in that instance take the opportunity of being on the upper decks to rebel. Boskin, *Sambo*, 44–45.

9. Pryor acted in over thirty Hollywood films, but most of them, especially films such as *The Toy*, do not showcase his talents. *Which Way Is Up?* (1977) and *Stir Crazy* (1980) are perhaps the only films that come close to showing the Pryor of stand-up. The former showcases his talent for adopting characters; Pryor plays three different roles, a preacher, a grouchy old man, and the lead role, using costume changes. It is also a film that implicitly connects slave labor and migrant labor in its opening scenes, wherein blacks and Latinos work side by side for minimal wages for racist white landowners. An adaptation of an earlier film entitled *The Seduction of Mimi*, *Which Way Is Up?* was written in collaboration with Pryor's Berkeley friend Cecil Brown. Pryor occasionally translated his talent as a stand-up comedian into film scripts, as when he collaborated in the script for *Blazing Saddles*, a film that bears many similarities to the work of another one of Pryor's Berkeley friends, Ishmael Reed's novel *Yellow Back Radio Broke-Down* (1969).

10. In one of many instances in which Pryor is quoted in a hip-hop cultural production, the group Public Enemy begins their song "Can't Trust It" with this line from Pryor's work.

11. Ellison, *Shadow and Act*, 131.

12. Ibid., 78.

13. See Pryor, "Bicentennial Nigger," on *Richard Pryor . . . and It's Deep Too*.

14. Turner, *Anthropology of Performance*, 34–35. In *Dramas, Fields and Metaphors*, Turner defines redress as one of four main phases in social dramas: (1) breach (a situation that divides a social unit); (2) crisis (in which the breach can no longer be overlooked;

the crisis "dares the representatives of order to grapple with it"); (3) redressive action ("ranging from personal advice and informal meditation or arbitration to formal juridical and legal machinery . . . to the performance of public ritual"); and (4) "re-integration of the disturbed social group or the social recognition and legitimation of irreparable schism between contesting parties." Sometimes, however, "a phase of a social drama may seethe for years and years with nothing much happening on the surface"; sometimes too "there is no resolution even after a climactic series of events." Turner, *Drama, Fields and Metaphors*, 37–41.

15.   In his autobiographical film, *Jo Jo Dancer, Your Life Is Calling You* (1986), Pryor por-trays the incident as a suicide attempt.

16.   Levine, *Black Culture and Black Consciousness*, 326.

17.   Pryor's albums also created different communities of listeners. As Greg Tate observes, Pryor's *That Nigger's Crazy* was the "greatest pop album of 1974," a year in which "you couldn't go to any Black home in Chocolate City, from Anacostia to the Gold Coast, and not find it on infinite repeat and folk laid out convulsed with hysteria" Greg Tate, "Richard Pryor, 1940–2005," December 12, 2005, *Village Voice* (www.villagevoice.com/news/0550,tate,70905,2.html). Testimonials make references to listening to Pryor in barbershops, retelling his skits at street corners and city stoops. Chris Rock remem-bers stealing away to listen to Pryor behind the backs of parents who considered him inappropriate. See the liner notes in *Richard Pryor . . . and It's Deep Too.*

18.   Because each concert film is also available as a sound recording, we have the oppor-tunity of comparing slight variations between performances.

19.   It is also known as *Prison Play*. Pryor, *Richard Pryor Evolution/Revolution.*

20.   Pryor's gift has also been compared to that of Lenny Bruce, although not necessarily in just terms. Pryor and Bruce both presented joke-free, character-driven routines colored by obscene language. They were both master mimics who could conjure dif-ferent characters and jump between them. But, as Jeff Rovin notes, Bruce "was an autocrat who beat up his audiences with irreverence and raped them with language," whereas Pryor, "even at his bluest and most vitriolic, couldn't molest an audience if he tried." Rovin adds that while most critics concentrate on the similarities between the styles of the two comedians, few discuss the "history of persecution" that they both shared. Rovin, *Richard Pryor*, 79–80.

21.   Debby Thompson rephrases the work of Judith Butler in "Is Race a Trope?" 132. See also J. Reed, "Lily Tomlin's *Appearing Nightly*," 437.

22.   D. Thompson, "Is Race a Trope?" 132.

23.   In yet another instance in which Pryor is quoted in hip-hop culture, the group De La Soul splices parts of this skit, this section in particular, in a version of their song "Buddy."

24.   Lott, *Love and Theft*, 122.

25.   Ibid., 117.

26.   Richard Pryor, *Recorded Live at the Troubadour*, West Hollywood, September 1968, produced by Robert Marchese, Dove/Reprise November 1968, released on *Richard Pryor . . . and It's Deep Too.* See also Pryor and Gold, *Pryor Convictions*, 106. Sub-sequent references are cited parenthetically as *PC*.

27. Joseph Boskin notes that as proliferation of the racist iconography of past decades lessened, mainstream media did not promote other images of African Americans. Instead, they largely omitted the presence of African Americans altogether. Boskin, *Sambo*, 202–204.

28. As quoted in R. Kennedy, *Nigger*, 22–23. The first quote is attributed to the journalist Farai Chideya and the second to Judge Stephen Reinhart.

29. Kate E. Brown and Howard I. Kushner rightly argue that "cursing is central rather than gratuitous" in Pryor's comedy. They examine how Pryor exploits "the grammatical and semantic mobility that attends obscene words" to create a poetry of cursing. K. E. Brown and Kushner, "Eruptive Voices," 554. In using curse words in such fashion, Pryor works in the African American folk tradition. Motherfucker, for example, is often inserted in toasts to break up the "regular feet" and thus avoid "a doggerel meter." William Labov et al., "Toasts," in Dundes, *Mother Wit*, 339.

30. Brown and Kushner, "Eruptive Voices," 550.

31. R. Kennedy, *Nigger*, 4.

32. Ibid., 31.

33. Watkins, *On the Real Side*, 559–60.

34. See "A Flying Fool" (1997), in Gates and McKay, *Norton Anthology of African American Literature*, 142.

35. See J. Brown, "Comic Book Masculinity and the New Black Superhero," 27.

36. Singer, " 'Black Skins' and White Masks," 1062.

37. Labov et al., "Toasts," 330–31. "The Signifying Monkey" is one of the best-known toasts. See Gates, *Signifying Monkey*, especially chapter 2, where Gates carefully explores different definitions (and misdefinitions) of signifying in black linguistic practices. Other well-known toasts include "The Titanic," "Shine," and "Stagolee." The toasts that Labov and colleagues examine concern urban life, whereas the more traditional toasts, such as "The Signifying Monkey," do not take place in urban settings. Migrations of black Americans from rural areas to cities have allowed for the perpetuation of the tradition of toasting, which has incorporated new situations and characters.

38. Labov et al., "Toasts," 334, 336.

39. See H. C. Brearley, "Ba-ad Nigger," in Dundes, *Mother Wit*, 578–85. Correct use and semantic interpretation of these words, as Claudia Mitchell-Kernan notes, "depend on a good deal of shared cultural knowledge." The words serve not only to "emphasiz[e] group solidarity" but also to signal that an instance of black verbal art is occurring and that, as such, the terms need to be interpreted according to "subcultural rules." Claudia Mitchell-Kernan, "Signifying," in Dundes, *Mother Wit*, 326.

40. See Freud, "Humour"; Levine, *Black Culture and Black Consciousness*, 343.

41. Alan Dundes sees the boasting and hyperbole that are integral to toasts in "light of the brutal history of slavery." "No one could take pride in being 'too light to fight or too thin to win' " amid the violence of slavery, "but one could find much needed ego support in maintaining one's roughness, toughness, meanness, or badness." Dundes, introduction, "Ba-ad Nigger," *Mother Wit*, 578.

42. The heroes of toasts "reject chivalry, exploit women and show even more violence toward them than toward men." Labov et al., "Toasts," 336.

43. Stone, *Laughing in the Dark*, 19.
44. Pryor, *Richard Pryor . . . Here and Now*. All further references to this performance are to this recording.
45. In the audio recording of the performance, Pryor segues into his travels to Zimbabwe, a country in which, as he puts it, "black people kicked ass." He gives a quick account of the independence struggle by which Southern Rhodesia became Zimbabwe and thus balances the memory of black subjugation in America against the reality of black liberation in contemporary Africa. This is one of many instances in which Pryor alludes to the liberation movements in Africa in the context of addressing slavery in America.
46. John Limon, who argues that "the usual stand-up posture" is that of abjection, claims that Pryor refuses it because of "his self-identification with an abjected race." What Limon means by abjection is twofold: its common definition as "abasement, groveling, prostration" and Julia Kristeva's definition as "a psychic worrying of those aspects of oneself that one cannot be rid of . . . for example, blood, urine, feces, nails, and the corpse." While Pryor does indeed reject abjection in the second sense—although not because of his identification with an "abjected race"—it is clear, especially in the *Here and Now* performance, that he does not reject it in the first sense. Limon, *Stand-up Comedy in Theory*, 5, 4.
47. Lott, "Aesthetic Ante," 550.
48. Ibid.
49. Richard Pryor, *That Nigger's Crazy*, (1974), on *Richard Pryor . . . and It's Deep Too*.
50. Beavers, "Cool Pose," 262, 264, 262, 260, 261.
51. Of his days in Berkeley, Pryor writes, "I indulged in every thought that popped into my sick head. I read and reread a copy of Malcolm X's collected speeches. I put Marvin Gaye's song 'What's Going On' on my stereo and played it so often that it became the soundtrack for my life up there" (*PC* 115). Pryor evokes Gaye's song in a previous instance, literally making the song part of the soundtrack in his autobiographical film *Jo Jo Dancer, Your Life Is Calling* (1986).
52. Pryor, *Richard Pryor Live on the Sunset Strip* (1982). Pryor was able to "fly high" through his art too. In his autobiography he writes, "The comedy gods have many tentacles. . . . And they swoop down and touch you at different times. But when they do it's like salvation. Or deliverance. It's as close to flying as man gets" (*PC* 144).
53. In "How to Tell a Story" (1895), Twain distinguishes between the comic or witty story, which focuses on content, or "*matter*," and "the humorous story," which "depends for its effects upon the *manner* of the telling." He adds, "To string incongruities and absurdities together in a wandering and sometimes purposeless way, and seem innocently unaware that they are absurdities, is the basis of American art. . . . Another feature is the slurring of the point. A third is the dropping of a studied remark apparently without knowing it, as if one were thinking aloud. The fourth and last is the pause." Twain, *Complete Essays*, 155, 158.
54. "Mudbone, Part One and Two," on Richard Pryor, *Is It Something I Said?* Warner Brothers, 1975. See Pryor, *Richard Pryor . . . and It's Deep Too!*
55. Douglas, *Implicit Meanings*, 149.

56. Beavers, "Cool Pose," 259, 266, 266–67.
57. *The Richard Pryor Show*, NBC, 1977. Available on DVD, Image Entertainment, March 23, 2004.
58. See, for example, Coleman, *African American Viewers.*
59. Beavers, "Cool Pose," 263.
60. Rock, *Rock This!* 17. Subsequent references are cited parenthetically as *RT.*
61. Rock's critique also suggests a change in black humor. As Levine notes, black humor has always contained a measure of self-criticism, but usually the criticism has been kept within the group. Rock uses humor to critique black culture, but he does so in front of mixed audiences. At the same time, he does not open that critique to white subjects, performing it while clearly providing limits. As in the use of the "N" word, black folk can critique themselves, Rock suggests, and do so in front of whites. But whites cannot join in.
62. See Reilly, "Betye Saar at Michael Rosenfeld," 112.
63. See Shaw, *Seeing the Unspeakable*, 32.
64. "Chappelle: 'An Act of Freedom,'" *60 Minutes II*, CBS News, December 29, 2004.
65. Unlike Pryor, Chappelle is not as interested in stereotypes of gender. In fact, as Bambi Haggins notes, his sexual politics can be "regressive and sophomoric." Haggins, *Laughing Mad*, 196.
66. For an extensive discussion of how differences in age, region, and class between Rock and Chappelle inform their distinct types of post–civil rights comedy, see ibid., especially chapters 2 and 5. Rock, a gifted comedian of a different kind, is clearly situated in a politics of grievance with respect to slavery and its legacy. Yet his sometimes reactionary perspectives on race and gender clash with the politics of grief, with the "freedom dreams" that we have explored in Pryor and that are, to some extent, also part of Chappelle's work. A thin, short man, Rock uses his trademark shrill voice and grin to productive ends. As Jack Chung notes, Rock seems to make his voice "purposely grate against the ear," creating a kind of "caustic pain" that keeps the tension between pleasure and discomfort during his performances. In some respects, this tension recalls *Bicentennial Nigger*'s mock laughter. In his live performances, the contrast between Rock's lithe frame and his characteristic grin against his aggressive sound makes for another sort of humorous contrast: he is the little guy with the outrageous voice. Still, unlike Pryor and Chappelle, Rock is sometimes willing to espouse conservative politics. Regarding anti-Semitism in the black community, for example, Rock writes:

> I'm around brothers every day, all the time, and I've *never ever* heard a bunch of black people talking about Jews. Never.
> Black people don't hate **Jews**.
> **Black people hate white people**.
> Just because we can tell the difference between one white guy and another doesn't mean we have time to dice them up into little groups.
> "The Jews are fucked up but the Irish are cool."
> You're **all** white to us. (*RT* 14)

Rock's cadences, which he here marks typographically, tend to replicate those of an opinionated barbershop customer. But whereas Pryor would imitate the voice and gestures of that customer, and thus highlight the theatricality of the character, Rock simply adopts his obstinacy, emphatically embracing perspectives that Pryor would have declined. Unlike Pryor's preacher in the Church of Understanding and Unity, Rock speaks, albeit hyperbolically, of hate. The routine is clearly a "cap" on hateful sentiments such as "All coons look alike to me," since it suggests that black people *can* see whites as individuals but that they hate them nonetheless. The live performance of the routine in *Bigger and Blacker* softens the intensity of the lines in boldface because Rock delivers them in the context of the laughter he generates throughout the show and as one of various instances in which the comedian critiques (even abuses) other people. Occasionally, his critiques reveal "reactionary impulses" regarding gender; see Haggins, *Laughing Mad*, 82. See also Jack Chung, "Burden of Laughter," 89.

67. Haggins, *Laughing Mad*, 207.
68. Ibid., 182.
69. See Weiner, "Funny Business." See also Haggins, *Laughing Mad*, 207, 182.
70. Kelley, *Freedom Dreams*, 133.
71. Neal Brennan and Dave Chappelle, interviewed by Charlie Rose, *The Charlie Rose Show*, PBS, April 28, 2004.
72. Haggins, *Laughing Mad*, 207. In her analysis of Chappelle's stand-up, Haggins examines how the comedian's lackadaisical "nice guy" persona can take the "sting out" of social critique (191–205).
73. Ault, "Latest Chappelle DVD Is Selling Like Crazy."
74. Rovin, *Richard Pryor*, 112.
75. As quoted in Michele Wallace, "The Enigma of the Negress Kara Walker," in Berry et al., *Kara Walker: Narratives of the Negress*, 179.
76. Mark Reinhart, "The Art of Racial Profiling," in Berry et al., *Kara Walker: Narratives of the Negress*, 111.
77. "Chappelle: 'An Act of Freedom,'" *60 Minutes II*, CBS News, December 29, 2004.
78. Dave Chappelle, interviewed on *Inside the Actor's Studio*, February 12, 2006.
79. I. Reed, *Flight to Canada*, 82.
80. Chappelle's performances in this film and Pryor's involvement in the concert film *Wattstax* are worthy of extensive comparison, for in both the comedians celebrate black culture from different vantage points and connote a sense of community and solidarity without losing the edge and mirth of their humor.

Chapter 3

1. See Vaidhyanathan, "Now's the Time," 43.
2. I. Reed, *Flight to Canada*, 9. Subsequent references are cited parenthetically as *FC*.
3. Walsh, "'Man's Story Is His Gris-Gris,'" 59.
4. Morrison, "Site of Memory," 109, 110.
5. Foster, *Witnessing Slavery*.

6. Samuel A. Cartwright, "Diseases and Peculiarities of the Negro Race," in Paskoff and Wilson, *Cause of the South*, 42. See also Otter, *Melville's Anatomies*, 119–20, 122–23, 148.

7. Although "it is rarely explicit," notes Deren, Guede, also spelled Gede or Ghede, is neither male nor female but might be a hermaphroditic deity (*Divine Horsemen*, 111). For simplicity's sake, I use the male pronoun. I also use Guede as the spelling of the loa's name in keeping with Reed's own spelling in *Flight to Canada*. Reed's different spelling reflects not only his improvisatory use of voodoo but also the fact that the orthography of voodoo sometimes varies because Haitian orthography generally bears the marks of different, sometimes opposing, colonial ideologies. See Joan Dayan, "Notes on Orthography," in *Haiti, History, and the Gods*, xxiii. A counterpart to Legba, who is the sun god, the provider of life, the guardian of destiny, Guede is the loa who has crossed "the cosmic threshold to the underworld" and is "everything that Legba once was at the prime of his life." Deren, *Divine Horsemen*, 102.

8. Deren, *Divine Horsemen*, 103. Leslie Desmangles observes that Guede "is the most complex character in Haitian folklore, for he reveals more than thirty personae." Guede's delight in assuming diverse personae brings to mind Pryor's chameleonlike transformations. Taking on more than thirty different characters, he sometimes appears as a "poor wandering beggar" dressed in a "motley assortment of bits and pieces of garments, one worn over the other, and proudly sporting a peculiar multicolored little cap." At other times he wears his "formal" costume: a tall, black top hat, long black coattails, and smoked glasses, and carries a cigarette or cigar and a cane. In all of his disguises, he can be deliberately vulgar in matters of sex and food for he has an insatiable appetite, one that represents his dual role as lord of death (he is thought to consume the dead) and lord of eroticism (he lusts for life but is free of shame or guilt). Vulgar as he can be in one disguise, he can also assume the personality of Mr. Entretoute (literally Mr. In-the-middle-of-all-things), a gentleman who is slyly erotic, witty, and "cosmopolitan *par excellence*." Guede's shape-changing manifestations suggest the challenge he presents to categorization; he also frequently appears at ceremonies intended for other loa and, as the houngans, or ritual leaders put it, "spoil" it, frustrating all attempts at controlling him. Deren, *Divine Horsemen*, 111; Desmangles, *Faces of the Gods*, 116.

9. Deren, *Divine Horsemen*, 103.

10. Desmangles, *Faces of the Gods*, 116.

11. Ibid.

12. Ibid.

13. "While he would seem to prefer the role of the witty clown," writes Deren, Guede "will also use his wisdom in a more serious manner. . . . He may be playing the clown, but if you will call him aside and humbly ask him, in all seriousness, an important question, he will generally answer you thoughtfully and carefully, and it will usually be the best possible advice." Deren, *Divine Horsemen*, 104, 112. See also Desmangles, *Faces of the Gods*, 116.

14. Deren, *Divine Horsemen*, 16.

15. Dayan, "Vodoun," 41.

16. Reed's dual performance as houngan and boco is actually in keeping with voodoo practices. As Dayan notes, "The division between a *houngan* and *boco* is not absolute (in the North of Haiti *boco* means *houngan*). And the *houngan* must be familiar with magic in order to fight against the machinations of sorcerers." Dayan, "Vodoun," 49. Zora Neale Hurston makes a similar observation in *Tell My Horse*, 189.

17. Rhys, *Wide Sargasso Sea*, 107, quoted in Dayan, "Vodoun," 54. Edward Rochester, from Charlotte Brontë's *Jane Eyre*, is not named in full (he is referred to only as Rochester), but all evidence points to him as the speaker.

18. Dayan, "Vodoun," 55.

19. Deren, *Divine Horsemen*, 338.

20. The phrase "fantastic process of reification" is by René Depestre, the Haitian novelist and poet whom Dayan quotes; "Vodoun," 55.

21. Dayan, *Haiti*, 264.

22. As David Mikics argues, Reed operates through an "aesthetic of 'sampling,' of inventively assembling snippets" of multiple traditions. Mikics, "Postmodernism, Ethnicity and Underground Revisionism in Ishmael Reed," paragraph 16.

23. For Reed's "Neo-HooDoo Manifesto," see I. Reed, *Conjure*, 21–22. Rather than presenting a definitive aesthetic, Reed offers an open vision of his aesthetic, one that foregrounds cultural syncretism, individual inventiveness, improvisation, and artistic freedom.

24. Ludwig, "Dialogic Possession," 330.

25. Deren, *Divine Horsemen*, 112–13.

26. See Lock, " 'Man's Story Is His Gris-Gris,' " 67–68.

27. Metz, "Photography and Fetish," 86.

28. See Kristeva, *Powers of Horror*.

29. Rushdy, "Ishmael Reed's Neo-HooDoo Slave Narrative," 132. See also Rushdy's *Neo-Slave Narratives*.

30. As we have seen in chapter 1, Zora Neale Hurston invokes High John de Conquer as a similar ancestral spirit.

31. Ishmael Reed, interview by the author, June 14, 1999.

32. "Interview with Ishmael Reed," by Stanley Crouch (1976), in Dick and Singh, *Conversations with Ishmael Reed*, 96.

33. Benshoff, "Blaxploitation Horror Films," 37.

34. Ibid., 39.

35. Quoted in Parish and Hill, *Black Action Films*, 289.

36. As quoted in Benshoff, "Blaxploitation Horror Films," 37.

37. MacDonald, *Blacks and White TV*, 182.

38. See Bogle, *Toms, Coons, Mulattoes*, 242.

39. Ibid., 44.

40. See Davis, "Strange, History," 752–53.

41. Reed suggests that Swille, like Napoleon III depicted in Karl Marx's *The Eighteenth Brumaire of Louis Napoleon*, makes a travesty of power in the name of a reactionary obsession with nobility. Sitting at a desk "rumored to have been owned" by his "good friend Imperial Majesty Napoleon Bonaparte III," Swille expounds on the pleasures

of his southern dream (*FC* 23–24). The American master, Reed implies, could use the power of capital to buy secondhand remnants of Europe's decaying signs of monarchical power. For an analysis of Reed's allusion to Edgar Allan Poe in this passage, see Weixlmann, "Ishmael Reed's Raven."

42. For a discussion of how the sexual licentiousness of slave masters fueled fears and solidified the need to abolish slavery, see Walters, "Erotic South."

43. N. Harris, "Gods Must Be Angry," 114.

44. MacDonald, *Blacks and White TV*, 184.

45. Davis, "*Strange, History*," 752.

46. Ibid., 751–52.

47. Reed acknowledges both William Wells Brown and Charles Chesnutt as his literary predecessors who transfigured "conjure" into narrative form. Ishmael Reed, interview by the author, June 14, 1999.

48. Ibid. As Reed told me in conversation, Alice Walker wanted "to ban [his] books" based on her reaction to Barracuda. For a discussion of Reed and misogyny, see T. Harris, *Saints, Sinners, Saviors*; O'Neale, "Ishmael Reed's Fitful *Flight to Canada*," 174–77. See also Nazareth, "Heading Them Off at the Pass."

49. N. Harris, "Gods Must Be Angry," 118.

50. For a discussion of Barracuda's crucifix and its blinding powers, see Spillers, "Changing the Letter," 31.

51. For an exploration of the visual and literary birth and commodification of the mammy stereotype, see Morgan, "Mammy the Huckster." See also McElya, *Clinging to Mammy*.

52. As Donald Bogle observes, films of the Depression era, particularly Mae West features, presented black domestics who were "always overweight, middle aged, and made up as jolly aunt jemimas. . . . Their naïve blackness generally was used as a contrast to Mae West's sophisticated whiteness . . . [and] served to heighten the hot white sexuality of their bawdy mistress. . . . The implications throughout the films were that black women could not possibly be rivals to Mae West's femininity and that only black women were fit to wait on whores." Commenting on the strange intimacy of mistress-maid relations, Bogle adds, "Because both blacks and whores were at the bottom of the social scale, Mae West could rely on her colored maids and enjoy a livelier camaraderie with them than she would with whites." Bogle, *Toms, Coons, Mulattoes*, 45–47.

53. Quoted in St. John, "It Ain't Fittin'," 134.

54. St. John, "It Ain't Fittin'," 127.

55. Ibid.

56. Mikics, "Postmodernism," paragraph 12.

57. See Metz, "Photography and Fetish," 82, 87.

58. Davis notes that when they were antislavery lecturers, Brown had flour thrown at him and Douglass was beaten up; "*Strange, History*," 747.

59. Reed suggests that Stowe's charge of pornography against Lord Byron revealed her prurient interest in it and aligns this "naughtiness" with her purported stealing of Henson's story, since Stowe's co-optation of Henson for economic profit suggests a sort of prostitution.

60. Quoted in Walsh, " 'Man's Story Is His Gris-Gris,' " 66. For further discussion of this rumor, see Benesch, "From a Thing into an I Am," 257.

61. James Baldwin, "Everybody's Protest Novel," in *Notes of a Native Son*, 13–23.

62. Reed suggests that novelists like Stowe work more as bocos or magicians that conjure for profit rather than for healing or insight. Taking Stowe's claim that she "was an instrument of the Lord" when she wrote *Uncle Tom's Cabin*, Reed writes: "Harriet saying that God wrote Uncle Tom's Cabin. Which God? Some gods will mount any horse" (*FC* 10–11). Here Reed refers to the boco's magic that can seduce certain loa for material rather than spiritual purposes.

63. Dayan, "Vodoun," 51.

64. Byerman, *Fingering the Jagged Grain*, 233.

65. Bernard Bell coined the term "neo-slave narrative" to describe "residually oral, modern narratives of escape from bondage to freedom"; *The Afro-American Novel*, 289. Among the first texts to focus on slavery in the mid-1960s and early 1970s are Margaret Walker's *Jubilee* (1966), Ernest Gaines's *The Autobiography of Miss Jane Pittman* (1971), and Gayl Jones's *Corregidora* (1975). These works were followed by Ishmael Reed's *Flight to Canada* (1976), Alex Haley's *Roots* (1976), Octavia Butler's *Kindred* (1979), Charles Johnson's *Oxherding Tale* (1982) and *Middle Passage* (1990), and J. California Cooper's *Family* (1991) and *In Search of Satisfaction* (1994). Similar texts include Caryl Phillips's *Higher Ground* (1989), *Cambridge* (1991), and *Crossing the River* (1993); Derek Walcott's epic poem, *Omeros* (1990); Kamau Brathwaite's three-part epic *The Arrivants* (1992); Barbara Chase-Riboud's *The President's Daughter* (1994); and Fred D'Aguiar's *The Longest Memory* (1994). For a discussion of factors contributing to the emergence of these fictional narratives, see Rushdy, *Neo Slave Narratives*, 3–22. Rushdy has shown the extent to which Reed corrects not only historical texts on slavery but also fictional works, such as Harriet Beecher Stowe's *Uncle Tom's Cabin* (1852) and William Styron's *The Confessions of Nat Turner* (1968). A thorough and compelling argument, Rushdy's discussion on *Flight to Canada* overstresses Reed's desire to revise slavery's record; see in particular 99–110. Reed does more than rewrite master texts. Other texts that Rushdy examines, such as Sherley Anne Williams's *Dessa Rose*, are more adamantly revisionist enterprises. For examples of criticism in Rushdy's revisionist vein, see Beaulieu, *Black Women Writers*. Beaulieu shows how fiction can be used to "reinscribe history from the point of view of the black woman" (2).

66. Ellison, *Going to the Territory*, 193–94. See the introduction where I first allude to "perspective by incongruity," a term Ellison borrows from Kenneth Burke.

Chapter 4

1. Ellison, *Going to the Territory*, 174.

2. Ibid., 194.

3. Ibid., 193.

4. Ibid., 197, 185.

5. See also ibid., 193–94.

6. Robert Colescott, as quoted in Colman, "Pretty on the Outside," 118.

7. See Groseclose, *Emanuel Leutze*, 36.

8. Ibid., 34.

9. I am quoting the response of one of my students to my query, "Does anyone know who George Washington Carver was?" during a seminar at Harvard University.

10. Groseclose, *Emanuel Leutze*, 36.

11. Included among these images are paintings of the "unsuccessful efforts of the Jews to prevent their expulsion from Spain . . . the Tudor Dissolution, and Cromwellian Puritanism." Leutze hoped to "paint a series of pictures illustrating the struggle of the religiously and politically oppressed, citing landmarks on the road to the New World freedoms." Groseclose, "Washington Crossing the Delaware," 70–71, 74–75, 73.

12. Fitz, "Dusseldorf Academy of Art," 30–31. Fitz refers to David Hackett Fischer, who notes the use of the painting to help the Union cause and who claims Leutze was a "strong supporter for antislavery movements throughout the world." See Fischer, "Historiography: Images and Interpretations of the Event," in *Washington's Crossing*, 425–57.

13. For an exemplary "literal" reading of Colescott's stereotypes, see Douglass, "Robert Colescott's Searing Stereotypes." Douglass insists that artists should ennoble the "victims" of the difficult history that produced the stereotypes Colescott depicts. "A question which plagues many African Americans," he writes, "is, does Colescott's presentation place them in history in a manner they point to with pride?" (34). He misses the point, however: Colescott's images do not represent "African Americans"; rather, they signify on racial and sexual myths and ideologies.

14. Harpham, *On the Grotesque Strategies of Contradiction*, 3.

15. Connelly, introduction, 2. As Connelly notes, because grotesque images are "typically characterized by what they lack: fixity, stability, order," they are hard to define. "The grotesque," she writes, "is defined by what it does to boundaries, transgressing, merging, overflowing, destabilizing them." It has been associated with notions of the "primitive, the uncanny, the abject," with the imagery and practices of the carnival and the aesthetics of bricolage, caricatures, and comic books (4–5).

16. Bergson, *Laughter*, 96.

17. See Lott, *Love and Theft*; Lhamon, *Raising Cain*.

18. See Goya, *Los Caprichos*; Gassier, *Francisco Goya Drawings*.

19. Ellison, *Going to the Territory*, 187–92.

20. See Cummings, *Willem de Kooning*, 177–86.

21. Merkert, "Stylelessness as Principle."

22. Polcari, *Abstract Expressionism*, 284.

23. Merkert, "Stylelessness as Principle," 120.

24. For reproductions of these images see Cummings, *Willem de Kooning*, 178–82.

25. These are the words Polcari uses to describe de Kooning's *Woman I*, but his description could well have been for Colescott's image. Polcari, *Abstract Expressionism*, 284.

26. See Wallace, *Black Macho*, 107.

27. For an incisive reading regarding the historical realities of Mammy, see D. G. White, *Ar'n't I a Woman?* 27–61. For a view of Mammy as complicit with the master see Peter Nazareth's reading of Reed's Barracuda. In an otherwise astute and sensitive essay,

Nazareth argues that Barracuda is overbearing because through her, Reed wants to stress the "hidden," "incestuous" relationship between slave women and masters. "We cannot mistake that she is in charge of the plantation/multinational corporation" because she is enslaved. But Barracuda "terrorizes the underlings, including Swille's pale wife," because she has "power within the household," a power that comes out of "her [sexual] relationship to Swille" and her position as mammy. As such, "she is as dangerous [as] . . . the middlemen in the slave trade, who handed the slaves over to the white men." As we saw in chapter 3, however, Reed's Barracuda is outrageous because, pace Nazareth, she is a representation of an ideological fixation that distorts the way we perceive the place of women under slavery. To read her at face value is to miss the signifying power of Reed's conjure. Nazareth, "Heading Them Off at the Pass," 216.

28. Merkert, "Stylelessness as Principle," 124; Polcari, *Abstract Expressionism*, 284.
29. Boime, *Art of Exclusion*, 1–2.
30. See Dubey, *Black Women Novelists*, especially 75.
31. Gilman, "Black Bodies, White Bodies."
32. Gilman in fact argues that in European painting of the eighteenth and nineteenth century, blacks predominantly figured as servants and that one of their central functions as such "was to sexualize the society in which [they are] found." Ibid., 228.
33. See Albert Boime on Manet's use of black and white for aesthetic and political contrast in *Olympia*; *The Art of Exclusion*, 2–4.
34. Tucker, *Le Déjeuner sur l'herbe*, 10–11.
35. See W. N. Burns, *Robin Hood of El Dorado*. For an exploration of the use of humor in myths about Murietta, see Lowe, "Joaquin Murieta."
36. Fried, "Manet's Sources," 49.
37. Lipton, "Manet," 49, 52.
38. For an excellent reading of Manet's painting in this context, see Nochlin, *Realism*, 116.
39. Rubin, "*Les Demoiselles d'Avignon*," 33.
40. Rubin, "*Primitivism*," 252.
41. Rubin, "*Les Demoiselles d'Avignon*," 58.
42. Ibid.
43. I follow William Rubin, who capitalizes the word "Primitive" to differentiate his use of it from common pejorative and ethnocentric associations and who presents Primitivism as the interest modern artists showed in African and Polynesian tribal art and culture.
44. In Picasso African plasticity designates masklike faces marked by scarification and other distortions, sharp profiles, and bodies made of contrasting shapes such as bent knees. The coloring includes raw oranges, blues, and whites applied to exaggerated noses and grins. Some of the Oceanic art Picasso saw at the Trocadéro exhibited such a palette and served him as a model. Rubin, "*Primitivism*," 256–58, 266–67.
45. Ibid., 268.
46. Recalling the care that black Americans had to keep in focus to ensure their safety in the South of his youth, Ralph Ellison writes, "You had to avoid even friendly whites when they were in company of their fellows. Because it was in crowds that hate, fear,

and blood-madness took over. . . . Most of all, you [had to] avoid them when women of their group were present. For when a Negro male came into view, the homeliest white woman became a goddess, a cult figure deified in the mystique of whiteness, a being from whom a shout or a cry or expression of hand or eye could unleash a rage for human sacrifice." Ellison, *Going to the Territory*, 173.

47. Colescott also painted another version of the painting, *Les Demoiselles d'Alabama: Desnudas* (1985), in which, as the title indicates, the women figures are naked. This version of the painting is decidedly less kitschy, although it retains some of the satiric edge of the version I discuss. The second figure from the left, for instance, looks mannish and bored as she poses in a pink bra (the only item of clothing in the frame) that is too small for her prominent breasts. The blonde figure, meanwhile, retains more of the frightful look of Picasso's original. For a reproduction of both versions of the painting, see Colescott, *Robert Colescott: A Retrospective*, 16–17.

48. Rubin, "*Les Demoiselles d'Avignon*," 16.

49. In *Les Demoiselles D'Alabama*, Colescott concentrates on how racial ideologies inform women's sexuality vis-à-vis men across racial lines; in his painting *Ecole de Fontainebleu* (1978) Colescott, like Reed, evokes the libidinal pull of racial fantasies *within* gender. The image is Colescott's appropriation of the sixteenth-century French painting of Gabrielle d'Estree and the Duchess de Villiers, a painting that plays on the suggestion of lesbian interplay between two white, upper-class women. Colescott transports the suggestion from the canonical painting to the realm of racial and sexual fantasy in the United States, presenting two pretty women, one black, one white, in cowgirl outfits and bare breasts. In the original both women touch each other's nipples; in Colescott's painting only the white woman touches the black, while the latter stares back in distrust. For a reproduction of this painting, see Kultermann, "Reconstitucion pictorica de la historia negra."

50. Princenthal, "New York: Kara Walker at Wooster Gardens," 106.

51. Quoted in "Paper Trail," *On Paper* 2 (March/April 1998): 11.

52. For reasons of space I do not discuss them here, but Walker's series of watercolor drawings *Negress Notes* (*Brown Follies*; 1996–97), resonate more immediately with *Los Caprichos*. Like Goya's images, Walker's *Brown Follies* present single figures, pairs, or small groups of people engaged in absurd and violent behavior. Some of the drawings, like each one of Goya's *Caprichos*, include captions that comment indirectly on the images presented. Walker's images are reproduced in Walker, *Kara Walker: Narratives of a Negress*, 23–35.

53. Charles Baudelaire, "Some Foreign Caricaturists," in *The Painter of Modern Life*, 192–23.

54. Goya initially named these etchings *Sueños* (dreams), following the eighteenth-century practice of presenting social commentary or satire within the context of a dream. See Goya, *Los Caprichos*, 15.

55. See Bakhtin, *Rabelais and His World*. See also Storr, "Reason's Dream," 212.

56. See Barasch, "Meaning of the Grotesque," xiii.

57. Alberro, "Interview with Kara Walker," 25–28.

58. Baudelaire, *Painter of Modern Life*, 193.

59. Connelly, "Profound Play," 200.

60. Each one of *Los Caprichos* is numbered and bears a phrase written by the artist or an aphorism common at the time that indirectly comments on the images presented. They are also accompanied by contemporary commentaries, the Ayala, Prado, and Biblioteca Nacional texts. See Goya, *Los Caprichos*, 21–22.

61. Ibid., 23–24, 24–25.

62. Baudelaire, *Painter of Modern Life*, 193.

63. Lott, *Love and Theft*, 159, 147.

64. Alberro, "Interview with Kara Walker," 25–28.

65. Wagner, "Black-White Relation," 94.

66. Reinhardt, "Art of Racial Profiling," 114.

67. Ibid.

68. Quoted in Saltz, "Kara Walker," 82.

69. Alberro, "Interview with Kara Walker," 25–28.

70. Johann Caspar Lavater (1741–1801) was a Swiss physiognomer who proposed a large lexicon of distinguishing signs and wrote a widely popular treatise, *L'Art de connaitre les hommes par la physionomie.* He argued for "the science or knowledge of the correspondence between the external and internal man, the visible superficies and the invisible contents." Wechsler, *A Human Comedy*, 23–24. For a fuller account of the silhouette's history in art and the pseudo-science of race, see Shaw, *Seeing the Unspeakable*, chapter 1.

71. Alberro, "Interview with Kara Walker," 25–28.

72. Saltz, "Kara Walker: Ill-Will and Desire," 82.

73. Significantly, voodoo rituals include the use of flags to call the spirits into being. These flags feature bead-embroidered silhouette inscriptions and figures "identifying the power" of the loa "for whom they are made"; they are noted for their beauty. See R. F. Thompson, *Flash of the Spirit*, 184–88.

74. "What scared me," Walker told an interviewer about her initial use of racial stereotypes, "was that I didn't know what these comments were going to be like. They were floating around in an unknown place in my mind. I just decided that the easiest way to figure out what was going on in my head was by free associating blackness . . . with my own self-impression, with situations I was in, with everything actually." Alberro, "Interview with Kara Walker," 25–28.

75. Tilley, "Interview with Kara Walker," 3, 2.

76. Alberro, "Interview with Kara Walker," 25–283.

77. Reid-Pharr, "Black Girl Lost," 32.

78. Elizabeth Armstrong, "Kara Walker Interviewed by Liz Armstrong 7/23/96," in Armstrong et al., *No Place (Like Home)*, 107.

79. For an exemplary reading of Walker as an artist who visualizes the "unspeakable" aspects of slavery, see Shaw, *Seeing the Unspeakable*, in particular chapter 2.

80. Alberro, "Interview with Kara Walker," 25–28.

81. See the introduction where I first discuss these ideas. Lott, *Love and Theft*, 143, 145, 149.

82. Walker's detractors often point to her lack of specific references to orient the viewer. If Walker does not provide guidance, museum curators could. But, as Shaw argues,

art curators often adopt a hands-off approach when presenting Walker's work, declining (often because they do not feel suited) to provide didactic explanations through brochures or exhibition plaques. Shaw, *Seeing the Unspeakable*, 111–12.

83. Frankel, "Kara Walker: Wooster Gardens," 122–23.

84. Francis, "Embodied Fictions," 831, 836.

85. Gubar, *Racechanges*, 115.

86. Francis, "Embodied Fictions," 836.

87. As quoted in and translated by Francis, ibid.

88. Francis notes that the costume's "designer is uncertain. . . . The paternity is attributed to different people, particularly Jean Cocteau." Ibid.

89. Borshuck, "Intelligence of the Body," 53.

90. Rose, *Jazz Cleopatra*, 114.

91. Francis, "Embodied Fictions," 836. Baker walked a tightrope between colluding with and mocking that colonialist fantasy. She also, Francis notes, enticed "audiences to forget that she was American" even though she included black American movements and reinvented herself as "*noire*—a fictional ethnicity elastic enough to encompass a variety of perceptions of Africans variously located in the diaspora" (834, 837).

92. Walker, *Kara Walker*, n.p.

93. Unger, "Contested Histories," 29.

94. Alberro, "Interview with Kara Walker," 25, my emphasis.

95. Kara Walker, interview by the author, May 13, 1999.

96. See www.bcaatlanta.com.

97. The frieze is reproduced in photograph form in Dixon, *Kara Walker*, 64.

98. Goddu, *Gothic America*, 131, 135, 134.

99. For examples, see Dixon, *Kara Walker*, 90; Berry et al., *Kara Walker*, 78–79.

100. Bowles, "Extreme Times," 8.

101. Newkirk, "Controversial Silhouette," 45. Currently, the New York Public Library's Division of Prints and Photographs owns the piece. See Shaw, *Seeing the Unspeakable*, chapter 4, for a history of censorship and reception of Walker's work, especially as Shaw links the controversy over Walker's work to a similar one provoked by Colescott's.

102. Saar initiated a letter-writing campaign condemning Walker's work and the institutions that chose to show it. She also petitioned the MacArthur Foundation to rescind the award recently given to Walker.

103. Bowles, "Extreme Times," 11.

104. Unger, "Contested Histories," 29.

105. As quoted in Kelefa, "Debate Continues," 42.

106. As quoted in Bowles, "Extreme Times," 13–14, 11.

107. Ibid., 11.

108. For a reproduction of *Successes* (1998), see Dixon, *Kara Walker*, 65. The image is reproduced on the same page as *Consume* and provides an interesting contrast. For a reproduction of *Letter from a Black Girl*, see 96.

109. Princenthal, "New York: Kara Walker at Wooster Gardens," 106.

110. Entitled *Cut*, the piece is reproduced in Dixon, *Kara Walker*, 67, and on the cover of Shaw's book. Shaw argues that the image is Walker's self-portrait, one that examines her "role as an African American woman artist in the public sphere." See Shaw, *Seeing the Unspeakable*, 125–51.

111. Quoted in Walker, interview with Liz Tilley, 3.

112. Quoted in Frankel, "Kara Walker: Wooster Gardens," 123.

113. As quoted in Dalton, "Past Is Prologue," 21.

114. As quoted in Bowles, "Stereotypes Subverted," 46. Held on March 18–19, 1998, the conference title comes from Ralph Ellison's essay on African American caricatures and humanity in folklore and literature. See Ellison, *Shadow and Act*, 45–60.

115. As quoted in Dalton, "Past Is Prologue," 18.

116. Ibid., 22.

117. For a reproduction of some of its pages, see Berry et al., *Kara Walker*, 132–39.

118. Cameron, "Kara Walker," 11.

119. As quoted in ibid.

120. I can't help but note a loaded coincidence in Walker's benefactors' name. Norton is, after all, the eponymous hero's well-intentioned but ultimately blind benefactor in Ralph Ellison's novel.

121. Ellison, *Going to the Territory*, 145–46.

122. The first show (March 21, 2006 to August 6, 2006) juxtaposed a variety of objects chosen by the artists from the museum's collection with her own work to expose the knots of race and poverty that Hurricane Katrina highlighted. The second show (October 11, 2007 to February 3, 2008) was a major retrospective of Walker's work.

Chapter 5

1. Parks, *America Play and Other Works*, 175. Subsequent references are cited parenthetically as *AP*.

2. Hartman, *Scenes of Subjection*, 3. For Hartman, the crucial issue is how "we are called to participate" in scenes of black suffering in nineteenth-century literature about slavery. Echoing Elaine Scarry, she asks: "Are we witnesses who confirm the truth of what happened in the face of the world-destroying capacities of pain, the distortion of torture, the sheer unrepresentability of terror, and the repression of the dominant accounts? Or are we voyeurs fascinated with and repelled by exhibitions of terror and sufferance? . . . Or does the pain of the other merely provide us with the opportunity for self-reflection?" Ultimately, Hartman calls attention to the "precariousness of empathy and the uncertain line between witness and spectator" even in scenes in which "terror can hardly be discerned," such as those of slaves dancing or of the minstrel stage (4).

3. In this respect, Parks's work is similar to Hartman's more recent writing. In "The Time of Slavery," Hartman examines the potential for a commercialism of grief in current tourism to African slave ports.

4. In "The Re-Objectification and Re-Commodification of Saartjie Baartman in Suzan-Lori Parks's Venus," Jean Young firmly critiques the artistic license that Parks

takes with the historical facts of Baartman's story. Additionally, Young argues that Parks further obfuscates Baartman's voice and wrongly attributes blame to Baartman by portraying her as complicit with her own demise. Young takes special issue with what she sees as Parks's reobjectification of Baartman in "re-displaying" her for the gaze of others. In a much more nuanced way than Young, Harry Elam Jr. and Alice Rayner examine the risks that Parks takes in staging the story of the Venus Hottentot but ultimately argue that her "representation of Venus actively embraces contradiction and complexity" and calls for a "rigorous and repeated interrogation of ourselves as well as the history of oppression." Elam and Rayner, "Body Parts," 280.

5. Oxford English Dictionary, 3rd edition.

6. Elam and Rayner, "Body Parts," 265–66.

7. Ibid., 266.

8. Ibid., 267.

9. Miller, "Bottom of Desire," 132.

10. Parks is certainly not alone in thinking of time in relationship to African American culture along these lines. See the introduction where I first discuss how in much contemporary African American literature, "non-linear time is juxtaposed with linear processes, to the effect that they intersect with and perspectivize each other." In particular, fictional revisions of the history of slavery, as in Gayl Jones's novel, *Corregidora* (1975), intertwine the traumatic repetition of the past "with a tentative progressive movement: by repeating the past, by revisiting it imaginatively and dialogically, they sketch a possible future that might help their characters to break out of . . . the after-effects of the past of slavery." Reichardt, "Time and the African American Experience," 479.

11. Wilmer, "Restaging the Nation," 448.

12. Roach, "Great Hole of History," 309.

13. Wilmer, "Restaging the Nation," 446.

14. A. Solomon, "Signifying on the Signifyin'," 75–76.

15. Bernard, "Musicality of Language," 692.

16. Parks also consciously makes reference to Henry Louis Gates Jr.'s *Signifying Monkey*, which proposes tropological revision through repetition with a difference as a key aspect of African American culture, especially in literature. At a reading that she gave at Harvard University in the spring of 2003, she acknowledged the influence of Gates's book on her concept.

17. Beckett, *Watt*, 48.

18. Orr, *Tragicomedy and Contemporary Culture*, 1, 4, 3, 1.

19. Robert Storr rearticulates Mann's argument in "Reason's Dream, Reason's Nightmare," 211.

20. Diamond, "Shudder of Catharsis," 159.

21. Orgel, "Play of Conscience," 134.

22. Ibid., 134. Here Orgel paraphrases Gerald Else's *Aristotle's Poetics*.

23. Orgel, "Play of Conscience," 136–37.

24. See Francis Sparshott's "The Riddle of Katharsis."

25. I here borrow a term used by R. Darren Gobert in "Cognitive Catharsis in the *Caucasian Chalk Circle*," 13. Gobert analyzes a shift in Brecht's conception of Aristotelian

catharsis. According to Gobert, Brecht first understood catharsis as "an empathetic identification of spectators with a hero," one that "concentrates their collective emotion in a single direction" and therefore ensnares "them in a somatic, uncritical experience." Later, Brecht had a much more "nuanced understanding of emotion" and ultimately of catharsis. He came to understand the "role that emotions . . . might play in ethical decision making" and in cognitive processes more generally and therefore let go of his hostility toward emotional effects of the theater. This hostility was always rooted in "his refusal to view spectators as objects to be conditioned" (15, 13). With his more expansive understanding of emotions, Brecht believed that their production did not necessarily make passive audiences.

26. Ibid., 16.

27. Brecht eventually embraced the importance of emotions in drama, especially in "the sense of justice," in "the urge of freedom and righteous anger," and to see them as playing an integral role in the "ethical decision making" of audiences (ibid., 18, 13). As Gobert notes, this shift coincided with an updating of the meaning of the term catharsis. Until 1940, catharsis was defined as the process of "purging" or "purification," but that year "clarifying" was added as a denotation. This new denotation "heralded an entirely new interpretation of Aristotle's notoriously vague clause," starting with a series of articles by Leon Golden (1962, 1969, 1976) and continuing more recently with Stephen Halliwell's *Aristotle's Poetics* and Martha Nussbaum's *The Fragility of Goodness* (both 1986). The two latter critics in particular argue that we can derive pleasure from the vicarious experience of the pitiable and the fearful because we gain knowledge and insight from it (Gobert, "Cognitive Catharsis," 16). This is particularly suggestive with regard to Parks, whose expert signifying on the signifyin(g) produces the pleasure to be gained not only from insight but also from the aesthetic experience of her formal creativity. See Bertolt Brecht, "Formal Problems Arising from the Theatre's New Content," in *Brecht on Theatre*, 226–30.

28. From R. Williams, *Marxism and Literature*: "Structures of feeling can be defined as social experiences in solution, as distinct from other social semantic formations which have been precipitated and are more evidently and more immediately available" (133–34).

29. See chapter 3. Elam and Rayner would argue against a reading of Parks's "spirit world" in terms of voodoo. In "Unfinished Business" they declare that it is not necessary to refer to "shamanistic practices or mythic reality belonging to 'primitive' cultures" to account for Parks's enactment of burial rites. They prefer to find the "clues" to Parks's dramaturgy in Lacan's work. Yet the choice they make (a vested one, no doubt) implicitly undermines the fact that Parks's use of voodoo, like Reed's, is an inventive use of a practice that is not merely "primitive" but actually in flux and in dialogue with other practices, most notably postmodernism.

30. Roach, *Cities of the Dead*, 36.

31. See Robinson, "Four Writers," 31. In her introduction to Stein's *Last Operas and Plays*, Bonnie Marranca writes, "As early as her first play, [Stein] had decided that a play did not have to tell a story. What happened was the theater experience itself. In other words, the creation of an experience was more important than the representation of

an event" (ix). Stein's drama "placed a supreme value on the experience of the mind, and therefore, presence or, in her sense, the continuous present" (x).

32. Kennedy describes the first scene of *The Owl Answers* as such: "The scene is a New York subway is the Tower of London is a Harlem hotel room is St. Peter's." A. Kennedy, *Adrienne Kennedy Reader*, 29.

33. A. Solomon, "Signifying on the Signifyin'," 80.

34. Ben-Zvi, "Aroun the Worl," 197.

35. Roach, *Cities*, 69, emphasis added.

36. Bernard, "Musicality of Language," 693, 697 n. 6. See also Sherley Ann Williams, "The Blues Roots of Contemporary Afro-American Poetry," in Harper and Stepto, *Chant of the Saints*, 127.

37. Ironically, I must insert my own note here to clarify the fact that the section also includes real footnotes; these have also to do with the slave trade but include references to housing laws, the real estate market, and the Jewish Holocaust. These footnotes subtly suggest connections between the confinement of slave ships and housing for the poor, between the marketing of bodies that slavery represented and the marketing of property, as well as between the representation of two major forms of genocide in history.

38. In Liz Diamond's 1989 production, the voices of the Seers were taped and projected on a darkened stage, empty except for black-and-white slides projected onto black screens with pictures of people's bodies, hands, and feet in thick mud. Suzan-Lori Parks, *Imperceptible Mutabilities in the Third Kingdom*, Brooklyn Academy of Contemporary Arts Downtown, September 26, 1989. See Frieze, "*Imperceptible Mutabilities*," 528.

39. Ben-Zvi, "Aroun the Worl," 197.

40. For example, Kin-Seer says, "I was standing with my toes stuckted in thuh dirt. Nothin in front of me but water. And I was wavin. Wavin. Wavin at my uther me who I could barely see Over thuh water on thuh uther cliff I could see my uther me but my uther me could not see me. And I was wavin wavin waving" (*AP* 38). Later Kin-Seer adds, "My uther me then waved back at me and then I was happy. But my uther me whuduhnt wavin at me. My uther me was waving at my Self" (38). Finally, Kin-Seer condenses his/her narrative into a chant: "Me waving at Me. Me waving at I. Me waving at my Self" (39).

41. Banerjee, "Stir within Stasis," 523–24.

42. Garrett, "Return of the Repressed," 37. Shange also experiments with language to exorcise the demon of minstrelsy. But, as Linda Ben-Zvi notes, while there are similarities between Parks's language and Shange's, the differences between the two playwrights are more significant:

> Both are language-based; both use dialect, omitting conventional punctuation and capitalization. . . . [But, while Shange] attempts to break free of [what she calls] an imposed "white version of blk speech" . . . Parks . . . stages the process of linguistic deformation itself, the imposition of language and culture and those strategies of survival encoded in Black vernacular. She offers less a face beneath

a mask . . . than the play between discourses: the intertextuality of dominant and muted forms, foregrounding the very process of linguistic containment, commensurate culture, and political effacement, indicating both the sickness and the healing: the development of a counterlanguage. (Ben-Zvi, "Aroun the Worl," 191)

43. Included among these plays are Robert Alexander's *I Ain't Yo' Uncle—The New Jack Revisionist of Uncle Tom's Cabin*, Matt Robinson's *The Confessions of Stepin Fetchit*, Michael Henry Brown's *King of Coons*, Bob Devin Jones's *Uncle Bends—A Home Cooked Negro Narrative*, Carlyle Brown's *The Little Tommy Parker Celebrated Colored Minstrel Show*, Breena Clarke and Glenda Dickerson's *Re/membering Aunt Jemima: A Menstrual Show*, Marcia L. Leslie's *The Trial of One Short-Sighted Black Woman vs. Mammy Louise and Safreeta Mae*, and Kim Dunbar's *Porch Monkey*. See Euell, "Signifyin(g) Ritual."

44. Euell, "Signifyin(g) Ritual," 668.

45. Elam and Rayner, "Unfinished Business," 453.

46. A. Solomon, "Signifying on the Signifyin'," 78.

47. Wilmer, "Restaging the Nation," 444–46.

48. Elam and Rayner, "Unfinished," 453–54.

49. Ibid., 457.

50. The play also suggests that anger can transform into shame. Black Man, for instance, must plead forgiveness for having let himself be persecuted when it is entirely clear that he is not to blame. His shame is so potent that Black Woman at one point smells it: "Whiff it!" she says, "you smell" (*AP* 120). In the BACA production, Black Man responds, "On me? In my bones? . . . Ah, my shame . . . on me, in my bones." Similarly, when Ham lists a certain uncle in the ancestral tree—the uncle of minstrelsy, the one that was spawned from Stowe's Tom, the one "who from birth was gifted with great singin and dancin capabilities which helped him make his way in life but tended tuh bring shame on his family"—the choir sings out, "Shame on his family, shame on his family" (122).

51. Spillers, "Mama's Baby," 67, 77, 73, 68, 79.

52. Elam and Rayner, "Unfinished Business," 459.

53. Parks's grammar also recognizes the loss of gender distinction that Spillers highlights in her essay. Her use of the gender-neutral pronouns It and That and the way she repeatedly interchanges Wasshername and Wasshisname recalls Spillers's poignant observation that the slave trade robbed captive people of the "*potential* for gender differentiation as it might express itself along a range of stress points, including human biology and its intersection with the project of culture." For Spillers, focusing on such possibility is not a reactionary insistence on female/male gender distinctions but a way of describing how captive people were jettisoned out of systems of human meaning. Spillers, "Mama's Baby," 66.

54. Elam and Rayner, "Unfinished Business," 459.

55. Spillers, "Mama's Baby," 56.

56. "The debate still ranges," writes Saidiya Hartman, "as to how many were transported to the Americas, killed in the raids and wars that supplied the trade, perished on the

long journey to the coast, committed suicide, died of dehydration in the Middle Passage, or were beaten or worked to death—22 million, 30 million, 60 million, or more? Isn't it enough to know that for each captive who survived the ordeal of captivity and seasoning, at least one did not?" Hartman, "Time of Slavery," 772.

57. Lott, *Love and Theft*, 122.

58. A. Solomon, "Signifying on the Signifyin'," 76.

59. In Reed's novel, "Jes Grew" is a contagion, connected with the improvisational spirit of ragtime and jazz. James Weldon Johnson used the term "jes grew" earlier in *The Book of American Negro Poetry* (1922) to describe African American music's purportedly unstructured development.

60. Dayan, "Vodoun," 43.

61. Deren, *Divine Horsemen*, 62.

62. The Petro are New World loa whose manifestations are to be differentiated from the most powerful West African nation of loa, the Rada. The Rada are known as peaceful and kind, with rituals that center around celebration and healing; the Petro are known for their anger and aggressiveness. The third major group of loa is named after Guede.

63. Deren, *Divine Horsemen*, 62.

64. Styan, *Dark Comedy*, 252.

65. Louis, "Body Language," 143.

66. Bernard, "Musicality of Language," 696; Elam and Rayner, "Unfinished Business," 460.

67. See Garrett, "Possession of Suzan-Lori Parks," 26. Monte Williams has also said, "Some blacks have complained that Ms. Parks's work is too abstract to accurately capture the black experience." M. Williams, "From a Planet Closer to the Sun," C, p. 14.

68. Garrett, "Possession of Suzan-Lori Parks," 134, 24, 16.

69. Roach, "Great Hole of History," 308, 307.

70. Garrett, "Possession of Suzan-Lori Parks," 24.

71. Kushner, "Art of the Difficult."

72. Elam and Rayner, "Body Parts," 274.

73. Ibid., 271.

74. Parks, *Venus*, 31. Subsequent references are cited parenthetically.

75. Elam and Rayner, "Body Parts," 276, 271.

76. Ibid., 276, 278.

77. Ibid., 279.

78. Hartman, *Lose Your Mother*, 6.

BIBLIOGRAPHY

Adamson, Jeremy Elwell, ed. *Niagara: Two Centuries of Changing Attitudes, 1697–1901*. Washington, D.C.: Corcoran Gallery of Art, 1985.

Alberro, Alexander. "An Interview with Kara Walker." *Index* 1, no. 2 (1996): 25–28.

Alis, Hilton. Introduction. *Clotel, or, The President's Daughter*. New York: Modern Library, 2000.

Andrews, William L. *The Literary Career of Charles W. Chesnutt*. Baton Rouge: Louisiana State University Press, 1980.

Apter, Emily. "Acting Out Orientalism: Sapphic Theatricality in Turn-of-the-Century Paris." In *Performance and Cultural Politics*, ed. Elin Diamond. 15–34. London: Routledge, 1996.

Apter, Emily, and William Pietz, eds. *Fetishism as a Cultural Discourse*. Ithaca, N.Y.: Cornell University Press, 1993.

Armstrong, Elizabeth, and Douglas Fogle, eds. *No Place (Like Home)*. Exhibition catalogue. Minneapolis: Walker Art Center, 1997.

Ault, Suanne. "Latest Chappelle DVD Is Selling Like Crazy." June 3, 2005, www.videobusiness.com/article/CA627685.html (accessed January 14, 2008).

Bakhtin, Mikhail. *Rabelais and His World*. Trans. Helen Islowsky. Bloomington: Indiana University Press, 1993.

Baldwin, James. *Notes of a Native Son*. Boston: Beacon Press, 1984.

Banerjee, A. "Stir within Stasis in 'Waiting for Godot.'" *English Studies* 72, no. 6 (1991): 520–29.

Baraka, Amiri [Leroi Jones]. *Blues People: Negro Music in White America*. New York: William Morrow, 1963.

Barasch, Francis. "The Meaning of the Grotesque." Introduction to *A History of Caricature and Grotesque in Literature and Art* by Thomas Wright. New York: Ungar, 1968.

Bass, George Houston, ed. *Mule Bone: A Comedy of Negro Life*. New York: HarperCollins, 1991. First published in 1931.

Baudelaire, Charles. *The Painter of Modern Life and Other Essays*. Trans. Jonathan Mayne. London: Phaidon Press, 1986. First edition originally published in 1964.

Beardslee, Karen E. "Through Slave Culture's Lens Comes the Abundant Source: Harriet A. Jacobs's 'Incidents in the Life of a Slave Girl.'" *MELUS* 24 (Spring 1999): 37–59.

Beatty, Paul. *Hokum: An Anthology of African American Humor*. New York: Bloomsbury, 2006.

Beaulieu, Elizabeth Ann. *Black Women Writers and the American Neo-Slave Narrative*. Westport, Conn.: Greenwood Press, 1999.

Beavers, Herman. "'The Cool Pose': Intersectionality, Masculinity and Quiescence in the Comedy and Films of Richard Pryor and Eddie Murphy." In *Race and the Subject of Masculinities*, ed. Harry Stecopoulos and Michael Uebel, 253–85. Durham, N.C.: Duke University Press; 1997.

Beckett, Samuel. *Waiting for Godot: A Tragicomedy in Two Acts*. New York: Grove Press, 2006. [First published in French as *En Attendant Godot* (1952) and in English as *Waiting for Godot: A Tragicomedy in Two Acts* (1954)]

————. *Watt*. 1953. New York: Grove Press, 1970.

Bell, Bernard. *The Afro-American Novel and Its Tradition*. Amherst: University of Massachusetts Press, 1987.

Benesch, Klaus. "'From a Thing into I Am': Ishmael Reed's *Flight to Canada.'"* In *Historiographic Metafiction in Modern American and Canadian Literature*, ed. Bernd Engler and Kurt Muller. 358–65. Paderborn, Germany: Ferdinand Schoningh, 1994.

Benshoff, Harry M. "Blaxploitation Horror Films: Generic Reappropriation or Reinscription?" *Cinema Journal* 39, no. 2 (2000): 31–51.

Ben-Zvi, Linda. "'Aroun the Worl.': The Signifyin(g) Theater of Suzan-Lori Parks." In *The Theatrical Gamut: Notes for a Post-Beckettian Stage*, ed. Enoch Brater. 189–208. Ann Arbor: University of Michigan Press, 1995.

Bergson, Henri. *Laughter: An Essay on the Meaning of the Comic*. Trans. Cloudesley Brereton and Fred Rothwell. London: Macmillan, 1921. First published in 1911.

Bernard, Louise. "The Musicality of Language: Redefining History in Suzan-Lori Parks's *The Death of the Last Black Man in the Whole Entire World*." *African American Review* 31, no. 4 (Winter 1997): 687–99.

Berry, Ian, Darby English, Vivian Patterson, and Mark Reinhart, eds. *Kara Walker: Narratives of the Negress*. Cambridge, Mass.: MIT Press, 2003.

Best, Stephen, and Saidiya Hartman. "Fugitive Justice." *Representations* 92 (Fall 2005): 1–15.

Bogle, Donald. *Toms, Coons, Mulattoes, Mammies and Bucks: An Interpretative History of Blacks in American Film*. New York: Continuum, 1996.

Boime, Albert. *The Art of Exclusion: Representing Blacks in the Nineteenth Century*. Washington, D.C.: Smithsonian Institute Press, 1990.

Bone, Robert. *Down Home: A History of Afro-American Short Fictions from Its Beginnings to the End of the Harlem Renaissance*. New York: G. P. Putnam's Sons, 1975.

Borshuck, Michael. "An Intelligence of the Body: Disruptive Parody through Dance in the Early Performances of Josephine Baker." In *EmBODYing Liberation: The Black Body in American Dance*, ed. Dorothea Fischer-Hornung and Alison D. Goeller. 41–57. Piscataway, N.J.: Transaction, 2001.

Boskin, Joseph. *Sambo: The Rise & Demise of an American Jester*. New York: Oxford University Press, 1986.

Bowles, Juliette. "Editor's Response." *International Review of African American Art* 15, no. 2 (1998): 50–52.

———. "Extreme Times Call for Extreme Heroes." *International Review of African American Art* 14, no. 3 (1997): 2–16.

———. "Stereotypes Subverted." *International Review of African American Art* 15, no. 2 (1998): 44–51.

Brawley, Benjamin. *The Negro in Literature and Art.* New York: Duffield & Company, 1918.

Breau, Elizabeth. "Identifying Satire: Our Nig." *Callaloo* 16, no. 2 (1993): 455–65.

Brecht, Bertolt. *Brecht on Theatre: The Development of an Aesthetic.* Trans. John Willet. London: Methuen, 1964.

Brodhead, Richard, ed. *The Journals of Charles Chesnutt.* Durham, N.C.: Duke University Press, 1993.

Brown, Jeffrey A. "Comic Book Masculinity and the New Black Superhero." *African American Review* 33, no. 1 (1999): 25–43.

Brown, Kate E., and Howard I. Kushner. "Eruptive Voices: Coprolalia, Malediction, and the Poetics of Cursing." *New Literary History* 32, no. 3 (2001): 537–62.

Brown, Michael K., Martin Carnoy, Elliot Currie, Troy Duster, David Oppenheimer, Marjorie M. Shultz, and David Wellman, eds. *Whitewashing Race: The Myth of a Color-Blind Society.* Berkeley: University of California Press, 2003.

Brown, William Wells. *Clotel; or, The President's Daughter.* New York: Penguin Classics, 2004.

———. *The Escape; or, A Leap for Freedom: A Drama in Five Acts.* Ed. John Ernest. Knoxville: University of Tennessee Press, 2001. First published in 1858.

———. *My Southern Home.* 1880. Upper Saddle River, N.J.: Gregg Press, 1968.

Burns, Mark K. "'A Slave in Form but Not in Fact': Subversive Humor and the Rhetoric of Irony in *Narrative of the Life of Frederick Douglass.*" *Studies in American Humor* 3, no. 12 (2005): 83–96.

Burns, Walter Noble. *The Robin Hood of El Dorado: The Saga of Joaquin Murietta, Famous Outlaw of California's Age of Gold.* Albuquerque: University of Mexico Center for the American West and University of New Mexico Press, 1999. First published in 1932.

Byerman, Keith. *Fingering the Jagged Grain: Tradition and Form in Recent Black Fiction.* Athens: University of Georgia Press, 1985.

Cameron, Dan. "Kara Walker: Rubbing History the Wrong Way." *On Paper* 2 (September–October 1997): 10–14.

Carretta, Vincent, ed. *Unchained Voices: An Anthology of Black Authors in the English Speaking World in the 18th Century.* Lexington: University Press of Kentucky, 1996.

Chappelle, Dave. *Dave Chappelle's Block Party.* Dir. Michel Gondry. Rogue Pictures, 2006.

Chappelle, Dave, and Neal Brennan. *Chappelle's Show.* Comedy Central. January 22, 2003–July 23, 2006.

Chesnutt, Charles Waddell. *Charles W. Chesnutt: Selected Writings.* Ed. SallyAnn H. Ferguson. Boston: Houghton Mifflin, 2001.

———. *The Short Fiction of Charles W. Chesnutt.* Ed. Sylvia Lyons Render. Washington, D.C.: Howard University Press, 1974.

Chesnutt, Charles Waddell. *Stories, Novels and Essays*. Ed. Werner Sollors. New York: Library of America, 2002.

Chung, Jack. "The Burden of Laughter: Chris Rock Fights Ignorance His Way." Honorable mention, Boothe Prize Essays (Winter 2002), available at www.pwr.stanford.edu/publications/index.html.

Cohen, Sarah Blacher, ed. *Comic Relief: Humor in Contemporary American Literature*. Chicago: University of Illinois Press, 1978.

Coleman, Robin R. Means. *African American Viewers and the Black Situation Comedy: Situating Racial Humor*. New York: Garland, 1998.

Colescott, Robert. *Robert Colescott: A Retrospective, 1975–1986*. San Jose, Calif.: San Jose Museum of Art, 1987.

Colman, David. "Pretty on the Outside." *George* (June/July 1996): 117–19.

Connelly, Frances S. Introduction. *Modern Art and the Grotesque*. Cambridge, England: Cambridge University Press, 2003.

———. "Profound Play: The Image Tradition of the Comic Grotesque." In *The Comic Grotesque Wit and Mockery in German Art*, ed. Pamela Kort. 193–209. New York: Neue Gallery, 2004.

Cory, Mark. "Comedic Distance in Holocaust Literature." *Journal of American Culture* 18, no. 1 (1995): 35–41.

Critchley, Simon. *On Humour*. London: Routledge, 2002.

Cumber Dance, Daryl. *Honey Hush! An Anthology of African American Women's Humor*. New York: Norton, 1998.

Cummings, Paul, ed. *Willem de Kooning: Drawings Paintings, Sculpture*. New York: Whitney Museum of American Art, 1983.

Dalfiume, Richard. "The Forgotten Years of Negro Revolution." *Journal of American History* 55 (June 1968): 1–5.

Dalton, Karen C. C. "The Past Is Prologue but Is Parody and Pastiche Progress? A Conversation." *International Review of African American Art* 14, no. 3 (1997): 17–29.

Davis, Cynthia J. "Speaking the Body's Pain: Harriet Wilson's *Our Nig*." *African American Review* 27, no. 3 (1993): 391–404.

Davis, Matthew R. "'*Strange, History. Complicated, Too*': Ishmael Reed's Use of African American History in *Flight to Canada*." *Mississippi Quarterly* 49 (Fall 1996): 743–53.

Dayan, Joan. *Haiti, History and the Gods*. Berkeley: University of California Press, 1995.

———. "Vodoun, or the Voice of the Gods." *Raritan: A Quarterly Review* 10, no. 3 (1991): 32–57.

DeCosta-Willis, Miriam, Reginald Martin, and Roseanne P. Bell, eds. *Erotique Noire: Black Erotica*. London: Doubleday, 1992.

de Kooning, Willem. *Willem de Kooning: Drawings, Paintings, Sculpture*. Ed. Paul Cummings. New York: Whitney Museum of American Art, 1983.

Deren, Maya. *Divine Horsemen: The Living Gods of Haiti*. New Paltz, N.Y.: McPherson, 1983. First published in 1953.

Desmangles, Leslie G. *The Faces of the Gods: Vodou and Roman Catholicism in Haiti*. Chapel Hill: University of North Carolina Press, 1992.

Diamond, Elin. "The Shudder of Catharsis in Twentieth Century Performance." In *Performativity and Performance*, ed. Andre Parker and Eve Kosofsky Sedgwick. 152–72. New York: Routledge, 1995.

Dick, Bruce, and Amritjit Singh, eds. *Conversations with Ishmael Reed*. Jackson: University Press of Mississippi, 1995.

Dickinson-Carr, Darryl. *African American Satire: The Sacred and the Profane Novel*. Columbia: University of Missouri Press, 2001.

Dines, Gail, and Jean M. Humez. *Gender, Race, and Class in Media: A Text-Reader*. Thousand Oaks, Calif.: Sage, 1995.

Dixon, Annette, ed. *Kara Walker: Pictures from Another Time*. Ann Arbor: University of Michigan Press, 2002.

Dollard, John. *Caste and Class in a Southern Town*. New York: Anchor: 1949. First published in 1937.

Douglas, Mary. *Implicit Meanings: Selected Essays in Anthropology*. New York: Routledge, 1999.

Douglass, Robert L. "Robert Colescott's Searing Stereotypes, Perceptions and Perspectives." *New Art Examiner* 16 (June 1989): 34–37.

Dubey, Madhu. *Black Women Novelists and the Nationalist Aesthetic*. Bloomington: Indiana University Press, 1994.

———. *Signs and Cities: Black Literary Postmodernism*. Chicago: University of Chicago Press, 2003.

du Cille, Ann. "Where in the World Is William Wells Brown? Thomas Jefferson, Sally Hemings, and the DNA of African-American Literary History." *American Literary History* 12, no. 3 (2000): 443–62.

Dundes, Alan, comp. *Mother Wit from the Laughing Barrel: Readings in the Interpretation of Afro-American Folklore*. Jackson: University Press of Mississippi, 1990. First published in 1973.

Elam, Harry J. "The Black Performer and the Performance of Blackness: *The Escape; or, A Leap for Freedom* by William Wells Brown and *No Place to Be Somebody* by Charles Gordone." In *African American Performance and Theater History: A Critical Reader*, ed. David Krasner. 288–305. Oxford: Oxford University Press, 2001.

Elam, Harry, and Alice Rayner. "Body Parts: Between Story and Spectacle in *Venus* by Suzan-Lori Parks." In *Staging Resistance: Essays on Political Theater*, ed. Jeanne Colleran and Jenny S. Spencer. 265–82. Ann Arbor: University of Michigan Press, 1998.

Elam, Harry, and Alice Rayner. "Unfinished Business: Reconfiguring History in Suzan-Lori Parks's *The Death of the Last Black Man in the Whole Entire World*." *Theater Journal* 16, no. 4 (1994): 447–61.

Ellis, R. J. "Body Politics and the Body Politic in William Wells Brown's *Clotel* and Harriet Wilson's *Our Nig*." In *Soft Canons: American Women Writers and Masculine Tradition*, ed. Karen L. Kilcup. 99–122. Iowa City: University of Iowa Press, 1999.

Ellis, Trey. "The New Black Aesthetic." *Callaloo* 38 (Winter 1989): 233–43.

Ellison, Ralph. *Going to the Territory*. New York: Random House, 1986.

———. *Shadow and Act*. New York: Vintage International, 1995.

Else, Gerald. *Aristotle's Poetics: The Argument*. Cambridge, Mass.: Harvard University Press, 1963.

Ernest, John. Introduction. *The Escape; or, A Leap for Freedom. A Drama in Five Acts*, by William Wells Brown. 1858. ix–li. Knoxville: University of Tennessee Press, 2001.

———. "The Reconstruction of Whiteness: William Wells Brown's *The Escape; or, A Leap for Freedom*." *PMLA* 113, no. 5 (1998): 1108–21.

———. *Resistance and Reformation in Nineteenth Century African-American Literature: Brown, Wilson, Jacobs, Delaney, Douglass, and Harper*. Jackson: University Press of Mississippi, 1995.

Euell, Kim. "Signifyin(g) Ritual: Subverting Stereotypes, Salvaging Icons." *African American Review* 31, no. 4 (1997): 667–75.

Farrison, William Edward. *William Wells Brown, Author and Reformer*. Chicago: University of Chicago Press, 1969.

Ferguson, Jeffrey B. *The Sage of Sugar Hill: George Schuyler and the Harlem Renaissance*. New Haven: Yale University Press, 2005.

Ferguson, SallyAnn H. Introduction. *Charles W. Chesnutt: Selected Writings*. 1–11. Boston: Houghton Mifflin, 2001.

Fischer, David Hackett, ed. *Washington's Crossing*. New York: Oxford University Press, 2004.

Fisher Fishkin, Shelley. "The Bondwoman's Escape: Hannah Crafts Rewrites the First Play Published by an African American." In *In Search of Hannah Crafts: Critical Essays on "The Bondwoman's Narrative,"* ed. Henry Louis Gates Jr. and Hollis Robbins. 117–26. New York: Civitas Books, 2004.

Fitz, Karsten. "The Dusseldorf Academy of Art, Emanuel Leutze, and German-American Transatlantic Exchange in the Mid-Nineteenth Century." *Amerikastudien* 52, no. 1 (2007): 15–34.

Foner, Philips S., ed. *Life and Writings of Frederick Douglass*. Vol. 2: *Pre-Civil War Decade*. New York: International Publishers, 1950.

Forman, Gabrielle, and Reginald H. Pitts. Introduction. *Our Nig or; Sketches from the Life of a Free Black*, by Harriet Wilson. xxiii–l. New York: Penguin Books, 2005.

Foster, Francis Smith. *Witnessing Slavery: The Development of Ante-Bellum Slave Narratives*. Madison: University of Wisconsin Press, 1994.

Francis, Terri. "Embodied Fictions, Melancholy Migrations: Josephine Baker's Cinematic Celebrity." *Modern Fiction Studies* 51, no. 4 (2005): 824–45.

Frankel, David. "Kara Walker: Wooster Gardens." *Artforum* 37, no. 8 (1999): 122.

Freud, Sigmund. "Humour." *International Journal of Psycho-Analysis* 9 (1928): 1–6.

———. *Jokes and Their Relation to the Unconscious*. Trans. James Strachey. New York: Norton, 1960. First published in 1905.

Fried, Michael. "Manet's Sources: Aspects of His Art, 1859–65." *Artforum* 7 (March 1969): 28–82.

Frieze, James. "*Imperceptible Mutabilities in the Third Kingdom*: Suzan-Lori Parks and the Shared Struggle to Perceive." *Modern Drama* 41, no. 4 (1998): 523–32.

Fuller, Hoyt. "Towards a Black Aesthetic." In *Within the Circle: An Anthology of African American Literary Criticism from the Harlem Renaissance to the Present*, ed. Angelyn

Mitchell. Durham, N.C.: Duke University Press, 1994. [First printed in *The Critic* 26, no. 5 (1968)]

Ganter, Granville. "'He Made Us Laugh Some': Frederick Douglass's Humor." *African American Review* 37, no. 4 (2003): 535–52.

Gardner, Eric, ed. *Major Voices: The Drama of Slavery.* New Milford, Conn.: Toby Press, 2005.

Garrett, Shawn-Marie. "The Possession of Suzan-Lori Parks." *American Theatre* 17, no. 8 (2000): 22–26, 132–34.

———. "Return of the Repressed." *Theater* 32, no. 2 (2002): 27–43.

Gassier, Pierre. *Francisco Goya Drawings: The Complete Albums.* Trans. James Emmons and Robert Allen. New York: Praeger, 1973.

Gates, Henry Louis, Jr. Introduction. *Our Nig; or, Sketches from the Life of a Free Black*, by Harriet Wilson. New York: Random House, 1983.

———. *The Signifying Monkey: A Theory of Afro-American Literary Criticism.* New York: Oxford University Press, 1988.

Gates, Henry Louis, Jr., and Nellie Y. McKay. *The Norton Anthology of African American Literature.* New York: Norton, 2004.

Gayle, Addison. *The Way of the World: The Black Novel in America.* New York: Anchor, 1976.

George, Nelson. *Hip-Hop America.* New York: Viking, 1998.

———. *Post-Soul Nation: The Explosive, Contradictory, Triumphant, and Tragic 1980s as Experienced by African Americans (Previously Known as Blacks and before That Negroes).* New York: Viking, 2004.

Gilman, Sander. "Black Bodies, White Bodies: Toward an Iconography of Female Sexuality in Late Nineteenth Century Art, Medicine, and Literature." In *"Race," Writing, and Difference*, ed. Henry Louis Gates Jr. 223–61. Chicago: University of Chicago Press, 1985.

Gilmore, Paul. "'De Genewine Artekil': William Wells Brown, Blackface Minstrelsy, and Abolitionism." *American Literature* 69, no. 4 (1997): 743–80.

Gobert, R. Darren. "Cognitive Catharsis in the *Caucasian Chalk Circle.*" *Modern Drama* 49, no. 1 (2006): 12–40.

Goddu, Teresa. *Gothic America: Narrative, History and Nation.* New York: Columbia University Press, 1997.

Gone with the Wind. Dir. Victor Fleming. Selznick International and Metro-Goldwyn-Mayer, 1939.

Goya, Francisco. *Los Caprichos.* Text and translation by R. Stanley Johnson. Chicago: R. S. Johnson Fine Art, 1992.

Gray, Frances. *Women and Laughter.* London: Macmillan, 1994.

Groseclose, Barbara. *Emanuel Leutze, 1816–1868: Freedom Is the Only King.* Washington, D.C.: Smithsonian Institution Press, 1975.

———. "'Washington Crossing the Delaware': The Political Context." *American Art Journal* 7, no. 2 (1975): 70–78.

Gubar, Susan. *Racechanges: White Skin, Black Face in American Culture.* New York: Oxford University Press, 1997.

Haggins, Bambi. *Laughing Mad: The Black Comic Persona in Post-Soul America.* New Brunswick, N.J.: Rutgers University Press, 2007.

Hall, Stephen, Larry Keeter, and Jennifer Williamson. "Toward an Understanding of Humor as Popular Culture in America." *Journal of American Culture* 16, no. 2 (1993): 1–6.

Harper, Michael, and Robert B. Stepto, eds. *Chant of the Saints: A Gathering of Afro-American Literature, Art and Scholarship.* Urbana: University of Illinois Press, 1979.

Harpham, Geoffrey Galt. *On the Grotesque Strategies of Contradiction in Art and Literature.* Princeton, N.J.: Princeton University Press, 1982.

Harris, Joel Chandler. *The Complete Tales of Uncle Remus.* Boston: Houghton Mifflin, 1983.

———. *Uncle Remus, His Songs and His Sayings: The Folklore of the Old Plantation.* New York: D. Appleton, 1880.

Harris, Michael D. *Colored Pictures: Race and Visual Representation.* Chapel Hill: University of North Carolina Press, 2003.

Harris, Norman. "The Gods Must Be Angry: *Flight to Canada* as Political History." *Modern Fiction Studies* 34, no. 1 (1998): 111–23.

Harris, Trudier. *Saints, Sinners, Saviors: Strong Black Women in African American Literature.* New York: Palgrave Macmillan, 2001.

Hartman, Saidiya. *Lose Your Mother: A Journey along the Atlantic Slave Route.* New York: Farrar, Straus & Giroux, 2007.

———. *Scenes of Subjection: Terror, Slavery and Self-Making in Nineteenth Century America.* New York: Oxford University Press, 1997.

———. "The Time of Slavery." *South Atlantic Quarterly* 101, no. 4 (2002): 757–77.

Hirsch, Faye. "L'Ecole de Paris Is Burning; Robert Colescott's Ironic Variations." *Arts Magazine* 66 (September 1991): 52–57.

Hurston, Zora Neale. *Tell My Horse: Voodoo and Life in Haiti and Jamaica.* New York: Harper & Row, 1990. First published in 1938.

Jackson, Bruce, comp. *Get Your Ass in the Water and Swim Like Me: African American Narrative Poetry from Oral Tradition.* New York: Routledge, 2004.

Jacobs, Harriet [pseud. Linda Brent]. *Incidents in the Life of a Slave Girl Written by Herself.* Ed. and introduction by Jean Fagan Yellin. Cambridge, Mass.: Harvard University Press, 1987. First published in 1861.

Kelefa, Sanneh. "The Debate Continues: Much Ado." *International Review of African-American Art* 15, no. 2 (1998): 44–47.

Kelley, Robin D. G. *Freedom Dreams: The Black Radical Imagination.* Boston: Beacon Press, 2002.

Kelley, Robin D. G., and Earl Lewis, eds. *To Make Our World Anew: A History of African Americans.* New York: Oxford University Press, 2000.

Kennedy, Adrienne. *The Adrienne Kennedy Reader.* Introduction by Werner Sollors. Minneapolis: University of Minnesota Press, 2001.

Kennedy, Randall. *Nigger: The Strange Career of a Troublesome Word.* New York: Vintage Books, 2002.

Kort, Pamela, ed. *The Comic Grotesque: Wit and Mockery in German Art, 1870–1940.* New York: Neue Gallery, 2004.

Krasner, David, ed. *African American Performance and Theater History: A Critical Reader.* Oxford: Oxford University Press, 2001.

Kreger, Erika M. "The Nineteenth-Century Female Humorist as 'Iconoclast in the Temple': Gail Hamilton and the Myth of Reviewer's Disapproval of Women's Comic-Ironic Writings." *Studies in American Humor* 3, no.11 (2004): 5–38.

Kristeva, Julia. *Powers of Horror: An Essay on Abjection.* Trans. Leon S. Roudiez. New York: Columbia University Press, 1982.

Kultermann, Udo. "Reconstitucion pictorica de la historia negra: La obra de Robert Colescott." *Goya* 260, no. 9 (1997): 492–99.

Kushner, Tony. "The Art of the Difficult." *Civilization* 4 (August–September 1997): 62–67.

Levine, Lawrence. *Black Culture and Black Consciousness.* New York: Oxford University Press, 1977.

———. *Highbrow/Lowbrow.* Cambridge, Mass: Harvard University Press, 1988.

Lhamon, W. T. *Raising Cain: Blackface Performance from Jim Crow to Hip-Hop.* Cambridge, Mass: Harvard University Press, 1998.

Limon, John. *Stand-up Comedy in Theory; or, Abjection in America.* Durham, N.C.: Duke University Press, 2000.

Lipton, Eunice. "Manet: A Radicalized Female Imagery." *Artforum* 13 (March 1975): 48–53.

Lock, Helen. " 'A Man's Story Is His Gris-Gris': Ishmael Reed's Neo-HooDoo Aesthetic and the African-American Tradition." *South Central Review* 10, no. 1 (1993): 67–77.

Lott, Eric. "The Aesthetic Ante: Pleasure, Pop Culture, and the Middle Passage." *Callaloo* 17, no. 2 (1994): 545–55.

———. *Love and Theft: Blackface Minstrelsy and the American Working Class.* New York: Oxford University Press, 1993.

Louis, Yvette. "Body Language: The Black Female Body and Word in Suzan-Lori Parks's *The Death of the Last Black Man in the Whole Entire World.*" In *Recovering the Black Female Body: Self-Representations by African American Women,* ed. Michael Bennett and Vanessa Dickerson. 141–64. New Brunswick, N.J.: Rutgers University Press, 2001.

Lowe, John W. "African-American Humor." In *Comedy: A Geographic and Historical Guide,* ed. Maurice Charney. Vol. 1. 34–47. Westport, Conn.: Praeger, 2005.

———. "Joaquin Murieta, Mexican History, and Popular Myths of Freedom." *Journal of Popular Culture* 35, no. 2 (2001): 25–39.

———. "Theories of Ethnic Humor: How to Enter, Laughing." *American Quarterly* 38, no. 3 (1986): 439–59.

Lubiano, Wahneema, ed. *The House That Race Built: Black Americans, U.S. Terrain.* New York: Pantheon Books, 1997.

Ludwig, Sami. "Dialogic Possession in Ishmael Reed's *Mumbo Jumbo*: Bakhtin, Voodoo, and the Materiality of Multicultural Discourse." In *The Black Columbiad: Defining Moments in African American Literature and Culture,* ed. Werner Sollors and Maria Diedrich. 390–420. Cambridge, Mass.: Harvard University Press, 1994.

MacDonald, J. Fred. *Blacks and White TV: African Americans in Television since 1948.* 2nd ed. Chicago: Nelson-Hall, 1992.

Massey, Douglas S. "American Apartheid: Segregation and the Making of the Underclass." *American Journal of Sociology* 96, no. 2 (1990): 329–57.

McDowell, Deborah, and Arnold Rampersad, eds. *Slavery and the Literary Imagination.* Baltimore: Johns Hopkins University Press, 1989.

McElva, Micki. *Clinging to Mammy: The Faithful Slave in Twentieth-Century America.* Cambridge, Mass: Harvard University Press, 2007.

McKinsley, Elizabeth. *Niagara Falls: Icon of the American Sublime.* Cambridge, England: Cambridge University Press, 1985.

Mercer, Kobena. "Reading Racial Fetishism: The Photographs of Robert Mapplethorpe." In *Fetishism as Cultural Discourse,* ed. Emily Apter. 223–46. Ithaca, N.Y.: Cornell University Press, 1993.

Merkert, Jörn. "Stylelessness as Principle: The Painting of Willem de Kooning." In *Willem de Kooning: Drawings Paintings, Sculpture,* ed. Paul Cummings. 115–239. New York: Whitney Museum of American Art, 1983.

Metz, Christian. "Photography and Fetish." *October* 34 (Autumn 1985): 81–90.

Mikics, David. "Postmodernism, Ethnicity and Underground Revisionism in Ishmael Reed." *Postmodern Culture: An Electronic Journal of Interdisciplinary Criticism* 1, no. 3 (1991).

Miller, Greg. "The Bottom of Desire in Suzan-Lori Parks." *Modern Drama* 45, no. 1 (2002): 125–37.

Morgan, Jo-Ann. "Mammy the Huckster: Selling the Old South for the New Century." *American Art* 9, no. 1 (1995): 87–109.

Morrison, Toni. "The Site of Memory." In *Inventing the Truth: The Art and Craft of Memoir,* ed. William Zinsser. 103–24. New York: Houghton Mifflin, 1995.

Nazareth, Peter. "Heading Them Off at the Pass: The Fiction of Ishmael Reed." *Review of Contemporary Fiction* 4, no. 2 (1984): 208–24.

Neal, Mark Anthony. *Soul Babies: Black Popular Culture and the Post-Soul Aesthetic.* New York: Routledge, 2002.

Newkirk, Pamela. "Controversial Silhouette." *Art News* 98, no. 8 (1999): 45.

Nichols, Charles H. "Comic Modes in Black America (A Ramble through Afro-American Humor)," In *Comic Relief: Humor In Contemporary American Literature,* ed. Sarah Blacher Cohen. 105–27. Urbana: University of Illinois Press, 1978.

Nochlin, Linda. *Realism.* New York: Penguin, 1971.

Omi, Michael, and Howard Winant. *Racial Formation in the United States from the 1960s to the 1980s.* New York: Routledge & Kegan Paul, 1986.

O'Neale, Sondra A. "Ishmael Reed's Fitful Flight to Canada: Liberation for Some, Good Reading for All." *Callaloo* 4 (October 1978): 176–78.

Orgel, Stephen. "The Play of Conscience." In *Performativity and Performance,* ed. Andre Parker and Eve Kosofsky Sedgwick. 133–51. New York: Routledge, 1995.

Orr, John. *Tragicomedy and Contemporary Culture: Play and Performance from Beckett to Shepard.* Houndmills, England: Macmillan, 1991.

Otter, Samuel. *Melville's Anatomies.* Berkeley: University of California Press, 1999.

Parish, James R., and George H. Hill. *Black Action Films.* Jefferson, N.C.: McFarland, 1989.

Parks, Suzan-Lori. *The America Play and Other Works.* New York: Theater Communications Group, 1995.

———. *Venus.* St. Paul, Minn.: Theatre Communications Group, 1997.

Paskoff, Paul F., and Daniel J. Wilson, eds. *The Cause of the South: Selections from De Bow's Review, 1846–1867.* Baton Rouge: Louisiana State University Press, 1982.

Patterson, Orlando. *The Ordeal of Integration; Progress and Resentment in America's "Racial" Crisis.* Washington, D.C.: Civitas /Counterpoint Publishers, 1997.

Paulson, Ronald. *The Fictions of Satire.* Baltimore: Johns Hopkins University Press, 1967.

Pirandello, Luigi. *On Humor.* Introduced, translated, and annotated by Antonio Illiano and Daniel P. Testa. Chapel Hill: University of North Carolina Press, 1974.

Polcari, Stephen. *Abstract Expressionism and the Modern Art Experience.* New York: Cambridge University Press, 1991.

Pratofiorito, Ellen. "'To Demand Your Sympathy and Aid': *Our Nig* and the Problem of No Audience." *Journal of American and Comparative Cultures* 24, nos. 1–2 (2001): 31–48.

Princenthal, Nancy. "New York: Kara Walker at Wooster Gardens." *Art in America* 87, no. 2 (1999): 106.

Pryor, Richard. *Live and Smokin'.* 1971. Dir. Michael Blum, MPI Home Video, 1981.

———. "*Black Ben, the Blacksmith*" *(1968).* In *Richard Pryor Evolution/Revolution: The Early Years (1964–1974).* Prod. Reggie Collins and Steve Pokorny. Rhino Records, 2005.

———. *Richard Pryor . . . and It's Deep Too! The Complete Warner Bros. Recordings (1968–1992).* Prod. Reggie Collins and Steve Pokorny. Warner Bros. Records, 2000.

———. *Richard Pryor Evolution/Revolution: The Early Years (1964–1974).* Prod. Reggie Collins and Steve Pokorny. Rhino Records, 2005.

———. *Richard Pryor . . . Here and Now.* Dir. Richard Pryor. Columbia Pictures, 1983.

———. *Richard Pryor—Live in Concert.* Dir. Jeff Margolis. SEE Theater Network, 1979.

———. *Richard Pryor Live on the Sunset Strip.* Dir. Joe Layton. Columbia Pictures, 1982.

Pryor, Richard, with Todd Gold. *Pryor Convictions and Other Life Sentences.* New York: Pantheon Books, 1995.

Ramsdell, George A. *The History of Milford, with Family Registers.* Concord, N.H., 1901.

Randle, Gloria T. "Between the Rock and the Hard Place: Mediating Spaces in Harriet Jacobs's *Incidents in the Life of a Slave Girl.*" *African American Review* 33, no. 1 (1999): 43–56.

Reed, Ishmael. *Conjure: Selected Poems, 1963–1970.* Amherst: University of Massachusetts Press, 1972.

———. *Flight to Canada.* New York: Simon & Schuster, 1998. First published in 1976.

———. *Yellow Back Radio Broke-Down.* Normal, Ill.: Dalkey Archive Press, 2000. First published in 1969.

Reed, Jennifer. "Lily Tomlin's *Appearing Nightly*: Performing Difference before Difference Was Cool." *Journal of Popular Culture* 37, no. 3 (2000): 436–49.

Reichardt, Ulfried. "Time and the African American Experience: The Problem of Chronocentricism." *Amerikastudien/American Studies* 45, no. 4 (2000): 465–84.

Reid-Pharr, Robert F. "Black Girl Lost." In *Kara Walker Pictures from Another Time*, ed. Annette Dixon. 27–41. Ann Arbor: University of Michigan Press, 2002.

Reilly, Maura. "Betye Saar at Michael Rosenfeld." *Art in America* 87, no. 2 (1999): 112–13.

Reinhardt, Mark. "The Art of Racial Profiling." In *Kara Walker: Narratives of the Negress*, ed. Ian Berry, Darby English, Vivian Patterson, and Mark Reinhart, 109–29. Cambridge, Mass.: MIT Press, 2003.

Rhys, Jean. *Wide Sargasso Sea*. London: Andre Deutsch, 1966.

Roach, Joseph. *Cities of the Dead: Circum-Atlantic Performance*. New York: Columbia University Press, 1996.

———. "The Great Hole of History: Liturgical Silences in Beckett, Osofisan and Parks." *South Atlantic Quarterly* 100, no. 1 (2001): 307–17.

Robinson, Marc. "Four Writers." *Theater* 24, no. 1 (1993): 31–42.

Rock, Chris. *Rock This!* New York: Hyperion, 1997.

Rose, Phyllis. *Jazz Cleopatra: Josephine Baker In Her Time*. New York: Doubleday, 1989.

Rovin, Jeff. *Richard Pryor: Black and Blue*. New York: Bantam Books, 1984.

Rubin, William. "*Les Demoiselles d'Avignon*." Special issue of *Studies in Modern Art* 3 (1994): 13–144.

———. "*Primitivism*" *in 20th Century Art: The Affinity of the Tribal and the Modern*. New York: Museum of Modern Art, 1984.

Rushdy, Ashraf. "Ishmael Reed's Neo-HooDoo Slave Narrative." *Narrative* 2 (May 1994): 112–39.

———. *Neo-Slave Narratives: Studies in the Social Logic of a Literary Form*. New York: Oxford University Press, 1999.

Saltz, Jerry. "Kara Walker: Ill-Will and Desire." Interview. *Flash Art*, international ed. (November/December 1996): 82–86.

Schechner, Richard. *Performance Theory*. London: Routledge, 2003. First published in 1988.

Seidel, Michael. *Satiric Inheritance: Rabelais to Sterne*. Princeton, N.J.: Princeton University Press, 1979.

Shaw, Gwendolyn DuBois. *Seeing the Unspeakable: The Art of Kara Walker*. Durham, N.C.: Duke University Press, 2004.

Singer, Marc. "'Black Skins' and White Masks: Comic Books and the Secret of Race." *African American Review* 36, no. 1 (2002): 107–20.

Sochen, June. *Women's Comic Visions*. Detroit: Wayne State University Press, 1991.

Solomon, Alisa. "Signifying on the Signifyin': The Plays of Suzan-Lori Parks." *Theater* 21 (Summer—Fall 1990): 73–80.

Solomon, William. "Secret Integrations: Black Humor and the Critique of Whiteness." *Modern Fiction Studies* 49, no. 3 (2003): 469–95.

Sparshott, Francis. "The Riddle of Katharsis." In *Centre and Labyrinth: Essays in Honour of Northrop Frye*, ed. Eleanor Coo, Chaviva Hošek, Jay Macpherson, Patricia Parker, and Julian Patrick. 14–37. Toronto: University of Toronto Press, 1983.

Spillers, Hortense. "Changing the Letter: The Yokes, the Jokes of Discourse or, Mrs. Stowe, Mr. Reed." In *Slavery and the Literary Imagination*, ed. Deborah McDowell and Arnold Rampersad. 25–61. Baltimore: Johns Hopkins University Press, 1989.

———. "Mama's Baby, Papa's Maybe: An American Grammar Book." *Diacritics* 17, no. 2 (1987): 64–81.

St. John, Maria. " 'It Ain't Fittin': Cinematic and Fantasmatic Contours of Mammy in *Gone with the Wind* and Beyond." *Qui Parle* 11, no. 2 (1999): 127–36.

Stein, Gertrude. *Last Operas and Plays*. Ed. Carl Van Vechten. Introduction by Bonnie Marranca. Baltimore: Johns Hopkins University Press, 1995. First published in 1949.

Stern, Julia. "Excavating Genre in *Our Nig*." *American Literature* 67, no. 3 (1995): 439–67.

Stone, Laurie. *Laughing in the Dark: A Decade of Subversive Comedy*. Hopewell, N.J.: Ecco Press, 1997.

Storr, Robert. "Reason's Dream, Reason's Nightmare." In *The Comic Grotesque: Wit and Mockery in German Art 1870–1940*, ed. Pamela Kort. 210–17. New York: Neue Gallery, 2004.

Stott, Andrew. *Comedy*. New York: Routledge, 2005.

Styan, J. L. *The Dark Comedy; The Development of Modern Comic Tragedy*. London: Cambridge University Press, 1968.

Sundquist, Eric. *To Wake the Nations: Race in the Making of American Literature*. Cambridge, Mass.: Harvard University Press, 1983.

Talley, Thomas W. *Negro Folk Rhymes, Wise and Otherwise, with a Study*. Port Washington, N.Y.: Kennikat, 1968.

Thompson, Ayanna, ed. *Colorblind Shakespeare: New Perspectives on Race and Performance*. New York: Routledge, 2006.

Thompson, Debby. "Is Race a Trope? Anna Deavere and the Question of Racial Performativity." *African American Review* 37, no. 1 (2003): 127–39.

Thompson, Robert Farris. *Flash of the Spirit: African and Afro-American Art and Philosophy*. New York: Vintage Books, 1984.

Thorston, James A. "Did You Ever See a Hearse Go By? Some Thoughts on Gallows Humor." *Journal of American Studies* 16, no. 2 (1993): 17–25.

Tilley, Liz. "Interview with Kara Walker." In *Switch*. Oakland: California College of Arts and Crafts, 1998.

Tucker, Paul H. *Le Déjeuner sur l'herbe*. New York: Cambridge University Press, 1998.

Turner, Victor *The Anthropology of Performance*. New York: PAJ Publications, 1988.

– –– –. *Drama, Fields and Metaphors; Symbolic Action in Human Society*. Ithaca, N.Y.: Cornell University Press, 1974.

Twain, Mark. *The Complete Essays of Mark Twain*. Ed. Charles Neider. Cambridge, Mass.: Da Capo Press, 2000.

Tynes Cowan, William. "Plantation Comic Modes." *Humor* 14, no. 1 (2000): 1–24.

Unger, Miles. "Contested Histories." *Art New England* 19, no. 4 (1998): 29.

Vaidhyanathan, Siva. "Now's the Time: The Richard Pryor Phenomenon and the Triumph of Black Culture." In *New Directions in American Humor*, ed. David E. E. Sloane. 40–50. Tuscaloosa: University of Alabama Press, 1998.

Van Deburg, William L. *Slavery and Race in American Popular Culture*. Madison: University of Wisconsin Press, 1984.

Van Vechten, Carl. *Nigger Heaven*. New York: Octagon Books, 1973. First published in 1926.

Virtanen, Simo V., and Leonie Huddy. "Old-Fashioned Racism and New Forms of Racial Prejudice." *Journal of Politics* 60, no. 2 (1998): 311–32.

Wagner, Ann M. "The Black-White Relation." In *Kara Walker: Narratives of a Negress*, ed. Ian Berry, Darby English, Vivian Patterson, and Mark Reinhardt. 91–101. Cambridge, Mass.: MIT Press, 2003.

Walker, Kara. Interview with Liz Tilley. In *Switch*. Oakland: California College of Arts and Crafts, 1998.

———. *Kara Walker*. Chicago: Renaissance Society at the University of Chicago, 1997.

———. *Kara Walker: Narratives of the Negress*. Ed. Ian Berry, Darby English, Vivian Patterson, and Mark Reinhardt. Cambridge, Mass.: MIT Press, 2003.

———. "Kara Walker's Response." *International Review of African American Art* 15, no. 2 (1998): 48–50.

Wallace, Michele. *Black Macho and the Myth of the Superwoman*. New York: Dial, 1979.

Walsh, Richard. " 'A Man's Story Is His Gris-Gris': Cultural Slavery, Literary Emancipation and Ishmael Reed's *Flight to Canada*." *Journal of American Studies* 27, no. 1 (1993): 57–71.

Walters, Ronald. "The Erotic South: Civilization and Sexuality in American Abolitionism." *American Quarterly* 25, no. 2 (1973): 177–201.

Watkins, Mel. *African-American Humor: The Best Black Comedy from Slavery to Today*. Chicago: Lawrence Hill Books, 2002.

———. *On the Real Side: A History of African American Humor from Slavery to Chris Rock*. Chicago: Lawrence Hill Books, 1994.

Wechsler, Judith. *A Human Comedy: Physiognomy and Caricature in 19th Century Paris*. Chicago: University of Chicago Press, 1982.

Weiner, Allison Hope. "Funny Business." *Entertainment Weekly*, August 20, 2004, http://www.ew.com/ew/article/0,681698,00.html (accessed June 23, 2007).

Weixlmann, Joe. "Ishmael Reed's Raven." *Review of Contemporary Fiction* 4, no. 2 (1984): 205–208.

———. "Politics, Piracy, and Other Games: Slavery and Liberation in *Flight to Canada*." *MELUS* 6, no. 3 (1979): 41–50.

West, Cornel. *The Cornel West Reader*. New York: Basic Civitas Books, 1999.

White, Barbara. "*Our Nig* and the She-Devil: New Information about Harriet Wilson and the 'Bellmont Family.' " *American Literature* 65, no. 1 (1993): 19–52.

White, Deborah Gray. *Ar'n't I a Woman? Female Slaves in the Plantation South*. New York: Norton, 1985.

White, Jeannette S. "Baring Slavery's Darkest Secrets: Charles Chesnutt's Conjure Tales as Masks of Truth." *Southern Literary Journal* 27, no. 1 (1994): 85–103.

Williams, Monte. "From a Planet Closer to the Sun." *New York Times*, April 17, 1996, C1, C8.

Williams, Raymond. *Marxism and Literature*. Oxford: Oxford University Press, 1977.

Wilmer, S. E. "Restaging the Nation: The Works of Suzan-Lori Parks." *Modern Drama* 43, no. 3 (2000): 442–52.

Wilson, Harriet E. *Our Nig or; Sketches from the Life of a Free Black*. Ed. P. Gabrielle Forman and Reginald H. Pitts. New York: Penguin Books, 2005. First published in 1853.

Winston, Mathew. "Humour noire and Black Humor." In *Veins of Humor*, ed. Harry Levin. 269–84. Cambridge, Mass.: Harvard University Press, 1972.

Wonham, Henry B. *Charles W. Chesnutt: A Study of the Short Fiction*. New York: Twayne Publishers, 1998.

——. "'The Curious Psychological Spectacle of a Mind Enslaved': Charles W. Chesnutt and Dialect Fiction." *Mississippi Quarterly* 51, no. 1 (1997): 55–69.

Wright, Richard. "Between Laughter and Tears." *New Masses*, October 5, 1937, 22–23.

Wright, Thomas. *A History of Caricature and Grotesque in Literature and Art*. New York: Ungar, 1968.

Young, Jean. "The Re-Objectification and Re-Commodification of Saartjie Baartman in Suzan-Lori Parks's *Venus*." *African American Review* 31 (1997): 699–708.

INDEX

Abjection, 63, 71, 95–98, 113, 175, 247n46

Abolition/abolitionists, 13, 16, 31–33, 51–52, 68, 70, 112, 119, 133, 171, 229; "Sentimental Abolitionism," 37–38, 44–48, 243n121

African American humor, 4–7, 16–17, 21, 27–31; books about, 20; and segregation, 5–6, 22–23, 95, 104, 110–11; whites' conception of, 5, 31. *See also* Black humor

Andrews, William, 35, 56

Apter, Emily, 34

Baker, Josephine, 16, 176–78

Bakhtin, Mikhail, 6, 26, 146, 163, 256n55

Baldwin, James, 79–80, 137–38, 253n61

Bambara, Toni Cade, 17

Baraka, Amiri (Leroi Jones), 19, 65, 230, 235n57

Baudelaire, Charles, 26, 162, 165, 190

Beatty, Paul, 17, 23, 236n73

Beavers, Herman, 100, 104

Beckett, Samuel, 196–97, 204, 208, 210

Bergson, Henri, 27, 56, 76, 103, 241n95

Best, Stephen, 9–10, 73

Birth of a Nation (Griffith), 102

Blackface, and farce, 22–24, 37–46, 75–76, 211–16; and gender, 66; and whiteface 24, 205. *See also* Minstrel show

Black humor, as artistic mode, 6–7, 20, 35–46, 51–71, 73–80, 82–91, 99–103, 117–18, 122–33, 141–44, 148–62, 168–84, 192, 205–17, 229–231; and catharsis, 11, 72–74, 84, 87–89, 98, 102, 114, 119, 124, 140–42, 228–231; and conjure, 16, 46–49, 51–63, 75–78, 81–87, 96, 106, 122–39, 170–80, 199–201; criticism of oppression, 5, 38–46, 51–54, 66, 72, 79–80, 87–95, 117, 192–94, 202–5, 222–31; definition of, 8, 140; and grief, 11, 36, 54–70, 77–78, 99–103, 186–90, 197–99, 209–14, 221–24, 229–31; and laughter, 7, 14, 16, 30, 32, 36–38, 51–63, 192, 196–97, 205–17, 229–31; and modernism, 149–53, 157–58; and postmodernism, 8, 15, 17, 106–8, 121–22, 139, 192, 200–201; and redress, 6, 11–16, 80, 85–102, 107–16, 122–27, 194, 198, 211–17, 221; and slavery, 7–12, 35–46, 48–63, 73, 79–82, 88, 91, 95–96, 100–105, 108, 112–16, 122–27, 194, 198, 221, 224; and stereotypes, 14–15, 17, 21, 35, 48, 72–75, 122–24, 129, 132–36, 140–62, 172, 177, 178, 180, 185–88, 190, 199, 206–9, 218, 229; whites' conception of, 5, 31; and women, 65–70, 151–53. *See also* Humor

Black Power Movement, 9–12, 17–21, 73, 80, 95, 107

Body, and blackness, 4, 24, 86, 104, 172, 175, 178, 192–94, 216; comedy of, 16, 37, 49, 54–57, 60, 65, 81, 87; as effigy, 78–79, 96, 98, 100, 200–201; of the enslaved, 4, 16, 37,